THE CONSTITUTION OF ELECTORAL SPEECH LAW

THE CONSTITUTION OF ELECTORAL SPEECH LAW

THE SUPREME COURT AND FREEDOM OF EXPRESSION IN CAMPAIGNS AND ELECTIONS

Brian K. Pinaire

STANFORD LAW BOOKS
An imprint of Stanford University Press
Stanford, California

Stanford University Press
Stanford, California

Library of Congress Cataloging-in-Publication Data

Pinaire, Brian K., 1974-
The constitution of electoral speech law : the Supreme Court and freedom of expression in campaigns and elections / Brian K. Pinaire.
p. cm.
Includes bibliographical references and index.
ISBN 978-0-8047-5724-9 (cloth : alk. paper)
1. United States. Supreme Court. 2. Freedom of speech--United States. 3. Election law--United States. 4. Political campaigns--Law and legislation--United States. 5. Political parties--Law and legislation--United States. I. Title.

KF4770.P56 2008
342.7308'53--DC22 2007049506

Designed by Bruce Lundquist
Typeset at Stanford University Press in 10/15 Sabon

To Team Baird-Pinaire

con·sti·tu·tion

1. The way in which a thing is composed or made up; makeup; composition
2. The act or process of constituting; establishment
3. The state of being constituted; formation

Contents

Tables and Figures

TABLES

FIGURES

Preface

AS A GOOD FRIEND and teacher of mine determined in the preface to one of his books (and this would be the only thing that his opus and my modest effort have in common), "every book needs an excuse . . . "[1] And so the excuse I offer for *The Constitution of Electoral Speech Law* is that the complexity and distinction of this legal domain have not been sufficiently appreciated (or examined), meaning that electoral speech has tended to be subsumed within either the general categories of "free speech" or "electoral process" jurisprudence. In failing to evaluate electoral speech law as the particular intersection of both its contributing doctrinal lines, one misses what I contend is its two-fold significance for American democracy: that it implicates the means by which a polity deliberates and makes decisions (freedom of expression), and it keeps those structures and practices in place to record collective preferences and reflect the public will (campaigns and elections). Thus, *my* "excuse" for this work confronts us every election day; with every broadcast of the evening news during campaign season; every time we attend a campaign rally; perhaps each time we hope to be involved in the political process, but are confined by the nature of our employment; as we distribute leaflets, post signs, or write checks in support of our preferred candidate; and through the myriad other means by which we attempt or desire to express ourselves within the electoral process.

Before proceeding to elaborate on the substantive aims of this work, allow me to state what this book is *not* about. This study is not a work of normative theory. It is not my intention here to devise a system of meta-principles—airtight in the abstract—only to apply them to the considerations and conclusions of the Supreme Court, which would, of course, be faulted for failing to have decided particular cases within my proffered theoretical parameters or in accord with my political or philosophical disposition. Books and law review articles setting out some grand design for free expression in this mode are legion; and, while I draw upon the insights and perspectives in these works, as I explore the constitution of this body of law, my purpose is comprehension not prescription.

Nor do I intend this book to be a partisan or otherwise castigatory assault on judicial review, jurisprudence, or decision-making methods. My study will perhaps leave some to be critical of the Supreme Court's rulings in certain cases, but I leave such conclusions to the reader. I certainly address the important questions regarding the rôle of the Court—or courts—in a democracy, but I do so as a scholar intrigued by the distinct problems, origins, development, and implications attendant to this legal domain, rather than as an advocate hoping to coax or cajole the Court in one direction or another.

What I do intend here is to provide a thorough investigation of the constitution of electoral speech law in the United States. An understanding of, and appreciation for, the principles and parameters of this domain requires attention to the universe of relevant cases considered by the United States Supreme Court; it requires an exploration of the nature of the high Court's conclusions; it calls for scrutiny of the tactics and techniques by which such appraisals are articulated; it necessitates a thorough review of the modes of argument and analysis that facilitate the cultivation of certain understandings of the issues in question; and it benefits from a probing of the above predicates in the form of in-depth case studies. What it obliges, in short, is a study of both the *elements* and *episodes* that comprise and facilitate the constitution of electoral speech law in the United States.

Acknowledgments

I HAVE LEARNED from inspiring educators throughout my life: from my first principal at Hartman Elementary, who taught me something about dedication—and discipline!; to those teachers who put up with me and gave of themselves to public education in Omaha, Nebraska; to my college professors who taught me to question and who showed me how to translate my talents; and to my primary Ph.D. advisors, Milton Heumann and Carey McWilliams, individuals who always demonstrated, by their own example, the meanings of "mensch" and "fraternity," respectively.

I have also been fortunate to work with some model professionals in the course of writing this book, from my colleagues at Lehigh University; to my editor, Amanda Moran, who saw—and somehow *kept* seeing—the promise of this book, from its earlier form as a stripped-down mess of a manuscript to, well, . . . whatever it is now; to the multiple reviewers who have seen this project in a variety of stages and who have provided immensely helpful advice along the way; and to the first student of the law I ever knew, Tom Lucas, who always gets me thinking.

But none of this would have been possible if it had not been for the continued encouragement and assistance of my parents, William and Janet Pinaire; my wife's parents, William and Nancy Baird; my wife, Dr. Emily Baird; and my son, Lucas Baird Pinaire. Words cannot sufficiently express my gratitude to each of them.

THE CONSTITUTION OF ELECTORAL SPEECH LAW

INTRODUCTION

The Constitution of Electoral Speech Law

THE ELECTION NIGHT PARTY was still going strong when I left at two o'clock in the morning. Oversized check marks, set against the background of the newly instituted (though now institutionalized) "blue"- and "red"-state graphics, provided intermittent consolation or consternation—depending on one's political orientation—and suggested that slowly, but surely (right?), *someone* would be named the winner and bring the festivities to a proper close. But, of course, when the country woke up the next day, there still was no president-elect. Thirty-six days *later*, however, there was—and *how* this came to be is a story of legal wrangling, political innovation, and constitutional development authored primarily and (in)famously by the U.S. Supreme Court.[1]

With the Court effectively awarding the election of 2000 to George W. Bush, in 7–2 and 5–4 splits, respectively, on the critical issues of the constitutionality of existing recount standards and the potential for employing better standards to resolve the dispute, this five-week constitutional drama brought to the forefront the significance of election laws in general (e.g., ballot design, recount schedules, and statutes governing the hours of polling places, standards for ascertaining voter "intent," etc.), and specifically the role and reach of the U.S. Supreme Court as an institution that—through its interventions and interpretations—sets the terms, structures the rules, supervises, and ultimately "constitutes" the electoral process in the United States. In accepting this case for review and rendering its decision literally and figuratively at the eleventh hour (saving the republic, for some commentators),[2] the Court established a precedent—a historical, if not a legally binding one[3]—for Supreme Court endeavors into what is arguably the most profound and consequential "political thicket" in this nation's electoral process: the selection of the president of the United States.[4]

Books and articles by esteemed scholars and analysts have exhaustively covered this case and its conjectured consequences,[5] and so my intention in revisiting *Bush v. Gore* is not to reconsider the decision on its merits, or to contemplate its impact necessarily,[6] but simply to showcase it as one of the most vivid illustrations of the manner by which the Supreme Court constitutes the process within and by which politics occurs in the United States. Such constitutive possibilities have been well documented in studies of reapportionment;[7] of the role of parties;[8] the development of the ballot box in America;[9] the Court's treatment of racial identity in redistricting cases;[10] the politics of proportional representation;[11] the evolving understandings of "equality" expressed by and inferred from the Court's engagement with political process cases;[12] evaluations of a particular Court's "vision of political representation";[13] historical and critical surveys of the Court's involvement in voting rights disputes;[14] and various other elements of election law and their implications for American campaigns and elections. But what has not received sufficient treatment—the theme to which this book is addressed—is the nature and process of freedom of *speech* within the course of campaigns and elections, or what I will refer to as *the constitution of electoral speech law.*

THE CONSTITUTION OF ELECTORAL SPEECH LAW

Given that constitutional guarantees have their "fullest and most urgent application precisely to the conduct of campaigns for political office,"[15] one might expect special protection for this variety of speech,[16] because it implicates both the method by which citizens deliberate (speak) and the means established to facilitate the translation from voice to action in a self-governing system (the institutions and structures of the electoral process—the "bedrock of our political system").[17] So, I contend, such speech is unique because of its situation within and impact upon the electoral process, necessarily requiring consideration of the customs, values, and inclinations associated with the maintenance of democratic forms, institutions, and practices *themselves.*

Put differently, electoral speech is more than simply speech *about* politics; significantly, the adjudication of free speech cases during campaigns and elections arises within an environment of the state's proprietary authority and as such is conditioned by and rooted in concerns for order,[18] integrity,[19] and participatory parity,[20] for example, in that such interests comprise so much of the law of democracy. And thus we have something of an irony: while this class of communication is by definition "political," and hence deserving of an elevated degree of protection, it is also inextricably "procedural," in that it necessarily arises in the midst of the electoral *process*, meaning that the state's regulatory antennae are also extended in a manner that would not necessarily appertain to other forms of speech, or even other varieties of political speech seeking purchase in environments beyond the electoral arena.

Electoral Speech Constitution(s)

Manifest in at least four interrelated ways in this study, my use of "constitution" relates first and perhaps most obviously to the "speech" clause of the First Amendment to the United States Constitution and the various ways this provision has been construed since about the middle of the twentieth century, when the first state restriction on electoral speech was reviewed. We will see, however, that the emphasis is more directed at the period since the early 1970s, when such cases came to be regularly reviewed in *constitutional* terms, as opposed to merely along the lines of statutory interpretation.

The invocation of "constitution" in the second sense appreciates the manner by which "practices are *constituted* by concepts" in the political world,[21] and emphasizes the particularly "constitutive" significance of electoral speech law[22]—or how, in other words, this body of law "constitutes,"[23] or structures,[24] the terms of our electoral process and thus conditions the (s)election of the agents populating and animating the institutions that draft, execute, and interpret the laws in the first place. Put differently, "before the first vote is cast or the first ballot counted, the possibilities for democratic politics are already constrained and channeled," because the acts of self-government "must operate through pre-existing laws, rules, and institutions," meaning that "the kind of democratic politics we have is always and inevitably itself a product of institutional forms and legal structures."[25] Thus, "a paradox rests at the core of democratic politics: this politics is in part a contest over the structure of state institutions, and yet those very institutions define the terms in which the contest of democratic politics proceeds."[26] The Supreme Court—as the "architect of election law"[27]—has the power, then, to tangibly and formatively affect "how the electoral process works and how effectively it satisfies its democratic objectives."[28]

Still though, the "constitutional" process—that is, the *act* of constitution—often requires a blueprint of sorts: a kind of theoretical overview for the project; a design that details its features, intentions, and purposes. To wit, the Court, in its electoral process decisions, has offered a host of political theories to justify its conclusions—theories which have been criticized as lacking in coherence at the abstract *and* applied levels;[29] as being too scattered to allow for coherence or development;[30] as flowing from incomplete information,[31] or from "faulty assumptions";[32] and as working with models, expectations, and values that may be unacknowledged or unrealized.[33] At the same time, the Court has also been *applauded* for not acceding to *one* distinct "theory" of politics,[34] and at least one justice famously refused to "freeze" in any specific "theory of political thought" with respect to the nature and attendant structures of representation.[35]

In a third sense, the use of "constitution" portrays my interest in investigating the basic *nature* (i.e., "constitution" in a more organic sense) of the Court's essential understanding of free speech rights within this domain. We have been told, for example, that the "free exchange of ideas provides *special* vitality to the process traditionally at the heart of American constitutional democracy—the political campaign."[36] Does this imply that there exists a theoretical core from which we might divine a *distinct* vision for the place, power, and potential for expression within the electoral process? What is the essence of the above "vitality"? That is, what are those values that appear to both orient and animate this body of law, or those principles that simultaneously conceive and condition the course of its development?

Fourth and finally, I wonder *how* the Court's understanding of electoral speech law is "constituted"—that is, not what the constitution *is*, but how it comes to be that way. Specifically, my interest is in how the Court's reasoning is both realized and rendered, or the manner by which conclusions are arrived at and articulated. In uniting these various "constitutional" inquiries then, we will see that the attention is distributed between the *elements* that comprise and the *episodes* that facilitate the constitution of this body of law.[37] It is by way of this convergence of "elemental" and "episodic" analyses—where the concepts, confluences, modes, and contours divined from the universe of cases meld from the top-down with the organic investigation of the origins, considerations, developments, and configurations of outcomes in key cases coming from the bottom-up—that the constitution of electoral speech law is best adduced.

The Constitutional Universe

While the Supreme Court has for some time reviewed electoral *process* cases,[38] its consideration of electoral *speech* cases did not begin until 1947. Since that time, the domain has come to include a total of thirty-nine cases,[39] flowing from various communicants and distributed across five distinct *dimensions* of speech (see below), wherein the Supreme Court either reviewed a law that specifically restricted freedom of speech during campaigns and elections, or where a more general law restricted freedom of speech as *applied* within the course of the electoral process. My focus in this study is on only those cases wherein the *primary* (though not necessarily exclusive) claim involves a constitutional challenge (on speech grounds) to a state or federal law restricting expression during campaigns and elections, as opposed to merely a request for statutory interpretation, for example.

Given these parameters, my review does not include some cases that may appear worthy, such as the late nineteenth-century case *Ex parte Curtis*,[40] involving transfers of money within the sphere of politics; a Depression-era case involving ongoing federal attempts to stamp out corruption in state elections (*Burroughs and Cannon v. United States*);[41] a mid-twentieth-century case involving restrictions on political lobbying (*United States v. Harriss*);[42] a case involving the nature of the contributions to union funds used for political purposes (*Pipefitters Local Union No. 562 v. United States*);[43] the well-known "right of reply" case, *Miami Herald Publishing Co. v. Tornillo*;[44] and, the "as-applied" case (as *anticipated* in *Buckley v. Valeo*'s discussion of disclosure and the rights of smaller political parties), *Brown v. Socialist Workers '74 Campaign Committee (Ohio)*.[45]

As a frame of reference for considering this relatively "young" but quickly expanding universe, consider that, as Richard Hasen has demonstrated, from 1901 to 1960 the Supreme Court decided with a written opinion an average of 10.3 general election law cases per decade, or about 0.7 percent of all its decisions during that period. In the time between 1961 and 2000, however, the number of cases increased to sixty per decade, or about 5.3 percent of all the decisions during this time span.[46] Within this context, note

FIGURE I.1 *The Universe of Electoral Speech Cases*

The Vinson Court (June 1946–September 1953) → 2 cases
Rate: One case decided every 3.5 years

United Public Workers of America v. Mitchell (1947)
United States v. Congress of Industrial Organizations (1948)[a]

The Warren Court (October 1953–June 1969) → 4 cases
Rate: One case decided every 4 years[b]

United States v. Auto Workers (1957)[c]
Mills v. Alabama (1966)
St. Amant v. Thompson (1968)
Red Lion Broadcasting Co. v. FCC (1969)

The Burger Court (June 1969–September 1986) → 16 cases
Rate: One case decided every 1.06 years

Monitor Patriot Co. v. Roy (1971)
Ocala Star-Banner Co. v. Damron (1971)
United States Civil Service Commission v. National Association of Letter Carriers (1973)
Lehman v. City of Shaker Heights (1974)
Buckley v. Valeo (1976)
Greer v. Spock (1976)
Hynes v. Mayor of Oradell (1976)
First National Bank v. Bellotti (1978)
California Medical Assn. v. FEC (1981)
CBS, Inc. v. Federal Communications Commission (1981)
Citizens Against Rent Control v. Berkeley (1981)
Brown v. Hartlage (1982)
Common Cause v. Schmitt (1982)[d]
FEC v. National Right to Work Committee (1982)
Members of the City Council of the City of Los Angeles v. Taxpayers for Vincent (1984)
FEC v. National Conservative Political Action Committee (1985)

The Rehnquist Court (September 1986–September 2005) → 15 cases
Rate: One case decided every 1.27 years

FEC v. Massachusetts Citizens for Life (1986)
Meyer v. Grant (1988)
Eu v. San Francisco Cty. Democratic Central Committee (1989)
Austin v. Michigan Chamber of Commerce (1990)

that, as Figure I.1 demonstrates below, following the first electoral *speech* case in 1947, there was one more during the Vinson Court (one case every 3.5 years); there were four cases during the sixteen terms of the Warren Court (one case every 4 years); after which there was a dramatic increase in the Court's constitution of this domain, with sixteen cases during the seventeen terms of the Burger Court (one case every 1.06 years), and fifteen cases during the nineteen terms of the Rehnquist Court (one case every 1.27 years), with two cases thus far for the Roberts Court (one case every 0.5 years), and one case awaiting oral argument as this book goes to press.[47]

Renne v. Geary (1991)[e]
Burson v. Freeman (1992)
McIntyre v. Ohio Elections Commission (1995)
Colorado Republican Federal Campaign Committee v. FEC (1996)
Arkansas Educational Television Commission v. Ralph P. Forbes (1998)
Buckley v. American Constitutional Law Foundation (1999)
Nixon v. Shrink Missouri Government PAC (2000)
FEC v. Colorado Republican Federal Campaign Committee (2001)
Republican Party of Minnesota v. White (2002)
FEC v. Beaumont, et al. (2003)
McConnell v. FEC (2003)

The Roberts Court (September 2005–present) → 3 cases
Rate: One case decided every 0.5 years

Randall v. Sorrell (2006)
Wisconsin Right to Life v. FEC (2006)
FEC v. Wisconsin Right to Life (forthcoming, 2007)

a Note that in this case, while the parties offered constitutional challenges to the Federal Corrupt Practices Act, the Court resisted this invitation and limited its review to considering whether the indictment in question charged acts within its scope. See 335 U.S. 106, 110.

b It is worth noting that while there were only four electoral speech cases decided during Earl Warren's tenure as the chief justice, one of them, *Red Lion Broadcasting Co. v. FCC*, was of great consequence in several domains. Note as well that the latter three (of the four) were decided during what Lucas Powe, Jr., has deemed "History's Warren Court," a term apparently directed at law professors who came of age in the 1960s and who have a tendency to simply associate this Court with the progressive rulings with which they agree, while failing to acknowledge the historical context in which those decisions were rendered and the various external political influences that made them possible in the first place. That this is news to academic lawyers is unfortunate, because, as Powe appropriately acknowledges, this is something that "political scientists have been preaching for decades on end." See *The Warren Court and American Politics* (Cambridge, Mass.: Belknap Press of Harvard University Press, 2000), 209–462, 500–501.

c As it did in *CIO*, and despite being urged to assess the First Amendment implications of 18 U.S.C. § 610, the Court once more found that a "refusal to anticipate constitutional questions is peculiarly appropriate in the circumstances of this case." 352 U.S. 567, 591.

d Per curiam opinion (no written judgment); 4-4 affirmation of the district court decision finding for the respondents, with Justice O'Connor not participating.

e The Court found the issue in *Renne* to be nonjusticiable and thus avoided consideration of the First Amendment issues, though the dissent vigorously rejected this conclusion.

But it is important for analytical purposes to extricate from the general class of electoral speech law the specific forms (i.e., "dimensions") of "speech" desiring entry to the electoral marketplace of ideas. As we will see in later chapters, approaching the universe in these terms sheds important light on the various understandings of electoral expression adopted by the individual members of the Court vis-à-vis other cases implicating similar claims. As Table I.1 demonstrates, the domain includes five cases involving *political activists*, advocating a cause or issue, as distinguished from those *candidates* (or their agents) attempting to communicate with the public—of which there are eleven instances. There are eighteen cases involving *money* as the speech form in question, broken down more specifically by the form of the "speaker" who challenged the law (e.g., committees, political parties, corporations, or multiple actors). There are three cases involving the distinctly "speech" (as opposed to "press") rights of *newspapers*, and there are two cases pertaining to "speech" (as opposed to "association") interests of *political parties*.

TABLE I.1 *The Dimensions of Electoral Speech Law*

Activist	Candidate	Money	Newspaper	Party
Mitchell	*St. Amant*	*CIO*	*Mills*	*Eu*
Letter Carriers	*Red Lion*	*Auto Workers*	*Ocala*	*Renne*
Meyer	*Shaker Heights*	*Buckley*	*Monitor Patriot*	
McIntyre	*Greer*	*Bellotti*		
ACLF	*Hynes*	*CARC*		
	CBS	*CMA*		
	Hartlage	*Common Cause*		
	Taxpayers	*NRWC*		
	Burson	*NCPAC*		
	AETC	*MCFL*		
	White	*Austin*		
		Colorado I		
		Shrink		
		Colorado II		
		Beaumont		
		McConnell		
		WRTL		
		Sorrell		

CONSTITUTIONAL ELEMENTS

The notion that the "law" is conditioned by devices, articles, and concerns beyond (or perhaps *besides*) "logic," with rules based on more than "syllogisms," was, of course, famously announced by Justice Oliver Wendell Holmes, Jr., who found at least as much explanatory leverage in the "felt necessities of the time," the "prevalent moral and political theories, intuitions of public policy, avowed or unconscious, [and] even the prejudices which judges share with their fellow-men" as an account for the "life of the law."[48] Indeed, since the early legal realists,[49] scholars have known that "the development of legal doctrine is as firmly rooted in politics, institutional change, judicial personalities, social context, and organizational dynamics as it is in logic, historical precision, and formal argumentation."[50] Such are the sorts of elements—legal and extralegal—that comprise the constitution of the law in general.[51] Thus, I am interested in such characteristics, not simply to acknowledge their presence, but rather to take stock of their particular instances and influences in understanding how they coalesce in an elemental sense to structure this body of law. As we will see in the chapters to follow, and in the subsections below, predominant foci in this regard are (a) constituent concepts; (b) the confluences of these organizing concepts; (c) rhetorical modes of analysis, argument, and articulation; and (d) cognitive contours affecting images, preferences, persuasion, and perception.

Constituent Concepts

Chapter 1 examines two constructs—"electoral superintendence" and the "marketplace of ideas," the former an admittedly more expansive notion (or trend) than a precise "concept" as such, and the latter the primary metaphor adopted by the U.S. Supreme Court in its freedom of expression jurisprudence since about the mid-twentieth century. "Superintendence" in this respect serves as shorthand for the general regulation of the processes of democracy, forecast by footnote 4 in the *Carolene Products* case, while the "marketplace of ideas" concept is derived from what one scholar has referred to as a "canonical" dissenting opinion,[52] by Justice Oliver Wendell Holmes, in *Abrams v. United States*.[53] Finding that the expression of Abrams and his colleagues did not constitute a "clear and present danger," Holmes famously posited that when men came to realize that time had "upset many fighting faiths," they would come to "believe even more than they believe the very foundations of their own conduct that the ultimate good desired is better reached by *free trade in ideas*," and that the "best test for truth is the power of the thought to get itself accepted in *the competition of the market*. . . ."[54] As we will see, "superintendence" and the "marketplace of ideas" are the critical conceptual constituents in the constitution of electoral speech law, and thus this chapter serves to establish their context and consequences.

Conceptual Confluence

As a way of explaining why and how the constituent concepts examined in Chapter 1 have shaped the constitution of electoral speech law, I open Chapter 2 with a discussion of what I refer to as "confluence," in order to offer a theoretical account for the phenomenon by which the core concepts of electoral process and free speech law meet, merge, and develop as one distinct entity, within this domain—and, critically, how this is manifest in the form of competing *conceptions* of the marketplace of ideas.[55] In this regard, the integration and implications of confluence are informed by the notion of "conjuncture,"[56] particularly as I emphasize not simply the *intersection* of ideas,[57] or "streams" of thought, but also the *joining together* of the two and the reciprocal implications realized as these relatively autonomous lines of doctrine mutually constitute—and consistently *re*-constitute—each other within the electoral arena.[58]

As a function of this confluence, what we will see, in Daniel Polsby's terms, is the "multivalency of the First Amendment,"[59] whereby the basic market principle (stressing exchanges—via "free trade"—in the pursuit of the social good) remains intact, but yields new manifestations as the calibration is adjusted in the confrontation with novel complications in practice. In a certain sense, this tracks the movement observed by Jack Balkin in his discussion of "ideological drift," wherein "legal ideas and symbols will change their political valence as they are used over and over again in new contexts"[60]—though here what has "drifted" is not so much the "political valence" of the concept, as it is the particular *core* speech value around which the marketplace framework is constructed. To imagine this effect in perhaps more familiar terms, consider the analogy to the modern economic marketplace.

Individuals seeking to trade goods and carry out commercial activities in the United States face a wide range of regulations ostensibly intended to encourage, rather than restrain, transactions.[61] And, with the exception of the most libertarian-minded economists,[62] most seem to accept some measure of government supervision of the economy (e.g., the Federal Reserve or the Federal Trade Commission) and the prophylactic structures, restrictions, and rules in place to discourage monopolization, corruption, collusion, intimidation, chicanery, or any other putative tendencies of laissez-faire platforms. At the same time, most would still think of the American economy as a "free market" and would still conceive of this nation as encouraging an open exchange in goods and services. In the same way, alternative conceptions of the speech marketplace concept still assume and encourage "free" exchanges, but they take seriously the potential for "market failures" and stress the state's role in sustaining values in addition to (not instead of) the liberty of speakers, such as opportunities for broader participation and access, or the promotion (or discouragement) of certain forms of speech based on their perceived effects on the democratic process.[63]

Put differently, an approach of this sort "recognizes the possibility that, just as a restraint of trade is sometimes lawful because it *furthers*, rather than restricts, competition, so a restriction on speech, even when political speech is at issue, will sometimes prove reasonable," as Justice Stephen Breyer has recently argued in the context of the Court's campaign finance jurisprudence.[64] The affirmative role for the state in this sense is to facilitate free(r) trade by acting, as Owen Fiss has argued, "as the much-needed countervailing power, to counteract the skew of public debate attributable to the market and thus preserve the essential conditions of democracy," meaning that intervention is designed not to supplant the market, nor to perfect it, but rather to "supplement" it and act as a "corrective."[65] Growing out of the notion of "free trade" as originally theorized by Justice Holmes then, we will see in Chapter 2 evidence for three distinct though nonmutually exclusive models: the *classic*, *equality*, and *custodial* conceptions of the marketplace of ideas.

Rhetorical Modes

Whereas the focus in the first two chapters is the nature and development of the central conceptual elements in electoral speech law, Chapter 3 is addressed to the orientation and significance of the rhetorical modes of argument and articulation invoked by the justices in the process of *constituting* this body of law. Borrowing from the approaches of both Philip Bobbitt, who in his *Constitutional Fate* a generation ago set forth six "archetypes" of constitutional argument legitimizing judicial review, and more recently Erwin Chemerinsky, who has reasserted the importance of the fact that "Supreme Court opinions are rhetoric" because they convey "reasoned arguments intended to persuade,"[66] my focus is on only those primary forms that arise within and organize this legal domain, namely the *historical*, *empirical*, *aspirational*, and *precautionary* modes.

As we will see, the historical constitution of electoral speech law makes appeals to the past, as one would expect, but does so in a manner that diverges in important ways with respect to the merits of institutional *practices* versus inferred historical *principles*. The thrust of the empirical constitution, evident most often in campaign finance cases, is to stress the nature of evidence itself—not the amount of evidence or its persuasive value, necessarily, but rather the qualitative variety of evidence required to rationalize restrictions on electoral expression, as well as the epistemological implications of justifying state action when the requisite "proof" is either inaccessible or inconceivable. The aspirational constitution of the law governing freedom of speech during campaigns and elections is, as the name would suggest, premised on the notion of "aspiration" as the operant posture for the review of electoral speech restrictions. By contrast, a precautionary mode, while not necessarily "pessimistic," starts from less sublime assumptions about the people and processes that comprise electoral politics, and thus paints a picture of democratic life as functioning best with certain safeguards in place.

Cognitive Contours

Chapter 4 continues the investigation of elements by examining the significance of the actions, incidents, implements, and influences most salient in facilitating the constitution of this body of law in a cognitive sense.

Central to this portion of the overall examination is the notion that our political discourse "is constituted not only by concepts and the kinds of statements and assertions that they make possible but also—and arguably, even more deeply—by the *imagery* that gives these concepts their place and point."[67] And so, I argue here that the justices of the Supreme Court have something fairly distinct "in mind," so to speak—that is, some working "mental construct"—when they assess free speech claims: a "something" in the form of speech images that underlie the Court's rulings and that shed light on the nature and process by which this body of law is constituted.[68] A central premise here is that while "speech" in the sense of *a* "speech," or "speakers," is tangible—something we can see, hear, or feel—"*freedom* of speech" exists as an abstraction; and, as such, requires coloring in (or fleshing out), and generally an "imagination" of its particular forms to give it meaning and substance. In this vein, as Steven Winter argues, legal actors need "something like a cognitive map of the cultural models and other social constructs that animate thinking and decisionmaking among lawyers, judges, and laypersons alike."[69] Drawing on Winter's analogy, then, one might envision this chapter as a "cartographic" effort to discern and depict these "contours."

My attention to both preferences and persuasion in this chapter is an effort to better understand the process by which such images are cultivated—that is, how specific visions were constructed and why certain rhetoric was employed. In terms of preferences, legal scholars and practitioners are certainly well aware of traditional theories relying on the ostensible political ideologies of the justices—as well as the inferred implications and/or extrapolated consequences of these values for purposes of decision making. So, too, has scholarship demonstrated the significance of language and rhetoric in shaping perception(s)[70]—and thus one would certainly expect advocates to appeal to a host of potential influences beyond formal legal arguments when attempting to sway courts that sit in judgment of their cases and controversies.[71]

I will outline here and explore in the case study chapters (5 through 8) how the cognitive constitution of electoral speech law is facilitated by *communicative frames*, or "central organizing idea[s] for making sense of relevant events and suggesting what is at issue."[72] In the course of the argument, what we will see in this exploration of the capacity to shape language, meaning, and emphasis is that the act of framing "essentially involves selection and salience," or the decision to emphasize "some aspects of a perceived reality and make them more salient in a communicating text, in such a way as to promote a particular problem definition, causal interpretation, moral evaluation, and/or treatment recommendation for the item described."[73]

But working in an obviously related fashion with imagery, preferences, and persuasion, we will also see that *perception* is critical to the cognitive constitution of this domain, especially regarding the "schemata" that condition the way that individuals perceive phenomena. Such schemata, or those "sets of rules or generalizations derived from past experience that organize and guide information processing about ourselves and others in our social experience,"[74] are critical contributing forces in the act of "constitution," particularly in that they serve as a sort of lens, shaping and filtering what the justices "see" in a given case vis-à-vis other would-be images of expression.

CONSTITUTIONAL EPISODES

The case study component of this book attends to key constitutional episodes in an effort to explore how the above elements are manifest, how they coalesce, how they develop, and how they collectively facilitate this constitutive process. My analysis of each episode begins at the point of controversy and traces the case through the lower courts and ultimately to the U.S. Supreme Court, because, as much recent scholarship suggests, an analytical disposition such as this is essential to an appreciation of the contributions and interconnections of *non*judicial institutions, actors, and interests.[75] In looking to case studies for such guidance, I do not purport to have discerned *the* precise arrangements for the causal arrows accounting for particular decisions;[76] rather, I suggest that this nuanced and comprehensive approach to key episodes has explanatory value in that it serves both to isolate the relevant contributions shaping the outcome of the case and to explicate the process by which these elements emerged and evolved in their various permutations.

Each chapter in this section of the book is organized in the same fashion: After a brief introduction to the controversy, the asserted speech claims and state interests, and the ultimate conclusion reached by the U.S. Supreme Court, I turn to a more detailed examination of the context, concerns, and considerations of each case, taking a step away from the instant dispute to discuss the larger debate(s) within which it is situated and offering some historical and theoretical background for evaluating the matter. Following this, I discuss the development of the case, from the trial or initial proceedings, through the appellate courts, and on to the Supreme Court, tracing the evolution of the issues and setting the stage for the final half of each chapter where I explore the *constitution* of the case, bringing together essential data drawn from interviews with the various participants (e.g., the parties that brought the case, their attorneys, state officials, and other relevant legal and political actors), archival research, rulings at all levels, as well as briefs and various supplemental materials to offer an analytical framework for understanding how the various elements configured the case and ultimately shaped the constitution of the larger domain.

Before reviewing the specific episodes, I should note that they were selected because in at least three ways they are representative of the larger domain. First, with respect to the form of speech involved, I sought a balanced and even distribution by choosing only one campaign finance case (speech as *money*); by selecting two cases involving *activist*-speech (the distribution of leaflets and the solicitation of signatures); and a final case involving traditional *candidate* speech (in this case that of an advocate seeking the last-minute support of voters). As such, my scope incorporates three of the five potential dimensions—but, more importantly, its coverage includes thirty-four of the possible thirty-nine cases (see Table I.1). Second, regarding the Court's ultimate resolution of the controversy, in two of the cases the *asserted* speech interest prevailed, while in the other two the alleged state interest succeeded. And third, two of the cases began in federal district court, while the other two originated in some form of municipal court and then proceeded through the state system on their way to the U.S. Supreme Court.

Where the cases are less representative, I concede, is in regard to their relatively recent adjudication—a choice that was made on account of my interest in securing interviews with the parties involved in the development of the arguments that defined and helped to constitute the case. (For a brief discussion of interview methods and protocol, see the Appendix.) However, the benefit of erring on the side of gatherable data was that the study allowed for the episodic comparison of three of the four cases (*McIntyre*, *ACLF*, and *Shrink*) amid a stable cohort of Supreme Court justices, a group that sat on the high Court together for a remarkably long and nearly record-setting period from 1994 to 2005.[77]

Burson v. Freeman

The focus of Chapter 5 is *Burson v. Freeman*,[78] a case involving Tennessee's prohibition on "electioneering" (the solicitation of votes and the display/distribution of campaign literature) within one hundred feet of the entrance to the polling place on election day. Desiring both to advocate for a candidate "down the ballot" and to take advantage of the opportunity for last-minute campaigning, generally, Rebecca Freeman challenged this provision of the state's electoral code, alleging that the law violated her First Amendment right to communicate with voters in this quintessentially political environment. But for the state, while the grounds of the polling place may avail themselves to such activities 364 days a year, on *election day* they took on a different character, acting as a kind of embodiment of the premise of a "secret ballot"—meaning that, as the Court agreed, "campaign free zones" of this sort were necessary to protect voters and the process itself, in light of the increased potential for fraud, harassment, and intimidation where electioneering was allowed.

McIntyre v. Ohio Elections Commission

In Chapter 6 we will turn from polling place advocacy to political leafleting and the case of *McIntyre v. Ohio Elections Commission*,[79] inspired by Margaret McIntyre's refusal to pay a $100 fine for distributing "anonymous" fliers outside a school board meeting in the midst of a campaign over a school tax levy, and in violation of the state's electoral code requiring that election materials contain the name and business address of the party responsible for the literature. While the state defended its provision as necessary to police fraud, to facilitate libel prosecutions, and to serve the public interest in disclosure during political campaigns, we will see that the Court considered her case in light of a long and storied tradition of anonymous political discourse in Western society and issued a ruling with potentially vast implications for multiple constitutional domains. In its essence, *McIntyre* involved the intersection—or clash—of individual privacy and autonomy claims and the state's (and/or public's) interests in having "sunlight" serve as a deterrent for scurrilous speech.

Buckley v. American Constitutional Law Foundation, Inc.

In Chapter 7, we turn to *Buckley v. American Constitutional Law Foundation, Inc.* (*ACLF*),[80] and consider a challenge brought by various parties to several of Colorado's restrictions governing the "petition" phase of the direct democratic process, whereby advocates act as "spokespersons" of sorts and work to procure signatures from registered voters in order to qualify propositions for the general election ballot. *ACLF*, which was essentially a follow-up to *Meyer v. Grant*[81]—also a Colorado case involving restrictions on signature collection decided by the Supreme Court eleven years before—called for the justices to consider requirements instituted in response to the increased reports of fraud (e.g., phony names, misrepresentation of proposition issues, forged signatures) that came in the wake of the *Meyer* decision. In evaluating the new provisions (identification badges, more comprehensive disclosure requirements, and voter registration for circulators, among others), we will see that the Court found that the state had failed to sufficiently justify such restrictions on the capacity for communication with voters during this phase of the direct democratic process.

Nixon v. Shrink Missouri Government PAC

In the final case study, in Chapter 8, *Nixon v. Shrink Missouri Government PAC*,[82] we will examine the state of Missouri's effort to establish campaign contribution limits for state officials paralleling those upheld in *Buckley v. Valeo*. Challenging the $1,000 limit ($1,075, as applied in this case), Shrink Missouri Government PAC argued that the caps on contributions unconstitutionally restricted its ability to support its preferred Republican candidate in the primary election for state auditor. But for the Court, the state had shown that the limits were necessary to diminish (the "appearance" of) "corruption," to encourage more positive perceptions of the political process, and even to facilitate particular *forms* of speech (e.g., *time* as opposed to money) in the electoral marketplace of ideas.

A CONSTITUTION WE ARE EXPOUNDING

Drawing upon the argument developed in the preceding chapters, in the Conclusion I will offer some final thoughts on the significance of this approach and its findings, taking time as well to contemplate *this* constitution in "living" terms as we anticipate some potentially important elemental issues and episodes on the horizon. I will consider the future of electoral speech law in three respects, regarding: (a) its *evaluation* by the justices presently on the Court; (b) its *expansion* and growth as a domain; and (c) its *extension* deeper and wider into existing dimensions of speech questions covered throughout this book. Constitutions, of course, err on the side of "great outlines," as the borrowed title for this chapter reminds us,[83] and so we will consider here how the received outlines of the electoral speech "constitution" of today might bear on the electoral expression debates of tomorrow.

PART ONE

Constitutional Elements

CHAPTER 1

Constituent Concepts

OUR ATTENTION in this chapter is directed toward those constituent concepts that figure most prominently in the constitution of electoral speech law: "electoral superintendence" and the "marketplace of ideas." As we will see, "electoral superintendence" represents, for my purposes, the general supervisory capacity the U.S. Supreme Court has assumed in electoral process cases since about World War II, while the concept of a "marketplace of ideas" has developed (over approximately the same period of time) from Justice Oliver Wendell Holmes's famous contemplation of the potential for "free trade in ideas" to serve as the vehicle for evaluating competing claims and ultimately realizing the social good in the realm of expression. We begin first with an exploration of the essence and evolution of "superintendence," as this notion encapsulates the Court's involvement in the organization of American politics.[1]

ELECTORAL SUPERINTENDENCE

While the justices may, at times, appear "confused, or indifferent, about what politics is for,"[2] as one commentator has suggested, at least since the judicial construction of *Baker v. Carr* and the spawning of the "Reapportionment Revolution" in the early 1960s,[3] the U.S. Supreme Court has assumed the role of electoral superintendent, a development that has consistently and increasingly involved the justices in the regulation of politics. Indeed, as election law scholars have stressed, judicial oversight has increased to a degree "unimaginable when the Supreme Court first entered the political thicket" in *Baker*.[4] Before proceeding further then, a brief recap of the road leading here is appropriate. While the first three of the *White Primary Cases* (*Nixon v. Herndon* in 1927, *Nixon v. Condon* in 1932, and *Grovey v. Townsend* in 1935)[5] are probably the most well known of the Court's early twentieth-century interventions in the political process, what is in effect the theory—or *a* theory—for why the justices would superintend in such a fashion was not articulated as such until 1938, in *United States v. Carolene Products Co.*[6]

Sweet Carolene

Announcing a routine-enough assertion of the deference to be paid to legislation having a rational relationship to a professed concern for the health and well-being of the public and its markets, *Carolene* is, of course, most known for the significance of its fourth footnote: a signal, if you will, of the heightened scrutiny to be paid to particular, noncommercial, classes of legislation. As Chief Justice Harlan Fiske Stone suggested in this forecast, the operative scope for the presumption of constitutionality may be "narrower" when "legislation appears on its face to be within a specific prohibition of the Constitution, such as those of the first ten amendments, which are deemed equally specific when held to be embraced within the Fourteenth."[7]

Following the *Carolene* invitation over the course of the next generation, the Court, in *United States v. Classic,*[8] *Smith v. Allwright,*[9] and *Terry v. Adams,*[10] appeared to demonstrate its intention to "unclog" the "channels of political change," as John Hart Ely put it—acting as a sort of "referee" for the political process.[11] Election law scholars such as Samuel Issacharoff and Richard Pildes, informed by Ely's work and looking to the *White Primary Cases* for evidence of prototypical problems, have applauded this mode for the Court and theorized that the justices should adopt a "structural" or "functional" approach to guide their review of political process cases,[12] intervening "only when the 'market,'" (in their case, the "political market") was "systematically malfunctioning"—that is, essentially when the process is undeserving of trust because "the ins are choking off the channels of political change to ensure that they will stay in and the outs will stay out,"[13] as Ely put it.

What this emphasis on "structure" or "function" would do for practical purposes, Issacharoff and Pildes contend, would be to present democratic politics as akin to a "robustly competitive market," whose "vitality depends on both clear rules of engagement and on the ritual cleansing born of competition."[14] Only within a system of *competitive* party politics, in other words, can the "policy outcomes of the political process be responsive to the interests and views of citizens," and thus they advocate a "theory of legal regulation of politics premised on a skeptical view of political lockups, akin to the 'hard look' given to managerial self-protection in the corporate setting."[15]

Critics of this approach, such as Richard Hasen, find it to be a "shallow theory" that "says nothing about *how* the courts should intervene in the face of political market failure."[16] For Hasen, the Court should focus instead on substantive equality principles, working to distinguish between "core political equality rights," such as not discriminating against individuals on the basis of race, and "contested political equality rights," such as the right espoused by some that minorities should have the right to generally proportional representation in legislatures, for example. Hasen admits that "most core rights are socially constructed," meaning that they are the product of social consensus, but his recommendation is that when the Court intervenes regarding contested political equality rights, it should craft a "murky (or vague) political rule," whereas intervention in cases implicating *core* political equality rights calls for the use of "bright-line rules."[17] But he contends that this more articulate focus clarifies "for both members of the Court and the public at large what normative value judgments the Court is making," meaning, too, that "the Court is more likely to consider whether the case's holding might have unintended consequences on other political issues," an approach he finds to be "more honest than a focus on process, because the Court will not always provide process protection absent a threat to a substantive equality principle recognized by a Court majority."[18]

"Platonic Guardianship"

But critics of intervention—for *any* reason and however cabined by theoretical partitions—contend that such authority vested in the Court necessarily envisions the justices as "Platonic Guardians" summoned for their wisdom in the arrangements of political life and operations.[19] Beyond this sort of normative resistance, however—rooted as it typically is in the perception that the Court's involvement is somehow un- or antidemocratic—a separate argument for resisting the lure of *Carolene* would point to the various and prominent examples of electoral reform that successfully emerged *without* courts (i.e., through the *political* process), such as the institution of the Australian "secret ballot" system; the direct primary; the direct election of senators; various campaign finance regulations; term limits; and the extension of the franchise to blacks, women, those over age eighteen, and recently, in some states, to ex-felons who have completed their sentences—a class which has actually been stymied in its efforts to regain voting rights through the courts,[20] and which has, instead, relied on unequivocal public support for the eventual return of the franchise in the course of political mobilization campaigns, grassroots lobbying of state legislatures, and appeals to state executives.[21]

But the concept of electoral superintendence invites us as well to consider the theoretical implications and consequences of the phenomenon that Richard Pildes has recently referred to as the "constitutionalization of democratic politics"[22]—or the tendency over the last generation for "issues concerning the design of democratic institutions and the central processes of democracy" to "increasingly become questions of constitutional law throughout the world."[23] Regarding this "constitutionalization," Pildes explains that "the contours of fair political representation and political equality," the constitution of "group identities in the design of democratic institutions," and the campaign voices and political participation of corporations, interest groups, unions, and parties, "are now substantially constrained by constitutional law."[24] Indeed, even in the *rejection* of particular claims, he continues, "constitutional law has been credibly invoked and has generated divided Court decisions over other central aspects of elections, governance, and politics," such as the "role of third parties in American politics, the place of write-in candidacies, the structure of campaign debates, and the role of partisanship in the design of election districts."[25]

Thus, with the "stakes for the practice of democracy, and the role of constitutional law" as "dramatic" as they are,[26] and with "hardly any issue concerning the institutions of governance or the conduct of elections . . . outside the reach of contemporary constitutional law,"[27] Pildes contends that in the coming years, constitutional law will be "shaped, in part, by the collision of these two developments: a Supreme Court increasingly constitutionalizing the structures of democracy, and political circumstances that spawn recurring challenges to existing democratic structures."[28] In this context then, the Supreme Court "remains well entrenched in the political thicket and is likely to remain there."[29]

As we will see in the next section, a concept of equal constituent significance has evolved within the Court's free speech jurisprudence. While more of an interpretive device than a historical trend or tendency, the "marketplace of ideas" warrants attention in understanding the constitution of this domain because it presents the framework, or design, which effectively absorbs and animates the characteristics drawn from the "superintendent" construct. Next we will review the marketplace concept in terms of its development, doctrinal establishment, discontents, and ultimate dominion in free speech law.

THE "MARKETPLACE OF IDEAS"

An enormous literature contemplating its historical origins, philosophical justifications, political values, contemporary applications, and doctrinal evolution confronts anyone writing on the topic of freedom of speech in the United States. While I will draw on free speech scholarship generally in my scrutiny of the domain of electoral speech law, space constraints preclude me from delving deep into those academic debates that antedate or exist only in the general atmosphere of my particular interest in this book. Obviously, the broader historical background and development of freedom of speech in the United States must be scrutinized, and recent studies have done this quite well,[30] but the terms of this project confine my temporal focus to the latter half of the twentieth century for three reasons.

First, most scholarly discussion tends to focus on freedom of speech issues since about the turn of the twentieth century and more specifically the World War I era and into the 1920s, primarily because it was at this point that the U.S. Supreme Court first began to seriously review restrictions on freedom of speech as violations of the U.S. Constitution,[31] though of course it was not until 1931 that the Court actually *upheld* a free speech claim.[32] Second, it was not until just after World War II that the Court first reviewed an *electoral* speech case as defined in the Introduction.[33] Third, as we will see below, the "marketplace of ideas" metaphor was written into American law in *Abrams v. United States*,[34] though it would take at least another generation before it came to be regularly invoked by the Supreme Court in free speech cases.

Development

In what has been called the most memorable dissenting opinion of the twentieth century,[35] Justice Oliver Wendell Holmes, Jr., reasoned that the "ultimate good" could be "better reached by free trade in ideas" and that the "best test for truth is the power of the thought to get itself accepted in the competition of the market."[36] As initially envisioned, the "marketplace" metaphor was both a mechanism and a method for serving the social good by protecting the liberty of expression for individuals and by situating them within a dynamic arrangement relying on the power of collective choice (competition) to sort good from bad, right from wrong, true from false, and so on, suggesting that it was the aggregation of individual preferences—in the absence of state intervention—that itself functioned to "regulate" the commodities and exchanges within this arena. These being the theoretical assumptions underlying the metaphor, it is important now to consider the context and philosophical ancestry from which Holmes's construct emerged.

While the notion that citizens are fulfilled in the polis—and must employ the power of speech (or "voice") as they share in the governance of the community—has been around at least since the time of Aristotle,[37] the modern understanding of political speech embraced by our legal system finds its most immediate roots in the British tradition. While a full exploration of John Milton's intellectual contribution to this concept is not possible in this space, for purposes of a general overview it is important to stress here that—while his *Areopagitica* obviously predated modern *economic* ("marketplace") theory—this work did provide the "roots" of marketplace thinking, at least in the sense that there was, as he imagined it, a *clash* of ideas where Truth "grappled" with Falsehood.[38] And so, while his portrayal was not the "free trade" we find in American jurisprudence, it does rely on the same underlying principle—that of a contest of forces—as it argues against Parliament's resolved efforts to license the press.

Milton's contribution, then, was to offer the base layer in the development of modern free speech theory: that is, the notion that *if* allowed to compete in a "free and open encounter,"[39] "Truth" could be realized. Expanding on this premise, John Trenchard and Thomas Gordon, in *Cato's Letters*, provided some additional insight to sustain the general development of this concept in the early 1700s, urging, "Whilst all opinions are equally indulged, and all Parties equally allowed to speak their Minds, the Truth will come out."[40] However, it is John Stuart Mill who is most often acknowledged to have offered the theoretical blueprint for what would become the "marketplace of ideas," stressing, as he did, open inquiry, consideration, and investigation.

Certainly Mill's influence on the marketplace concept could be a book unto itself; but in essence, as he portrayed it, freedom of expression was valuable on individual *and* social grounds, essential to the development of the rational capacity of man *and* instrumental in the quest for the social good of Truth. While not every "exchange" would inexorably lead to such conclusions, of course, intellectual liberties were necessary to allow for corrections over time and for at least the pursuit of truth to remain a possibility. More specifically, while Mill's contemplation of "liberty" in terms of untethered individual freedom did not necessarily apply to issues beyond the intellectual domain,[41] his rejection in *On Liberty* of the prescribing of opinions by the state,[42] his emphasis on minority rights to expression in the face of majority opposition,[43] his vision of "truth" as the objective to be reached in the consideration of ideas,[44] his skepticism of "certainty" as a claim in intellectual debate,[45] his concern over assumptions of "infallibility,"[46] his unease with the complacency that settles in over time,[47] and his assertion that "discussion" is both a central device in the collective reasoning endeavor[48]—*and* a kind of "life support" instrument (my term) for the above-noted pursuit of "truth,"[49] *over time*—all provided essential theoretical materials in the mental construction of the "marketplace of ideas" metaphor. Thus, Mill's claim that free speech was essential to the permanent interests of man as a progressive being adjusted the model from that of "grappling" to "discovery," or a search engaged in by free and equal individuals, meaning that his argument was to provide the "best formulation" for what would later become the "marketplace" metaphor,[50] inferred from Holmes's depiction of "free trade" in ideas.[51]

Complicated thinker and jurist that he was,[52] Holmes's enshrinement of "exchange" logic was a bit of an about-face from his majority opinions in *Debs v. United States* and *Schenck v. United States*,[53] issued only months before, especially as he reconceived the role of freedom of speech in a democratic society by stressing, as noted above, that "the ultimate good" would be "better reached by free trade in ideas"—a move that did not displace the "clear and present danger" test established in *Schenck*, but one that certainly suggested a higher burden for demonstrating the "clarity" and "present-ness," if you will, of the alleged danger. *Why*, exactly, Holmes altered his opinion is the subject of much speculation,[54] ranging from strategic reasons,[55] to his discussions of the issues with legal and academic peers,[56] to his reading of various texts and treatises in the time between cases,[57] and to his personal epistemology and general outlook on and understanding of social relationships and obligations[58]—though it is important to stress, as well, the larger trends under way in this era, specifically the significant reconceptualization of individual rights.[59] Whatever the reason or combination of forces that generated the shift, the upshot was to cull together the philosophic components and craft the conceptual core of the "market" for free trade in ideas and information—which, in the post–World War II era would become, as we will see, the dominant paradigm for the contemplation of freedom of speech in the United States.

Doctrine

As I will demonstrate in this section, whether or not marketplace precepts are completely accepted by certain free speech theorists ("discontents" to be considered below), the metaphor that developed from Justices Holmes's dissent has become the Supreme Court's preferred conceptual framework for deciding free speech cases and controversies—a claim sustained by a host of scholars, including Frederick Schauer;[60] Lee Bollinger;[61] Craig Smith;[62] C. Edwin Baker;[63] Rodney Smolla;[64] Cass Sunstein;[65] Gerald Rosenberg and John Williams;[66] Samuel Issacharoff, Pamela Karlan, and Richard Pildes;[67] Jerome Barron;[68] and Steven K. Winter.[69] And so, while commentators may criticize the theory and applicability of the marketplace, jurists continue to rely on this approach and presume that the *best* (not the *only*, but the "best") test for "truth" (or optimal results) is the "free trade" of ideas in society, because the open exchange of information, opinions, and insights is perceived to be the best procedural means by which to protect both individual *and* social interests in expression. Whether or not judges should or should not be paying more attention to academic criticism is not my concern here; nor does it matter for my descriptive claim whether such invocations are, or are not, generally sincere, because, for whatever reason or purpose, the marketplace remains the preferred construct for deciding questions of free expression.

We turn then to a consideration of when and how the marketplace concept has been invoked across various domains of constitutional law. In explicit terms, my research[70] indicates that it was *Thornhill v. Alabama* that first referred to the testing of the "merits of ideas by competition,"[71] though *Bridges v. California* was the first case to use the exact phrase "free trade in ideas,"[72] as Holmes articulated it in *Abrams*.[73] *Terminiello v. Chicago* offered a synonymous and perhaps more common version in its reference to the "free *exchange* of ideas,"[74] while it was *United States v. Rumely* which took the next step—situating these "trades" and "exchanges" in a distinct *locale*: that is, a "market *place*" (two words).[75] Finally, nearly fifty years after its blueprint was sketched out, we have the grand opening of the "marketplace of ideas" in *Lamont v. Postmaster General*.[76]

While a calculation of the total number of *explicit* references over time, in one form or another, provides an interesting quantitative perspective,[77] such an approach is considerably more narrow than the claim I am making here, which is that the logic, assumptions, and values of the "marketplace" concept are sufficiently imbued within our modern legal tradition and popular culture that they can easily govern the contemplation of a case even *without* citations to *Abrams*;[78] even absent patent prefatory exclamations in the form of: "We decide the following case in light of the marketplace of ideas . . ."; and, even when appeals to the associated conceptual vernacular of "free trade," "competition," "exchange," and so on, are lacking.

That said, a review of literal invocations is still instructive in some sense because it affords a measure of influence, given the appearance of such appeals within some of the most prominent civil liberties cases of the last half-century. More specifically, the status and situation of these invocations reveal two phenomena portraying the significance of the marketplace concept in the canon of constitutional law. On one hand, we see that, after taking a few decades to become established, the momentum of the metaphor has picked up considerably in some of the key free expression cases since World War II; on the other hand, the emerging mobility, or even malleability, of the concept is evident in its influence on cases *beyond* the speech domain.

Considering momentum first, the concept of the speech "marketplace" figured prominently in majority, concurring, or dissenting opinions in critically important post–World War II and developing Cold War cases (*Terminiello v. Chicago,*[79] *Beauharnais v. Illinois,*[80] and *Dennis v. United States*),[81] as well as one of the key Vietnam–War era speech cases of the 1960s (*Tinker v. Des Moines*).[82] In the 1970s, the marketplace was implicated in the primary "obscenity" standard case of the last half-century (*Miller v. California*),[83] as it had been in the preceding analysis (*Roth v. United States*);[84] it appeared in an important case involving "erogenous zoning" (*Young v. American Mini Theatres*);[85] and it arose in the paradigm case for campaign finance (*Buckley v. Valeo*)[86]—as well as one of its most immediate and significant follow-up cases (*First National Bank v. Bellotti*).[87] Two critical cases contemplating the proper scope of "commercial speech" rights, *Bigelow v. Virginia*[88] and *Virginia State Board of Pharmacy v. Virginia Citizens Consumer Council,*[89] looked to the marketplace, as did the famous "seven dirty words" case involving radio broadcasts (*FCC v. Pacifica*).[90]

In the 1980s, the "marketplace" concept arose in the consideration of: a community's attempt to keep "big money" from overwhelming its direct lawmaking process (*Citizens Against Rent Control v. Berkeley*);[91] the right of speakers to communicate with the public on private property (*Pruneyard Shopping Center v. Robins*);[92] "captive audience" problems (*Consolidated Edison v. Public Service Commission*);[93] further commercial speech claims (*Metromedia, Inc. v. San Diego*);[94] "public forum" debates

(*Perry Educational Association v. Perry Local Educators Association*);[95] clarifications of the "public figure" standard with respect to defamation of character (*Hustler Magazine v. Falwell*);[96] and a prohibition on offensive and incendiary speech (*Texas v. Johnson*).[97]

The 1990s saw prominent rulings explicitly invoking the marketplace concept in the Court's unanimous rejection of hate speech legislation (*R.A.V. v. St. Paul*),[98] as well as in a concurrence for that seminal case;[99] in yet another important "public forum" case (*International Society for Krishna Consciousness, Inc. v. Lee*);[100] in the paradigm case regarding anonymous political speech (*McIntyre v. Ohio Elections Commission*);[101] in the Court's statement on an important melding of the speech and establishment clauses of the First Amendment (*Rosenberger v. Rector and Visitors of the University of Virginia*),[102] as well as in a concurrence in that case;[103] in the ongoing review of commercial speech rights (*44 Liquormart v. Rhode Island*);[104] and, in the *then*-emerging realm of Internet speech (*Reno v. American Civil Liberties Union*).[105] And since 2000, the marketplace concept can be seen in an important case "mopping up" the paradigm established by *Buckley*, with respect to contribution limits at the state level (*Nixon v. Shrink Missouri Government PAC*);[106] in another prominent Internet speech case (*Ashcroft v. ACLU*);[107] in this post-*Buckley* generation's major (re)statement of the entire rationale for campaign finance (*McConnell v. FEC*);[108] and in the consideration of a post-*R.A.V.* prohibition on cross-burning (*Virginia v. Black*),[109] among many others.

With respect to the mobility of the marketplace concept, note that the basic principles and assumptions of marketplace reasoning have served as the logical and/or rhetorical grounds in prominent cases in the following domains: ballot access (*Williams v. Rhodes*,[110] *Anderson v. Celebrezze*);[111] freedom of the press (*Houchins v. KQED, Inc.*);[112] libel and defamation of character (*Time, Inc. v. Hill*,[113] *Gertz v. Welch*);[114] freedom of association—surely a right "ancillary" to free speech, as it is often said, but still analytically distinct in its own right (*Thornhill v. State of Alabama*,[115] *NAACP v. Button*,[116] *Roberts v. United States Jaycees*,[117] *Timmons v. Twin Cities Area New Party*);[118] equal protection, in a rather odd, albeit still informative manner (*Stanton v. Stanton*);[119] and, more recently, religious establishment, specifically in one of the two "Ten Commandments" cases (*McCreary County v. ACLU*).[120]

Discontents

Despite—or perhaps due to—its prominence in the Court's jurisprudence, scholars have leveled extensive criticism at the underlying assumptions and practical application of the "marketplace" concept,[121] though some, too, have demonstrated faith in the long-term benefits of free trade in ideas.[122] The thrust of this criticism centers on a few basic themes. First, some scholars question the propriety of importing theories and frameworks from the *economic* realm to describe (and dictate) human action in this distinctly *social* sphere.[123] David Strauss, for example, wonders how we "know what constitutes perfect competition or the equivalent of market power in the realm of ideas," because "no matter how we define the ground rules, there is no theory that explains why competition in the realm of ideas will systematically produce good or truthful or otherwise desirable outcomes."[124] In this respect, Vincent Blasi suggests that Holmes's figure of speech may be better imagined as a "choice-proliferating marketplace, a site for spontaneous and promiscuous browsing, comparing, tasting, and wishing, a paean to peripatetic subjectivity amid abundance" rather than a "market" with its economic implications and assumptions. Such an application, he continues, "evokes intellectual serendipity."[125]

On a different level, some wonder whether there is an inherent—and perhaps irreconcilable—contradiction in assuming that any *unitary* end, such as "Truth," can be achieved by *adversarial* means, such as the "competition" of ideas.[126] Indeed, a theory built on the collective search for Truth necessarily requires that human beings are functionally qualified to—and sufficiently interested in—carrying on the exchange. In assuming fitness to engage in such an exchange, markets (of economy and expression) are predicated on the assumption that individuals are rational. The marketplace of ideas, in fact, expects human reason to be the engine that drives the "exchange"—allowing us to distinguish true from false and good from bad; thus it is essential that individuals have "access" to the arena *and* that they be willing and able to apply their faculties in such a manner.[127] Form and function are often difficult to disentangle, given

Madison Avenue–style political campaigns, our basic cognitive processes,[128] and the "background limitations," "indoctrination," "mediation," and "manipulation" that inhibit genuinely critical analysis of social conditions, questions, and concerns. Thus some scholars question whether individuals within the current system and given the existing distribution of power and resources are even capable of independently and critically evaluating the world around them.[129]

Meanwhile, in a world where traditional outlets of information are waning, where a dizzying array of alternatives have sprung up in their place,[130] and where vast income disparity, decreasing political participation, vanishing public fora in a cyber age,[131] diminished social capital,[132] the fixedness of our views on salient issues,[133] the general desire to avoid confrontations with those with whom we disagree,[134] and the increasing potential for "polarization" as groups and individuals are exposed only to those opinions, outlooks, Web sites, and chat rooms that affirm and amplify their preexisting beliefs and values,[135] critics and theorists wonder whether citizens are really willing (or able) to be exposed to the diverse informational input assumed by the marketplace metaphor.[136] Beyond this is the problem of bias and privilege built into the very structure itself.[137] Indeed, argues Stanley Fish, the marketplace "does not exist in nature" and thus must be constructed, meaning that the "way it is to be set up will often be a matter of dispute," and decisions about its "very shape" will "involve just the ideological considerations it is meant to hold at bay."[138] Finally, others ask the question: without the benefit of some external referent, is "Truth" simply "the 'thought' that wins acceptance in the market"[139]—that which "survives" . . . in the "long run"?[140]

But discontentment with the "marketplace" model is also manifest in alternative theoretical explications of the value, purpose, and relationship of free speech in a democracy. Perhaps the most prevalent competing approach is what I will refer to as the "self-government" rationale[141]—though it is sometimes referred to as the "argument from democracy,"[142] the "progressivist" approach,[143] or a "Madisonian" conception of speech[144]—a general notion that speech should enjoy vigorous protection principally because it better prepares citizens for participation in democratic life. This understanding, which could arguably be traced at a basic level back to Athens,[145] finds its clearest articulation in speech law in Justice Louis Brandeis's eloquent concurrence in *Whitney v. California*,[146] with its emphasis on the role of political speech in promoting the development of the citizen. "Those who won our independence," Brandeis wrote, "believed that the final end of the State was to make men free to develop their faculties; and that in its government the deliberative forces should prevail over the arbitrary."

> Moreover, valued "both as an end and as a means," he offered, they "believed liberty to be the secret of happiness and courage to be the secret of liberty," and believed that freedom to think as you will and to speak as you think are means indispensable to the discovery and spread of political truth; that without free speech and assembly discussion would be futile; that with them, discussion affords ordinarily adequate protection against the dissemination of noxious doctrine; that the greatest menace to freedom is an inert people; that public discussion is a political duty; and that this should be a fundamental principle of the American government.[147]

While the above passage is plainly informed by Justice Holmes's "marketplace" framework for conceiving of and protecting free speech (with the stress on the "discovery and spread of political truth," the suggestion that discussion would be "futile" without "free speech and assembly," and certainly the notion of "liberty" valued as a "means"), Brandeis goes further by imagining the expansive domain of individual development as tied to self-expression,[148] and especially in the notion of "public discussion" as a "political duty" for citizens and intrinsically good for democracy.[149]

Drawing to some degree on the Brandeis vision of political speech, Alexander Meiklejohn provided some of the first significant commentary on First Amendment theory and doctrine in the post–World War II era. In a series of books and articles, Meiklejohn argued variously that the First Amendment is an "absolute,"[150] and that it "stands alone, as the cornerstone of the structure of self-government."[151] For Meiklejohn, "public" speech was deserving of special protection in the American constitutional system because for citizens not to enjoy this opportunity for shared governance, and collective inquiry, would be to offend one of the fundamental principles of the republic.[152] Thomas Emerson, for his part, sought in the 1960s to devise a general theory of the First Amendment,[153] reasoning that the four-fold "function of freedom of expression in a democratic society" was to assure individual self-fulfillment, to preserve the means for attaining the truth, to provide a method for securing the participation of the polity, and to maintain the balance between stability and change in society.[154] The various strands of Emerson's thought (especially the aim of self-fulfillment and the place for participation) worked together "to imply a notion of freedom oriented toward self-realization and self-determination"[155]—the upshot of which was to demonstrate how the broader objectives of self-rule were to be realized at both the micro (individual) and the macro (societal) levels through the free flow of expression. Finally, as but one example of subsequent theorizing in this vein, Cass Sunstein has argued that "our constitutional system is one of deliberative democracy," prizing "both political (not economic) equality and a shared civic culture" in seeking to "promote, as a central democratic goal, reflective and deliberative debate about possible courses of action."[156]

Resisting the instrumental presuppositions of the marketplace and self-government approaches, other scholars argue that the First Amendment should be construed to protect a broader domain of expressive liberty and a more expansive notion of individual autonomy. This argument presents the individual as sovereign, autonomous, singularly in control of his or her mind and able to make the final choice on any matter.[157] As Thomas Scanlon contended along these lines, "an autonomous person cannot accept without independent consideration the judgment of others as to what he should believe or what he should do,"[158] though it is Martin Redish who is arguably more associated with this line of thinking, especially in his introduction of the concept of "self-realization," a deliberately broader term that protects all forms of expression that serve this goal and that encompasses autonomy, liberty, and human development.[159] Following Redish, C. Edwin Baker has registered discontentment with marketplace theory in several works, arguing instead that "the first amendment protects a broad realm of nonviolent, noncoercive, expressive activity," that "individual self-fulfillment and participation in change are fundamental purposes of the first amendment," and ultimately that "speech is protected because, without disrespecting the autonomy of other persons, it promotes both the speaker's self-fulfillment and the speaker's ability to participate in change."[160]

But even beyond these models, legal scholars have proposed a host of additional free speech theories, including Vincent Blasi's notion of the First Amendment as a "safety valve" (and, more recently, as essential to the development of "character");[161] Lee Bollinger's conception of the First Amendment as a device to promote tolerance;[162] Steven Shiffrin's contemplation of the place for "romance" in our thinking about free expression;[163] Ronald Collins and David Skover's urging of a "bottom-up" approach to the First Amendment;[164] and "antitheory" approaches suggesting that "free speech" is simply verbal behavior that serves the substantive agendas of those in power.[165]

Dominion

And yet, in anticipation of the argument to come in Chapter 2, I contend that in many ways discontentment with the marketplace framework actually works to sustain it. That is, a conceptual absorption is evident as competing models rely on similar structures, intentions, and premises in their effort(s) to (re)adjust, (re)orient, and/or (re)arrange input, actors, and outlets in such a way that the market model functions *better*—or, more to the point, that it *delivers* on its promises. The effect of this, I suggest, is to *entrench* the "marketplace" in American law. Consider, for example, that even the "market failures" mindset is essentially a "reformist marketplace theory,"[166] meaning that those of this disposition first highlight flaws *in practice* and then proceed to "advocate repair" or "governmental intervention,"[167] such as Jerome Barron's "right of access statute" to protect the "right to be heard" via media outlets,[168] in order to improve its functional capacity. Thus, even this line of argument does not actually dismiss the *virtues* of an "exchange" of ideas; what it rejects is the premise that the process can be sufficiently engineered by the operations of an "invisible hand."[169]

In the same sense, the regulation of campaigns "may indicate not so much the rejection of a market ideal for elections as the recognition that supervision can *improve* the working of the marketplace."[170] Indeed, as the campaign finance scholar Herbert Alexander asks in this spirit of electoral reform,

> How can political dialogue be improved, a more attentive and well-informed electorate be attracted, and citizens be encouraged to participate in the political process as workers, contributors, and voters, while financial inequalities among candidates and political parties are diminished, the dominance of big money is reduced, and opportunities for well-qualified persons to become candidates are opened up?[171]

And how, too, he continues can "democratic principles be applied to elections in an age of media politics, seemingly dominated by an atmosphere of dollar politics, in ways consonant with constitutional guarantees?"[172]

Consider as well the contrast that I would argue is too often, and too dramatically, drawn between the objectives of "truth" and "self-government" as functions and derivatives of "free trade"—portraying the two theories as mutually exclusive and conceptually incompatible given their allegedly divergent intentions and operating principles.[173] Cass Sunstein, offering but the foremost example of such a tendency, seems to draw too sharp a distinction between his approach to free speech and the reigning marketplace concept. Consider the purported benefits that Sunstein finds in his "Madisonian" approach and notice how much these virtues resonate with the imagery and assurances of the marketplace: "Public deliberation may reveal the *truth or falsity* of factual claims about the state of the world or about the likely effects of policy proposals." Thus, Sunstein contends,

> through *confrontation* among people who disagree, errors of fact may be *revealed* as such. A candidate for electoral office claims that a tax on gasoline will have good effects on the environment, by reducing automobile pollution; another candidate disagrees. At least if *reasoned* analysis can be made to play a large role in public debate, *better outcomes* should result from public deliberation simply through this *process of correction*.[174]

There are some important parallels here with Holmes's dissent in *Abrams*. Not only does Sunstein speak first of the instrumental potential for deliberation to reveal "truth or falsity," but he relies on the "confrontation" (at least a cousin of "competition" or the "War" Milton imagined) to demonstrate "errors of fact" (again moving toward "truth"), and assumes that "better outcomes" are the logical by-product of "deliberation" (certainly the assumed procedural method for exchanges in the marketplace) and the general "process" by which speakers and listeners encounter competing ideas and their advocates. One can also see a consonance between the "market" and "Madison" approaches, as indicated by Sunstein's conclusion that "a New Deal may therefore be necessary" for freedom of speech in America.[175] Here, even more than in the quotation above, the historical analogy to a period famously associated with *regulated* markets (rather than the absence of markets) seems inconsistent with his apparent interest in moving away from the logic (and, for him, constraints) of a "market" approach to speech because "New Deal" economic programs were most of all a departure only from a laissez-faire market.[176]

CONCLUSION

And so, it is to this idea of regulated—or, in this case, *superintended*—markets for electoral speech that we now will turn. As we will see, the constituent concepts explicated in this chapter are both necessary—and thus neither is itself sufficient—to explain the conceptual constitution of this body of law. The argument in Chapter 2 will begin with an elaboration on the notion of "confluence" in the abstract, followed by an explication of its effects in this domain. What this investigation will demonstrate is that the merging of these general notions has yielded competing understandings of the very nature, purpose, and possibilities of electoral expression in the United States—or what I will refer to as the classic, equality, and custodial conceptions of the marketplace of ideas.

CHAPTER 2

Conceptual Confluence

THE PREVIOUS CHAPTER'S EXPLORATION of constituent concepts prepares us for the present consideration of the outcomes and implications of what I will refer to as "conceptual confluence," or the phenomenon whereby two relatively autonomous lines of doctrine—electoral process and free speech law—have merged and melded, affording an accommodation of the values and precepts central to *both* jurisprudential traditions. While cases involving free speech claims *within* the electoral process might be appealed to the Court as "speech" cases rather than "process" cases, I contend that issues of electoral expression are intrinsically different from speech cases outside this domain and thus efforts to decouple "speech" from "process" law will, as an intellectual endeavor, fail to appreciate the particular essence of the intersection and development of the two—as one—over time. And thus we begin this chapter with the requisite attention to how this development might take place.

CONCEPTUAL CONFLUENCE

There is a sense in which "conceptual confluence" portrays tendencies similar to the observed qualities of "path dependency," which as James Mahoney has argued "characterizes specifically those historical sequences in which contingent events set into motion institutional patterns or event chains that have deterministic properties."[1] One of the implications of such "dependency" is, of course, that "previously viable options may be foreclosed in the aftermath of a sustained period of positive feedback," while "cumulative commitments on the existing path will often make change difficult and will condition the form in which new branchings will occur."[2] The upshot of this, as political development scholars will recognize, is increased "stickiness,"[3] not in terms of a "mechanistic form in which choices, once made, lock in forever," but rather in the sense that "*particular aspects* of social relations . . . become deeply embedded."[4]

But even more specifically, Thomas Keck, in his excellent study of the Rehnquist Court, captures something close to what I am suggesting here, by explaining that "constitutional development is a 'path dependent' historical process [in the sense that] the particular sequence by which competing norms become entrenched within constitutional discourse has a substantial effect on subsequent events."[5] That said, my preferred metaphor here is that of "streams," rather than "paths"—and thus I look to "confluence" as the phenomenal shorthand, given its definitional accessibility in accounting for both a point of contact *and* a process by which tributaries flow in from multiple sources. In the course of confluence, then, the domain of electoral speech law constantly and irrevocably gathers sediment as it shifts with the momentum, influences, and confines of contributing forces,[6] proceeding in such a way that both the conjoined waters and the supporting landscape are fundamentally reshaped in and through their interaction.[7] And so, the merger of these two lines of doctrine may proceed in a meandering, less-than-direct manner, but this is merely the stream itself charting new directions—which may involve lateral twists and turns, but which always continues to move downstream as an amalgam of its constitutional elements.[8]

SUPERINTENDING THE MARKETPLACE(S) OF IDEAS

The significance of this confluence of concepts, we shall see, is that it modifies versions of the marketplace metaphor, similarly oriented toward reaching the social good through the exchange of ideas, but predicated on and oriented toward interests beyond that of individual *liberty*, with which the metaphor is most associated in its original form.[9] Put simply, we will see the "superintendence" *of* the "marketplace of ideas," specifically in the influx of equality principles (e.g., "one person, one vote") drawn generally from the cases comprising the Reapportionment Revolution in the early 1960s and stressing values of parity and participation. We will also see the influence of what I refer to as "custody," an admittedly less contained notion that stresses primarily, though not exclusively, the state's proprietary claim to and supervision of the mechanisms and institutions that animate the democratic process.

To be more precise, in addition to the original understanding of the marketplace concept—essentially manifest here as the classic conception—we can also see within this domain an equality conception, directed toward promoting access and opportunities for involvement in the realm of electoral expression for more people, and a custodial conception, privileging those manners and methods of expression (in the eyes of the "custodian"—i.e., the state) that best serve the structural intentions, interests, purposes, and designs of the political process itself. As we will see below in the analysis of the reasoning employed in deciding electoral speech cases, these alternative conceptions of the marketplace are also committed to the putative good to be achieved through the exchange of ideas, though they differ in their understanding of the state's role,[10] their estimation of the proper means for facilitating the exchange, and in their endorsement of the paramount value or principle toward which such expression is properly focused.

To flesh this out a bit more, and to demonstrate how the "core" of the "exchange" concept survives its reconceptualization, let us shift the analogy from the economic realm to the classroom. As teachers well know, in any random sample of students in institutions of higher learning there are going to be some individuals who—if left to their own devices—will tend to monopolize the conversation; there will be some whose mannerisms and/or methods of argument tend to be disruptive of the learning process; some who have contributions to make, but who are more reserved because they lack the confidence, characteristics, or perhaps *volume* to interject their thoughts; and, of course, there will be some who are simply thinking about lunch. Or their iPod. So, a discussion-centered pedagogy almost certainly confronts the following dilemma: while a laissez-faire attitude toward class discussion *may* "in the long run" accomplish the desired results, sometimes intervention may seem appropriate to encourage a wide(r) array of perspectives, to compel minimum standards of civility, or (perhaps) to redirect wayward discussions and encourage their adherence to the method (i.e., deliberation) and the particular mission (i.e., education) of the institution itself.

Put differently, the classroom "marketplace" may call for the regulation of the manner of exchange or the commodities being traded. In this respect, an instructor might, for example, deliberately *not* call on certain students who always raise their hands in class, in the interest of increased diversity and "equalization" of voices and opinions.[11] Doing so would surely "restrict the speech of some,"[12] but it would also allow the teacher to invite more participants (more reserved students, for example) into the conversation and thus avoid situations wherein a few voices (ideas) tend to dominate the discussion. Such an approach represents the sort of values evident in a conception of the marketplace of ideas that orients itself less toward the unmitigated liberty of the individual speaker, and more toward equality (of opportunity) for more, and more diverse speakers even—and this is vitally important—as it remains committed to the concept of "free trade" in ideas as the *means* by which to reach the desired democratic *end*.

For an example of how the concept of "custody" might be manifest in the marketplace of ideas, consider the operational mode and mission of "cyber marketplaces," such as bulletin boards and e-mail Listservs. Mediums of this sort play an important role in the exchange of information and ideas between scholars, activists, and advocates, but practically speaking there is always someone overseeing the posts—typically referred to as the custodian, in fact—who enforces the rules of the medium and who generally works to see that the objectives, intentions, and spirit of the endeavor are respected by the contributors. In such settings, exchanges can tend to veer off their intended course—devolving, perhaps, into partisan, ideological, and even ad hominem attacks. While the individuals posting such messages may assert that they are "free" to do so—that it is within their "liberty"—such expression could be entirely inconducive to, or incompatible with the mission or purpose of the instituted medium itself; as such, a "custodian" may intervene to curtail such posts, to remind all of the parameters for exchanges within this environment, and to keep the contributors working toward the social good in the most productive way possible.

The remainder of this chapter provides more elaborate theoretical attention to the nature and origins of these conceptions and then uses passages from the cases as evidence to flesh out the character of (and distinctions between) them as they arise in this domain. Given my particular interest in how the chosen language and style of argument illuminate the critical conceptual elements in the passages, my discussion of the facts, history, and consequences of these cases will perhaps be more abbreviated than some readers may like. That said, I err on the side of breadth in teasing out the major themes evident across the domain as a whole.

THE CLASSIC CONCEPTION

As suggested above, in its original form the marketplace concept emphasized a laissez-faire role for government; it rejected the idea of state regulation, even for the "good" of the market; it envisioned a vibrant economy of speech in the form of numerous and uninhibited "sellers" (speakers) and "buyers" (listeners); and it, more than the other two versions that have emerged, generally expected that the social good—in the form of "truth" and its ancillary benefits for democracy—would emerge from the "natural" and uninhibited flow of ideas and information.

While Holmes only sketched out the general parameters of "free trade" in ideas in his *Abrams* dissent,[13] my study of the application of this concept to the domain of electoral speech law demonstrates that, at least within this particular context, the classic conception stresses three distinct, though complementary, tenets. First, there is a clear attention to *quantums*, with the implication that more communicants—able to offer more "speech"—is necessarily better than its alternative. (Ten speakers on soap boxes in the public square is, in other words, ipso facto superior to five.) Second, we also see state supervision of the speech arena rejected as inherently unacceptable evidence of *paternalism*. Third, there is a consistent adherence to the notion that *truth* or the best possible results can and *will* flow only from the exchange of ideas enjoyed by agents unmitigated in the electoral marketplace.

Quantums

Viewing the marketplace as a bazaar with speakers peddling their wares, the particular affinity for quantums finds an intrinsic value in *more* speech—not better, clearer, more persuasive, informed, or prescient speech, necessarily, just more speech as the precondition for a better result *from* speech, in that an environment with more parties and products will have the tendency to better realize the good of society. As Justice Scalia succinctly put it, capturing this theme while dissenting (in part) in *McConnell v.*

FEC, the landmark campaign finance case upholding major provisions of the Bipartisan Campaign Reform Act (BCRA) of 2002 (also known as "McCain-Feingold"), "Given the premises of democracy, *there is no such thing as too much speech*."[14]

But to track the development of the emphasis on quantums within the classic conception, we begin with the principal holding in *Buckley v. Valeo*,[15] which involved a challenge to the Federal Election Campaign Act of 1971 (and as amended in 1974) brought by a wide array of interests and parties and which is certainly one of the most significant and controversial free speech cases of the twentieth century. The per curiam opinion of the eight justices sitting at the time (Blackmun, Brennan, Burger, Marshall, Powell, Rehnquist, Stewart, and White—Stevens did not participate) in essence found various limitations on contributions to candidates for federal office, certain disclosure and record-keeping provisions, and the public financing of presidential elections to be *constitutional*; while finding limitations on expenditures by candidates and their committees (except for presidential candidates accepting public funds), the $1,000 limitation on independent expenditures, the limitation on expenditures drawn from candidates' personal funds, and the method of appointment for FEC members to be *unconstitutional*.[16] While the disclosure and public funding provisions are of critical importance to the operations of modern campaigns, it was the Court's distinction between campaign contributions and expenditures that has had the greatest lasting significance.

Though accepting the claim that the state's legitimate interest in preventing corruption and the "appearance of corruption" justified the limits on contributions to candidates for federal office,[17] the Court found expenditure limits to be an offense to the First Amendment because, among other reasons, a "restriction on the amount of money a person or group can spend on political communication during a campaign necessarily reduces the *quantity* of expression by restricting the number of issues discussed, the depth of their exploration, and the size of the audience reached";[18] and thus, such limitations represented "substantial rather than merely theoretical restraints on the *quantity* and diversity of political speech."[19] By contrast, limits on *contributions* to candidates entailed "only a marginal restriction upon the contributor's ability to engage in free communication," because "the *quantity* of communication by the contributor does not increase perceptibly with the size of his contribution, since the expression rests solely on the undifferentiated, symbolic act of contributing."[20] Along with the problems thought to flow from corruption and its "appearance" then was the conjectured impact of the distinction in raw number terms.

This same thrust is evident in the Court's ruling in *Citizens Against Rent Control v. Berkeley*,[21] involving the review of a Berkeley, California, statute passed by citizen initiative (the Election Reform Act of 1974), limiting contributions by corporations or individuals to $250 in direct democracy campaigns. While the California Supreme Court had upheld the statute as serving a compelling state interest in preventing undue influence—in effect reducing speech *quantity* to achieve a certain degree of speech *quality*—the Court struck down the ordinance on speech grounds. Writing for an eight-member majority, Chief Justice Burger explained, "The Court has long viewed the First Amendment as protecting a marketplace for the clash of different views and conflicting ideas," and the challenged ordinance in this case "places restrictions on that marketplace."[22]

Here, Burger shifts the emphasis on the *quantity* of voices in a different direction—stressing that the *many* voices may not be denied access to the marketplace that allows admittance to the *one*. Under the Berkeley ordinance, an affluent person acting alone can "spend without limit to advocate individual views on a ballot measure," whereas the unconstitutional prohibition applies only when "contributions are made in concert with one or more others."[23] To be sure, he continued, there are some activities open to individuals, but foreclosed to groups, though it is clearly unconstitutional to "place a Spartan limit—or indeed any limit—on *individuals wishing to band together* to advance their views on a ballot measure, while placing none on individuals acting alone."[24] Thus, the limit on contributions "imposes a significant restraint on the freedom of expression of groups and those individuals who wish to express their views through committees."[25]

In another case involving state restrictions on speech within the initiative process and directing similar attention to the *quantifiable* as the focal point for the form and function of speech to be protected—that is, to the number of speakers as, in effect, a "market" indicator—the Court, a few years later in *Meyer v. Grant*,[26] struck down a Colorado law that prohibited payments to petition circulators in campaigns to present constitutional amendments to the voters on the general election ballot. Agreeing with the Tenth Circuit Court of Appeals that "the statute trenches upon an area in which the importance of First Amendment protections is 'at its zenith,'" the Court, in a unanimous opinion by Justice Stevens, concluded that the circulation of petitions was "interactive communication concerning political change that is appropriately described as 'core political speech,'"[27] with the state's burden under such conditions "well-nigh insurmountable."[28]

Though Colorado had introduced evidence of fraud to justify the prohibition on payments to circulators,[29] and while such a restriction did not seem to stifle the citizens' use of the direct democratic method of lawmaking,[30] notice that the Court's attention in this case remains fixed on the purported "limits" put on the "*number* of voices that will convey appellees' messages," an imposition that, when combined with restrictions on when they can speak, "limits the *size* of the audience they can reach."[31] Thus, for the justices, such restrictions make it "less likely that appellees will garner the number of signatures necessary to place the matter on the ballot, thus limiting their ability to make the matter the focus of statewide discussion" and having the "inevitable effect of reducing the total *quantum* of speech on a public issue."[32]

Consider too, *Hynes v. Mayor of Oradell*,[33] a case involving a challenge by a candidate for political office to a municipal ordinance that prohibited door-to-door canvassing without the permission of the local police department. Writing for the majority and finding the law to be unconstitutionally vague, Justice Brennan stressed the importance of removing impediments to citizen speech in the political process. But he did so in a way that expanded the concern for quantums into the realm of the conjectural. "The oppressive financial burden of campaigns makes reliance on volunteers absolutely essential," he wrote, "and, in light of the enormous significance of citizen participation to the preservation and strength of the democratic ideal, absolutely desirable, indeed indispensable."[34] Thus, identification requirements, which he speculated were "offensive to the sensibilities of private citizens," must "even in their least intrusive form" tend to "discourage that participation."[35] What is significant here is that the constitutional problem with the ordinance for Brennan was the *supposition* that the law would reduce the number of participants, meaning that this tenet of the classic model resists as well those regulatory efforts which may be inferred or assumed to have the effect of limiting the number of speakers, even if the amount of actual speech may be otherwise unaffected.

Paternalism

In other cases portraying a marketplace orientation in its classic form, the contours of the justices' reasoning will stress the inherent dangers concomitant to any state effort to supervise speech "for the good of" either the electoral process or the electors themselves. To be sure, while this particular subcategory is *also* concerned with quantums, it is principally expressed as a rejection of the proposition that the state could be trusted to set the terms of the discussion that, in effect, determines who and what the government shall be in the first place.[36] In this vein, the supervision of political discourse is condescendingly censorial,[37] representing an inherent conflict of interest since government agents themselves generally participate in the process over which they extend their regulatory reach. Or, as Senator Howard Baker remarked during the debate on the amendments to the FECA, "I think it is extraordinarily important that the Government not control the machinery by which the public expresses the range of its desires, demands, and dissent."[38] In this spirit, Justice Douglas, writing in dissent in *United States v. Auto Workers*,[39] argued that because the people "determine through their votes the destiny of the nation," it is "therefore important—vitally important—that all channels of communication be open to them during every election, that no point of view be restrained or barred, and that the people have access to the views of every group in the community."[40]

Note too the Court's holding in *First National Bank of Boston v. Bellotti*,[41] a case involving a Massachusetts law prohibiting corporations from contributing to ballot issue campaigns not materially affecting the property, business, or assets of the corporation. Having repeatedly failed to pass a constitutional amendment calling for a graduated personal income tax, with much of the resistance coming from Massachusetts-based corporations, the legislature amended the law in question to entirely prohibit corporate expenditures on ballot proposals concerning "taxation of income." Finding that a referendum issue involved "the type of speech indispensable to decisionmaking in a democracy," a five-member majority concluded that while the state certainly had an interest in maintaining the integrity of its elections, it was beyond its prerogative to simply *assume* that corporate spending would exert an undue influence on the electoral process. More important, reasoned Justice Powell for the Court, what the law did was to single out a class of "speaker" and effect a prior restraint that did damage to the interests of free expression because it is "*the people* in our democracy [who] are entrusted with the responsibility for judging and evaluating the relative merits of conflicting arguments."[42]

Along the same lines, consider Justice Brennan's opinion for a unanimous Court in *Brown v. Hartlage*,[43] a case dealing with a constitutional challenge to a Kentucky statute prohibiting the offering of material benefits to voters for consideration of their votes. In this challenge, brought by a candidate for county commissioner who had pledged to lower salaries if elected, the justices concluded that political speech during campaigns and elections deserved full protection because the First Amendment "embodies our trust in the free exchange of ideas as the means by which the people are to choose between good ideas and bad, and between candidates for political office."[44] And so, "the State's fear that voters might make an ill-advised choice does not provide the State with a compelling justification for limiting speech," because "it is simply not the function of government to 'select which issues are worth discussing or debating' in the course of a political campaign."[45]

A series of campaign finance cases in the 1980s fluctuated back and forth with regard to state supervision of the campaign finance system, sometimes trumpeting,[46] sometimes tempering the state's role,[47] but it was *Austin v. Michigan Chamber of Commerce* that evoked some of the most vigorous antipaternalism in this domain.[48] Though this case will be discussed in more detail in the equality conception section to follow, in essence *Austin* involved a challenge to a section of the Michigan State

Campaign Finance Act that prohibited corporations from using general treasury funds for, among other things, independent expenditures in connection with state candidate elections—though expenditures could be made with monies allocated to segregated funds used exclusively for political purposes. And yet, because it desired to purchase a newspaper advertisement from its general treasury fund in support of a candidate, the Chamber challenged the constitutionality of the provision. Justice Marshall, writing for a six-member majority, found for the state and reasoned that, while the section did burden political expression, it was justified by a compelling governmental interest in preventing corruption—or the *appearance* thereof—and reducing the potential for corporate treasuries to overwhelm the political process and unfairly influence electoral outcomes.

For the dissenters, however, singling out corporate entities assembled for economic purposes—and requiring that they create and maintain a separate "political" fund—constituted an unduly burdensome restriction on the speech rights of these organizations. Justice Scalia in particular took the majority to task for its "Orwellian" attempt to regulate the marketplace of ideas. "Attention all citizens," he wrote, offering his own rejoinder in the spirit of Orwell: "To assure the fairness of elections by preventing disproportionate expression of the views of any single powerful group, your Government has decided that the following associations of persons shall be prohibited from speaking or writing in support of any candidate: ______."[49] What the Court had done, as Scalia put it, was to endorse the "principle that 'too much speech is an evil that the democratic majority can proscribe,'" one which was "contrary to case law" and "incompatible with the absolutely central truth of the First Amendment: that government cannot be trusted to assure, through censorship, the 'fairness' of political debate."[50]

Taking the argument a step further in a separate dissent, Justice Kennedy offered his own iteration on this theme, finding that "the suggestion that the government has an interest in shaping the political debate by insulating the electorate from too much exposure to certain views is incompatible with the First Amendment."[51] "By constructing a rationale for the jurisprudence of this Court that prevents distinguished organizations in public affairs from announcing that a candidate is qualified for public office," he continued, "the Court imposes its own model of speech, one far removed from economic and political reality."[52] And so it was an "unhappy paradox," he continued, that "this Court, which has the role of protecting speech and of barring censorship from all aspects of political life, now becomes itself the censor."[53]

In the next two major campaign finance cases to reach the Court, we can see this criticism developed further. In *Colorado Republican Federal Campaign Committee v. FEC*,[54] the Court reviewed the "party expenditure" provision of the Federal Election Campaign Act (FECA) of 1971, which imposed expenditure limits on political party expenditures "in connection with the general election campaign of a [congressional] candidate." Justice Breyer's opinion for the Court found that the FECA did not apply to this particular case, but in his concurring opinion, Justice Thomas more forcefully rejected paternalist pretensions and the entire *Buckley* framework, asserting that the very idea of regulating electoral speech was akin to "letting the fox stand watch over the henhouse."[55]

Beyond the campaign finance battleground the particular resistance to state supervision of the electoral speech marketplace has been strengthened by cases involving parameters placed on political speech during state judicial elections. Unlike federal judges, who are appointed for life, nonfederal judges in thirty-nine states must run for election or are subject to various forms of retention elections, though in twenty-eight of these states, candidates for judicial offices faced restrictions on what they could say while campaigning.[56] In *Republican Party of Minnesota v. White*, the Court found unconstitutional a section of Minnesota's Judicial Code of Conduct (as promulgated by the Minnesota Supreme Court in 1974) that prohibited a "candidate for a judicial office, including an incumbent judge" from "announc[ing] his or her views on disputed legal or political issues."[57]

While Justice Scalia's five-member majority professed that the Court has "never allowed the government to prohibit candidates from communicating relevant information to voters during an election,"[58] Justice Kennedy's concurrence provides a more forceful exposition of this tenet of the classic conception of the marketplace. "Minnesota may choose to have an elected judiciary," Kennedy reasoned; it "may strive to define those characteristics that exemplify judicial excellence"; it "may enshrine its definitions in a code of judicial conduct"; and it "may adopt recusal standards more rigorous than due process requires, and censure judges who violate these standards."[59] "What Minnesota may not do, however, is censor what the people hear as they undertake to decide for themselves which candidate is most likely to be an exemplary judicial officer," because "deciding the relevance of candidate speech is the right of the voters, not the State," and the state's imposition "contradicts the principle that unabridged speech is the foundation of political freedom."[60]

Nor could the state choose to elect judicial officers and then "assert that its democracy, in order to work as desired, compels the abridgement of speech," Kennedy continued, because if Minnesota believed that "certain sorts of candidate speech disclose flaws in the candidate's credentials," then "democracy and free speech *are their own* correctives."[61] Rather than paternalistically restricting speech during an election in the ostensible interest of the election, as the state had urged and as the four dissenters accepted along custodial lines (see below), the various agents and associations in civil society such as the "legal profession, the legal academy, the press, voluntary groups, political and civic leaders, and all interested citizens" were quite well suited to also rely on the First Amendment as a means of "protest[ing] statements inconsistent with standards of judicial neutrality and judicial excellence,"[62]—meaning that *choice*, rather than state regulation ("censorship"), was the proffered regulatory mechanism to discourage speech of some concern in the electoral marketplace. Notice here that the context of the speech claim—that of an election—trumps the state's argument for preserving the integrity of its judicial officers. Minnesota was free to appoint judges, importantly, and to thereby restrict the sorts of political communication they may engage in, but when the method of selection takes the form of an election, then as the majority and Justice Kennedy in concurrence tell us, the state may not filter information reaching the voters in the course of a campaign.[63]

"Truth"

The final tenet of the classic conception stresses an uninhibited exchange of ideas, information, and voices as an essential precondition for the discovery of "truth," or at least the attainment of the most desirable social results. In this sense, the people are ultimately served—and thus can best govern—when they have full and complete information as a means for reaching that outcome that can only come from the process of unmitigated inquiry, though as with the previous tenets, this is not to the exclusion of the other assumptions that underwrite this conception.

St. Amant v. Thompson afforded the Supreme Court its first opportunity to apply the reasoning of the recently decided *New York Times v. Sullivan* to a case involving freedom of speech in the electoral process.[64] In this case, having to do with a televised political speech wherein St. Amant falsely charged Thompson with criminal conduct, Justice White wrote for an eight-member Court and reasoned that while "knowingly false speech" did not deserve constitutional protection, and while "neither lies nor false communications serve the ends of the First Amendment," in order to "promote the publication of the *truth* about public affairs," it was still "essential that the First Amendment protect some erroneous publications as well as true ones."[65]

Two years later the Court further extended the *Sullivan* reasoning to reach as well the situation presented by *Ocala Star-Banner Co. v. Damron*,[66] a case pertaining to a libel action brought by the mayor of Ocala, Florida (Damron), who was also a candidate for the office of county tax assessor.[67] Following libel rulings at all levels of the Florida courts, the U.S. Supreme Court, in an opinion by Justice Stewart, reversed and concluded that charges of criminal conduct were always relevant to a candidate's fitness for office and, as such, in the interest of reaching the truth, it was necessary to err on the side of uninhibited exposure to information.

Concurring with the majority, in this case, Justice White issued a host of qualifications stressing that the First Amendment is not construed "to award merit badges for intrepid but mistaken or careless reporting"; that "misinformation has no merit in itself"; that it "is as antithetical to the purposes of the First Amendment as the calculated lie," that it contributes nothing to "intelligent decisionmaking by citizens or officials"; and that it achieves "nothing but gratuitous injury," before reaching his crescendo, concluding that the "sole basis for protecting publishers who spread false information is that otherwise the *truth* would too often be suppressed."[68] But the build-up, despite its protestations and dissenting spirit, actually serves to make the point in an even more powerful fashion: that is, acknowledging the range of misdeeds and maladies incumbent in the search for "truth," and *still* finding the lemonade to be worth the squeeze.

THE EQUALITY CONCEPTION

By contrast to its classic counterpart, the equality conception did not really emerge as a distinct alternative until the end of the Warren Court era in the late 1960s, and has developed primarily, though not exclusively, in the course of campaign finance debates since the mid- to late 1970s.[69] The impetus for this conception, I argue, was the Reapportionment Revolution spawned by *Baker v. Carr* and its construction of a particular notion of "equality" in political life.[70] This revolution, as its "biographer" Robert Dixon has argued, "may be as significant for the development of the theory and practice of representative democracy as the equally bloodless Glorious Revolution of 1688 in England,"[71] because it virtually remade the political map of America within the span of five years—and, perhaps most importantly, directed itself toward changing the "*ideas* men live by, not just the *power* men live under."[72] The most consequential of these "ideas," for the purposes of the development of electoral speech law and *this* conception of the marketplace of ideas, was the principle of "one person, one vote," almost certainly the defining theoretical capsule of the Warren Court's political process jurisprudence.

Reversing course from its previously and famously articulated reticence,[73] the Court in *Baker* announced that it would now hear constitutional challenges to state apportionment schemes and ruled in this paradigm case that the Tennessee General Assembly, in failing to reapportion the assembly since 1901 (when the state had a very different population distribution), had violated the equal protection of its citizens "by virtue of the debasement of their votes." At stake in *Baker* then was, obviously, the concept of political representation—but also an underlying notion of "fairness,"[74] and for lack of a more precise term, the "spirit" of political competition. Indeed, as Dixon summarized, the "ultimate rationale" for *Baker* and its numerous progeny is that when political avenues for redressing political problems become dead-end streets, "some judicial intervention in the politics of the people may be essential in order to *have* any effective politics."[75] Yet the preconditions for such "effective politics" do not exist "except in the context of state-created rules and regulations," and "democratic politics cannot exist without fairly rigidly prescribed rules of conduct imposed from outside the political process itself."[76]

And so *Baker* set the tone for the equality conception of the electoral speech marketplace, though the mantra of "one person, one vote" would not appear until *Gray v. Sanders*.[77] Coining the term in the course of striking down on equal protection grounds Georgia's "county unit system" for conducting primary elections for statewide office, because it accorded victory to the candidate who received a plurality of the *counties* as opposed to a plurality of the *voters*, Justice William O. Douglas reasoned that "the conception of political equality from the Declaration of Independence, to Lincoln's Gettysburg Address, to the Fifteenth, Seventeenth, and Nineteenth Amendments can mean only one thing: one person, one vote."[78]

Developing the concept further, it was the Court's ruling in *Reynolds v. Sims* that made the important linkage to participation,[79] a notion broad enough to eventually accommodate the claim that electoral speech rights, as well, were deserving of the protection accorded to political representation, in that expression is itself a function of electoral participation. Finding that the malapportionment of the Alabama legislature violated the Equal Protection Clause, the Court predicated its ruling in *Reynolds* on the critical distinction that "legislators represent people, not trees or acres,"[80] and asserted that "representative government is in essence self-government through the medium of elected representatives of the *people*," meaning that "each and every *citizen* has an inalienable right to full and effective participation in the political processes of his State's legislative bodies."[81] The upshot of this was that because "most citizens can achieve this participation only as qualified voters through the election of legislators to represent them," then "full and effective participation by all citizens in state government requires . . . that each citizen have an *equally effective voice* in the election of members of his state legislature."[82] Here then the Court explicates—in what would be the foundation for the development of the equality conception of the electoral speech marketplace—that what the Equal Protection Clause guarantees is "the opportunity for *equal participation* by all voters in the election of state legislators."[83]

Moreover, on the same day that it announced the judgment in *Reynolds*, the Court explained in *Lucas v. the Forty-Fourth General Assembly of the State of Colorado* that even though Colorado voters had recently approved a referendum calling for the apportionment by population of only one of the two state houses of government—a design paralleling that in operation at the federal level—"an individual's constitutionally protected right to cast *an equally weighted vote* cannot be denied by a vote of a majority of a State's electorate, if the apportionment scheme adopted by the voters fails to measure up to the requirements of the Equal Protection Clause."[84] Taken together, what the emphasis on equal "weight" and "voice" means for electoral speech purposes is that "opportunity" (or access) is the essence to be teased out and applied to other domains as the operational value informing the design and maintenance of systems predicated on *choice*—be they elections or marketplaces for expression—because arenas open to more interested parties benefit the people individually and collectively by arranging for a more diverse selection than would be possible within a scheme left to its own tendencies.[85]

Of relevance, too, for the emphasis on participatory equality symbolized by "one person, one vote," is *Harper v. Virginia Board of Elections*,[86] wherein the Court found Virginia's poll tax unconstitutional, because the Equal Protection Clause of the Fourteenth Amendment is violated whenever a state makes "the affluence of the voter or payment of any fee an electoral standard."[87] But what is especially pertinent with respect to the debate over campaign finance is the fact that the *Harper* Court concluded that "the principle that denies the State the right to dilute a citizen's vote on account of his economic status or other such factors by analogy bars a system which excludes those unable to pay a fee to vote or who fail to pay."[88] What such an articulation amounts to, as Richard Hasen has appropriately observed, is a kind of "Antiplutocracy Principle"—meaning that the state "may not condition the ability to participate fundamentally in the electoral process on wealth or the payment of money."[89]

To be sure, the constitution of "equality" in these political representation cases—in principle and in practice—was the subject of considerable criticism,[90] with some portraying the Court as a "Crusader" on a quest for the "Holy Grail" of "One Man-One Vote,"[91] and others depicting the justices as rooted in a "Guardian Ethic," profoundly patronizing in its distrust of political practices and institutions.[92] Notwithstanding these normative critiques, my purpose in including this section in the discussion is simply to make the point that the Court's promulgated equality principles dramatically reconceived the practice of politics in such a wholesale manner that they *necessarily* transcend their doctrinal categories (i.e., "representation" cases) and flow as steadily into the domain of electoral speech law where similar concerns and inequities exist. Manifest in the course of the Court's review of restrictions on speech during campaigns and elections, we can see two distinct tendencies in the equality conception, sometimes intertwined in principle but still analytically distinguishable as applied.[93]

One tendency stresses the need for restrictions on the "volume" of particular voices (lowering the "ceiling" as it were), in order to deter such groups or individuals from drowning out other contributors to the marketplace; while the general thrust of the other is to stress facilities that could amplify those voices presently un- or underinvolved in the political process (raising the "floor"), by designing a more expansive and accommodating geography of opportunity that would allow for greater diversity (and thus expanded competition) in the electoral marketplace. This conception is concerned not only with those speakers who *would* be competing for attention within the process, but also those *would-be* speakers who could be drawn (back) into the process if they believed their "voice" genuinely had the potential to be "equally effective."

One of the influences on the First Amendment side of the merger that has encouraged this equality-inclined reconceptualization has been the gradual entrenchment and reification of moneyed interests, arising via the free speech tradition of the modern First Amendment. This phenomenon, which Morton Horwitz has deemed the "Lochnerization" of the First Amendment,[94] portrays a trend whereby wealthier interests, positioning themselves as "speakers" in the marketplace of ideas are perceived as having infiltrated and, in effect, *captured* the speech market[95]—signifying one version of "market failure"[96]—while then, ironically, relying on laissez-faire logic to ward off state regulatory efforts and all the while pretending that the status quo is "natural."[97] As a corrective measure of sorts—a kind of counterbalance—the last three decades have seen increased attention to a more affirmative state role in regulating the electoral marketplace, driven by the assumption that for the market to *truly* afford citizens a free exchange of ideas, honestly promote diversity of thought, and preserve genuinely open access and opportunities for all, the government must assume an interventionist role—regulating the system of exchanges in order to better serve the ultimate interests and values of the people.[98]

While criticized by some as being unworkable, or inconsistent with the idea of "free exchange,"[99] what we see in the decisions below is that the equality conception appreciates the potential for *freer* exchanges when the state assumes the role of "promoter" in the debate on public issues:[100] that is, functioning as a facilitator of sorts, committed to the project of providing for and sustaining genuinely open deliberation that brings a wide(r) array of perspectives to the table in the interests of both speakers and listeners.[101] In this respect, Owen Fiss argues that we should "learn to recognize the state not only as an enemy but also as a friend of speech," because "like any social actor, it has the potential to act in both capacities," and thus, "using the enrichment of public debate as the touchstone, we must begin to discriminate between them." "When the state acts to enhance the *quality* of public debate," he concludes, "we should recognize its actions as consistent with the first amendment."[102] Or, as Michael Kent Curtis argues, "efforts to enrich our public dialogue by expanding free speech opportunities for those with limited resources do not abridge free speech. They expand it."[103]

Turning now to the cases to flesh out the theory and development of this conception of the electoral speech marketplace, the Court's holding in *Red Lion Broadcasting Co. v. FCC* presents us with the first evidence of the merger of equality and expression principles in the electoral speech domain.[104] In this case, the Court shifted the emphasis away from the interest asserting the free speech claim (the broadcaster in this case), and toward a general notion of *equality* in consideration, manifest here as a commitment to "access" whereby the public, not private, interest was the starting point for the review. To wit, the Court explained in this important case dealing with the relative "scarcity" of the government-controlled "spectrum" that facilitated such expression, the "fairness doctrine," as promulgated by the Federal Communications Commission (essentially requiring that broadcast licensees provide a balanced presentation when dealing with controversial ideas and issues of public consequence), was properly suited to sustain a wider dissemination of views for the listening public—expanding opportunities within the marketplace of ideas.

More specifically, the Court's consideration in this case was directed toward the element of this doctrine addressing "personal attacks" (including attacks on political candidates, as was the case here), whereby an individual was to be granted by the broadcaster an equivalent opportunity and amount of time to reply. Reviewing Red Lion's challenge to the Commission's mandate, Justice White concluded for a unanimous Court that with respect to the rights asserted by the purveyor of ideas, broadcasting was qualitatively different from the medium of print and thus a different degree of consideration was appropriate given the difference in the manner and mode of dissemination.[105] But, he went on to explain in important language emphasizing the state's role in affording equal opportunity for speakers in the interest of the social good of receivers, "It is the right of the *viewers and listeners*, not the right of the broadcasters, which is paramount." Indeed, it is the "purpose of the First Amendment to preserve an uninhibited *marketplace of ideas* in which *truth* will ultimately prevail, rather than to countenance *monopolization* of that market. . . . It is *the right of the public* to receive suitable *access* to social, political, esthetic, moral, and other ideas and experiences which is crucial here."[106] And thus *Red Lion*, perhaps more explicitly than any other case, announces its realization of "market failure" (recall that the "purpose" of the First Amendment was not to "countenance monopolization" of the speech market) to lay the theoretical groundwork for an equality conception of the marketplace of ideas. Note, for example, that Justice White's opinion expressly adheres to the "marketplace" concept as a means for realizing "truth," but the Court also accepts here that the state has a role to play in sustaining some modicum of equity and parity in terms of opportunities for expression, both for those desiring the equally effective "voice" discussed above and for the audience whose decision-making potential turns on the exposure to ideas that may not arrive without intervening governmental assistance.

Along similar conceptual lines, the justices in *CBS, Inc. v. FCC*,[107] found an affirmative right for political candidates to use the broadcast airwaves. *CBS* invited the Court to consider a complaint to the FCC, made by a presidential campaign committee after the three major networks had declined to provide time for a thirty-minute program, contending that such a refusal constituted a violation of the "reasonable access" rule of the Communications Act of 1934. Ruling against the networks, a six-member majority reasoned that access and opportunity were key; thus "Section 312 . . . makes a significant contribution to freedom of expression by enhancing the ability of *candidates* to *present*, and the *public* to *receive*, information for the effective operation of the democratic process."[108]

Stressing the state's role in expanding opportunity in a similar way, though in a different space, Justice Brennan argued in dissent in *Members of the City Council of the City of Los Angeles v. Taxpayers for Vincent* that for the underresourced to equally compete in the electoral speech marketplace, public property must be construed as a "public forum,"[109] in that it "entails a relatively small expense in reaching a wide audience,"[110] and might therefore be the only accessible (affordable) arena of expression for many candidates and organizations.[111] In this case, involving supporters of a Los Angeles City Council candidate seeking an injunction against the enforcement of a city ordinance prohibiting the posting of signs on public property, the majority found that the parties had failed to demonstrate that their asserted speech interests were sufficient to overcome the municipal interest(s) in aesthetics and public safety.

But Brennan reasoned that, conversely, the "City of Los Angeles has not shown that its interest in eliminating 'visual clutter' justifies its restriction of appellees' ability to communicate with the local electorate."[112] Stressing the "critical importance in the posting of signs as a means of communication" for such parties,[113] Brennan's logic here recalled that of the early free speech scholar Zechariah Chafee, Jr., who noted that "handbills are almost the only available way for poor men to express ideas to the public or announce a protest meeting,"[114] and emphasized a fundamental tenet of the *equality* conception, which is that rather than assuming that groups and individuals are simply "free" to "bring their goods to market" in other ways or by other means, careful attention must be given to the realistic potential that contributions from such parties will actually be "voiced" (and heard) if their adopted methods of communicative participation are foreclosed by the state.[115]

There must be, in other words, genuinely "ample alternative avenues of communication" available.[116] Or, as Geoffrey Stone has suggested, if the "right to *communicate*" is the essential presupposition underlying the freedom of speech, then "in the absence of *an effective and meaningful opportunity to reach the relevant audience* the theoretical right of free expression would be hollow."[117] Under such conditions, place—with its geography of opportunity—is essential if parties of disproportionate resources are to fairly compete in the electoral marketplace. And yet, while the preceding examples emphasize the equality concerns implicated by the allocation of space—on the "spectrum" or the highway median—most cases reflecting the equality conception involve the translation of economic power into political influence, and the disproportion of the latter that flows from the distribution of the former.

In that it is the signature campaign finance case, *Buckley* is the proper starting point for the consideration of efforts to restrict the flow of money into the electoral speech marketplace, an agenda referred to as "enhancement." "It is argued," the per curiam opinion explained, "that the ancillary governmental interest in equalizing the relative ability of individuals and groups to influence the outcome of elections serves to justify the limitation on express advocacy of the election or defeat of candidates imposed by 608 (e) (1)'s expenditure ceiling." "But," the Court held,

> *the concept that government may restrict the speech of some elements of our society in order to enhance the relative voice of others is wholly foreign to the First Amendment*, which was designed "to secure 'the widest possible dissemination of information from diverse and antagonistic sources,'" and "to assure unfettered interchange of ideas for the bringing about of political and social changes desired by the people."[118]

And so, for the Court "the First Amendment's protection against governmental abridgement of free expression cannot properly be made to depend on a person's financial ability to engage in public discussion."[119] And yet, from the moment it was issued, the general equation of money with speech has inspired strenuous objections.[120] Moreover, as campaign finance cases came before the Court in the 1980s, the *Buckley* framework was reconsidered and, at times, transformed in light of concerns over the volume of the corporate "voice" (e.g., *Bellotti* and *Austin*) and the potential for "war chests" to distort the public debate.[121]

Given this sentiment then, we return to *Austin v. Michigan Chamber of Commerce*, the first majority ruling to embrace the equality conception within a campaign finance case. Recall that in *Austin* a majority of the justices for the first time upheld the constitutionality of a sort of expenditure limit, finding that a state regulation prohibiting corporations from "speaking" through *general* treasury funds, while allowing *segregated* funds, served a compelling governmental interest in eliminating the "distortion caused by corporate spending";[122] in minimizing the "corrosive effect of political 'war chests'";[123] and in discouraging both corruption and its "appearance" in the political process.[124] But in terms of the values sustaining the equality conception, Marshall also reasoned that the Michigan Campaign Finance Act reduced the "threat that huge corporate treasuries amassed with the aid of favorable state laws will be used to influence *unfairly* the outcome of elections"[125]—a claim deserving of emphasis here because the implication of "fairness" as a standard or measure for marketplace functioning suggests that too much speech or a particular form of expression (e.g., the "voice" of corporate interests) might in fact *deter* or crowd out entry to the marketplace for interested participants.[126] As such, the state has an affirmative obligation to "equalize" the opportunity for more and more diverse parties to "speak" in the course of campaigns and elections—not to make it equal, of course, but to strive for a *more* equal set of conditions.

In this same spirit, Justice Stevens, joined by Justice Ginsburg, contemplated a kind of "equalization" of voices, dissenting in *Colorado Republican Federal Campaign Committee v. FEC*, the case involving a challenge to the FECA's bar on party expenditures. "I believe the Government has an important interest in *leveling the electoral playing field* by constraining the cost of federal campaigns," Stevens explained: "It is quite wrong to assume that the net effect of limits on contributions and expenditures—which tend to protect *equal access to the political arena*, to free candidates and their staffs from the interminable burden of fund-raising, and to diminish the importance of repetitive 3-second commercials—will be adverse to the interest in informed debate protected by the First Amendment."[127] Finding that the state had established a compelling governmental interest in limiting the expenditures of political parties—thus lowering the costs of elections overall—Stevens argued that restrictions on the amount of money spent would not only serve as an antidote to the purported distortion observed in *Austin* but would also measurably increase the quality of political debate. Like the rationale in Affirmative Action cases, then, a "leveling" of the "playing field" is promoted as an appropriate compensation for the preexisting and/or state-conferred advantages enjoyed by those with easier access to financial resources.

THE CUSTODIAL CONCEPTION

The marketplace of ideas concept in its *custodial* conception embraces those means and manners of expression thought to best promote the values, mechanics, and structures of the electoral process itself—those ostensibly most conducive to the systems and operations by which democratic decision making is carried out. In an operational sense, this conception asks first and foremost: how can the conditions, arrangements, and activities of electoral politics be structured in such a way that best meets the needs not just of the individual speaker, but also, and perhaps instead, of the democratic process—or those institutions and arrangements toward which electoral expression is directed in the first place? Certainly the other two conceptions also evince such concerns, and so the significance here is really one of where the emphasis is placed: on speech existing as a value distinct from the particular context in which it seeks purchase, or on speech as a value conditioned by the character of the context in which it develops? From the latter, we divine the concept of "custody," manifest in at least two distinct ways.

First, it works under the premise that the state properly asserts proprietary control over the processes and practices of democratic politics—implicating speech as one of multiple systemic concerns as a society engages in campaigns and elections. Stressing a variation on this claim, Justice White, in one of the more important electoral process cases of the last generation, reasoned that because the Constitution affords the states the authority to prescribe the "Times, Places and Manner of holding Elections for Senators and Representatives,"[128] the Court has "recognized that States retain the power to regulate their own elections."[129] White concluded: "Common sense, as well as constitutional law, compels the conclusion that government must play an active role in structuring elections"; indeed, in a practical sense, "there must be *substantial* regulation of elections if they are to be fair and honest and if some sort of order, rather than chaos, is to accompany the democratic process."[130] In this environment, then, with its inherent institutional interests in "order,"[131] "stability,"[132] and "integrity,"[133] among other concerns, speech claims are necessarily conceived of as arising within an electoral context, meaning that the custodial conception is in this sense primarily oriented toward promoting "speech" that best facilitates the *process* by which campaigns and elections are conducted.

Consider, for example, as Frederick Schauer and Richard Pildes have recently written, that because elections are "extensively regulated, state-structured processes," which are "designed to achieve specific instrumental purposes,"[134] they "should be constitutionally understood as (relatively) bounded domains of communicative activity"—wherein due to the "defined scope of this activity, it would be possible to prescribe or apply First Amendment principles to electoral processes that do not apply through the full reach of the First Amendment."[135] Put differently, as Pildes has suggested separately, the "content of political rights" should properly be derived from the "purposes of the institutional structures within which those rights exist,"[136] meaning that "government should have considerable leeway to design democratic institutions on the basis of different substantive views of the aims of democracy, as long as laws neither constitute forms of self-entrenchment nor violate intrinsic political rights."[137]

At the risk of mixing metaphors, one might imagine the state in this sense as the "chairperson" of a meeting. Those attending such an assembly certainly have the "freedom" to speak; but at the same time, there is a fairly well defined institutional *purpose* to the gathering itself, meaning that the chair may have to either limit his or her speech or promote particular forms of speech by curtailing debate on an issue, limit access to the microphone for certain periods of time, or prohibit certain forms of expression because they interfere with the general effort to organize an orderly, efficient, civilized, and temporally bounded experience that at least *strives* to allow for deliberation over some set of issues with some mode of decision making to follow.[138] Along the same lines, the notion of "custody" would lead us to the conclusion that, as in the above meeting, speech during elections is also "institutionally bound" expression, meaning that, as C. Edwin Baker has argued, it "refers to situations where resources and activities are authoritatively organized to further or accomplish particular objectives within a limited realm of social life," whereby "rules—including rules related to speech—are introduced to help achieve those objectives."[139]

In the same sense, Baker continues, "schools, military bases, prisons, and all governmental employment—as well as all state institutions involved in governing" are institutionally bound contexts;[140] in such environments, "explicitly political and fully protected speech is often subject to severe limits"—limits which are "justified by the goal of making the particular institutional element of government better perform its democratic and governing functions."[141] By extension, then, with elections as a "part of a formal, legally structured realm of the governmental apparatus," and with campaign speech as a "central part of this electoral realm," then *campaign* speech "must be distinguished from the much broader category of political speech or speech about public issues," meaning that regulations could be justified according to this logic as long as they "aim at increasing the democratic quality of the institutionalized process of choosing public officials or making binding legal decisions."[142]

Having explicated the general thrust of the concept of "custody" in its first basic form, we turn now to the notion in its second sense, whereby the framework is—and you will have to pardon the pun—at least ostensibly committed to "cleaning up" the political process. As Justice Frankfurter reasoned in *Auto Workers*, for example, congressional legislation that prohibits corporations and labor unions from making contributions or expenditures "in connection with" any election was "designed to *cleanse* the political process" because the very nature of such a marketplace commodity was thought to do harm to the integrity of electoral institutions and the exchange of ideas itself.[143] Whether or not such posturing is sincerely committed to "clean" politics, or strategically intended to serve the self-interest of entrenched incumbents is an excellent question, but not the one I pursue here. Whatever the actual motivations in some or all of the cases considered below, the notion of "custody," at least at the conceptual level, presents itself as committed to preserving the conditions by which and context in which freedom of speech is most conducive to the purposes and function of the electoral process.

Taken together, the two manifestations of the custodial conception to be considered below (privileging time or manpower as the marketplace input and discouraging certain forms of speech) are both oriented in practice toward promoting some modicum of civility;[144] "purifying" campaigns;[145] encouraging more "respectable" discourse;[146] attempting to root out "corruption" and its equally troubling and detrimental "appearance";[147] accepting transparency and disclosure as disinfecting devices;[148] and, at times, promoting more *citizen*-style participation in political life.[149] There is, then, a kind of political vision at the heart of the custodial conception: an understanding of democracy as committed to a particular variety of involvement in the affairs of public life, and one generally accepting of regulatory arrangements with the announced purpose of encouraging such involvement. Conceiving of speech in custodial terms is not code for an "antispeech" mentality, as compared with what we might reflexively assume to be the "pro-speech" alternative in the classic conception. Indeed, such a binary approach misses entirely the theoretical significance of electoral speech law as a distinct domain.[150] It is rather more about locating speech interests of various political actors within the substance and space of process interests in the course of campaigns and elections.

To flesh this out a bit, as we will see in Chapter 8, one manifestation of the custodial inclinations would be to privilege *time* over money as a contribution for citizens to make to the political process, based on the assumption that donating one's hours might suggest a more profound commitment to, and investment in, the democratic process than the mere writing of a check.[151] In this sense, laws regulating campaign finance would be construed as critical protections *of*, not prohibitions *on* "speech," because such efforts ultimately seek to "maintain the integrity of the political process—a process that itself translates political speech into governmental action."[152] And thus, custodial care for the electoral speech marketplace is predicated on a pronounced and substantive notion of politics and political life *itself*—a particular form of "moralism,"[153] in fact—meaning that the argument for regulatory supervisions to prevent moneyed interests from overwhelming the "market" also necessarily assumes that voters actually desire those facilities and features of a "properly" functioning speech market.[154]

Drawing on the same custodial energy, we may see that certain commodities of expression are classified as "harmful" to democratic institutions and have a potentially "corrosive influence" on the speech marketplace.[155] In this sense, the concept of "corruption," which figures prominently in electoral speech jurisprudence, necessarily implies custodial sentiments in that referring to something as "corrupt," as Peter Euben explains, suggests "decay, where the original or natural condition of something becomes infected," meaning that corruption also "involves enervation, a loss of health and power" and "implies degeneration and disintegration."[156] Which means that, at the same time, any discussion of this sort necessarily assumes the existence of an ideal form, a pure state, or a better day that has been lost, unrecognized, or perverted in some capacity;[157] and so a benchmark or standard of *right* functioning is in some respect *required* if "corruption" (that is, the deviation, deterioration, departure, or distance from that form) is to be recognized and *remedied*.[158]

Having outlined the theoretical precepts of this reconceived marketplace model, but before proceeding to the relevant cases for support, let us enrich the frame of reference for understanding the essence of "custody" by considering some analogies with similarly oriented concerns. Specifically, note that the emphasis in the examples below is also on the *process*, *structures*, and *institutions* of the particular environment *within* which the speech occurs, and consider the practical effect of such a thrust, allowing for associations with a wide array of ideological and theoretical traditions, including communitarianism, civic republicanism, conservatism, and progressivism: "isms" that, depending on the issue, can be associated with individuals on both the left and the right of the traditional political spectrum. We turn first to the controversy over speech codes on university campuses.[159]

As demonstrated in the debate over regulations on expression in this environment at several universities during the 1980s and 1990s, those on the political "left" (as distinguished in important ways from those we might think of as "liberals") were often inclined to accept perhaps severe restrictions on certain speakers and *varieties* of expression because such messengers, and/or messages, were deemed to be threatening to the concept and *process* of discourse *itself*, or at the very least detrimental to the larger purposes, aims, and aspirations of the institution *itself*. That is, expression of this sort was inconsistent with the objectives toward which free inquiry is directed and to which it is intended to lead, such as those implicating the proffered "mission" of the institution, the cultivation of a sense of citizenship, the development of critical thinking skills, an increase in tolerance and appreciation for diversity, and so on.[160] "Liberals," meanwhile, at least of the "classical" sort (e.g., John Locke), as manifest in the political values and legal action of groups such as the American Civil Liberties Union (at least on freedom of expression issues),[161] tended to *oppose* codes of this kind, because, among other reasons, they were thought to replace the process of inquiry with substantive conclusions to be reached.

The same phenomenon can be seen in debates over pornography where, for example, many on the "left" stress both the literal harm (i.e., violence) and the more subtle, unrealized, even unconscious harms (i.e., a culture of objectification) that confront women, generally, as a result of pornographic images and entities,[162] while many on the "right" root their antipathy to such behaviors in religion or some culture of faith[163]—but where *both* find themselves in common cause *against* liberals and conservative-libertarians who resist (and resent) such top-down prescriptions on speech and conduct for the reasons implied by the alliances seen in the debate over speech codes. The point in these analogies is simply to emphasize that the concept of "custody" in a democracy has roots running in multiple directions and, as such, does not necessarily act as a proxy for one particular political viewpoint or institutional perspective.

Turning then to the cases, we start with *United Public Workers of America, CIO, v. Mitchell*,[164] a controversy that reflects well the values and tensions of this conceptual framework. *Mitchell* involved a suit brought by employees of the executive branch of the federal government to enjoin members of the Civil Service Commission from enforcing the provision of the Hatch Act forbidding such employees from taking "any active part in political management or in political campaigns." Conceding that the prohibition did cause a "measure of interference . . . with what otherwise would be the freedom of the civil servant" under the First Amendment,[165] the Court, in a seven-member majority decision authored by Justice Reed, accepted this congressional effort to preserve the dignity, discipline, integrity, and efficiency of public service. And so it was for the majority that even legislation that "muzzles several million citizens," as Justice Black protested in dissent,[166] could be constitutional because the act left "untouched full participation by employees in political decisions at the ballot box" and forbade "only the partisan activity of federal personnel deemed offensive to efficiency."[167]

Three decades later, *Lehman v. City of Shaker Heights* afforded the Court the opportunity to consider the constitutionality of a municipal prohibition on political advertisements in vehicles of public transit.[168] Harry Lehman, a candidate for state representative in 1970, sought to promote his candidacy to the several thousand daily riders who were residents of his district.[169] Joined by four other justices in a majority opinion for the Court, Justice Blackmun found that the statute avoided First Amendment violation because the city consciously "limited access to its transit system advertising space in order to minimize chances of abuse, the appearance of favoritism, and the risk of imposing upon a captive audience"—all "reasonable legislative objectives advanced by the city in a *proprietary* capacity."[170]

And while *commercial* advertising *was* allowed on these vehicles, the Court reasoned around the incongruity by finding that a transit vehicle was not a traditional "public forum" and thus First Amendment rights must yield to state interests in a way that they would not be in a different geography or context (e.g., a park or a parade). Thus, Blackmun reasoned, while American First Amendment jurisprudence "has been jealous to preserve access to public places for purposes of free speech," the "nature of the forum" and "conflicting interests" were essential to the question.[171] Indeed, in the instant case there were "no open spaces, no meeting hall, park, or street corner, or other public thoroughfare"; rather, the city was "engaged in commerce" and as such in the provision of service to commuters, it was to be afforded the "discretion to develop and make reasonable choices concerning the type of advertising that may be displayed in its vehicles."[172]

Presented in such a fashion, the decision not to allow a political advertisement was really just a *business* decision—"little different from deciding to impose a 10-, 25-, or 30-cent fare, or from changing schedules or the location of bus stops"—and a necessary one for the Court because in addition to jeopardizing long-term commercial advertising by affording short-term candidacy or issue advertisements space on car cards, "users would be subjected to the blare of political propaganda."[173] Moreover, the majority opinion continued, "there could be lurking doubts about favoritism, and sticky administrative problems might arise in parceling out limited space to eager politicians. . . ."[174] Indeed, were the Court to hold otherwise, finding discretion offensive to the First Amendment, then "display cases in public hospitals, libraries, office buildings, military compounds, and other public facilities immediately would become Hyde Parks open to every would-be pamphleteer and politician."[175]

Concurring with the judgment of the Court, but offering a different rationale, Justice Douglas emphasized not the constitutional rights of the *candidate*, but rather those of the *commuter*, finding that while Lehman did have a right to express his positions to willing listeners, "he has no right to *force* his message upon an audience incapable of declining to receive it." Indeed, Douglas continued, stressing the particularly invasive and nonconsensual nature of such expression, "In my view the right of the commuters to be free from forced intrusions on their privacy precludes the city from transforming its vehicles of public transportation into forums for the dissemination of ideas upon this captive audience."[176] What makes this logic distinctly custodial is that the "marketplace" of ideas is, Douglas suggests, a *place*—meaning that it requires, as a first step, *entry* (where one would be "confronted" with its commodities), but meaning as well that it now necessarily implicates the government as the surveyor of the *space* within which exposure may legitimately occur.

Put differently, while "markets" might be "places," not all "places" are necessarily "markets," and so especially because commercial speech was *not* subject to the same prohibition, the restriction on electoral speech in this case implies that the "marketplace" is a place that we go *to* for political exchange and education, rather than an atmosphere that happens to surround us at any given moment.

But an intriguing subtextual theme, evident in the majority and concurring opinions here, is the difference between a collection and a clutter of voices—or between a *marketplace* and in effect a *morass* of ideas—a distinction that appears to have been significant as the Court contemplated the application of the public forum doctrine to the facts of the case. Ultimately, we see the adoption of a custodial conception in light of the state's interest in setting the literal and figurative boundaries of political space in order to—and this does seem to be the correct verb to use—*shield* the public from the confrontation with candidate messages (the "blare of political propaganda," as Blackmun put it),[177] a motive unquestionably incompatible with a classic conception yet comfortably consistent with custodial inclinations toward process concerns.

In a similar vein, the Court, two years later in *Greer v. Spock*, determined that, while the military post was a public entity in some ways, it was not traditionally open to democracy as such (i.e., it was not a "traditional public forum") and thus restrictions prohibiting the conventional activities of electoral politics were constitutional.[178] Denied permission to enter the military reservation at Fort Dix, New Jersey, for purposes of distributing campaign literature and discussing election issues with service personnel, Benjamin Spock and Julius Hobson, candidates for president and vice-president for the People's Party, respectively, as well as their counterparts with the Socialist Workers Party, asserted a First Amendment violation, sought an injunction, lost at the District Court level, but won at the Third Circuit Court of Appeals. The U.S. Supreme Court reversed, however, with a seven-member majority finding, in an opinion by Justice Stewart, that it was essential that the military remain "insulated from both the reality and the appearance of acting as a handmaiden for partisan political causes or candidates," and that there was an important and necessary "distinction between the role of the soldier and that of the citizen."[179]

But while speaking much to tradition, as we will see in the following chapter, the adoption of this distinction also portrays a vision akin to that of *Shaker Heights*, whereby politics is compartmentalized, in a literal and figurative manner, meaning that the responsibilities (and opportunities) of the "soldier" are segregated from those of the "citizen." And so, what makes *Greer* custodial in its marketplace orientation is the message that is sent by the statute as it asserts a proprietary claim over the conditions of self-rule, whereby soldiers are not precluded from exposure to the commodities of the electoral marketplace of ideas but simply must: (1) go *to* the arena (rather than having it come to them); and (2) preserve the "insulation" from partisanship and its "appearance" (as critical here as it is with "corruption") by having such encounters during the hours when they are out of uniform.

Developing the sort of argument he had alluded to in *Buckley* and spelled out more clearly in *Bellotti*,[180] Justice White's dissent in *CARC* is rooted in the logic of "custody" in that he argues that the purpose of the citizen initiative option as a means of direct democracy was to "reform" the political process—putting government in the hands of the people and taking it away from the corrupting influence of money and special interests—and so the city's $250 limit on contributions to committees formed to support or oppose ballot measures was constitutional because it promoted the procedural interests to be enjoyed by increased citizen participation. "The role of the initiative in California cannot be separated from its purpose of preventing the dominance of special interests," White explained, because such "is the very history and purpose of the initiative in California, and similarly it is the purpose of ancillary regulations designed to *protect* it."[181]

Indeed, he noted of the initiative *and* its regulation, "*Both* serve to maximize the exchange of political discourse"; and thus, "the Court's fundamental error is its failure to realize that the state regulatory interests . . . are *themselves* derived from the First Amendment."[182] Clearly the construction of "protection" is essential here, in that White's reasoning begins with the premise that the initiative is a state-created entity and thus preservation was a logical implication flowing from the initial theoretical charge and citizen-oriented reform mandate. But note as well the emphasis on the fact that "both serve to maximize the exchange of political discourse," which goes to the point often underappreciated by the binary approach that pervades much free speech debate: that a disinclination to accept the posited speech claim by an affected party ipso facto renders the regulatory agent "antispeech" in some regard, an assertion we will consider in greater detail in Chapter 4.

More recently, the four members of the Court, dissenting in *White*, argued that a state restriction prohibiting judicial candidates for office from "announcing" their views on disputed legal and political issues was not only constitutional but was in fact a prudent (i.e., "custodial") effort to maintain institutional integrity in the democratic process. At the outset of her dissent, joined by Justices Stevens, Souter, and Breyer, Justice Ginsburg emphasized the unique role responsibilities of the judiciary and the distinct function of the judge in American democracy, arguing that such individuals are "expected to refrain from catering to particular constituencies or committing themselves on controversial issues in advance of adversarial presentation."[183] Put simply, she insisted, though judges may be elected in most states, they nonetheless "are not political actors."[184]

Moreover, while the electorate may have an "interest" (a reference to the majority's emphasis placed on the "interests" of the voting public) in knowing the explicit intentions and policy preferences of U.S. Supreme Court nominees, for example, "every Member of this Court declined to furnish such information to the Senate, and presumably to the President as well."[185] Certainly, in the post-Bork era of Supreme Court nominations and confirmation hearings, a declination of this sort is at least in some sense *strategic* (e.g., avoiding the entanglements of analogizing the ambiguity of the Ninth Amendment to that of a provision obscured by an "ink blot" in responses). At the same time, given the institutional expectations of jurists in our legal tradition, one would think that making "announcements" of the sort prohibited by the state would be thought of as highly improper and entirely inconducive to the values ascribed to judges (neutrality, objectivity, "blindness," etc.). Consider, for example, the stone-faced demeanor of the justices as they sit in the Chamber during the State of the Union Address, careful not to applaud, stand, or otherwise "announce" support for the proposals of the party in power.

But the *White* dissents collectively are of interest as well for the distinction made between being a *judge* and being a *candidate*, even in systems that elect their judges, because in essence the donning of (or at least desire for) the black robe renders the consideration moot, in that the *institutional* interests of the judiciary properly condition the exercise of free speech in such arenas. Context controls content, in other words, and situates itself within the sort of distinction drawn in *Greer*, whereby custody compels inhibitions on information in the interest of institutional implications. And so Ginsburg concluded: "Prohibiting a judicial candidate from pledging or promoting certain results if elected directly promotes the State's interest in preserving public faith in the bench,"[186] a point echoed by Justice Stevens, who explained that "there is a critical difference between the work of the judge and the work of other public officials," because in a democracy "issues of policy are properly decided by majority vote; it is the business of legislators and executives to be popular."[187]

And yet, critically, during the course of litigation, "issues of law or fact should not be determined by popular vote; it is the business of judges to be indifferent to unpopularity."[188] In fact, Stevens observed, the "very purpose of most statements prohibited by the announce clause is to convey the message that the candidate's mind is *not* open on a particular issue."[189] Such logic presents a somewhat counterintuitive twist in that the announcement clause existed here as a means of maintaining (at least the appearance of) an "open" judicial mind, liberating a candidate to *think* freely by prohibiting her from *speaking* freely—rendering a distinction that is ironic in some ways, but one that is perfectly consistent with the custodial anticipation of speech as intended to underscore, not undermine, the electoral process.

Finally, such custodial sentiments were again exhibited by Justice Stevens, dissenting most recently in *Randall v. Sorrell*,[190] a case involving Vermont's scheme of contribution and expenditure limits for candidates running for state office. As Stevens stressed in this case with six separate opinions, the proper conception of free speech is more easily and properly reached within a system that encourages, if you will, "free" speech—that is, speech that *costs* nothing and still persuades its audience by virtue of its eloquence rather than its expenditures. Indeed, Stevens emphasized (resisting the argument that candidates run on money just as cars run on fuel), "a candidate can speak without spending money" and, in fact, "there is no limit on the number of speeches or interviews a candidate may give on a limited budget."[191]

There was, Stevens acknowledged, "a certain threshold" required for reaching voters, but "just as a driver need not use a Hummer to reach her destination, so a candidate need not flood the airways with ceaseless sound-bites of trivial information in order to provide voters with reasons to support her."[192] Examples of "effective speech" in the political arena that did not require any "significant expenditure" by the campaigner were legion, he reasoned, citing the "Cross of Gold" speech by William Jennings Bryan and William McKinley's front porch addresses as political communication that succeeded on account of its content rather than its cost.[193] It was in this vein that Stevens reiterated his custodial concern that "without expenditure limits, fundraising devours the time and attention of political leaders, leaving them too busy to handle their public responsibilities *effectively*."[194] The vision of a proper mode of—and role for—speech in the political process is inescapable in these passages and sums up well the intentions and implications of a custodial orientation toward the marketplace of ideas.

CONCLUSION

What this chapter has offered is a theoretical explication and genealogy for the alternative conceptions of the marketplace of ideas evident in electoral speech jurisprudence. In addition to the classic model, with the closest connection to that imagined by Justice Holmes, we can see that the concept has taken the form of two alternative conceptions: one oriented principally toward *equality* (directed primarily toward people and opportunities for participation—i.e., "voice"), and the other rooted in what I have referred to as *custody*, or the state's proprietary claim over the mechanics and institutions of the process by which elections are carried out. Having examined the constituent concepts of this domain in Chapter 1, and the outcomes of their confluence above, we turn in the following chapter to the rhetorical modes of argument and analysis that facilitate the process of "constitution" in electoral speech law.

CHAPTER 3

Rhetorical Modes

WHILE THE FOCUS of the previous chapter was on the constitution of electoral speech law in *conceptual* terms, our attention here is to the means by which rhetorical modes of argument and analysis facilitate the articulation of this constitution. Assuming, as I do here, that arguments do, in fact, matter, whether they convey sincere sentiments or strategic sentiments (or more likely some combination of the two), it is essential to examine as well how this domain is constituted. Attention to rhetorical data is critical to this study, we will see, because, as one scholar has convincingly argued, such materials can "serve as a gateway" to a more sophisticated understanding of the nature of Supreme Court decision making and the composition of Court rulings.[1] In surveying these predominant modes we will examine appeals to historical materials, inclinations toward empirical data, and in a manner particular to this body of law, democratic dispositions of both an aspirational and precautionary nature, revealing important impressions of and inclinations toward the possibilities of political life.[2]

For purposes of introduction, we will see that the historical mode places great stock in how speech has functioned and how state regulations have been received in the past, with references ranging from legal practices or events (e.g., the Magna Carta, the Bill of Rights, etc.), to extralegal sources such as political, literary, or philosophical figures and arguments from earlier times—a capaciousness that, as applied in these cases, almost necessarily compels the tension evident in such appeals between the reliance on asserted speech *principles* of the people and the reference to established regulatory *practices* of political communities. The empirical mode stresses data and demonstrability as the factors to be privileged in the review of electoral speech regulations, meaning that this approach is self-consciously positivistic, as it puts the most emphasis on evidence, epistemology, and inference in the review of electoral speech restrictions, even while it may not deem the lack of "proof" necessarily dispositive in all cases. Finally, in a form that is equal parts description and prescription, the aspirational and precautionary modes both evince a mutual concern for the institutions of electoral politics and the people and processes on which a democracy is predicated. As with our examination of the conceptual constitution in the last chapter, the data supporting this classification of modes are divined from a global review of the entire domain, with particular attention to those passages, themes, and elements that typify the most commonly invoked approaches (or, if one prefers, the "modal" modes) facilitating the constitution of electoral speech law.

THE HISTORICAL MODE

As Court scholars are well aware, the use of history either to scrutinize legislation or to frame an opinion is a common expository approach to evaluating cases and explaining their holdings.[3] Such a tactic, what Alfred Kelley has referred to as "law office history,"[4] has been the subject of extensive criticism. Indeed, as Kelly argued in his well-known indictment, "The Court, in performing its self-assumed role as a constitutional historian, has been, if not a naked king, no better than a very ragged one." "Too often," he continues, the justices "reach conclusions that are plainly erroneous," though "more often they state as categorical absolutes propositions that the historian would find to be tentative, speculative, interesting, and worthy of further investigation and inquiry, but not at all pedigreed historical truth."[5] Both the Supreme Court justice and the "professional historian" turn to history, in other words, but the jurist or advocate does so to make her case, while the scholar does so to have it made for her.[6]

As we will see in the passages to follow and in the case study chapters, the appeal to history as a rhetorical mode in this domain warrants the same critical caution, but what distinguishes electoral speech jurisprudence in some respects is that it exists in a more expansive form than that of the conventional association of historical arguments with "original intent" or, alternatively, "original meaning."[7] To wit, as we will see below, there is an important distinction (and sometimes a contradiction) *within* this mode—between the reliance on actual practices, customs, and traditions on the one hand, and the appeal to alleged historic principles, precepts, and designs on the other. That is, one might make a historical argument by appealing to the founders to make the claim that statute *x* is contrary to the "intentions" (or principles) of those involved in the initial evaluation of what became the First Amendment, for example; but one might just as well argue that statute *x* is perfectly consistent with the Constitution because the fifty states have had such laws in place since some time just after the founding era.

The emphasis on practices portrays an approach less concerned with suppositions, conjectures, and abstractions than with the guidance to be realized from a consideration of the actual tendencies evident in the history of election regulation in various American communities. The concern here is less with the alleged or inferred beliefs of previous generations and more with their actual behavior. Let us return here to *Greer v. Spock*,[8] the case discussed in the previous chapter dealing with the denial of a request made by political candidates to distribute literature on the grounds of a military compound. Writing for the majority in this case and upholding the restrictions, Justice Potter Stewart reasoned that "such a policy is wholly consistent with the American constitutional tradition of a politically neutral military established under civilian control," a policy consistent with "numerous laws and military regulations throughout our history."[9]

Writing in concurrence, Chief Justice Burger, joined by Justice Powell, was more forceful on this note, arguing at the outset that "permitting political campaigning on military bases cuts against a 200-year tradition of keeping the military separate from political affairs, a tradition that in my view is a constitutional corollary to the express provision for civilian control of the military in Article II, § 2, of the Constitution."[10] And thus *custom* was controlling; history was more than simply "how things used to be," or "what happened in the past," and was instead a practical instantiation of—a "corollary" to—the values of the Constitution *itself*. But on another level, Burger noted, history indicated that the "real threat to the independence and neutrality of the military" came "not from the kind of literature that would fall within the prohibition of Reg. 210–27," but rather "from the risk that a military commander might attempt to 'deliver' his men's votes for a major-party candidate."[11] Like the distinctions we will see in the discussion of *Burson v. Freeman* in Chapter 5, then, here we have an argument justifying space restrictions based on *past*, as opposed to present, necessity—with the suggestion that "tradition" is effectively evidence by virtue of its lineage.

But for practices to be controlling, and to overcome First Amendment claims made by interested speakers, we learn from Justice Scalia's opinion for the majority in *Republican Party of Minnesota v. White* that they must not only have "roots," but sufficiently *deep* roots.[12] To wit, in this case—which, as we saw in Chapter 2, involved a challenge to the state's content restrictions on the campaign speech of judicial candidates—Scalia wrote that while "it is true that a 'universal and long-established' tradition of prohibiting certain conduct creates a 'strong presumption' that a prohibition is constitutional," the practice of prohibiting the speech of judicial candidates "is neither long nor universal."[13] Indeed, he explained, "at the time of the founding, only Vermont (before it became a State) selected any of its judges by election."[14] While more states began providing for judicial elections during the period of Jacksonian democracy, the Court pointed out that it could locate "no restrictions upon statements that could be made by judicial candidates (including judges) throughout the 19th and the first quarter of the 20th century."[15] Judicial elections were generally partisan, the majority concluded, and thus candidates typically discussed not only legal and political issues but also party affiliations.

By contrast, the reliance on historical principles puts the stress on those arguments and ideas that ostensibly define us as a people: looking more to the broad precepts, themes, and presumptions that are thought to underwrite American democracy and that are divined from historical materials (values, beliefs, myths, etc.) rather than actual activities, tendencies, or records. We return at this point to *Greer*, which is such an intriguing case because, like *Burson* and *McIntyre v. Ohio Elections Commission*,[16] which we will explore in more detail in the case studies, it captures the essence of the tension between principle and practice in the majority and the dissenting opinions. As Justice Brennan elaborated in this respect, "the Court gives no consideration to whether it is actually necessary to exclude all unapproved public expression from a military installation under all circumstances and, more particularly, whether exclusion is required of the expression involved here."[17] But more fundamentally, as Justice Marshall argued in his separate dissent, the majority's deference to custom suppressed the more significant and abiding principle, namely "the commitment of the Nation and the Constitution to an open society."[18] And "by its unblinking deference to the military's claim that the regulations are appropriate," he continued, the Court "has sharply limited one of the guarantees that makes this Nation so worthy of being defended."[19] It seems that, whether by intention or effect, the historical mode has within it the potential to deflect such *re*evaluations by reflexively accepting that which has been as a proxy for that which should be.

More recently, Justice Stevens has referred to the governing principles of the nation's founders, as a way of defending the premise of restrictions on expenditures in—and contributions to—campaigns for state office. Indeed, as Stevens argued in dissent in *Randall v. Sorrell*,[20] contribution and expenditure limits would have been supported by the founding fathers, because "at the time of the framing the accepted posture of the leading candidates was one of modesty, acknowledging a willingness to serve rather than a desire to compete."[21] And, while he stressed that "speculation about how the Framers would have legislated if they had foreseen the era of televised sound-bites" could not provide us with "definitive answers," he still went on to add that he was "firmly persuaded that the Framers would have been appalled by the impact of modern fundraising practices on the ability of elected officials to perform their public responsibilities."[22] What Stevens is arguing here is that the strain of civic republicanism alive at the time of the nation's founding would have served as its own deterrent for the founders,[23] accounting for their collective sense of the form that public service—as opposed, perhaps, to mere "politics"—should take.

THE EMPIRICAL MODE

What is most significant about the empirical constitution of electoral speech law is just how much issues implicating the evidentiary burden figure into the resolution of cases, even at this highest appellate level. Of course, debates over whether or not empirical data really "proves" the point toward which it is marshaled is a longstanding question in American constitutional law.[24] Some scholars question the basic capacity of courts to process "specialized information";[25] others have criticized the Supreme Court in particular for failing to consider the relevant data when evaluating constitutional questions;[26] and still others have faulted the Court for failing to consider the available social science materials in its electoral process jurisprudence.[27]

With these criticisms in mind, what my analysis reveals is that the empirical constitution implicates two basic themes. The first involves the qualitative nature of "evidence" and its burden; not simply whether there *is* evidence, or enough evidence, or whether it is persuasive—but rather, as a two-fold issue of ontology: "What *is* evidence?" and: "Could proof theoretically *be* provided—or must it be gleaned from skeletal remains by some modern-day archaeologist of the law?" The second general theme pertains to the epistemological and related problem of inference that flows from the first: "While we may know things when we see them, so to speak, how do we know that we really see that which we purport to see, and that which allows us to (think we) know?"

Regarding the first evidentiary theme, we see at least three specific manifestations, distinguishable but often interrelated within this domain. First, in certain cases (the more recent campaign finance cases like *Nixon v. Shrink Missouri Government PAC* and *McConnell v. FEC*, for example),[28] the Court accepts as sufficient a relatively scant amount of evidence to justify regulations on speech rights. As we will see in the discussion of *Shrink* in Chapter 8, the trial court, for example, relied extensively on newspaper op-eds and one affidavit from a legislator to divine the "culture" (my word) of campaign finance in the state at the time the regulations were enacted as a way of gauging the "appearance of corruption" that ostensibly justified limits on contributions to candidates for state office.

A second specific manifestation we will see quite clearly in the discussion of *Burson v. Freeman* in Chapter 5 involves the division of responsibility implied by the evidentiary burden, specifically regarding the relaxing of the state's traditional obligation of providing specific and tangible evidence documenting genuine harm.[29] One reason for the diminished nature of the burden, it would seem, is the inherently less precise nature of the *interest* with which it is associated (e.g., the "integrity" of the political process or the "appearance" of "corruption"). Meanwhile, a third specific variety of this first theme can be seen in cases where the Court has been provided extensive evidence to justify state restrictions on electoral speech, and yet has seemed unable or unwilling to find that such proof satisfied the evidentiary burden in the instant case—or, for that matter, in *any* case.

Consider the two cases the Court has reviewed involving Colorado's efforts to regulate signature gathering in the initiative process. In the first, *Meyer v. Grant*,[30] the Court was presented with detailed evidence demonstrating the prevalence of fraud involving payments to petition circulators, and in the second case, *Buckley v. American Constitutional Law Foundation*,[31] the justices scrutinized a host of regulations meant to reform the process in the wake of *Meyer* (which found the ban on payments to circulators to be unconstitutional) by requiring increased disclosure of information and thus offering the voters more to consider as they evaluated certain propositions. But with the protection for First Amendment rights in *Meyer* "at its zenith," writing for a unanimous Court, Justice Stevens went on to articulate that the standard here was "well-nigh insurmountable,"[32] a turn of phrase which really offers little in the way of actual guidance to the states or parties involved and may, in fact, simply be a coy way of saying: "It doesn't matter how many cases of fraud you provide, we still will not think it is enough, so stop trying to restrict this sort of speech." Such at least seems to have been practical consequence when, eleven years later in *ACLF* (the focus of Chapter 7), the Court revisited and relied once more on this obfuscation.

The second general theme of the empirical mode, involves, to borrow a celestial metaphor, a debate akin to whether the collection of stars in the sky represents merely a cluster or a discernible constellation. That is, as is particularly evident in debates over the deductions to be made from patterns of campaign giving and the relationships and reactions that flow from it, this second theme contemplates whether a high correlation between financial contributions and "access" to, or "responsiveness" of, elected officials suggest "corruption" in the political process. Or is it evidence of a well-functioning representative democracy? Consider the contrast along these lines in *FEC v. Colorado Republican Federal Campaign Committee*,[33] between Justice Souter's and Justice Thomas's interpretations of the trial declarations offered up by former elected officials and their political aides—Leon Billings, Timothy Wirth, and Robert Hickmott—regarding the connection of candidates to their political parties.

"Under the Act, a donor is limited to $2,000 in contributions to one candidate in a given election cycle," Souter wrote for the majority upholding the limits, though "the same donor may give as much as another $20,000 each year to a national party committee supporting the candidate," and thus, he gleaned, "What a *realist* would expect to occur has occurred," in that "donors give to the party with the tacit understanding that the favored candidate will benefit."[34] Moreover, Souter continues, while the relationship between donors and parties may "involve no definite commitment and may be tacit on the donor's part," a considerable amount of bookkeeping is required to track and trace such contributions—a practice, he notes, that the Democratic Party refers to as "tallying,"[35] and one that serves as "a sign that contribution limits are being diluted and could be diluted further if the floodgates were open." "Why," in other words, "does a party *bother* to tally?"—the "obvious answer" being that "it wants to know who gets the benefit of the contributions to the party, as the record quotations attest."[36] But Justice Thomas, looking to the same practices and testimonials, came to a very different conclusion, noting that two of the Court's four testimonials relied on as evidence do not necessarily support "the proposition that donations are funneled through parties to candidates," but reflect instead the "obvious fact" that "a candidate benefits when his party receives money"[37]—meaning that the suspicions sustaining Souter's induction may have been misplaced.

Or, one might consider *Arkansas Educational Television Commission v. Forbes*,[38] wherein the Court reviewed the Arkansas Educational Television Commission's decision to limit participation in a planned television debate to candidates with sufficient popular support—a standard which excluded Ralph Forbes, a third-party candidate running for the Third Congressional District. Finding for the commission, a state agency owning and operating a network of noncommercial television stations,

Justice Kennedy explained for the Court that this case did not implicate the "traditional public forum" doctrine, given the uniqueness of the setting, which presented environmental and/or structural limitations on speech—suggesting something like the quintessential "Chairman's Problem."[39] In coming to this conclusion though, the Court turned to data which indicated that in the 1988, 1992, and 1996 presidential elections, "no fewer than 22 candidates appeared on the ballot in at least one state."[40] Importantly, the majority reasoned, "were it faced with the prospect of cacophony, on the one hand, and First Amendment liability, on the other hand, a public television broadcaster might choose not to air candidates' views at all."[41]

The dissenters, however, construed these numbers in a very different light. For them, the Court misinterpreted the significance of Forbes's financial resources and his potential impact on the election. Though branded as "not a serious candidate" by the AETC staff, Justice Stevens, writing in dissent (with Justices Souter and Ginsburg), noted that the last Republican victor in the Third District race in 1992 received only 50.22 percent of the vote, while the Democrat received 47.2 percent, meaning that an independent candidate like Forbes could still have a very significant effect on the election in such a divided district, even if he was unlikely to actually *win* the seat. Further, while the majority tacitly accepted the AETC staff's evaluation of Forbes's financial resources—concluding that his limited financial backing implied less enthusiasm for his candidacy—the dissenters again drew the inverse conclusion: "The fact that Forbes had little financial support was considered as evidence of his lack of *viability* when the factor might have provided an independent reason for *allowing* him to share a free forum with wealthier candidates."[42]

Thus the nub of the case is the issue of the proper inferences to draw from data. On the one hand, we have the question of what makes one's candidacy "serious" or "viable": the potential to *win* or the potential to *influence* the selection of the winner. (Think, for example, of Ralph Nader's influence on the presidential election of 2000.) And, on the other hand, how does one demonstrate his or her "viability" if the channels for reaching and persuading the public are closed to those not already meeting such a standard? In a broader sense, what these cases illustrate is the general imprecision and inconsistent manner with which the Court appeals to data, the ambiguity of its holdings (with respect to the guidance offered to lower courts and political actors), the problems associated with multiple interpretations of the same statistical "evidence," and the questions that must be confronted when the Court extrapolates from "missing" data in certain situations.

THE ASPIRATIONAL MODE

While none of the modes of argument considered in this chapter is exclusive of the others (or others unmentioned), the aspirational and precautionary postures to be considered in the following two subsections appear to serve as modes of first appeal, in that they most likely frame the consideration and invocation of other modes. Put differently, these postures are informed by the concept of "cultural attitudes," which, as Richard Pildes has argued, "surely influence, if they do not completely dominate, how judges respond to empirical claims and open-ended precedents," a phenomenon that explains "why, perhaps, most justices end up consistently on the same side of these cases, despite differences in facts, partisan consequences, and precedents among the various cases involving democracy that have recently been before the Court."[43]

I rely on this general notion of a "cultural attitude" in order to discuss the significance of the justices' professed impressions of the possibilities of American politics, paying attention to arguments and assertions that portray perceptions of human nature and man's capacity for self-governance; various conceptions of citizenship; (mis)trust in the potential of our electoral institutions; and an articulated vision of the proper relationship between political speech and the ideals of representative government. At the most basic level, a vision of citizens engaged in the political process that is more prepared to concede that individuals will take advantage of speech liberties is obviously more inclined to support the state's proposed "reform" measures; but a rhetorical posture that presents the glass as "half-full" rather than "half-empty" is more willing to endure the occasional indiscretions of *some* in the greater interest of *all*.

Regarding the focus of this subsection, my appeal to "aspirationalism" draws on that view of the constitution as a "signal of the kind of government under which we would like to live."[44] What aspirationalism represents is a way of thinking that is specifically directed at realizing the promise of political institutions, practices, and actors, and one that evinces obvious teleological anticipations about the nature and development of self and society through the medium of politics. For a recent example of this mode from outside the electoral speech domain, consider Justice Stevens's majority opinion in a case challenging a municipal requirement that, among other things, required that those advocating a cause first register with city officials.

Rather than stressing the potential for annoyance, disruption, or distraction with such door-to-door interactions, Stevens conceived of these speakers as communicants engaged in the noble act of political dissent—and perceived this case through the lens of past and present political actors who may find their speech "chilled" by such an ordinance. "As our World War II-era cases dramatically demonstrate," he reasoned, "there are a significant number of persons whose religious scruples will prevent them from applying for such a license."[45] But certainly there are "other *patriotic citizens*, who have such firm convictions about their constitutional right to engage in uninhibited debate in the context of door-to-door advocacy, that they would prefer silence to speech licensed by a petty official," as well, he continued.[46]

By contrast to Justice Stevens's clearly aspirational constitution of the case, Justice Scalia portrayed a kind of "cultural attitude" or posture that rejected "the Court's fairy-tale category of 'patriot citizens,' who would rather be silenced than licensed in a manner that the Constitution (but for their 'patriotic' objection) would permit."[47] "If our free-speech jurisprudence is to be determined by the predicted behavior of such *crackpots*," he continued, "we are in a sorry state indeed."[48] Whether or not such would-be speakers are in fact "patriotic citizens," or "crackpots," is not my concern here; rather, my focus is on the way that each justice sought to portray the speakers/speech in question: a contrast that, I contend, speaks volumes about the justices' perceptions of various issues—though not in a traditional doctrinal sense. In the remainder of this section we will see that the aspirational and precautionary modes each implicate the capacity of the people to be self-governing and to properly enjoy freedom of speech in an open society and the potential of the electoral process to serve the aims of democratic governance.

We begin, in this first section, with a discussion of the Court's emphasis on the rational qualities of *individuals*—a vision of citizens capable of making difficult decisions and seeing liberty through to its proper end. Justice Hugo Black, in his dissent in *United Public Workers of America v. Mitchell*,[49] acknowledged that *some* engaged in the exchange of ideas might exploit the system but, he argued, problems of this sort were not endemic. In this case, in which the Court upheld provisions of the Hatch Act that prohibited federal employees from "taking any active part in political management or in political campaigns," Justice Black argued strongly that an *anticipated* impropriety should hardly be the starting premise. "It is argued that it is in the interest of clean politics to suppress political activities of federal and state employees," he wrote, but "all political corruption is not traceable to state and federal employees."[50] It is possible "that some higher employees, unless restrained, might coerce their subordinates or that government employees *might* use their official position to coerce other citizens," he conceded, though he wondered why such a possibility was thought to be limited to *governmental* employer-employee relationships?[51] Would not the same argument "support a law to suppress the political freedom of all employees of private employers, and particularly of employers who borrow money or draw subsidies from the Government"? he asked, as a way of making the point that it seemed an affront to "our system of equal justice to all to suppress the political and speaking freedom of millions of good citizens because a few bad citizens might engage in coercion."[52]

Justice Scalia stressed a similar faith in the discerning qualities of the people in his dissenting opinion in *Austin v. Michigan Chamber of Commerce*.[53] As he reminded those justices who accepted the state's requirement that corporations make expenditures from a segregated "political" (rather than general treasury) fund, "The premise of our system is that there is no such thing as too much speech—that the people are not foolish but intelligent, and will separate the wheat from the chaff."[54] Government need not patronizingly restrict particular voices because trusting in citizens' abilities to make distinctions and draw conclusions was preferable, returning power to the ultimate source and sustenance of any healthy democratic society: rational and engaged individuals. Indeed, "the premise of the First Amendment," he argued at the same pitch thirteen years later in the Court's most significant campaign finance cases since *Buckley*, is that "the American people are neither sheep nor fools," but in fact are "fully capable of considering both the substance of the speech presented to them and its proximate and ultimate source."[55] "If that premise is wrong," he surmised, "our democracy has a much greater problem to overcome than merely the influence of amassed wealth."[56]

Aspirationalism extends, as well, to the *institutions* of democracy. One specific manifestation of this message, expressed in several of the Court's decisions, is the notion that the political process benefits from the interjection and influences of speech coming from a wide array of sources. In this spirit, Justice Powell, in *First National Bank of Boston v. Bellotti*,[57] found that the corporate voice, too, deserved a place in the free and open evaluation of matters of public concern. The bank, in this case, wished to spend money in opposition to a referendum, but was barred from doing so by a Massachusetts criminal statute that prohibited various business entities from making expenditures of this sort when the public question did not "materially affect" them. In his decision, Powell expressed a notable faith in the referendum process itself, concluding that "the risk of corruption perceived in cases involving candidate elections . . . simply is not present in a popular vote on a public issue."[58] Corporate bodies, he explained, also have the right to "speak" for or against political proposals, because ultimately "the people in our democracy are entrusted with the responsibility for judging and evaluating the relative merits of conflicting arguments," meaning that as they make their judgment, they may also consider the "source and credibility of the advocate."[59]

Justice Marshall demonstrated a similar faith in the electoral process in *Eu v. San Francisco Democratic Committee*,[60] writing for the majority and explaining that parties, too, have essential First Amendment speech rights in political campaigns and elections. While the state has a legitimate interest in preventing corruption in the process, the Court found, it could not prohibit the governing boards of party committees from endorsing candidates in primary races. Abuse, deal making, and other compromising activities were surely possible where parties were involved, but, Marshall made clear, parties were still indispensable contributors to the debate. The problem with the state's ban on primary endorsements was that it prevented "party governing bodies from stating whether a candidate adheres to the tenets of the party or whether party officials believe that the candidate is qualified for the position sought."[61] And thus, as a kind of boundary line for the expression and association of a free people, the prohibition "directly hampers the ability of a party to spread its message and hamstrings voters seeking to inform themselves about the candidates and the campaign issues,"[62] constituting a "particularly egregious" example of "the State censor[ing] the political speech a political party shares with its members."[63]

More recently, Justice Kennedy embraced the virtues of open institutions in his concurrence in *Republican Party of Minnesota v. White*.[64] While the majority seemed to acknowledge that certain conflicts of interest attached to the unique situation of an "impartial" judge running for office and addressing controversial issues of public concern, Kennedy underscored his faith in the self-regulating character of electoral institutions. "If Minnesota believes that certain sorts of candidate speech disclose flaws in the candidate's credentials," he wrote, "democracy and free speech are their own correctives. . . . Free elections and free speech are a powerful combination: Together they may advance our understanding of the rule of law and further a commitment to its precepts."[65]

THE PRECAUTIONARY MODE

While the very nature of modern law may be rooted in the idea of the "bad man,"[66] the *precautionary* mode of argument, though not necessarily assuming the worst, does hedge its bet, so to speak, on the side of prudence. By contrast to its aspirational alternative, this posture is premised on the concession that defects, malfunctions, and malfeasance are inherent in a democracy, to be sure, but still warranting of preventative efforts. It is, in fact, "experience" which has "taught mankind the necessity of auxiliary precautions," as James Madison argued;[67] and so, given that "men are not angels,"[68] this mode accepts that electoral malfunctions, misunderstandings,[69] and machinations are possible—even probable—and that a solution comes in the form of deference to the state's prophylactic measures.[70]

While I have deliberately avoided terms like *realistic* in portraying this disposition—given the plasticity of this notion as applied,[71] and its freighted associations across various fields of study and practice (e.g., literature, art, foreign policy)—this approach is perhaps "realistic" in that it posits a somewhat grittier, possibly jaded, perhaps "conservative" (in dispositional terms), arguably self-interested,[72] and certainly skeptical view of political actors and institutions.[73] Of course, it behooves us to emphasize that "reform" is always *political*, no matter how it might be portrayed or rationalized,[74] and so, to be clear, it is not my intention for aspirationalism to serve as shorthand for "idealism," with the precautionary approach somehow its opposite.

Turning to the cases for support, we can see that, while this mode of argument has certainly been invoked in controversies involving people in democratic politics, the central concern is the vulnerability of the electoral process itself, but specifically the state's expressed concerns over the role of money in political campaigns.[75] Perhaps the most influential case to rely on suppositions and appearances of wrongdoing with respect to the role of money in politics (in this body of law and beyond) is *Buckley v. Valeo*. In this paradigmatic case—wherein the per curiam majority rejected the expenditure limitations of the FECA (as amended in 1974), but found the contribution limitations to be constitutional—the pervasive cynicism of the day colored the Court's acceptance of the state's interest in preventing both corruption and the appearance of corruption. "To the extent that large contributions are given to secure a political quid pro quo from current and potential office holders," the Court acknowledged, "the integrity of our *system* of representative democracy is undermined."[76] While the "scope of such pernicious practices can never be reliably ascertained," of course, "the deeply disturbing examples surfacing after the 1972 election demonstrate that the problem is not an illusory one."[77]

Significantly then, from a precautionary standpoint, "of *almost equal concern* as the danger of actual quid pro quo arrangements," the Court explained, "is the impact of the *appearance* of corruption stemming from public awareness of the opportunities for abuse inherent in a regime of large individual financial contributions."[78] Where the aspirational approach would construe financial contributions as an indication that a candidate and her supporters are committed to the same policies, or that money is the "voice" of the wealthy who lack the time to "speak" in a more conventional sense, the precautionary mode suggests that, instead—or, at least, as well—corruption is possible and/or likely once financial contributions pass a particular threshold. Perhaps more importantly, even if there is no evidence of actual corruption, most people are likely to assume some degree of impropriety, a fact which, in and of itself, is a state interest (see Chapter 8) because it could discourage participation and trust in the political process.

Later campaign finance cases, building on the reasoning set forth in *Buckley*, have continued to rely on this central premise. Consider, for example, *Colorado* II, where the justices, having determined, in *Colorado* I,[79] that "independent" expenditure limits on party spending were unconstitutional, were asked to consider whether expenditures "coordinated" between parties and particular candidates were equally problematic for First Amendment purposes. Finding these sorts of expenditure limitations to be constitutional—given that this type of "expenditure" was more akin to an evasive and indirect "contribution"—Justice Souter, writing for a five-member majority, concluded that the notion that parties should be exempt from such restrictions was "not so much metaphysics as myopia, a refusal to see how the power of money *actually* works in the political structure."[80] Indeed, as he stressed in precautionary terms—emphasizing less the sublime than the sober—"when we look directly at a party's function in getting and spending money, it would ignore *reality* to think that the party role is adequately described by speaking generally of electing particular candidates."[81] Of course, the money that parties spend "comes from contributors with their own personal interests."[82] To fail to take such interests and their implications seriously would be to fail to frankly take stock of politics as it is, not as we might like it to be.

CONCLUSION

While much more detailed attention to the significance of these modes can be found in the case study chapters, what we have above is the basic framework for those rhetorical devices facilitating the process of constitution in this domain. Chapter 4 directs us to the constitution of electoral speech law in cognitive terms, with a shift in focus from the nature of the argument and means of articulation, to the contours that serve to instantiate the conceptual and rhetorical possibilities discussed in this and the previous chapter, fleshing them out in terms that will, as we will see in considering the constitutive qualities of *images*, *preferences*, *persuasion*, and *perception*, have profound, formative consequences for the justices' contemplation of the speech cases in the constitutional episodes to come in Chapters 5 through 8.

CHAPTER 4

Cognitive Contours

IN RELYING ON the general notion of "contours" in this exploration of cognitive constitutional elements, I mean to accommodate the range of techniques, tactics, devices, and schemes that have the potential to constitute the manner in which and means by which the justices "see" the speech question before them. The constitutional episodes to follow will illustrate this point. Indeed, what the members of the Court "have in mind" here is especially important in that such contours color their impressions of the issues, the questions they ask, the evidence they consider, and the conclusions they reach.[1] And what is "in mind," I will demonstrate, depends—not exclusively or deterministically, but still critically—on how speech controversies are translated through competing communicative frames and/or how the questions presented either comport with or complicate existing cognitive schemata. And so, unlike the previous two chapters that turned to data from the larger domain to inductively classify conceptual intentions and rhetorical maneuvers, our purpose here is to establish the vocabulary and framework necessary to understand the evolution of each constitutional episode from its status as a controversy through its review by the U.S. Supreme Court.

To do this, I begin with a discussion of the general significance of the role of *imagery* in argument and develop the claim that the particular and literal "vision" of the case is critical to its ultimate resolution in the sense that the "picture" of speech in such cases really *is* worth a "thousand words," given the degree to which sufficiently compelling images of electoral expression can, in effect, control a case—profoundly governing the perception of the speech controversy and hence confining its consideration or review to a preferred realm. I move then to a discussion of evident preferences for certain dimensions of electoral expression, as they are revealed by the voting patterns and evident correlations between various constitutional elements within this domain. Following this, I focus on the role for persuasion in the constitution of electoral speech law, with special attention to the work of cognitive psychologists, linguists, sociologists, communications scholars, philosophers, and political scientists who have offered extensive explications of the principles and processes of "communicative framing"—generally the manner by which communicants (advocates and amici for my purposes) make certain elements or issues "more noticeable, meaningful, or memorable to audiences" and thus render it more likely that "receivers will perceive the information, discern meaning and thus process it, and store it in memory."[2] Finally, I turn to the role of and for perception, but specifically the significance of "schemata," or those categories of the mind which represent an individual's "complex set of beliefs and feelings about, or world view of, some area of experience."[3]

To be clear, I do not presume to know, from this exploration of elements, whether the "mental constructs" (the images that govern the consideration of the case) are cultivated by the process of communicative framing or whether schemata held over from previous cases or life experiences are activated in the normal course of perception and understanding—or *both*, as I would expect to be the case more often than not.[4] Decision making is too complex to afford an easy alignment of causal arrows explaining the path from review through reasoning to outcome. What I can and will do, however, is to provide a thorough inventory of the features and factors of the mind that figure most prominently in this constitutive process.

IMAGERY

"Political discourse," Terence Ball and J. G. A. Pocock have argued, "is constituted not only by concepts and the kinds of statements and assertions that they make possible but also—and arguably, even more deeply—by the imagery that gives these concepts their place and point."[5] Moreover, Murray Edelman has argued, to facilitate the expression of ideas "there must be an image as articulated in art, in words, or in other symbols."[6] "The notion that an idea can somehow exist without objectification in an expression of any kind is an illusion," he continues, "though the expression may take the form of a term or image in one's own mind: that is, as a contemplated exchange with others."[7] Images and imagery, or in psychological terminology "mental pictures,"[8] are, I will argue, central to the process of reasoning and evaluation, indeed to the fundamental nature of *how* we go about thinking.[9]

As one scholar has observed, in fact, "human beings link seeing so closely with thinking that we regularly use the verb 'to see' to indicate understanding or insight."[10] Thus, the ability to visualize—"to 'see' relationships, patterns, information, ideas, and facts—is one of the most powerful mental tools we have because it pushes us to think in a more specific, tangible way."[11] Consider that our contemporary understanding of the place, purpose, and essence of the speech clause of the First Amendment is still much governed by the prototype and incumbent imagery of the "basement press cranking out seditious leaflets" and of the "'individual mount[ed on] a soapbox on a corner in some large city . . . criticiz[ing] governmental policy.'"[12] Appraising an abstraction in such fashion, we will see, bears significantly on the consideration and constitution of this body of law, because novel controversies necessarily draw upon some such referent.

That such images still structure the way the justices approach speech questions is evident in the Court's invalidation of the Communications with Decency Act in *Reno v. ACLU*, for example.[13] As Steven Winter has observed of this case, "In striking down the act's prohibitions on 'indecent' material on the Internet, the Court drew a direct if somewhat awkward analogy to these free speech prototypes: 'Through the use of chat rooms, any person with a phone line can become a *town crier* with a voice that resonates farther than it could from any *soapbox*. Through the use of Web pages, mail exploders, and newsgroups, the same individual can become a *pamphleteer*.'"[14] The significance of such allusions is that the invoked metaphors, analogies, and symbols stand in for something like the "ideal" speech form—that which speech is *supposed* to be, or what we think of when we think of "speech," in other words—and thus become an embodiment of sorts for the First Amendment itself. This is a critical notion because "speech" qua speech is essentially *un*-imaginable, in that it is but an abstraction, manifest only in particular instantiations: the likes of which have historically referenced (and in some cases been represented by) the above-noted "town crier," "soapbox advocate," pamphleteer running the "basement printing press," or, obviously, the "marketplace of ideas."[15]

To be sure, we can imagine *a* "speech" (e.g., Irving Feiner's verbal denunciation of the "bum" mayor of Syracuse, New York);[16] we can conjure up notions of tangible "speakers" (e.g., individuals distributing literature);[17] we can see *un*-"spoken" expression (e.g., jackets with colorful critiques of conscription,[18] or of black arm bands);[19] we can calculate "speech" (e.g., the money received and expended by political candidates);[20] certain communities allow for an individual to feel "speech," as it were (e.g., various forms of "embodied" expression);[21] and so on. The upshot of this is that while we may infer from observable microlevel instances and incidents of speech to draw conclusions regarding the abstract macrolevel category, "freedom *of* speech," we do so while working with specific images such as these, which are gleaned from experience and which simultaneously inform *and* confine—though they do not foreclose—the scope of review to a space within the contours of the cognitive construct. Certainly new images emerge as the law evolves, but they arise only while on the "path" previously charted out by their ancestors.

Images of this sort pervade our "normal conceptual system," as George Lakoff and Mark Johnson have argued in their seminal study of metaphors. Indeed, they continue, "*because* so many of the concepts that are important to us are either abstract or not clearly delineated in our experience (the emotions, ideas, time, etc.)," we need to understand them "by means of other concepts that we understand in clearer terms (spatial orientations, objects, etc.)."[22] Or, as Lakoff has expressed in his assessment of the ways in which individuals at different ends of the political spectrum think—not simply *what* they think but *why* they think it—"salient exemplars" pertain here because, as "single memorable examples," they are "commonly used in making probability judgments or in drawing conclusions about what is typical of category members."[23] Such exemplars are commonly invoked in our discourse as if they were a typical case, he explains, such as the practice of "popularizing the case of a single welfare cheater to suggest that everyone on welfare cheats."[24] As we will see in the case study chapters to follow, images of electoral expression have the same potential to structure the entire perception of the speech claim(ant).

And thus we consider Winter's observation that a judge's "lawmaking activities are not only bounded but also *shaped* by the habits, practices, and understandings of his culture."[25] Considering cases involving gay rights, for example, "what ultimately decides the issue is not the legal rule but the concept of *intimacy* that the judges bring to the case."[26] That is, "if the judges know intimacy only in the context of a traditional heterosexual marriage, if they know lesbians and gays only as Other, then *Bowers* [*v. Hardwick*] is always and already lost."[27] So too, I will argue in the case studies below, the images of electoral expression that arise in the consideration of various cases and controversies—whether activated as schemata or cultivated by way of communicative framing—have a profound effect on the shaping of "lawmaking activities," to which Winter refers, in that judges require the capacity and materials to imagine the abstraction of "speech" by filling in the content with concrete and discernible images.

To be sure, the "figurative language" used "can also be the source of distortion and misrepresentation," given that "analysis is a function of the language we employ, and frequently 'our thoughts do not select the words we use; instead, words determine the thoughts we have.'"[28] And thus, for example, as communications scholar Haig Bosmajian suggests, "when attorneys and Supreme Court Justices metaphorized 'revolutionary' ideas into 'flames,' 'fire,' 'sparks,' and 'poisons,' and those advocating such ideas as 'snakes,'" the consequence was to direct society's thinking "not by the force of argument at hand, but by the interest of the image in our mind."[29]

PREFERENCES

Turning to the role for preferences as a contour influencing the evaluation in electoral speech cases, we can see intriguing patterns emerge by looking at the correlations between the constitutional elements discussed in Chapters 2 and 3. What these correlations reveal, as we would expect, are some clear tendencies to support one or another conception of the marketplace of ideas, or a particular rhetorical mode for purposes of analysis and articulation, but—by looking, as well, to the forms of speech implicated—we can see apparent preferences for particular dimensions of electoral expression within the larger domain. Let us, therefore, turn to these data.

Table 4.1 includes only those justices who have heard at least eight cases within this domain—a threshold adopted to afford sufficient jurisprudential exposure for analysis, but also one allowing for a "natural" break in that those justices who did not reach this point heard only four cases (at the next lowest level) or, below that, only one or two.[30] An implication of this is that not until *United States Civil Service Commission v. National Association of Letter Carriers, AFL-CIO*, in 1973,[31] is there a case where each justice on the Court is (or will at some point be) a member of the "eight-case club"; and not until *FEC v. National Conservative PAC*, in 1985,[32] is there a Court where each justice presently sitting has already heard at least eight cases, if *Common Cause v. Schmitt* is included in the count (a per curiam, 4-4 affirmation of the lower court decided in 1982).[33] Otherwise, such a threshold was not realized until *McConnell v. FEC* (in 2003).[34]

Regarding the coding for Table 4.1, the "cases heard" column omits those cases that may have occurred during a member's tenure, but in which she or he did not participate. The form of ruling is indicated in the "opinion" column, with bold implying authorship and parentheses indicating the degree of concurrence (in judgment or result)—or, in the case of *Buckley v. Valeo*,[35] which parts of the per curiam opinion the justice joined. Though it probably goes without saying, unless otherwise indicated by a parenthesis, a concurrence implies agreement in result *and* reasoning, while a dissent logically distances the justice from both components of the majority ruling.

The "Concept I" column indicates the conceptual framework that was clearly invoked or implied in the opinion authored or joined by the justice. As we saw in Chapter 2, a classic conception rationale bespeaks more than merely finding for the asserted speech interest; so, too, do custodial or equality conception justifications implicate more than reasoning in terms of purported or generic state interests. There may be no evident conception because the Court majority may not have reached the constitutional

TABLE 4.1 *Constitutional Correlations*

Justice[a]	Year	Case	Dimension	Opinion[b]	Concept I[c]	Concept II	Rhetoric I[d]	Rhetoric II
Black	1947	*Mitchell*	activism	**dissent**	classic		aspirational	
	1948	*CIO*	$ (union)	conc (result)	classic		aspirational	
	1957	*UAW-CIO*	$ (union)	dissent	classic		aspirational	
	1966	*Mills*	newspaper	**majority**	classic		na	
	1968	*St. Amant*	candidate	majority	classic		na	
	1968	*Red Lion*	candidate	majority	equality		na	
	1971	*Ocala*	newspaper	**conc (judgment)**	classic		aspirational	
	1971	*Monitor Patriot*	newspaper	**conc (judgment)**	classic		aspirational	
Douglas	1947	*Mitchell*	activism	**dissent**	classic		aspirational	
	1948	*CIO*	$ (union)	conc (result)	classic		aspirational	
	1957	*UAW-CIO*	$ (union)	**dissent**	classic		aspirational	
	1966	*Mills*	newspaper	**conc**	classic		na	
	1968	*St. Amant*	candidate	majority	classic		na	
	1971	*Ocala*	newspaper	conc (judgment)	classic		aspirational	
	1971	*Monitor Patriot*	newspaper	conc (judgment)	classic		aspirational	
	1973	*Letter Carriers*	activism	**dissent**	classic		na	
	1974	*Shaker Heights*	candidate	**conc**	custodial		precautionary	
Brennan	1957	*UAW-CIO*	$ (union)	majority	na		na	
	1966	*Mills*	newspaper	majority	classic		na	
	1968	*St. Amant*	candidate	majority	classic		na	
	1968	*Red Lion*	candidate	majority	equality		na	
	1971	*Ocala*	newspaper	majority	classic		na	
	1971	*Monitor Patriot*	newspaper	majority	classic		na	
	1973	*Letter Carriers*	activism	dissent	classic		na	

	1974	*Shaker Heights*	candidate	**dissent**	classic		na	
	1976	*Greer*	candidate	**dissent**	classic		historical	
	1976	*Hynes*	candidate	**conc**	classic		aspirational	
	1976	*Buckley*	$ (mult)	per curiam (join all)	classic	cust / equality	aspirational	precautionary
	1978	*Bellotti*	$ (corp)	dissent	custodial		precautionary	
	1981	*CARC*	$ (mult)	majority	classic		aspirational	
	1981	*CMA*	$ (comm)	majority	custodial		precautionary	
	1981	*CBS*	candidate	majority	equality		na	
	1981	*Common Cause*	$ (comm)	per curiam	na		na	
	1982	*NRWC*	$ (comm)	majority	custodial		precautionary	
	1982	*Hartlage*	candidate	**majority**	classic		aspirational	
	1984	*Taxpayers*	candidate	**dissent**	equality		aspirational	
	1985	*NCPAC*	$ (comm)	majority	classic		na	
	1986	*MCFL*	$ (corp)	**majority**	classic	custodial	aspirational	precautionary
	1988	*Meyer*	activism	majority	classic		empirical	aspirational
	1989	*Eu*	party	majority	classic		aspirational	
	1990	*Austin*	$ (corp)	**conc**	equality	custodial	precautionary	
Stewart	1966	*Mills*	newspaper	majority	classic		na	
	1968	*St. Amant*	candidate	majority	classic		na	
	1968	*Red Lion*	candidate	majority	equality		na	
	1971	*Ocala*	newspaper	**majority**	classic		na	

a Includes only those justices who have reviewed at least eight electoral speech cases.

b Form of opinion; bold implies authorship.

c "Concept I" indicates the conceptual invocation of this justice in this case; "Concept II" indicates an additional, though not necessarily secondary, invocation.

d "Rhetoric I" indicates the rhetorical mode of this justice in this case; "Rhetoric II" implies an additional, though not necessarily secondary, mode.

e Reflective only of the vote and reasoning on the primary elements, Titles I and II, involving the ban on "soft money" and electioneering restrictions.

continued

TABLE 4.1 *(continued)*

	1971	*Monitor Patriot*	newspaper	**majority**	classic		na	
	1973	*Letter Carriers*	activism	majority	custodial		historical	precautionary
	1974	*Shaker Heights*	candidate	dissent	classic		na	
	1976	*Greer*	candidate	**majority**	custodial		historical	
	1976	*Hynes*	candidate	majority	classic		na	
	1976	*Buckley*	$ (mult)	per curiam (join all)	classic	cust / equality	aspirational	precautionary
	1978	*Bellotti*	$ (corp)	majority	classic		aspirational	
	1981	*CMA*	$ (comm)	**dissent**	na		na	
	1981	*CBS*	candidate	majority	equality		na	
White	1966	*Mills*	newspaper	majority	classic		na	
	1968	*St. Amant*	candidate	**majority**	classic		na	
	1968	*Red Lion*	candidate	**majority**	equality		na	
	1971	*Ocala*	newspaper	majority	classic		precautionary	
	1971	*Monitor Patriot*	newspaper	majority	classic		precautionary	
	1973	*Letter Carriers*	activism	**majority**	custodial		historical	precautionary
	1974	*Shaker Heights*	candidate	majority	custodial		precautionary	
	1976	*Greer*	candidate	majority	custodial		historical	
	1976	*Hynes*	candidate	majority	classic		na	
	1976	*Buckley*	$ (mult)	conc / diss	custodial	equality	precautionary	
	1978	*Bellotti*	$ (corp)	**dissent**	custodial		precautionary	
	1981	*CARC*	$ (mult)	**dissent**	custodial		historical	
	1981	*CMA*	$ (comm)	majority	custodial		precautionary	
	1981	*CBS*	candidate	**dissent**	na		na	
	1981	*Common Cause*	$ (comm)	per curiam	na		na	
	1982	*NRWC*	$ (comm)	majority	custodial		precautionary	

	1982	*Hartlage*	candidate	majority	classic		aspirational	
	1984	*Taxpayers*	candidate	majority	na		precautionary	
	1985	*NCPAC*	$ (comm)	**dissent**	custodial		precautionary	
	1986	*MCFL*	$ (corp)	**conc / diss**	custodial		precautionary	
	1988	*Meyer*	activism	majority	classic		empirical	aspirational
	1989	*Eu*	party	majority	classic		aspirational	
	1990	*Austin*	$ (corp)	majority	equality	custodial	precautionary	
	1991	*Renne*	party	**dissent**	na		na	
	1992	*Burson*	candidate	plurality	custodial		historical	emp / prec
Marshall	1968	*St. Amant*	candidate	majority	classic		na	
	1968	*Red Lion*	candidate	majority	equality		na	
	1971	*Ocala*	newspaper	majority	classic		na	
	1971	*Monitor Patriot*	newspaper	majority	classic		na	
	1973	*Letter Carriers*	activism	dissent	classic		na	
	1974	*Shaker Heights*	candidate	dissent	classic		na	
	1976	*Greer*	candidate	**dissent**	classic		historical	
	1976	*Hynes*	candidate	concurrence	classic		aspirational	
	1976	*Buckley*	$ (mult)	conc / diss	classic	cust / equality	precautionary	
	1978	*Bellotti*	$ (corp)	dissent	custodial		precautionary	
	1981	*CARC*	$ (mult)	**conc (judgment)**	classic	custodial	precautionary	
	1981	*CMA*	$ (comm)	**majority**	custodial		precautionary	
	1981	*CBS*	candidate	**majority**	equality		na	
	1981	*Common Cause*	$ (comm)	per curiam	na		na	
	1982	*NRWC*	$ (comm)	majority	custodial		precautionary	
	1982	*Hartlage*	candidate	majority	classic		aspirational	
	1984	*Taxpayers*	candidate	dissent	equality		aspirational	
	1985	*NCPAC*	$ (comm)	**dissent**	equality	custodial	precautionary	
	1986	*MCFL*	$ (corp)	majority	classic	custodial	aspirational	precautionary

continued

TABLE 4.1 *(continued)*

	1988	*Meyer*	activism	majority	classic		empirical	aspirational
	1989	*Eu*	party	**majority**	classic		aspirational	
	1990	*Austin*	$ (corp)	**majority**	equality	custodial	precautionary	
	1991	*Renne*	party	**dissent**	classic		aspirational	
Blackmun	1971	*Ocala*	newspaper	majority	classic		na	
	1971	*Monitor Patriot*	newspaper	majority	classic		na	
	1973	*Letter Carriers*	activism	majority	custodial		historical	precautionary
	1974	*Shaker Heights*	candidate	**majority**	custodial		precautionary	
	1976	*Greer*	candidate	majority	custodial		historical	
	1976	*Hynes*	candidate	majority	classic		na	
	1976	*Buckley*	$ (mult)	conc / diss	classic	equality	na	
	1978	*Bellotti*	$ (corp)	majority	classic		aspirational	
	1981	CARC	$ (mult)	**conc (judgment)**	na		na	
	1981	CMA	$ (comm)	**conc / diss**	custodial		na	
	1981	CBS	candidate	majority	equality		na	
	1981	*Common Cause*	$ (comm)	per curiam	na		na	
	1982	NRWC	$ (comm)	majority	custodial		precautionary	
	1982	*Hartlage*	candidate	majority	classic		aspirational	
	1984	*Taxpayers*	candidate	dissent	equality		aspirational	
	1985	NCPAC	$ (comm)	majority	classic		na	
	1986	MCFL	$ (corp)	conc / diss	custodial		precautionary	
	1988	*Meyer*	activism	majority	classic		empirical	aspirational
	1989	*Eu*	party	majority	classic		aspirational	
	1990	*Austin*	$ (corp)	majority	equality	custodial	precautionary	
	1991	*Renne*	party	dissent	classic		aspirational	
	1992	*Burson*	candidate	**plurality**	custodial		historical	emp / prec

Burger	1971	*Ocala*	newspaper	majority	classic		na	
	1971	*Monitor Patriot*	newspaper	majority	classic		na	
	1973	*Letter Carriers*	activism	majority	custodial		historical	precautionary
	1974	*Shaker Heights*	candidate	majority	custodial		precautionary	
	1976	*Greer*	candidate	**conc**	custodial		historical	
	1976	*Hynes*	candidate	**majority**	classic		na	
	1976	*Buckley*	$ (mult)	conc / diss	classic		aspirational	
	1978	*Bellotti*	$ (corp)	**conc**	classic		aspirational	
	1981	*CARC*	$ (mult)	**majority**	classic		aspirational	
	1981	*CMA*	$ (comm)	dissent	na		na	
	1981	*CBS*	candidate	**majority**	equality		na	
	1981	*Common Cause*	$ (comm)	per curiam	na		na	
	1982	*NRWC*	$ (comm)	majority	custodial		precautionary	
	1982	*Hartlage*	candidate	**conc (judgment)**	classic		aspirational	
	1984	*Taxpayers*	candidate	majority	na		precautionary	
	1985	*NCPAC*	$ (comm)	majority	classic		na	
Rehnquist	1973	*Letter Carriers*	activism	majority	custodial		historical	precautionary
	1974	*Shaker Heights*	candidate	majority	custodial		precautionary	
	1976	*Buckley*	$ (mult)	conc / diss	classic	cust / equality		
	1976	*Greer*	candidate	majority	custodial		historical	
	1976	*Hynes*	candidate	**dissent**	custodial		precautionary	
	1978	*Bellotti*	$ (corp)	**dissent**	custodial		precautionary	
	1981	*CARC*	$ (mult)	majority	classic		aspirational	
	1981	*CMA*	$ (comm)	dissent	na		na	
	1981	*CBS*	candidate	dissent	na		na	
	1981	*Common Cause*	$ (comm)	per curiam	na		na	
	1982	*NRWC*	$ (comm)	**majority**	custodial		precautionary	

continued

TABLE 4.1 *(continued)*

	1982	*Hartlage*	candidate	**conc (result)**	na		na	
	1984	*Taxpayers*	candidate	majority	na		precautionary	
	1985	*NCPAC*	$ (comm)	**majority**	classic		na	
	1986	*MCFL*	$ (corp)	**conc / diss**	custodial		precautionary	
	1988	*Meyer*	activism	majority	classic		empirical	aspirational
	1990	*Austin*	$ (corp)	majority	equality	custodial	precautionary	
	1991	*Renne*	party	majority	na		na	
	1992	*Burson*	candidate	plurality	custodial		historical	emp / prec
	1995	*McIntyre*	activism	dissent	custodial		precautionary	historical
	1996	*Colorado* I	$ (party)	conc (judge) / diss	classic		aspirational	
	1998	*AETC*	candidate	majority	na		empirical	
	1999	*ACLF*	activism	conc / diss	custodial		precautionary	
	2000	*Shrink*	$ (comm)	majority	custodial	equality	empirical	precautionary
	2001	*Colorado* II	$ (party)	dissent	classic		empirical	aspirational
	2002	*White*	candidate	majority	classic		historical	aspirational
	2003	*Beaumont*	$ (corp)	majority	custodial		precautionary	historical
	2003	*McConnell*[c]	$ (mult)	**dissent**	classic		aspirational	empirical
Powell	1973	*Letter Carriers*	activism	majority	custodial		historical	precautionary
	1974	*Shaker Heights*	candidate	dissent	classic		na	
	1976	*Buckley*	$ (mult)	per curiam (join all)	classic	cust / equality	aspirational	precautionary
	1976	*Greer*	candidate	**conc**	custodial		precautionary	
	1976	*Hynes*	candidate	majority	classic		classic	
	1978	*Bellotti*	$ (corp)	**majority**	classic		aspirational	
	1981	*CARC*	$ (general)	majority	classic		aspirational	
	1981	*CMA*	$ (comm)	dissent	na		na	

	1981	*CBS*	candidate	majority	equality		na	
	1981	*Common Cause*	$ (comm)	per curiam	na		na	
	1982	*NRWC*	$ (comm)	majority	custodial		precautionary	
	1982	*Hartlage*	candidate	majority	classic		aspirational	
	1984	*Taxpayers*	candidate	majority	na		precautionary	
	1985	*NCPAC*	$ (comm)	majority	classic		na	
	1986	*MCFL*	$ (corp)	majority	classic	custodial	aspirational	precautionary
Stevens	1978	*Bellotti*	$ (corp)	majority	classic		aspirational	
	1981	*CARC*	$ (mult)	majority	classic		aspirational	
	1981	*CMA*	$ (comm)	majority	custodial		precautionary	
	1981	*CBS*	candidate	**dissent**	na		na	
	1981	*Common Cause*	$ (comm)	per curiam	na		na	
	1982	*NRWC*	$ (comm)	majority	custodial		precautionary	
	1982	*Hartlage*	candidate	majority	classic		aspirational	
	1984	*Taxpayers*	candidate	**majority**	na		precautionary	
	1985	*NCPAC*	$ (comm)	**conc / diss**	classic		na	
	1986	*MCFL*	$ (corp)	conc / diss	custodial		precautionary	
	1988	*Meyer*	activism	**majority**	classic		empirical	aspirational
	1989	*Eu*	party	majority	classic		aspirational	
	1990	*Austin*	$ (corp)	**conc**	custodial		na	
	1991	*Renne*	party	majority	na		na	
	1992	*Burson*	candidate	**dissent**	classic		aspirational	emp / hist
	1995	*McIntyre*	activism	**majority**	classic		aspirational	historical
	1996	*Colorado* I	$ (party)	**dissent**	custodial	equality	precautionary	
	1998	*AETC*	candidate	**dissent**	equality		empirical	aspirational
	1999	*ACLF*	activism	majority	classic		aspirational	empirical
	2000	*Shrink*	$ (comm)	**conc**	custodial		precautionary	
	2001	*Colorado* II	$ (party)	majority	custodial		empirical	precautionary

continued

TABLE 4.1 *(continued)*

	2002	*White*	candidate	**dissent**	custodial		precautionary	
	2003	*Beaumont*	$ (corp)	majority	custodial		precautionary	historical
	2003	*McConnell*[c]	$ (mult)	**majority**	custodial	equality	precautionary	empirical
	2005	*WRTL*	$ (corp)	per curiam	na		na	
	2006	*Sorrell*	$ (mult)	**dissent**	custodial		historical	
O'Connor	1981	*CARC*	$ (mult)	**conc (judgment)**	na		na	
	1982	*NRWC*	$ (comm)	majority	custodial		precautionary	
	1982	*Hartlage*	candidate	majority	classic		aspirational	
	1984	*Taxpayers*	candidate	majority	na		precautionary	
	1985	*NCPAC*	$ (comm)	majority	classic		na	
	1986	*MCFL*	$ (corp)	**conc (judgment)**	classic	custodial	aspirational	precautionary
	1988	*Meyer*	activism	majority	classic		empirical	aspirational
	1989	*Eu*	party	majority	classic		aspirational	
	1990	*Austin*	$ (corp)	dissent	classic		aspirational	
	1991	*Renne*	party	majority	na		na	
	1992	*Burson*	candidate	dissent	classic		aspirational	emp / hist
	1995	*McIntyre*	activism	majority	classic		aspirational	historical
	1996	*Colorado* I	$ (party)	plurality	classic		empirical	
	1998	*AETC*	candidate	majority	na		empirical	
	1999	*ACLF*	activism	**conc / diss**	custodial		precautionary	empirical
	2000	*Shrink*	$ (comm)	majority	custodial		empirical	precautionary
	2001	*Colorado* II	$ (party)	majority	custodial		empirical	precautionary
	2002	*White*	candidate	**conc**	classic		precautionary	
	2003	*Beaumont*	$ (corp)	majority	custodial		precautionary	historical
	2003	*McConnell*[c]	$ (mult)	**majority**	custodial	equality	precautionary	empirical
	2005	*WRTL*	$ (corp)	per curiam	na		na	

Scalia	1986	*MCFL*	$ (corp)	majority	classic	custodial	aspirational	precautionary
	1988	*Meyer*	activism	majority	classic		empirical	aspirational
	1989	*Eu*	party	majority	classic		aspirational	
	1990	*Austin*	$ (corp)	**dissent**	classic		historical	aspirational
	1991	*Renne*	party	majority	na		na	
	1992	*Burson*	candidate	**conc (judgment)**	na		historical	
	1995	*McIntyre*	activism	**dissent**	custodial		precautionary	historical
	1996	*Colorado* I	$ (party)	conc (judge) / diss	classic		aspirational	
	1998	*AETC*	candidate	majority	na		empirical	
	1999	*ACLF*	activism	majority	classic		aspirational	empirical
	2000	*Shrink*	$ (comm)	dissent	classic		aspirational	empirical
	2001	*Colorado* II	$ (party)	dissent	classic		empirical	aspirational
	2002	*White*	candidate	**majority**	classic		historical	aspirational
	2003	*Beaumont*	$ (corp)	dissent	na		na	
	2003	*McConnell*[c]	$ (mult)	**dissent**	classic		aspirational	empirical
	2005	*WRTL*	$ (corp)	per curiam	na		na	
	2006	*Sorrell*	$ (mult)	conc (judgment)	classic		empirical	
Kennedy	1988	*Meyer*	activism	majority	classic		empirical	aspirational
	1989	*Eu*	party	majority	classic		aspirational	
	1990	*Austin*	$ (corp)	**dissent**	classic		aspirational	
	1991	*Renne*	party	**majority**	na		na	
	1992	*Burson*	candidate	**conc**	custodial		historical	emp / prec
	1995	*McIntyre*	activism	majority	classic		aspirational	historical
	1996	*Colorado* I	$ (party)	**conc (judge) / diss**	classic		aspirational	
	1998	*AETC*	candidate	**majority**	na		empirical	
	1999	*ACLF*	activism	majority	classic		aspirational	empirical
	2000	*Shrink*	$ (comm)	**dissent**	classic		aspirational	

continued

TABLE 4.1 *(continued)*

	2001	*Colorado* II	$ (party)	dissent	classic		empirical	aspirational
	2002	*White*	candidate	**conc**	classic		aspirational	
	2003	*Beaumont*	$ (corp)	**conc (judgment)**	na		na	
	2003	*McConnell*[e]	$ (mult)	**dissent**	classic		aspirational	empirical
	2005	*WRTL*	$ (corp)	per curiam	na		na	
	2006	*Sorrell*	$ (mult)	**conc (judgment)**	classic		na	empirical
Souter	1991	*Renne*	party	majority	na		na	
	1992	*Burson*	candidate	dissent	classic		aspirational	empirical
	1995	*McIntyre*	activism	majority	classic		aspirational	
	1996	*Colorado* I	$ (party)	plurality	classic		empirical	
	1998	*AETC*	candidate	dissent	equality		empirical	aspirational
	1999	*ACLF*	activism	majority	classic		empirical	aspirational
	2000	*Shrink*	$ (comm)	**majority**	custodial	equality	empirical	
	2001	*Colorado* II	$ (party)	**majority**	custodial		empirical	precautionary
	2002	*White*	candidate	dissent	custodial		precautionary	
	2003	*Beaumont*	$ (corp)	**majority**	custodial		precautionary	historical
	2003	*McConnell*[e]	$ (mult)	majority	custodial		precautionary	empirical
	2005	*WRTL*	$ (corp)	per curiam	na		na	
	2006	*Sorrell*	$ (mult)	**dissent**	custodial		precautionary	empirical
Thomas	1995	*McIntyre*	activism	**conc (judgment)**	classic		historical	
	1996	*Colorado* I	$ (party)	**conc (judge) / diss**	classic		aspirational	
	1998	*AETC*	candidate	majority	na		empirical	
	1999	*ACLF*	activism	**conc (judgment)**	classic		na	
	2000	*Shrink*	$ (comm)	**dissent**	classic		aspirational	
	2001	*Colorado* II	$ (party)	**dissent**	classic		empirical	aspirational

	2002	*White*	candidate	majority	classic		historical	aspirational
	2003	*Beaumont*	$ (corp)	**dissent**	na		na	
	2003	*McConnell*[c]	$ (mult)	**dissent**	classic		aspirational	empirical
	2005	*WRTL*	$ (corp)	per curiam	na		na	
	2006	*Sorrell*	$ (mult)	**conc (judgment)**	classic		empirical	
Breyer	1995	*McIntyre*	activism	majority	classic		aspirational	
	1996	*Colorado* I	$ (party)	**plurality**	classic		empirical	
	1998	*AETC*	candidate	majority	na		empirical	
	1999	*ACLF*	activism	conc / diss	custodial		precautionary	empirical
	2000	*Shrink*	$ (comm)	**conc**	equality	custodial	empirical	precautionary
	2001	*Colorado* II	$ (party)	majority	custodial		empirical	precautionary
	2002	*White*	candidate	dissent	custodial		precautionary	
	2003	*Beaumont*	$ (corp)	majority	custodial		precautionary	historical
	2003	*McConnell*[c]	$ (mult)	majority	custodial		precautionary	empirical
	2005	*WRTL*	$ (corp)	per curiam	na		na	
	2006	*Sorrell*	$ (mult)	**plurality**	custodial		empirical	
Ginsburg	1995	*McIntyre*	activism	**conc**	classic		aspirational	historical
	1996	*Colorado* I	$ (party)	dissent	custodial	equality	precautionary	
	1998	*AETC*	candidate	dissent	equality		empirical	aspirational
	1999	*ACLF*	activism	**majority**	classic		empirical	aspirational
	2000	*Shrink*	$ (comm)	concurrence	equality	custodial	empirical	precautionary
	2001	*Colorado* II	$ (party)	majority	custodial		empirical	precautionary
	2002	*White*	candidate	**dissent**	custodial		precautionary	
	2003	*Beaumont*	$ (corp)	majority	custodial		precautionary	historical
	2003	*McConnell*[c]	$ (mult)	majority	custodial		precautionary	empirical
	2005	*WRTL*	$ (corp)	per curiam	na		na	
	2006	*Sorrell*	$ (mult)	dissent	custodial		precautionary	empirical

question (e.g., *United States v. Auto Workers*);[36] there may not have been a written explanation (e.g., *Common Cause*); the justices may have determined the case was nonjusticiable (e.g., *Renne v. Geary*);[37] the case may have been reviewed *exclusively* along doctrinal lines, finding for example, that an environment did not constitute a traditional "public forum" (e.g., the majority opinions in *Members of the City Council of the City of Los Angeles v. Taxpayers for Vincent*, or *Arkansas Educational Television Commission v. Forbes*, or Justice Scalia's concurrence in judgment in *Burson v. Freeman*)[38]—as distinguished from cases that also construe the constitutional question in terms of doctrinal categories, but which ground the analysis in larger conceptual foundations (e.g., the majority opinions in *Greer v. Spock* and *Burson*);[39] or precedent alone may have provided "ample basis" for the result reached (e.g., Chief Justice Rehnquist's concurrence [in judgment] in *Brown v. Hartlage*).[40]

The "Concept II" column, meanwhile, exists because certain opinions invoke distinct conceptual frameworks to be applied to different provisions (e.g., *Buckley*—wherein a joining of each part of the per curiam opinion would mean invoking the classic conception in the rejection of expenditure limits, the custodial conception in the acceptance of congressional grounds for placing restrictions on contributions, and the equality conception in the support for the principle sustaining public financing for presidential elections); or hybrid and/or reciprocal conceptual claims, where the concern, perhaps, is with *both* the "distortion" flowing from the excessive volume of certain voices *and* the especially deleterious influence of such varieties of expression on the democratic process itself (e.g., the majority rulings in *Austin v. Michigan Chamber of Commerce* and *Nixon v. Shrink Missouri Government PAC*).[41] Regarding the "Rhetoric" column, note that these are, as we saw in Chapter 3, only the modal modes that arise in this domain and therefore not every opinion will appeal to such devices, while some will appeal to several—and thus the "Rhetoric II" column.

Turning now to the data in Table 4.1, and moving chronologically from the earliest judicial appointment, note that—consistent with their general reputations on First Amendment questions—Justices Black and Douglas invoked the classic conception (with aspirational support) almost exclusively, with Black's only exception coming in *Red Lion Broadcasting Co. v. FCC*,[42] a unanimous decision pertaining to the unique concerns of that realm (spectrum scarcity) and Douglas's only departure coming in his last case in the electoral speech domain, *Lehman v. City of Shaker Heights*,[43] wherein one might construe his finding for the state as principally guided by his concern for the *privacy* rights of commuters more than anything else. Justice Brennan portrays similar tendencies, conceiving of nearly all dimensions of speech in classic terms (with the exception of "money" coming from certain speakers), though his tenure is significantly distinguished from those of Black and Douglas because he served during—and for fourteen years following—*Buckley*, meaning that his preferred classic conception approach was confronted by the emergence of money as a form of speech seeking entry to the marketplace. One wonders whether Black and Douglas would have been as resolutely "classical" had they been forced to make the same decisions.

Justice White presents an intriguing bookend to the tendencies of Justice Brennan. White, who heard twenty-five cases (compared to Brennan's twenty-four), was perhaps the most regularly custodial in his adopted conceptual approach, accepting or advocating such a construction of the case twelve times, or 48 percent of the time. Moreover, he was also perhaps the most inclined toward the precautionary mode of argument, adopting this approach thirteen times, or in 52 percent of the cases he heard. Of course "precautions" are a logical complement to "custody," but as White indicates, precautionary logic can also go to support (however reluctantly) a classic model of the marketplace, as was the case in *Ocala Star-Banner Co. v. Damron* and *Monitor Patriot Co. v. Roy*.[44] Justice Marshall presents a further distinction, as the justice showing the most consistent inclination toward the equality conception of the marketplace of ideas as evidenced by his joining the Court in *Red Lion*, his concurrence/dissent in *Buckley*, his membership in the majority in *CBS, Inc. v. FCC*,[45] his dissent in *NCPAC*, his joining in the dissent in *Taxpayers*, and, most significantly, his majority opinion in *Austin*.

Former Chief Justice Rehnquist, like Justice White, is notable for his precautionary inclinations (arising thirteen times in twenty-eight cases, or 46 percent of the time), and for the clear distinction in his classic approach to money as a dimension of speech—eschewing restrictions of a general variety, or those pertaining to committees or involving parties—but adopting a custodial concern when "corporate" voices were competing for acceptance.[46] And yet, a more general observation bears mention here as well: Rehnquist wrote an opinion in only seven of the twenty-eight cases he heard. More specifically, he was in the majority in eight of the fourteen cases that were reviewed while he was the chief (meaning, of course, that he has power to assign the opinion), and yet he did not write for the Court in *any* of these cases. This does not necessarily mean anything for his electoral speech jurisprudence, but it is worth noting and is perhaps ripe for study by those more closely attuned to the former Chief Justice's style and operational tendencies.

By contrast, Justice Stevens has written in thirteen of the twenty-six cases heard and decided thus far (50 percent of the time), and generally appeals to a classic conception of the marketplace (and an aspirational rhetorical mode) when activism is the dimension of speech in question; whereas he refers to the equality and/or custodial conceptual approaches (and argues along precautionary lines) when money (which he has asserted is *not* speech) is the dimension involved.[47] One might conclude from this that Stevens's free speech jurisprudence is especially committed then to "citizen"-speech—that is, expression carried out by people—and manifest in the sorts of imagery (soapboxes or basement printing presses) considered in the previous section. Such does seem to be his general jurisprudential trajectory, in that he has not construed a campaign finance case in classic terms since *NCPAC*, in 1985—which was a case fairly easily guided by *Buckley*—meaning that his vote in *Citizens Against Rent Control v. Berkeley*, in 1981,[48] may actually be a more accurate register of the last time that he was welcoming of money as speech in the marketplace of ideas.

Former Justice O'Connor's most lasting influence here may have come by routinely voting with the Court majority—a phenomenon consistent with her voting patterns in numerous other bodies of law. Specifically, of the twenty-one cases that she heard and decided, O'Connor ended up *not* in the majority only three times (14.3 percent of the time). Meanwhile, Justice Scalia is intriguing because, with the exception of *McIntyre v. Ohio Elections Commission*,[49] he *only* advocates the classic conception—even while his custodial exposition in *McIntyre* was arguably the most vigorous in the entire domain. Turning to Justice Kennedy, we see that he has written in ten of the sixteen cases he has heard thus far and, like Justices Scalia and Thomas, has *never* embraced the equality conception of the marketplace of ideas. Rather, Kennedy is, with the exception of *Burson*, an exclusively *classic* advocate.

Justice Souter's tendencies appear instructive as to the future of electoral speech law, given his custodial reasoning in six of the last seven cases decided, each of which involved money as the speech dimension under review. At the same time, Souter is one of the justices most inclined toward the empirical mode of rhetoric, articulating along these lines in eight of the thirteen cases he has considered. Justice Thomas is noteworthy for what may be his interest in carving out a name for himself as the Court's most consistent advocate of a particular vision of free speech—writing in eight of the eleven cases he has heard, and adopting an exclusively classic conception, amplified by not even the slightest hint of precautionary rhetoric. For their part, the two members appointed most recently (who have heard at least eight cases), Justices Ginsburg and Breyer, are both inclined toward the custodial approach, though significantly they also represent (with Justice Stevens) the only current voices on the Court for the equality conception (see *Colorado Republican Federal Campaign Committee v. FEC* and *Shrink*),[50] and neither has invoked the classic conception in more than two of the eleven cases they have reviewed. Moreover, as the compatibilities between conceptual and rhetorical elements would lead us to expect, neither tends toward the aspirational mode, adopting instead either a precautionary (especially where money is implicated) or an empirical approach.

What this consideration of correlations between constitutional elements presents is a two-fold challenge to the assumptions and implications of the traditional "liberal" versus "conservative" dichotomy that is a staple of scholarship on judicial decision making and that to some extent is conventional wisdom. A scholarly exemplar of this approach to understanding judicial behavior is the "attitudinal model,"[51] a theory that at its most basic level assumes that "the Supreme Court decides disputes in light of the facts of the case vis-à-vis the ideological attitudes and values of the justices," meaning that Chief Justice Rehnquist voted the way he did because he was "extremely conservative" while Justice Marshall voted the way he did because he was "extremely liberal."[52] Under this theory, the justices are relatively unconstrained as they vote their policy preferences, with "legal" factors simply employed as legitimizing devices.[53] In operational terms, the attitudinal model assumes that a "liberal" outcome or vote is one in "support of those alleging deprivation of First Amendment freedoms," while a "conservative" vote or outcome is "the opposite."[54] This definition and these distinctions are key, because the distinction between the two turns on the source "alleging the deprivation," meaning that "support" for *the* "speech" interest must track this *asserted* (or "alleged") speech claim, rather than sustaining an inferred, alternative, or equally compelling counterclaim to expression that may also be at stake within a given controversy.

To demonstrate the limits of this approach within the domain of electoral speech law, we turn to Table 4.2, which provides data regarding the ideological value (attitudinal score), the number of electoral speech cases reviewed, the number of cases wherein the constitutional question was reached, the number of "pro-speech" votes (meaning that the justice accepted the argument of the interest making the speech claim), and the "pro-speech" voting percentage (based on the number of pro-speech votes and the number of cases reaching the First Amendment issue). For purposes of discussion, let us consider the last stable Rehnquist Court cohort, just prior to the appointments of Chief Justice Roberts and Justice Alito. Attitudinalists scaled that panel of Supreme Court justices as follows, from "extremely conservative" to "extremely liberal": Scalia, Rehnquist, Thomas, Stevens, Souter, Kennedy, O'Connor, Breyer, and Ginsburg.[55]

Following the attitudinal ordering outlined above, Scalia should be the least supportive of "First Amendment freedoms," while Ginsburg should be the most, with the other justices falling between these two on the ordinal scale. But this is not the case, and thus the first complication: within this particular domain, it is actually Justice Thomas who shows the highest percentage support for the asserted speech claim (90), though he should show the third lowest, followed by Justice Scalia (80) (who should be the least, not the second most, supportive of First Amendment claims), and Justice Kennedy (78.5).[56] Justice Breyer, meanwhile, who should be the second most "supportive" of "First Amendment freedoms," and Justice Ginsburg, who should rank first in her "support," are tied for last in terms of their percentage of such support (30), putting them even below former Chief Justice Rehnquist (34.6), the second most "conservative" justice.[57]

TABLE 4.2 *Attitudinal Coding and "Pro-Speech" Voting Percentages*

Justice	Ideological Values[a]	Number of Cases Decided		Support for Electoral Speech Claims	
		Total	On the Merits[b]	# "Pro-Speech" Votes[c]	"Pro-Speech" %
Black	na	8	8	7	87.5
Douglas	na	9	9	8	88.8
Brennan	1.00	24	22	16	72.7
Stewart	.50	13	13	8	61.5
White	0.0	25	24	8	33.3
Marshall	1.00	23	22	14	63.6
Blackmun	–.77	22	21	12	57.1
Burger	–.77	16	15	7	46.6
Rehnquist	–.91	28	26	9	34.6
Powell	–.67	15	14	7	50
O'Connor	–.17	21	19	11	57.8
Stevens	–.50	26	23	10	43.4
Scalia	–1.00	17	15	12	80
Kennedy	–.27	16	14	11	78.5
Souter	–.34	13	11	5	45.4
Thomas	–.68	11	10	9	90
Breyer	–.05	11	10	3	30
Ginsburg	.36	11	10	3	30

a Values taken from Jeffrey Segal and Harold Spaeth, *The Supreme Court and the Attitudinal Model Revisited* (New York: Cambridge University Press, 2002), 322 (updating Jeffrey Segal and Albert Cover, "Ideological Values and the Votes of U.S. Supreme Court Justices," *APSR* 83 [1989]: 557). A score of "–1.00" represents "extremely conservative," while a score of "1.00" represents "extremely liberal."

b Represents the number of cases that were reviewed *and* for which this member of the Court considered the *constitutional* question presented to the Court. Note that *Common Cause v. Schmitt* is not included in this column because it was decided by a 4-4 affirmation of the lower court ruling, with no indication of which justices were on which side of the question. Note too that the majority (as opposed to the dissenters) did not reach the constitutional questions posed by *United States v. Congress of Industrial Organizations* or *United States v. Auto Workers*; the majority (though not Justice Marshall, in dissent) found the question nonjusticiable in *Renne v. Geary*; and a per curiam Court remanded *Wisconsin Right to Life* to the lower court for further consideration of the relevant constitutional question.

c Votes in *Buckley v. Valeo* are considered "pro-speech" so long as they find *expenditure* limitations unconstitutional. Votes in *McConnell v. FEC* are considered "pro-speech" only if they reject the provisions of Title I, regarding restrictions on "soft money," seemingly the single most pertinent question considered by all parties in this case.

Certainly, part of the inability to account for electoral speech decisions is due to the theory's failure to precisely account for what "conservatism" is,[58] especially with respect to the differences between its libertarian and prudentialist orientations. More to the point, though, while such labels and the freight that arrives with (and ahead of) them may well be instructive in other jurisprudential domains,[59] for purposes of electoral speech law—and, I would conjecture, freedom of speech, generally—it is hard to say what *the* "liberal" (or "left") or "conservative" (or "right") position is, or *ought* to be on speech rights per se.[60]

Further complicating the attitudinal approach in this respect is the fact that votes/outcomes do not necessarily engender the partisan advantages one would typically associate with the assumed ideological inclinations. Consider the recently decided *McConnell* case contemplating the constitutionality of the Bipartisan Campaign Reform Act of 2002. Here, we can see that the "liberals" on the *Court* (or, as some might say, the *less* "conservative" justices), though not necessarily the "liberal" amici,[61] were committed to preserving "reform" legislation that many perceived as more detrimental to the fundraising efforts of the Democratic Party, given the demographics of its "base" (with more wealth at the very top, perhaps [e.g., Hollywood celebrities], but with a larger percentage of members in the lower and lower-to-middle income brackets). Meanwhile, the more "conservative" members of the Court rejected the terms of such "reform," even though the Republican Party was likely to benefit from upholding the legislation (given the greater percentage of its support coming from individuals able to afford the maximum "hard money" contributions).[62]

A second and more fundamental complication with the attitudinal model, however, is the *mis*representation inherent in the reductionist assumption that a vote is essentially either "for" or "against" speech. Indeed, as Eugene Volokh has argued, it is an "unsound locution" to suggest that "Justice X believes in free speech" and "Justice Y doesn't" because it "suggests that there's only one True Vision of free speech, that it's a maximalist one, and that those who disagree with it therefore don't believe in free speech."[63] Consistent with this assessment, I would argue that it is quite unlikely that *any* justice should genuinely be described (or would describe himself or herself) as not "supporting" the First Amendment or freedom of speech; it is rather a question, as we saw in Chapter 2, of *which* among various popular (people) and institutional (process) values—or their combination—are to be privileged and what speech dimensions are thought to be truer to the intentions of the First Amendment. As such, I offer the percentages in Table 4.2 with some trepidation because it is central to my argument that such binary conceptions misperceive the nature of free speech itself, and particularly its role, purpose, and implications in the course of campaigns and elections.

PERSUASION

The cognitive constitution of electoral speech law is, we will see, significantly influenced by the communicative frames presented by advocates and amici who cultivate particular images in the course of argument. "Persuasion," while having a readily available and broad array of lay meanings,[64] represents for scholars "*human communication designed to influence the autonomous judgments and actions of others*,"[65] with the purpose of "effect[ing] the internalization or voluntary acceptance of new cognitive states or patterns of overt behavior through the exchange of messages."[66] That persuasion is central to the law is obvious: within an adversarial legal model, advocates are supposed to effectively lobby for their clients' interests;[67] they are supposed to, in essence, "conceive and structure a true story . . . that the trier of fact is most likely to believe or adopt."[68] The focus here is on *how* these stories function as "communication devices" in the course of legal proceedings (where their "interpretive power" takes on "special significance") and *how* they facilitate the constitution of the law in this domain.[69]

Assuming, as Jeremy Bentham famously suggested, that law is made by "judge and company," then we need to pay equal attention to contributions of the "company" as they condition the "judge's" review of the case. What we will see in the studies of constitutional episodes to follow in Chapters 5 through 8 is that effective persuasion has the potential to cultivate the controlling images for a case by channeling the review in such a way that the other party must argue within an at least uncomfortable, if not *incompatible*, frame (akin to the uncertainty and discomfort of playing an "away" game), meaning that the Court's adoption of a proffered image stands an advocate on unfamiliar ground and requires that arguments be transmitted through an interpretive framework that may be prohibitive of certain claims (like trying to push a square through the circle cut-out, for example). Put differently, I argue that communicative frames have the potential to design a kind of "cognitive space," if you will, *within which* issues are to be considered—but *by which* they are also confined.[70]

To flesh out this phenomenon, consider, as C. Edwin Baker has wisely observed, that "the lawyerly technique of imagining worst case scenarios and then proceeding to base analyses on the need to prevent it, no matter how unlikely," is successful because it frames "some outlandish, offensive, or otherwise costly behavior that the challenged regulation prohibits," and then proceeds to imply that "without the regulation we may be inundated with offensive behavior."[71] And yet, "the hypothesis of an inundation of the offensive behavior is usually implausible, and such scenarios usually predict an improbable series of worse cases."[72] For example, he offers, "How often will thousands of people be so incensed that they will want to take to the streets and block traffic as a means to protest current problems?" Or: "How often are people actually going to deliver a political message in the town center while locked in a nude, sexual embrace?"—results that, Baker notes, are typical of those that tend to be "*imagined* and then *feared*" by the justices, thus signaling the success of an advocate's frame for the case.[73]

Communicative Frames

The specific device that motors the persuasive process is the communicative frame. In his influential *Frame Analysis*, published in the early 1970s, Erving Goffman was the first to provide serious analytical precision to the concept of "frames,"[74] while Todd Gitlin built upon this work as he directed his focus to the manner by which mass media outlets position various stories for public consumption.[75] But since the late 1970s and early 1980s, the study of frames—in *thought* (involving an individual's perception of a situation more than a communicative property per se) and in *communication* (involving the words, images, phrases, and manners of presentation employed to present material)—has exploded across multiple academic domains, including economics, marketing, management, decision theory, psychology, communications, political science, law, sociology, and other disciplines directed toward studies of both macrolevel phenomena, such as the media or social movements,[76] and microlevel encounters and environments, such as appeals to juries in a courtroom.[77] But attention running constant across all fields pertains to *how* issues, debates, questions, and policies are presented, *why* these developments, arguments, and packages are received and interpreted as they are, and *what* we might learn about "framing effects" in their capacity to shape perceptions of electoral speech claims.[78]

As such, I focus on both sorts of frames in this chapter and in the case studies to follow (in the sense that schemata portray "frames in thought"),[79] but in the course of my discussion of persuasion in this subsection, I begin with frames in communication, which, as Donald Kinder and Don Herzog have observed, work by consisting of "metaphors, exemplars, catchphrases, depictions, and visual images"—often including "a rudimentary causal analysis and appeals to common principles"—and telling stories "about how problems come to be and what (if anything) needs to be done about them."[80] When actively framing an issue, decision, or for my purposes, a case, communicators craft and present their arguments through the use of frames which are "manifested by the presence or absence of certain keywords, stock phrases, stereotyped images, sources of information, and sentences that provide thematically reinforcing clusters of facts or judgments."[81] Moreover, as William Gamson and Andre Modigliani have argued, these "clusters" are typically displayed through signature elements that "imply the core frame and invoke the whole with handy condensing symbols"[82]—such as the "domino" in the famous "theory," that served as a shorthand reference to the arguments for intervention in Southeast Asia during the early 1960s and 1970s.[83]

Evocative imagery of this sort figures prominently in persuasion and is central to successful communicative frames in a variety of ways. Recent research has demonstrated, for example, that "while issue frames may affect the content of one's beliefs, they also affect the *importance* individuals attach to particular beliefs."[84] And thus the frame—or, the effort to "establish a dominant definition or construction of an issue" or to "highlight some bits of information about an item" so as to "elevat[e] them in salience"[85]—is just as significantly an attempt to declare what a dispute "is really all about, and what it has nothing to do with," and can influence opinion in the most important, if subtle, ways by "suggesting which of many, possibly conflicting, considerations should predominate."[86] One of the ways that bits of information in a frame can appear more salient is by "placement or repetition, or by associating them with culturally familiar symbols."[87]

As the Nobel Prize–winning scholars Daniel Kahneman and Amos Tversky have observed, in "selecting and highlighting some features of reality while omitting others," the choices individuals make—in this case between "likely deaths" and "likely lives saved"—can be essentially reversed simply by reversing the framing.[88] Or, as Shanto Iyengar puts it, because "people are exquisitely sensitive to contextual cues when they make decisions, formulate judgments, or express opinions," the "manner in which a problem of choice is 'framed' is a contextual cue that may profoundly influence decision outcomes."[89] Entman concludes, then, that "the frame determines whether most people notice and how they understand and remember a problem, as well as how they evaluate and choose to act upon it."[90] Moreover, the conclusions of Tversky, Kahneman, and other decision theorists "demonstrate that frames select and call attention to particular aspects of the reality described, which logically means that frames simultaneously direct attention *away from* other aspects"; and thus, "most frames are defined by what they *omit* as well as include, and the omissions of potential problem definitions, explanations, evaluations, and recommendations may be as critical as the inclusions in guiding the audience."[91]

Here then, we consider "framing effects," occurring when, "in the course of describing an issue or event, a speaker's emphasis on a subset of potentially relevant considerations causes individuals to focus on these considerations when constructing their opinions."[92] But note that, unlike standard persuasion models, framing effects "do not depend upon the recipient's acceptance of the messages assertions"; indeed, even if one *disagrees* with a frame's assertion (that welfare is bad policy because it breeds laziness, for example), "the frame may still make salient one's beliefs about the poor, positive or negative."[93] Which brings us to what James Druckman has observed: that a more subtle form of framing may be manifest in what he refers to as "emphasis framing effects," phenomena observed in experimental studies showing that by "emphasizing a subset of potentially relevant considerations, a speaker can lead individuals to focus on these considerations when constructing their opinions."[94] For example, he continues, "when a candidate frames a campaign in economic terms, it may cause voters to evaluate candidates based on their economic policies." And this, in turn, "may lead voters to prefer the candidate with the stronger economic policy," whereas, "if the candidate focuses on foreign affairs policy, voters may do the same and, as a result, support the candidate with the stronger foreign affairs policy."[95]

In conclusion, framing, as I will refer to it in the case studies, does not assume that an audience is told *what* to think;[96] rather, it stresses the potential for influencing what they think *about* what to think[97]—assuming not an audience of automatons, lacking "agency," but accepting instead a complicated and fluid social dynamic wherein any one or a number of influences and attributes could, taken together, profoundly alter the way a problem is perceived and the manner by which decisions are reached.[98] Which is to remind us of Murray Edelman's astute contention that the social world is a "kaleidoscope of potential realities, any of which can be readily evoked by altering the ways in which observations are framed and categorized."[99]

PERCEPTION

As Thomas Kuhn argued in his influential study two generations ago, "What a man sees depends both upon what he looks at and also upon what his previous visual-conceptual experience has taught him to see."[100] Perception, in other words, never does and never *can* take place in what we might think of as a "pure" form—that is, unconditioned by our attachments or associations, or as abstracted from the particular context within which we receive information and sensory input. Put differently, as the psychologist Hadley Cantril stressed in a classic study sketching out the concept of "binocular resolution," "our perception depends in large part on the assumptions we bring to any particular occasion."[101] "It would seem," he concluded, that "a person sees what is 'significant,' with significant defined in terms of his relationship to what he is looking at."[102] Consider, too, as Walter Murphy concluded in his study of judicial decision making (drawing on Cantril's conclusions), "on important issues each of us can perceive of only one *image*—that is, we cannot see a choice."[103] What this suggests is that images are critical as devices rendered in the course of argument to persuade an audience, but also in the way they exist in the mind *as* or *among* those "stored clusters of ideas," considered above, thus influencing the manner by which electoral speech law is constituted.

Schemata

Rounding out our evaluation of contours and representing the central element of perception for our consideration, we now turn to those features that play a central role in the process by which audiences consciously or unconsciously determine which messages—or which components or combinations of messages—register with them, meaning that for practical purposes they are inclined to hear what they want to hear and see what they want to see.[104] I will refer to these as *schemata* (the generally accepted plural version of "schema"), which are, in essence, "sets of rules or generalizations derived from past experience that organize and guide information processing about ourselves and others in our social experience"[105]—operating in essence as a "category in the mind which contains information about a particular subject,"[106] while representing a person's "complex set of beliefs and feelings about, or world view of, some area of experience."[107] Schemata facilitate the process and parameters by which we "filter out those stimuli which are irrelevant," attending only to those "important or useful,"[108] rendering some "coherence and structure to our experience."[109]

Frames are certainly important to this process, in that they help to "determine how people will connect the matter to their existing schemas, their internal networks of political thoughts and emotions,"[110] though at the same time—and this is what makes it difficult to outline the exact causal chain in the cognitive constitution of this domain—the "schema, as organized prior knowledge, shapes what is perceived and remembered,"[111] as well as "how quickly we perceive, what we notice, how we interpret what we notice, and what we perceive as similar and different."[112] The utility or instrumental function of these mechanisms is clear, then, in that "concepts such as categories, scripts, or stereotypes connote mentally stored clusters of ideas that guide individuals' process of information,"[113] and thus have the effect of describing "how the world is and how it works."[114]

Central to the relationship *between* frames and schemata is the concept of "priming," or the "process by which frames bring certain values and other beliefs to mind,"[115] thus increasing the "accessibility of some category or construct in memory."[116] In its most basic form, priming starts from the premise that "when people make decisions, they rarely take into consideration the entire array of available relevant evidence,"[117] preferring instead to rely on "intuitive shortcuts and simple rules of thumb": heuristics that privilege "information that is most *accessible*" as consumers make choices, voters make decisions, and so on.[118] Priming has its most noticeable effect in influencing "how information, especially ambiguous information, relevant to a judgment is interpreted or classified,"[119] meaning that, in the perception of a communicative frame and the framing effects flowing from it, various other images and elicitations come to mind in a manner that is not deterministic, but still as a relatively direct function of a prior persuasive framing endeavor.

CONCLUSION

What makes the process and consequences of the cognitive constitution of electoral speech law (or any domain, really) so significant can be expressed by reference to the familiar "nine-dot problem" that is a staple of motivational seminars and brain-teaser books. When confronted with nine dots (arranged in three rows and three columns) and asked to connect the dots with four straight lines without lifting one's pen, most people *assume*—and this is critical—that they cannot venture "outside the box," and thus they fail to consider that the solution involves something other than that they would typically imagine. But of course the "box" only "boxes" them in because they transmuted the image of "walls" into—or onto—the situation, perceiving it as a box because of prior experience with boxes, the habit of constructing boundaries, and so on.

So, too, do the cognitive contours mapped out above structure the development of the cases examined as constitutional episodes in the next four chapters. Specifically, we will see that the natural, if still risky response in making one's case is to slip into the mode of arguing *within* the competing frame, asserting, as the case may be, that one man's "gauntlet" is another man's vibrant democracy (Chapter 5);[120] that even the authors of *The Federalist Papers* would—and should—have had to disclose *their* identities in distributing political literature (Chapter 6); that "political conversations" motivated by profits are not really "conversations" at all—or at least not good ones (Chapter 7); or that there really is *not* the "appearance" of corruption that some people think is "apparent"—or that some people might "assume" or "perceive" is at work, even if it cannot be demonstrated (which is, ironically, all the more reason to regulate, because the harm unseen is the disease undiagnosed—and the failure to act is to "do harm") (Chapter 8).[121] In each of these cases, we will see, the framing of the question to the Court—and the justices' various reactions to these frames—had a profound effect on the outcome reached, and has had, by extension, a profound effect on the ultimate constitution of this body of law.

PART TWO

Constitutional Episodes

CHAPTER 5

Burson v. Freeman

AS A CANDIDATE and political advocate for various campaigns and causes, Rebecca Freeman had determined through years of experience that the grounds surrounding polling places afforded her a unique opportunity to engage in last-minute campaigning.[1] As various individuals interviewed for this book suggested, Freeman was motivated toward *this* form of and environment for electoral expression (as opposed to distributing literature in advance of the election or at a location more removed from voters) because somewhere along the way she had encountered a study indicating that about 15 percent of voters come to the polls undecided on at least *some* contests, meaning that the environment itself offered a prime—and ultimate—opportunity to solicit support as voters made their way into the polling place.[2] In this sense, an encounter at the polling place, however brief, had a potentially persuasive effect and, especially for low-budget or grassroots activist campaigns, represented an efficient, economic, and educative method of political advocacy. While "standing out in the sun for twelve hours and try[ing] to smile all day" may not be a pleasant experience, as advocates who have attempted to speak in this venue understand, those who do politick in this way are those who genuinely feel that they can "make a difference" for their candidates and causes.[3]

But while all fifty states maintained some sort of limitations on activity outside the polls, Tennessee (like forty-six other states) prohibited "electioneering,"[4] including campaign "speech," in various forms, within a hundred-foot radius from the door of the polling place[5]—an amount that, as Table 5.1 demonstrates, was the modal distance nationally. Those interested in interacting with voters were prohibited from entering what was in effect a "campaign free zone"; and, in some cases, depending on the size and landscape of the location, were relegated to a space entirely off the grounds of the polling place. As part of a larger effort to preserve the "purity" of its elections,[6] the state had initially passed polling place reform legislation in 1890, as the fervor for such policies was sweeping the nation, though the law under review here went through several amended versions before it reached its current form in 1974.[7] For Tennessee, we will see that the "zone" was, in essence, a geographic manifestation of

TABLE 5.1 *State Polling Place Speech Statutes*[a]

State	Distance (ft)	Criminal Offense	Election Related	Total Ban	Other
Alabama	30			x	
Alaska	200	x	x		
Arizona	150	x	x		
Arkansas	100	x	x		x
California	100	x	x		
Colorado	100	x	x		
Connecticut	75	x	x		x
Delaware	50	x	x		
Florida[b]	300	x	x		
Georgia	50		x		
Hawaii	1000	x	x		
Idaho	100	x	x		x
Illinois	100	x	x		
Indiana	50	x	x		
Iowa	300		x		
Kansas	250	x	x		x
Kentucky	500		x		
Louisiana	600		x		
Maine	250	x	x		
Maryland	100	x	x		
Massachusetts	150	x	x		
Michigan	100	x	x		x
Minnesota	100			x	
Mississippi	150	x	x		
Missouri	25	x	x		
Montana	200		x		
Nebraska	200	x	x		
Nevada	0	x	x		
New Hampshire	10	x	x		
New Jersey	100	x	x		
New Mexico	100	x	x		
New York	100		x		

the "secret ballot," that reform instituted in the nineteenth century to protect voting rights and maintain order at the polls.

While the Chancery Court upheld the provision, the Tennessee Supreme Court reversed this ruling, finding that the state had not located those means most narrowly tailored to satisfy the admittedly compelling

State	Distance (ft)	Criminal Offense	Election Related	Total Ban	Other
North Carolina	50		x		
North Dakota	100	x	x		
Ohio	100		x		
Oklahoma	300	x	x		
Oregon	100		x		
Pennsylvania	0		x		
Rhode Island	50		x		
South Carolina	200	x	x		
South Dakota	100	x	x		
Tennessee	100	x	x		
Texas	100	x	x		
Utah	150	x	x		
Vermont	0		x		
Virginia	40		x		
Washington[c]	300	x	x		
West Virginia	300			x	
Wisconsin	500		x		
Wyoming	300	x	x		

NOTES

"Distance": Some statutes refer to distances in yards, but these distances have been converted into feet for purposes of comparison.

"Crime": These states provide for a criminal penalty for violation of the regulation.

"Election related": "Election related" statutes regulate such things as distributing campaign materials, soliciting votes, etc.

"Total Ban": These states prohibit any persons except voters, election officials, and certain other individuals assisting disabled voters from being within the restricted zone.

"Other": These states ban other activities unrelated to the election, such as charitable and commercial solicitations.

a State polling place statutes in place as of 1992, when *Burson* was decided. Adapted from the "Brief for the State of Tennessee," *Burson.*

b This statute was declared unconstitutionally overbroad (due to the distance) in *Clean Up '84 v. Henrich*, 759 F.2d 1511 (11th Cir., 1985) and later repealed.

c This statute was declared unconstitutional in *Daily Herald Co. v. Munro*, 838 F.2d 380 (9th Cir., 1988).

interest of protecting voters and the political process. The U.S. Supreme Court, however, in a plurality opinion written by Justice Blackmun (and joined by Chief Justice Rehnquist, Justices White and Kennedy, and Justice Scalia in judgment only), noted from the outset that this case involved "a particularly difficult reconciliation: the accommodation of the right to engage in political discourse with the right to vote—a right at the heart of our democracy."[8] In negotiating this "reconciliation," as we will see in the discussion of the constitution of *Burson v. Freeman* below, the Court's conceptual emphasis was on "custody" as the organizing value in this marketplace of ideas—as opposed to the classic alternative proffered by Justice John Paul Stevens (with Justices Souter and O'Connor)[9]—and so the justices found compelling the state's argument for proprietary attention to the environs of elections as a means of properly ordering the democratic process. So too, we will see, the custodial conception sustaining the notion of a "campaign free zone" was reasoned to and articulated through a combination of historical, empirical, and precautionary modes of argument, while the cognitive constitution of this case was controlled by the state's communicative framing and its particular emphasis on the resonance of key images (e.g., "bottlenecks," "gauntlets," and "chaos") and their capacity to confine the consideration and draw out contributing schemata in shaping the Court's construction of freedom of speech at the polls.

CONTEXT, CONCERNS, AND CONSIDERATIONS

The Polling Place

Whether or not the area around the polling place has traditionally and technically been considered a "public forum,"[10] in doctrinal terms, is certainly important to the resolution of a case such as this—indeed, as we will see in the "development" section below, it was the basis for Justice Scalia's entire concurring opinion—but whether or not crowds have tended to assemble there as a matter of fact, with or without the state's approval, is at least as important an issue to consider. Recent scholarship suggests, indeed, that whether or not it was officially acknowledged as such, the polling place *has* at least "traditionally" been a "forum" at which the "public" may gather for political purposes. Thus, records of contested elections in the mid-1800s suggest that "the polling place was usually congested with milling throngs of men waiting their turn to vote or, having voted, simply enjoying the public spectacle."[11] Some were there to wager on elections,[12] and various forms of incentive and/or compensation were surely prevalent,[13] though many appear to have gone to polling places simply because they were exciting arenas and social events.[14]

The significance of the structure and design of the ballot box mechanism, and the process by which votes were registered, served to facilitate this open, public environment. As Alexander Keyssar has observed, at the nation's founding—and especially in the South—"voting was still an oral and public act: men assembled before election judges, waited for their names to be called, and then announced which candidates they supported."[15] By about the time of the Civil War, nearly all states had moved away from the "viva voce" method (the showing of hands),[16] and toward written ballots, which were either stuffed into ballot boxes or handed to election officials.[17] Eventually, standardized and printed ballots (usually prepared by the parties) became the norm, as well as various other safeguards meant to discourage electoral shenanigans, intimidation, and fraud at the polls.[18]

Moreover, while polling places today offer private booths or curtained-off quarters, and are in locations like schools or fire stations, it was quite common until the start of the twentieth century for elections to be conducted in private buildings such as saloons and for the *act* (if not the substantive preferences) of voting to remain a publicly observable process.[19] In this earlier period, then, the typical polling place was usually a large room where election officials worked, with a small window through which voters would hand their tickets. Outside the window—intended, as it was, to separate the election officials from the public, rather than separating voters from advocates—there were very few structural restrictions on movement and activities. Voters mingled with party agents and others without constraint.

As this would imply, in a significant fashion the place and the process of politics were, in this respect, mutually constitutive. A system wherein the parties printed, distributed, and even premarked (or *mis*-marked) their own tickets, *required* easy access to would-be voters as these individuals pursued competing propositions.[20] Party advocates, whether by financial incentives, libations,[21] intimidation,[22] possession,[23] persuasion, or even appeals to pride, patriotism, and duty, actively regulated the goings-on, ebb and flow, access-to, and geography-of the polling place. In this space and on this day, Richard Bensel concludes: "Almost anything was permitted."[24]

Part of this "anything" sometimes meant that while most elections were carried out in a peaceful and civil manner, harassment was still prevalent in many areas, so the operating standard for election etiquette at this the time was the "ordinary man of courage" test. That is, normal jostling was typically distinguished from excessive violence by reference to what such an "ordinary man" with his conjectured "courage" should be able to withstand. Those too meek to suffer a bit of pushing or some verbal barbs, in other words, could not argue that their right to vote had been denied, according to courts considering challenges at this time; by contrast, those conditions through which such a man could not or would not wade *were* deemed to be sufficiently hostile to invalidate the results of that precinct.[25]

One of the reasons for the violence and intimidation that did occur was that, at least in urban areas, the party that was in power would situate precincts near the locations of the clubhouses of various gangs associated with their party. Indeed, as Bensel writes, the "usual tactics used by these clubs on election day entailed the occupation of the area in front of the voting window by dozens of their members," and thus "would-be voters were then forced to make their way through the crowd in order to hand their tickets to the election judges."[26] Moreover, "as they moved through the crowd, club members would insist on seeing the ticket they wished to vote."[27]

And so, "the sheer physicality of voting" meant that in many ways those men with opinions (as opposed to those looking to be "persuaded" at the polls) were fairly resolute in their stance *before* they arrived at the polls. Such was the environment, then, that while men "shoved, poked, threatened, grabbed, and sometimes stabbed or shot at those they saw as politically damned," they "rarely engaged in an open and free debate of the issues that divided them"—meaning that, coupled with the various legal restrictions on the franchise in effect at this time, the polling place during this era was often, ironically, one of the "*less* democratic sites in the nation."[28] As we will see, the intentions of the law under review in *Burson* were rooted in these assumptions, though it is important to note that this era was obviously lacking in the numerous state and especially federal laws passed to protect voters in the twentieth century (e.g., the Voting Rights Act).

To address problems such as these, one of the reforms popular in the late nineteenth century was the institution of the secret or "Australian" ballot: ostensibly intended to offer voters the increased security of standardized, official ballots, to promote privacy in the form of polling booths, and to preserve the integrity and purity of the process in general.[29] The actual motives behind the adoption of the Australian ballot are a matter of some debate. While they did have the effect of standardizing election procedures and at least *suppressing* (or perhaps merely displacing) fraud at the polls, the indirect consequence (and, some would say, the intention) of such efforts was a further disenfranchisement of "illiterate" voters—often a proxy for black voters in the rural South or for new immigrant voters in the urban North—who now could no longer merely arrive at the polls with preprinted ballots containing their party's candidates and mark their selection, though some states did allow for the continued use of party emblems or the assistance of party officials.[30]

There was, then, during this early Progressive era, increased attention to electoral integrity and specifically the virtues to be realized by secret voting. The first experiment with the Australian system took place in the city of Louisville, Kentucky, in 1888,[31] while the state of Tennessee—in somewhat of a backlash against party machines (and most likely the foreign-born and/or black voters that they tended to represent in many locales)—switched to the secret ballot format in 1890 and continued to add new provisions until 1972, when the state enacted a comprehensive code to regulate the conduct of elections, the code that included the statute in question.[32] For the state, the buffer zone then was a logical extension of the secrecy accorded by the ballot: endeavoring to reduce the potential for threats, intimidation, corruption, bribery, and various forms of interference at the polls, this domain of privacy (akin to that enjoyed within an individual booth) would be off-limits to electioneering and persuasive political efforts of any kind.

It is important to consider this context, as Tennessee endeavored to frame *Burson* as an electoral regulation case that involved speech concerns within the conduct of campaigns, as opposed to a freedom of speech case that happened to arise within the context of the electoral process. The distinction may seem subtle, but it is of great significance, as we will see, given that the more voting rights are implicated—or *imagined* to be implicated—the greater the state's claim to proprietary control over the real estate surrounding those buildings where Americans congregate to record their will as a people.[33]

The "Market"-Place?

For Rebecca Freeman and other advocates who rely on the parity of proximity in this sense, the environment of the polling place was the truest sort of "marketplace of ideas," especially because it was the last—and often best—opportunity to reach "consumers" of information, to engage in dialogue with fellow citizens, and most importantly to actually interact with those individuals who had showed up to vote. Only a few years before, in a case to which Freeman looked for support, a unanimous Supreme Court had invalidated a Colorado statute that prohibited the use of paid petition circulators in large part because such a provision restricted access to the most "fundamental, and perhaps *economical* avenue of political discourse, *direct one-on-one communication.*" Significantly, the Court found that the First Amendment protects the right to not only advocate one's cause, "but also to select what they believe to be *the most effective means* for so doing."[34] John Herbison, counsel for Rebecca Freeman, argued that Freeman had been denied access to her most effective, fundamental, and economical "avenue of political discourse": "direct one-one-one communication" in the form of electioneering efforts at the polling place.

In this respect, notwithstanding the state's hyperbole in contemplating the deficiencies and dysfunction wrought by electioneering at the polls, Freeman's position was that polling place advocates actually have to be on their best behavior so that they represent their cause well. This marketplace is, in other words, *self*-regulating, because in an important sense the incentives are structured in such a way that improprieties are punished via the simple act of ("secret") selection, whereby voters will—immediately after this encounter—proceed into the building and express their sentiments in the privacy of a booth. Thus, in the words of one interviewee, "it's like a sales job," because "you don't want a negative for your candidate," and you would not want to hurt the chances of your cause by "insisting on putting a piece of paper in somebody's hand, or saying 'vote so and so.'" Polling place advocates must be "intelligent" in the way they talk to people, that is, because "if it is obvious that people don't want to talk to you, then you don't pursue them."[35]

THE DEVELOPMENT OF BURSON V. FREEMAN
"Down the Ballot"

As noted above, Rebecca Freeman contended that, to be effective as an advocate, she would need to be able to actually *engage* voters in order to persuade them to consider her candidate.[36] Research and the experience of advocates does confirm that, at least for candidates and offices "down the ballot" (those races that receive less attention or which require the voter to select multiple candidates for less competitive offices, for example), last-minute campaigning at the polling place may have a significant impact.[37] But the *possibility* of such encounters seemed to vary across polling place environments, in Tennessee and beyond. To wit, as Justice Stevens stressed in dissent in this case, "Campaign-free zones are noteworthy for their broad, antiseptic sweep," which, in the case of the Tennessee zone, "encompasses at least 30,000 square feet around each polling place," though "in some States, such as Kentucky and Wisconsin, the radius of the restricted zone is 500 feet—silencing an area of over 750,000 square feet."[38]

Indeed, at the particular precinct where Freeman hoped to advocate, according to the registrar at large for Davidson County at this time, there was "a parking area less than 100 feet away from the door of the polling place and . . . if a voter were to park 20 feet away from the door, persons who wanted to solicit that person's vote would not be able to do so unless the voter met them back of the 100-foot boundary."[39] Furthermore, the registrar added, "there are some polling places where the entire grounds of the polling place are inside the 100-foot radius."[40] Thus, much of the concern that initiated this case pertained to the inconsistencies in opportunity that resulted from the application of the hundred-foot requirement, perhaps providing a workable "buffer" in some instances but moving advocates to the "middle of the highway" at other locales.[41]

Concerned then about her capacity to effectively serve as campaign treasurer for a city council candidate in the upcoming election—and after hearing rumors that election officials had interpreted an opinion of the attorney general in such a way that they were going to begin prohibiting campaign workers from the grounds of the polling place *entirely* (even beyond the hundred-foot boundary)—Freeman filed for a temporary injunction and challenged the statute as a facial violation of the Tennessee and federal constitutions,[42] because, among other reasons, it statutorily precluded *only* "political" speech, that form of expression generally accorded the highest degree of protection.[43]

The Lower Courts

During the trial before the Honorable Irvin Kilcrease, Jr., at the Davidson County Chancery Court in Nashville, Tennessee, it was established that the prohibition applied only to electoral speech involving issues on the ballot that day, as opposed to political speech more generally.[44] Meanwhile, the only witness testified that "total havoc" would ensue if the zone were removed, with the prediction that "without the 100-foot boundary there would be room for error in [the] totaling of the votes, the voting location would be overcrowded, and people would campaign inside polling places."[45] Accepting this assertion over Herbison's contention that the statute was neither narrowly tailored, nor content-neutral, Chancellor Kilcrease concluded that TCA section 2-7-111 was a reasonable regulation, affecting only the "time, place, and manner" of the speech; that the law was content-neutral; and that the plaintiff had "alternate channels to exercise her speech."[46]

On appeal, Tennessee Supreme Court Chief Justice Frank Drawota, writing for a four-member (of five) majority, reversed the ruling of Chancellor Kilcrease and reminded the parties involved that "the First Amendment 'has its fullest and most urgent application' to speech uttered during a campaign for office."[47] For this Court, there were two central problems with the law and the state's argument. First, the law targeted only *electoral* speech, and thus the regulation was not properly construed as a general "time, place, and manner" restriction on free speech,[48] or as a doctrinally consistent effort to contain problematic "secondary effects,"[49] such as crowds, confusion, or the voter intimidation thought to result from "speech" in certain environments.[50] Second, while the state had "unquestionably" shown a "compelling interest in banning solicitation of voters or distribution of campaign material within the polling place *itself*,"[51] and while it certainly had "an interest in maintaining peace, order and decorum at the polls," it had failed to adequately demonstrate that the hundred-foot radius represented the "least restrictive means" available, a standard requirement for strict scrutiny review. Moreover, laws criminalizing voter intimidation and fraud were already on the books and so an additional regulatory overlay that functioned essentially to shield voters from "annoying campaign workers armed with cheap ball point pens and fingernail files embossed with a candidate's name" was both superfluous and, in its curtailment of speech rights, unconstitutional.[52]

William H. D. Fones, the lone dissenter, offered a succinct rejection of the majority's reasoning. Dismayed by the majority's refusal to recognize the validity and appropriateness of the legislature's rationale, Fones questioned why a *court* was better suited to consider the necessity or estimate the precise size of the buffer zone. Specifically, he wondered how it was that a twenty-five-foot zone (which the majority had suggested might pass constitutional muster) was really all that different from a hundred-foot zone and chided his brethren for their conjecture that "somewhere in the space of 75 feet a ban on vote solicitation becomes unconstitutional." "It takes approximately 15 seconds to walk 75 feet," he concluded, and "if the electorate of Tennessee is dependent upon the free speech available in the last 15 seconds before they enter the polling place, to cast an informed ballot, God help us."[53]

The United States Supreme Court

Reversing the Tennessee Court, Justice Blackmun in a plurality opinion for the U.S. Supreme Court,[54] acknowledged the "particularly difficult reconciliation" central to this case:[55] that, as noted above, the "right to engage in political discourse" must be made to accommodate the "right to vote," which is "at the heart of our democracy."[56] But while he adjudged "exacting scrutiny" to be the proper level of review for this "content-based restriction on political speech in a public forum,"[57] he reasoned that section 2-7-111(b) *did* advance the state's compelling interests in preventing voter intimidation and election fraud. The critical basis for this conclusion was the historical evidence for some sort of restricted area surrounding the polling place in order to protect the right to vote "freely and effectively."[58] The necessary dimensions of this space, the plurality opinion acknowledged, were less obvious; but, importantly, legislatures "should be permitted to respond to potential deficiencies in the electoral process with foresight, provided the response is reasonable and does not *significantly* impinge on constitutionally protected rights."[59] To be sure, there could be some distance staked out wherein the restrictions on the solicitation of votes could become an impermissible burden on First Amendment freedoms,[60] but "Tennessee, in establishing its 100-foot boundary, is on the constitutional side of the line."[61]

Each writing a separate concurring opinion, Justices Kennedy and Scalia emphasized different concerns. The object of Justice Kennedy's opinion was to offer some "observations"[62] on the use of the "compelling interest test" and provide some "elaboration on the meaning of the term 'content based'" as it had been used in the Court's recent jurisprudence.[63] In essence, and further developing the concerns set out in his concurrence in *Simon & Schuster, Inc. v. Members of the New York State Crime Victims Board*,[64] Kennedy urged caution, lest the Court assume the mindset that, in general, content-based restrictions on speech could survive strict scrutiny so long as they were "confined in a narrow way to serve a compelling state interest."[65] It was only in particular and exceptional cases such as *this one*—in that "narrow area in which the First Amendment permits freedom of expression to yield to the extent necessary for the accommodation of another constitutional right"[66]—where the justification for content restrictions could be deployed in a legitimate manner by the state.

Justice Scalia, for his part, concurred only in the judgment of the Court, and concluded in a brief opinion that "exacting scrutiny" was not called for in this case because the law was a reasonable, viewpoint neutral regulation of a physical space which was *not*—and historically had not been—a "traditional public forum," given the lineage of the laws proscribing vote solicitation and the distribution of literature in the area immediately surrounding the polls in the fifty states. "If the category of 'traditional public forum' is to be a tool of analysis, rather than a conclusory label," he reasoned, "it must remain faithful to its name and derive its content from *tradition*,"[67] and thus he stressed that by 1900, "at least 34 of the 45 States (including Tennessee) had enacted such restrictions" while "most of the statutes banning election-day speech near the polling place specified the same distance set forth" by the law—leading him to infer that "the streets and sidewalks around polling places have traditionally not been devoted to assembly and debate."[68] As such, he essentially adopted the state's argument that on this particular day, the polling place is necessarily a *non*-"public forum" because it serves as a "brick and mortar" embodiment of the electoral process itself.[69]

In dissent, Justice Stevens (joined by Justices O'Connor and Souter) conceded that there was "no question" that protecting orderly access to the polls was a compelling state interest; in light of the decision in *Mills v. Alabama*,[70] however, the prevention of last-minute campaigning in this environment was not necessary to ensure such access. Troubling because it "encompasses at least 30,000 square feet around each polling place,"[71] the Tennessee statute was excessive for the dissenters given that "some States have no problem maintaining order with zones of 50 feet or less,"[72] and because the statute appeared to be "informed by political concerns" in that a 300-foot zone was required in twelve of the state's ninety-five counties.[73] In essence, for the dissent, the Tennessee statute was "a police power regulation that also silences a substantial amount of protected political expression" and the state had failed to provide the evidence to support this sort of prohibition of political speech on Election Day.[74]

THE CONSTITUTION OF BURSON V. FREEMAN

While Justice Stevens stressed in dissent that Freeman's speech interest constituted "classic political expression,"[75] because she desired to engage in free and open political discussions in this environment affording maximum contact with voters, the ultimate conceptual constitution of this case was rooted in the concept of "custody," whereby the Court validated the state's effort to confine a certain form of democratic interaction, thus diminishing the persuasive potential (and, in some cases, the possibility) for last-minute campaigning,[76] and "constituting" politics in a manner deemed to preserve the state's proprietary process values. Accepting custody as such, what the Court's ruling speaks to is a vision of the "market" as, in fact, a place, where interested "consumers" may venture to, but which, importantly, does not encompass or even involve them in this locale.[77]

In rhetorical terms, *Burson* was constituted in a historical mode stressing electioneering restrictions of the past in order to demonstrate their *present* necessity (and constitutionality) in the state of Tennessee.[78] As Blackmun noted, writing for the plurality, statutes similar to section 2-7-111 have existed as a response to voter fraud and intimidation since the mid-nineteenth century;[79] but he was careful to stress as well that Tennessee at the end of the previous century had undergone a period of electoral reform and had also adopted the Australian (secret) ballot system, at about the same time—a conflation that allowed him to link the "campaign free *zone*" to the "secret *ballot*," and to thus conclude, "The only way to preserve the secrecy of the *ballot* is to limit access to *the area around the voter* . . . ," meaning that "*some* restricted zone around the voting area is necessary to secure the State's compelling interest."[80]

However, this inferential jump, from the need for the secret ballot to the need for a hundred feet of undisturbed space on the way into the building where the "secret ballot" would be procured and "secretly" marked, was quite tenuous in failing to account for the obvious structural barriers already in existence at the modern polling place. In other words, the "secrecy" of the *ballot* was not at issue in this case, never as a question presented to the Court and in no way implicated by the respondent or amici; but Blackmun's rhetorical constitution of the case turned on this claim, rationalizing the hundred-foot radius as an extension of this "secrecy" (which would somehow be in immediate jeopardy without the "buffer"), rather than taking the "secrecy" of the ballot as a sufficient protection unto itself. That is, given that the *act* of voting was already necessarily (secretly) encompassed within the four walls of the polling place—and, even more, in a curtained off containment within that locale, as opposed to taking place outside, in the open air, or among whatever "crowd" (or lone individual) may be assembled on the sidewalk.

But the reliance on the historical mode is instructive in other ways as well, specifically in terms of what we learn about the means by which—that is, *how*, or in what specific manner—history can "constitute" this body of law. Most enlightening in this regard is Blackmun's almost exclusive reliance on eight historical texts for purposes of analysis and articulation, each focusing on the intimidation of voters in particular periods, the power of political "machines," and the prevalence of electoral fraud that was common well over one hundred years before Freeman challenged the Tennessee law.[81] Most notable here is Blackmun's consistent emphasis on the portraits depicted in a book by Eldon Cobb Evans (written during the First World War),[82] but specifically Evans's discussion of isolated instances of problems occurring at the polls in the late 1800s, leading Blackmun to conclude, following Evans, that "in short, these early elections 'were not a very pleasant spectacle for those who believed in democratic government.'"[83] But, most significantly for the historical constitution of *Burson*, never does Blackmun's focus shift away from "these early elections"; never, in other words, is the logical link made between the necessity as demonstrated in the 1890s and that which was urged one hundred years later.

While the opinion musters some historical evidence justifying the establishment of such "campaign free zones" at the end of the nineteenth century, it does not even pretend to reach beyond such temporal confines and makes no expressed effort to consider whether such restrictions are *still* called for, one century and numerous state and federal protections removed from the initial period of election reform legislation.[84] Certainly there is merit in considering, as Cobb's text does, *a* "history" of the Australian ballot system in the United States, in order to gain some perspective on the original incidents of abuse and subsequent calls for reform, but when such historical depictions become the linchpin of the argument, as opposed to merely providing some context—that is, when they are cited fifteen times in the span of five pages and are thus the primary source for footnote anecdotes and examples of fraud, intimidation, and deception offered up to support the continued need for the law in Tennessee (as opposed to some other state) and over one hundred years later (as opposed to the 1880s)[85]—then the historical mode shows the capacity to constitute something quite different from that considered at trial.

Consider, too, that in response to Freeman's contention that the Tennessee statute was underinclusive, ironically, in that it only prohibited political speech, Blackmun—this time relying on a text published in 1889—wrote that "allowing members of the general public access to the polling place makes it more difficult for *political machines* to buy off all the monitors."[86] The constitutive significance of this rhetorical move is telling in many ways. Certainly political "machines" such as Tammany Hall in New York and Boss Curley's network in Boston have had a colorful influence on this nation's history, but even the most cursory glance at American politics since World War II suggests that the relevance—even the existence—of such operations is very much in question outside of particular wards in Chicago or certain counties in New Jersey. The shift to candidate-centered elections; changes in immigration patterns; the increasing significance of state primaries; the diminished affective ties to party and vanishing Tocquevillian "arts of association," in general—as well as a host of other factors help to explain this demise.[87] My purpose here is simply to emphasize the stasis in Blackmun's historical constitution of this case—unwilling or unable as he is to move beyond the rationale rooted in the politics of the previous century in his effort to justify the need for such campaign-free zones.

In a different sense, the rhetorical constitution of this case was curious for its concentration on what one interviewee referred to as "abstract problems."[88] That is, as we have seen now, Blackmun *does* document historic, periodic, and global incidents of abuse and anecdotal accounts of fraud from American history generally, but the Court's opinion does not offer much specific contemplation of the alleged problems within the state of Tennessee. Instead, he works toward an affirmation of the state's position by locating abuses over time and in a range of American states and foreign countries, and then infers from the aggregate that the specific state restrictions in question must also have been and thus *still be* necessary. The closest Blackmun comes to particularizing his reasoning is in his assertion that "the roots of Tennessee's regulation can be traced back to two provisions passed during this period of rapid reform," an assertion that situates the state's effort within the larger context and concerns for the period, generally, but which still does not establish a basis for *this* particular law in *this* particular state and at *this* particular time—even if other states were ostensibly responding to problems that one might expect to also have existed in Tennessee.

And yet, Blackmun still sees fit to assess in the end that "in sum, an examination of the history of election regulation in this country reveals a persistent battle against two evils: voter intimidation and election fraud," a statement that in many ways exemplifies how the predominant rhetorical mode can so significantly construct—or, in this case, *re*construct—a case. Notice, for example, that Blackmun "sums up" by professing to have carried out an "*examination* of *the* history of election regulation in this country," even as his scope is limited almost entirely to examples of specific problems—which were themselves carefully selected incidents and anecdotes (as opposed to an "examination," per se), from only one period in history, significantly, as opposed to portraying "*the* history"—a statement that would imply at a minimum, one would think, that he had actually reviewed the history of election regulation from the colonial era to the 1880s and then—following that period of election reform when such policies would have had their putatively prophylactic effect—that he had also considered the era emerging from this period of reform, leading into the 1990s when Rebecca Freeman—not a "political machine"—sought to address voters heading into the polls.

In this regard, Blackmun's use of "persistent" portrays a sleight of hand with the historical evidence, given the decidedly temporal confines within which he was working. That is, having established only that there were problems that called for attention at an earlier time—and summarily concluding that these problems were addressed with various regulations during that earlier era—it is dubious at best to refer to the problems as "persistent" without some historical evidence that tracks such "evils" beyond the initial period and through the course of twentieth-century elections, which logically ought to have confronted considerably fewer incidents of such "evils" if, in fact, such policies successfully achieved the objective to which they were directed.

But the confined temporal scope of review comports here with an equally truncated contemplation of evidence, revealed by the plurality's employment of this empirical mode of argument. Inquiring of the demonstrability of data to justify the state's "campaign-free zone," the Court determined that proof per se could not be provided (given how long these laws have been on the books), yet still upheld the zones as constitutionally sound efforts to protect the right to vote. "As a preliminary matter," the plurality opinion offered, "the long, uninterrupted, and prevalent use of these statutes makes it difficult for States to come forward with the sort of proof the dissent wishes to require."[89] And thus, because "the majority of these laws were adopted originally in the 1890's, long before States engaged in extensive legislative hearings on election regulations," it is "difficult for the States to put on witnesses who can testify as to what would happen without them."[90]

Moreover, the opinion stressed, "it is difficult to isolate the exact effect of these laws on voter intimidation and election fraud," since such acts of electoral malfeasance are "successful precisely because they are difficult to detect."[91] Significantly then, the "long period of time" was accepted as a substitution for the typical evidentiary requirement that evidence be sustained to justify the current need for such restrictions. Thus, ironically, the burden was diminished in this case because rather than requiring evidence in the *present*, the Court accepted conjecture and examples from the *past* and simply inferred from this to the present. The upshot of all this is a concededly "modified burden of proof" in cases such as this,[92] wherein the Court does not require the legislature to provide evidence proving that the zone *must* extend to hundredth foot (as opposed to the ninth or ninety-ninth foot, for example), because the longstanding tradition of campaign-free zones made it too difficult to contemplate such a counterfactual.[93] Rather than empirically demonstrating that a hundred feet was actually the "*least* possible distance" required to satisfy the state's compelling interests, the onus of the burden in *Burson* was *inverted*, as opposed to "modified,"[94] in the sense that practices that would generally require empirical verification were exempt from typical obligations because of the "tradition" that situated them—meaning that, in effect, the modes are merged here as history *becomes* "evidence" and the past constitutes "proof."

Noting as much, Justice Stevens's dissent honed in on the fact that the state's sole witness at trial offered justification for special restrictions only inside, not outside the polling place. On the "poverty" of that record from trial then, Stevens observed that the Tennessee Supreme Court, which was surely more attuned to the state's electoral tradition, had concluded that the hundred-foot ban was not justified by the evidence presented. More importantly though, as the dissent emphasized, the relevant facts, observations, evaluations, and data were not, in fact, unknowable, as the plurality seems to suggest; indeed, various lower courts, in challenges to similar restrictions in other states, had demanded empirical evidence demonstrating that the statutorily devised distances constituted the least possible restriction on political speech while still protecting access to the polling place.[95] These courts, Stevens argued, "having received evidence on this issue, were far better situated than we are to assess the contemporary necessity of campaign-free zones," and they had "concluded that such suppression of expression is unnecessary," with the suggestion that they were "something of a social atavism,"[96] meaning that "recent history . . . indicates that, whatever the original historical basis for campaign-free zones may have been, their continued 'necessity' has not been established."[97]

And yet, ironically, it was precisely because the "necessity" had not been "established" that the Court was more willing to adopt the state's precautionary posture toward electioneering. To be sure, wrote Justice Stevens, reasoning along aspirational lines, even "the most sanguine scenario of participatory democracy" made it hard to envision such heavy voter turnout that it was necessary to clear "hundreds of thousands of square feet simply to ensure that the path to the polling-place door remains open and that the curtain that protects secrecy of the ballot box remains closed." More to the point, though, he stressed that while "the hubbub of campaign workers outside a polling place may be a nuisance," it is also "the sound of vibrant democracy."[98] But the emphasis on such aspirations was not enough to overcome the inclinations of the plurality—ready, as it seemed to be, to accept the state's appeal to a "real world context"[99]—assuming the need for institutional safeguards to protect the public's right to an unmolested polling place experience.[100]

As the state and amici had urged in oral argument and in various briefs (potential) problems needed to be addressed "in anticipation";[101] unless those engaged in electioneering were going to be allowed into the polling place itself, Tennessee reasoned that the "line" must be drawn somewhere on the grounds and the legislature was properly situated to draft the lines of the enclosure. Such were the only means available to legitimately deter or discourage problems at the polls on election day, the state urged, because other elements of the electoral code (pertaining to voter intimidation and fraud) were by design *reactive* (i.e., allowing only for prosecutions after the fact), meaning that "once you enforce those laws, the damage is done to the election."[102] Accepting this, the plurality opinion stressed that "intimidation and interference laws fall short of serving a State's compelling interests because they 'deal with only the most blatant and specific attempts' to impede elections," and because, since "law enforcement officers generally are barred from the vicinity of the polls to avoid any appearance of coercion in the electoral process . . . many acts of interference would go undetected"—meaning that these and other less obvious incidents may "drive the voter away *before* remedial action can be taken."[103] *Pre*cautions, in other words, to put the emphasis on the temporal significance of the prefix, were essential because problems are possible—at least theoretically—even if not manifest or present in the instant controversy.

But it is to the cognitive constitution of this case that we now turn in order to better understand how the Court arrived at the above conceptual and rhetorical conclusions. When asked about the state's persuasive efforts, one state official—who admitted that even she had been frustrated by the law at times, when forced to campaign at the 101st foot in previous races[104]—suggested that Ms. Freeman's noble intentions were more the exception than the rule. Giving the voters "a little space,"[105] as this official put it—positioning (potentially) disruptive speakers beyond the perimeter—was necessary to preserve the balance of voting and expression rights that is inherent to this domain.

To accomplish such, Tennessee Attorney General Charles Burson established the "cognitive space" for the argument from the start of his appearance before the U.S. Supreme Court, suggesting for the justices a series of images that would prove central to the cognitive constitution of this case. Framing the relative insignificance of the distance, and thus the actual as opposed to abstract burden on speech, Burson demonstrated the exact parameters at stake in this case. Having arranged for the measurement of a distance a hundred feet from the podium the night before,[106] Burson used his opening statement to offer a communicative (physical) frame of reference for understanding the questions presented:

> This case presents a facial challenge to a Tennessee law which prohibits, on election day, campaigning within 100 feet to [*sic*] the entrance of the polling place. To put this distance into perspective, this courtroom is almost 100 [feet] wide. Now, the Tennessee Supreme Court suggested that 25 feet might meet constitutional muster. As measured from where I stand, 25 feet goes to the second row of the press section.[107]

Various state officials affirmed that at this point they "watched the heads of the justices turn" as Burson's outstretched arm traced the hundred-foot distance, and observed of this tactic that "you could see them looking—they all turned and looked—and you could see their minds working and saying 'you know, that's not that far.'"[108]

Within this frame, the state asked the Court to accept that the "mere presence of campaign workers soliciting votes in close proximity to polling places could undermine the perception of a secret ballot and chill the exercise of voting rights."[109] The state's cognitive capture then was in the depiction of exchanges outside polling places as necessarily susceptible to the rough and tumble realities of electoral politics, a claim underscored by the state's consistent emphasis on voters being forced to "run the gauntlet" on their way to the door of the polling place,[110] on the one hand, and—because they "may only vote at one location and within certain hours"—essentially held as "*captives*" on the other.[111] Importantly then for the state, "in the absence of some regulation on electioneering," a voter would need to choose to "not exercise their constitutional right to vote" or "face a *crowd* surrounding the entrance."[112]

Polling place speech must be imagined in this light, Burson stressed during oral argument, because on election day "all of this emotion, excitement, and tension is focused right on the polling place, [and] [c]ampaign workers aren't always cool and reasoned." Moreover, "polling places are in all kinds of neighborhoods, the peaceful and the rough," and most importantly for purposes of framing, the "entrances to polling places form a natural *bottleneck*." "Now," he continued, coloring in the outline of chaos he had put forth as the central image of electoral expression in this case,

> if you allow campaigning at those *bottlenecks*, you are going to get *crowds*. Voters and campaign workers alike are going to intermingle. The *sales pitches* are going to go through the crowd and over the crowd. They will not always be softly spoken. In many situations they'll be *shouting*, *jostling*, and *tempers* may flair. The effect of these conditions will be *disorder*, *disruptive* noises, reaching the polling place, *delays* in voting. These conditions elevate the chances for voter *intimidation*.[113]

And thus the linkage between the cognitive contours and the ultimate conceptual constitution: construed in these terms, and with these images in mind, "custody" *must* be the animating value of "marketplace" operations in order to promote public participation and eliminate impediments, fear, and potential intimidation at the polling place. "What may not be intimidating to a 30-year old lawyer going to the polls may well intimidate an elderly citizen going or a first-time voter," Burson explained. And more unfortunately, he argued, rather than running this "gauntlet," they may simply "turn around and go home."[114]

Apparently sympathetic to the state's argument from the outset, Justice Blackmun offered what turns out to have been an important signal for the defining schematic contour in this case, one that seems to have acted as a filter for his consideration of such electioneering methods in general. Interjecting himself into Burson's argument, Blackmun conceded: "I must confess that when I came, we happened to live across the river in Virginia, that I was almost *offended* by the presence of people handing out literature within 25 feet of the polling place," and added that "one would be put in the jug in Minnesota if he did that."[115] The author of the plurality opinion, then, conceded to having *personally* had a negative encounter with campaign workers outside the polls. One would have to expect that being "almost offended" by such activities would bear heavily on the justice's evaluation of this case—and, by implication and extension, the law governing electioneering in general.

On the ultimate significance of this "confessed" schematic contour, consider the perspective of one state official who was "struck by Justice Blackmun's comments . . . about his problems at the polling place and the *nuisance* he considered those hangers-on to be."[116] Especially given the justice's "place on the spectrum," this respondent explained, Blackmun was actually the one "that we were concerned about" and thus the ultimate significance and salience of this frame portrayed well the "learning that you have to do [about] the experience of the judges, the life experience," because as the official continued, for one of the justices himself to have had a "perhaps *annoying* experience at the polling place certainly affected the tenor of the argument and accomplished the concern about . . . problems for voters and perhaps for election officials."[117]

Suggesting similar sympathies and explicitly adopting the state's communicative frame for the case, another justice asked during oral argument whether voters were not "sort of a *captive audience*, when the only way you can get to the polling place is to *run the gauntlet* of electioneering?" But what if "I don't want to listen to electioneering?" wondered this justice, suggesting an alternative: "Suppose I am a citizen saying, you know, I've read the papers, I've made up my mind. I don't want to be *hassled* by these people. Now you're free to *hassle* me, but I'm free not to be *hassled* in a *coerced* situation. Isn't that a reasonable basis for these statutes?"[118] The constitutive significance of this language is profound. Within the course of the six sentences comprising the question, we see the "captive audience," "gauntlet," and "coercion" images once each, with the "hassle" image invoked three times, and with no indication that there could be any possible reason or intention for interacting with individuals other than to disturb, molest, annoy, or threaten. The "running of the gauntlet" image had been adopted as the Court's basic mental construct for evaluating this case, with helpless citizens held "captive," as opposed to being politely apprised of the merits of candidates or issues; with voters in a state of de facto disenfranchisement, "coerced" by throngs of menacing political mercenaries, instead of one conscientious activist; and with "hassling" as the default assumption for the intentions of such advocates, whether or not there was any evidence to support this in modern American politics. Such was the constitution of *Burson v. Freeman.*

CONCLUSION

Burson, in short, went from being about Rebecca Freeman to not being about her at all. As one state official mused, once Tennessee Supreme Court Chief Justice Frank Drawota had had the chance to read the U.S. Supreme Court's ruling in *Burson v. Freeman*, his reaction was: "What *is* this?"[119] Such had the case changed in its terms and tone between the two courts that the Tennessee chief no longer recognized the portrait of events surrounding Freeman's First Amendment challenge to the state's "campaign free zones." How this happened is one of the significant features of *Burson*—and how this *tends* to happen is obviously significant to the larger domain of electoral speech law, because it indicates what can take place within the course of particular constitutional episodes.

What we have seen, then, is that the justices were persuaded to accept what was in effect an institutional speech argument, urging a contemplation of context in this arena where speech and process were inextricably linked. "Custody" was the core value at stake here, in other words, because as Burson argued—and the Court agreed—exchanges between voters and campaign workers should be optional rather than mandatory, meaning that individuals interested in receiving additional information—or "pitches"—could meet advocates at the 101st foot, but that those interested in participating only with their votes, as opposed to their voices, need not endure such interactions (whether good or bad) simply as a function of their desire to execute that element of the electoral process, assigned to that particular building, on that particular day.

CHAPTER 6

McIntyre v. Ohio Elections Commission

IN THE WORDS of one Ohio State Supreme Court justice, *McIntyre v. Ohio Elections Commission* "should offer great hope to American citizens,"[1] because Margaret McIntyre felt her free speech rights were being violated and she and her estate pursued her case from a $100 fine to a landmark freedom of speech decision by the U.S. Supreme Court.[2] As part of a campaign against a tax levy in 1988, McIntyre distributed leaflets outside a middle school while a school board meeting was going on and was reported by the superintendent and later fined by the Ohio Elections Commission for violating a section of Ohio code requiring, among other things, that individuals distributing leaflets in the course of an issue election include a name and business address on their literature.[3] Though the U.S. Supreme Court had previously invalidated a municipal ban on anonymous pamphleteering in *Talley v. California*,[4] that case involved a categorical prohibition, while the Ohio statute was directed specifically at pamphlets distributed in the course of an election—a context implicating state interests in the orderly and efficient regulation of the ballot, as well as concerns for the integrity and accountability of political speech during a (perhaps heated) campaign season.

Such a distinction was appropriate, the state urged, in light of the public's interest in disclosure; that is, the polity would have access to *more*, not less, information in the marketplace of ideas, and the government would be better prepared to discourage fraud and those scurrilous attacks thought to flow from anonymous political expression. And yet, in the distribution of such materials, the anonymous nature of the expression may *itself* be a component of the overall message, meaning that such a requirement could qualitatively alter the content of their speech.[5] Indeed, requirements compelling the disclosure of one's name and address may invite a host of potential repercussions, retribution, and invasions of privacy: problems that typically render opportunities for anonymous expression appealing in the first place.[6]

Appealing her fine to the Franklin County Common Pleas Court, McIntyre secured a reversal of the commission's decision, though the Court of Appeals for the Tenth Appellate District reversed the trial court's holding and the fine was reinstated. The Supreme Court of Ohio then affirmed this ruling, though this decision was then reversed by the U.S. Supreme Court. Writing for the seven-member majority, including Justices O'Connor, Kennedy, Souter, Ginsburg, Breyer, and Thomas in judgment only, Justice John Paul Stevens reasoned that anonymous expression was protected by the First Amendment as "core political speech" that overwhelmed the state's asserted custodial interests in the electoral marketplace of ideas.

CONTEXT, CONCERNS, CONSIDERATIONS
The Freedom Not to Speak

While *Talley* is the only case wherein the U.S. Supreme Court had previously considered whether a categorical ban on anonymous "speech" (in leaflet form) could pass constitutional muster, the high Court has of course considered the constitutional implications of "compelled speech" in other forms—namely in the required recitation of the pledge of allegiance. In *West Virginia Board of Education v. Barnette*,[7] the majority famously determined that the mandatory salute of the flag and the recitation of the Pledge of Allegiance in the public schools violated the First Amendment rights of those individuals (Jehovah's Witnesses, in this case) who objected to such a compulsion on religious grounds. In one of the more quoted utterances in defense of such a First Amendment freedom *not* to "speak," Justice Robert Jackson announced: "If there is any fixed star in our constitutional constellation, it is that no official, high or petty, can prescribe what shall be orthodox in politics, nationalism, religion, or other matters of opinion, or force citizens to confess by word or act their faith therein. If there are any circumstances which permit an exception, they do not now occur to us."[8]

One might also consider the conclusions reached in the "license plate case," *Wooley v. Maynard*,[9] wherein the Court relied on the logic of

Barnette to find unconstitutional a New Hampshire law calling for most automobiles to bear license places including the state's motto, "Live Free or Die." Objecting to the message they found repugnant to their beliefs, a married couple (again Jehovah's Witnesses) covered the "message" portion of their plate and were charged with a misdemeanor offense. Writing for the majority, Chief Justice Burger reasoned that the statute in effect requires that individuals suffer a penalty unless they "use their private property as a 'mobile billboard' for the State's ideological message" and "display 'Live Free or Die' to hundreds of people each day."[10] Whether or not "most individuals agree with the thrust of New Hampshire's motto is not the test," he stressed, because "most Americans also find the flag salute acceptable."[11]

At the heart of both cases, then, was a state effort to render citizens official "spokespersons," as it were, for a particular (political) message. Such a requirement obviously procured at least tacit support for an official value or sentiment, but it also "put words in their mouth," so to speak, and—of particular significance for *McIntyre*—qualitatively altered, added to, or negated those views and perspectives they may hold as individuals, untethered to their purported obligations as citizens.

Anonymity concerns have also figured prominently in several cases involving compelled disclosure of group membership lists, thus implicating interests in *associational* anonymity as a form of political expression. In *NAACP v. Alabama*,[12] for example, the Court found unconstitutional the state's demand that the organization provide its membership lists in the course of an injunction action brought to stop the group from conducting activities on account of its status as a "foreign corporation" that was "doing business" in the state. Writing for the Court, Justice Harlan noted the "hardly novel perception that compelled disclosure of affiliation with groups engaged in advocacy" may tend to restrain association, particularly respecting groups with dissident beliefs;[13] but for the purposes of our exploration of *McIntyre*, it is important to stress too his assessment that in the instant case, the NAACP had demonstrated that the revelation of the identity of its rank-and-file members had exposed these individuals to "economic reprisal, loss of employment, threat of physical coercion, and other manifestations of public hostility."[14]

However, anonymity claims have been trumped in other cases by the asserted democratic interest in disclosure as a kind of mechanism for regulation in the political marketplace. Most notably, the Court located the balance on the side of the government in *Buckley v. Valeo*,[15] which, while perhaps most remarkable for its (in)famous distinction between "expenditures" and "contributions" (see Chapters 2, 3, and 8), also involved a challenge to the provision of the Federal Election Campaign Act requiring that every political candidate and "political committee" keep records of the names and addresses of individuals contributing more than $10 in a calendar year, among other stipulations, and that such information be made available for inspection by the Federal Election Commission.

Of most relevance to the evaluation of *McIntyre* is the per curiam Court's conclusion in *Buckley* that there were "governmental interests sufficiently important to outweigh the possibility of infringement" in this case,[16] because "disclosure provides the electorate with information 'as to where political campaign money comes from and how it is spent by the candidate.'" So too, this Court noted, disclosure has the effect of deterring actual corruption and avoiding the appearance of corruption exposing contributions "to the light of publicity," and is an important component in the larger regulatory effort to detect violations in the financing of political campaigns.[17] To be sure, such "sunlight" could have the same "chilling" effects on party associational freedom, especially minor parties with perhaps unorthodox or dissident credos, but evidence for such an effect was not provided in this case and thus exemptions would need to be—and later were—considered on an as-applied basis in future litigation.[18]

At a more general level, as Chief Justice Burger noted, dissenting in part from the per curiam opinion in *Buckley*, "The public right to know ought not be absolute when its exercise reveals private political convictions," in essence because "secrecy and privacy as to political preferences and convictions are fundamental in a free society."[19] At the same time though, as Kathleen Hall Jamieson has written, from the first days of the republic, "the basest attacks appeared in unsigned print." In 1781, for example, "Benjamin Franklin complained to Robert Morris that the public 'is often niggardly, even of its Thanks, while you are sure of being censured by malevolent Criticks and Bug-writers, who will abuse you while you are serving them, and wound your Character in nameless Pamphlets.'"[20] Or, from a more modern view, and directed at a different implication of anonymity, one might consider the claim that the very form of such expression diminishes the *quality* of our political debate because "real conversations" for purposes of "democratic problem solving" require "face-to-face interaction."[21] Moreover, "without immediate feedback, without being forced to examine our opinions under the light of other citizens' scrutiny, we find it easier to hawk quick fixes and to demonize anyone who disagrees." Anonymity, then, is "*fundamentally anathema to deliberation*."[22]

"Concerned Parents and Tax Payers"

Having outlined some of the basic legal and political issues associated with anonymity in political life, we turn now to the context of the controversy that inspired the *McIntyre* case. The source of Margaret McIntyre's discontent, and the cause of her efforts, was an operating levy proposed by Westerville, Ohio, school board officials in 1988. Elections involving school board policies and especially levy propositions, were "hot issues," famous for their bitterness and contention, as one member of the Ohio Elections Commission explained.[23] Indeed, "some of the thorniest cases" that the commission received involved "a roomful of people [on] some school issue." But significantly for the balance of power in this case, this official explained, "if somebody bucks the school establishment, they are unforgiving—the superintendent will try to cut their throat. And this is pervasive throughout the state."[24]

And yet, prior to the first of two meetings meant to provide the opportunity for public discussion of the proposed levy, McIntyre, with the help of her son and his girlfriend, was in front of Blendon Middle School distributing fliers urging opposition to the levy when Ernest Husarik, superintendent of schools, and J. Michael Hayfield, assistant superintendent, grabbed a copy of the leaflet from her son's girlfriend. Because the flier was "signed" only by "CONCERNED PARENTS AND TAX PAYERS" (see Figures 6.1 [Exhibit "A"] and 6.2 [Exhibit "C"]), Husarik and Hayfield confronted

FIGURE 6.1 *Exhibit "A"*

VOTE NO

ISSUE 19 SCHOOL TAX LEVY

Last election Westerville Schools, asked us to vote yes for new buildings and expansions programs. We gave them what they asked. We knew there was crowded conditions and new growth in the district.

Now we find out there is a 4 million dollar deficit - WHY?

We are told the 3 middle schools must be split because of over-crowding, and yet we are told 3 schools are being closed - WHY?

A magnet school is not a full operating school, but a specials school.

Residents were asked to work on a 20 member commission to help formulate the new boundaries For 4 weeks they worked long and hard and came up with a very workable plan. Their plan was totally disregarded - WHY?

WASTE of tax payers dollars must be stopped. Our children's ucation and welfare must come first. WASTE CAN NO LONGER BE TOLERATED.

PLEASE VOTE NO

ISSUE 19

THANK YOU,

CONCERNED PARENTS
AND
TAX PAYERS

FIGURE 6.2 *Exhibit "C"*

VOTE NO

ISSUE 19 SCHOOL TAX LEVY

Last election Westerville Schools, asked us to vote yes for new buildings and expansions programs. We gave them what they asked. We knew there was crowded conditions and new growth in the district.

Now we find out there is a 4 million dollar deficit - WHY?

We are told the 3 middle schools must be split because of over-crowding, and yet we are told 3 schools are being closed - WHY?

A magnet school is not a full operating school, but a specials school.

Residents were asked to work on a 20 member commission to help formulate the new boundaries For 4 weeks they worked long and hard and came up with a very workable plan. Their plan was totally disregarded - WHY?

WASTE of tax payers dollars must be stopped. Our children's education and welfare must come first. WASTE CAN NO LONGER BE TOLERATED.

PLEASE VOTE NO

ISSUE 19

THANK YOU,

CONCERNED PARENTS
AND
TAX PAYERS

Mrs. J.R. McIntyre
5278 Broadview Rd. Cols., OH.
Not paid with public funds.

McIntyre and informed her that she was in violation of Ohio's election code and that she should leave the premises immediately. Disregarding the administrators' instructions, she continued to distribute literature until the meeting began, and did so as well the next night, this time at Walnut Springs School, where the second meeting was being held.

Nearly one year later—and after the levy had finally passed on the third attempt—Hayfield filed a complaint with the Ohio Elections Commission,[25] alleging that McIntyre had violated section 3599.09 of the Revised Code, which required the name, residence, or business address of the person issuing or making the statement. But, because the leaflets included a reference to an apparent *organization*—again, "CONCERNED PARENTS AND TAXPAYERS"—Hayfield alleged as well a violation of section 3517.13(E), which required that political action committees file statements as required under section 3517.10. As interviews with those close to her indicated, McIntyre's opposition to the levy was driven by her political beliefs (she was part of a local group known as Citizens Against Tax Waste), but the motivation for her continued appeals of the commission's holding stemmed from her belief that Westerville, Ohio, school officials had grossly abused their power.[26] As she expressed in an op-ed, the fine and consequences flowing from it were "just an infringement upon the little guy, and I am standing up for what I believe, not only for myself, but for others."[27]

And yet, the great irony of this case is that while the U.S. Supreme Court ultimately carved out a new constitutionally protected right to engage in "anonymous political speech"—invalidating the laws of forty-nine states and the federal government in one fell swoop (see Table 6.1)—the fact is that *Mrs. McIntyre never intended for her speech to be anonymous.* As she explained in a letter to Donald McTigue (then counsel for the Ohio Elections Commission) and as she emphasized again during her hearing before the commission, "at no time was there any intent to hide my identity or to issue any false statements."[28] Not only did she inadvertently omit her name and address on some of the fliers, that is, but as she explained "at no time did I imply that I represented any group or organization. I was merely expressing my concerns and those of others that I had talked with in our school district."[29]

TABLE 6.1 *Disclosure Statutes for Political Literature*[a]

State	Candidate	Referendum	Pamphlets-Circulars-Handbills	Periodicals-Newspapers	TV-Radio
Alabama	x		x	x	x
Alaska	x	x	x	x	x
Arizona	x	x	x	x	x
Arkansas	x	x[b]	x	x	
Colorado	x	x[c]	x	x	
Connecticut	x	x	x	x	
Delaware	x		x	x	x
Wash. D.C.	x	x	x	x	
Florida	x	x[d]	x	x	x
Georgia	x	x	x[e]	x	
Hawaii	x		x[f]	x[g]	x
Idaho	x	x	x	x	x
Illinois	x	x	x	x	
Indiana	x	x	x[h]	x	x
Iowa	x	x	x	x	
Kansas	x			x	x
Kentucky	x		x	x	x
Louisiana	x	x	x	x[i]	x
Maine	x	x	x		
Maryland	x		x[j]		
Michigan	x	x	x	x	x
Minnesota	x	x	x[k]	x	x
Mississippi	x		x	x	x
Missouri	x	x	x	x	x
Montana	x	x	x	x	x
Nebraska	x	x	x	x[l]	x
Nevada	x	x	x	x	x
New Hampshire	x	x	x	x	x
New Jersey	x	x	x	x	
New Mexico	x	x	x		
North Carolina	x		x	x	
North Dakota	x	x	x	x	x
Ohio	x	x	x	x	x
Oklahoma	x	x	x	x	x
Oregon	x	x	x	x	x
Rhode Island	x	x	x	x	
South Carolina	x	x	x		x
South Dakota	x	x	x		x
Tennessee	x	x	x	x	x

State	Candidate	Referendum	Pamphlets-Circulars-Handbills	Periodicals-Newspapers	TV-Radio
Texas	x	x	x	x	x
Utah	x			x	
Vermont	x	x	x	x	
Virginia	x	x	x	x	x
Washington	x	x	x	x	x
West Virginia	x		x	x	
Wisconsin	x		x	x	x
Wyoming	x		x	x	x

a Disclosure statutes in place as of 1995, when *McIntyre* was decided. Adapted from the "Brief for the States of Tennessee et al.," as amici curiae supporting respondents, *McIntyre*.

b "any printed material of a political nature"

c "relating to any issue"

d "any advertisement intended to influence public policy"

e "distribute . . . circulate . . . disseminate"

f "circulated, distributed"

g "published"

h "circulates"

i "publish"

j "campaign material"

k "circulated"

l "printed matter"

THE DEVELOPMENT OF MCINTYRE V. OHIO ELECTIONS COMMISSION

The Commission and the Lower Courts

Margaret McIntyre had the opportunity to plead her case before the Ohio Election Commission on March 19, 1990.[30] Members of the commission were concerned about the anonymous and possibly misleading nature of the phrase "Concerned *Parents* and *Taxpayers*" (note the plural forms),[31] but particularly the flier's failure to offer the specific name and address of those responsible. The commission presented Mrs. McIntyre with the different versions of the flier it had been provided as evidence, though only one included her name and address. McIntyre conceded that there must have been some mistake in the printing or photocopying (implying that the name and address were somehow cut off), because her name and address "should have been written in on all of them."[32] Concluding her testimony, Mrs. McIntyre explained that "the ones I passed out, to the best of my knowledge, all of them had my name on them, all of them. I wouldn't have passed it out without my name on it."[33] But the commission had concluded that, whether intentional or not, Mrs. McIntyre's actions violated Revised Code 3599.09 and thus a unanimous panel fined her the sum of $100.

Refusing to pay the fine, Mrs. McIntyre appealed the commission's decision to the Franklin County Court of Common Pleas,[34] where Judge Tommy L. Thompson concluded that, in light of the reasoning spelled out in a state case, *Pestrak v. Ohio Elections Commission*,[35] the statute, while not facially infirm, was unconstitutional *as applied* to Mrs. McIntyre because it extended "too far in requiring Ms. McIntyre to have her name, residence, or further disclaimers upon the flyer."[36] On appeal, however, the Court of Appeals of Ohio, Tenth Appellate District, reversed the court below, relying primarily on an Ohio State Supreme Court precedent, *State v. Babst*,[37] and reasoning that GC 13343-1, the nearly identical predecessor to RC 3599.09, did not violate Section 11, Article I of the Ohio Constitution.[38]

While Judge Peggy Bryant's opinion for this court expressed some doubt about the applicability of the *Babst* precedent,[39] she concluded that the court's judgment was bound by this decision even in the face of *Talley v. California* (the above-mentioned U.S. Supreme Court case finding unconstitutional a municipal ban on *all* anonymous handbills) because "the state has a greater interest in prohibiting anonymous *political* communication to protect against fraudulent and corrupt election practices than it has in prohibiting anonymous communications *generally*."[40] Thus, political expression is significant, Judge Bryant contended, but its special place in American history and speech jurisprudence does not render it free from regulation; to the contrary, because electoral speech is so significant—and because it is the means by which ideas and information reach the voting public—it is even more essential that it be regulated and supervised by the state.[41]

At the Ohio Supreme Court, Justice William Sweeney, writing for a 6-1 majority that affirmed the lower court's ruling, found that the "minor requirement imposed by RC 3599.09 that those persons producing campaign literature identify themselves as the source thereof neither impacts the content of their message nor significantly burdens their ability to have it disseminated."[42] Furthermore, he reasoned, "this burden is more than counterbalanced by the state interest in providing the voters to whom the message is directed with a mechanism by which they may better evaluate its validity," while also allowing for the identification of those engaging in fraud, libel, or false advertising, interests that been found to survive constitutional scrutiny.[43] Moreover, because the Ohio statute implicated only political speech (leafleting), the court distinguished it from the U.S. Supreme Court's decision in *Talley v. California*,[44] and found it to be a necessary component of the larger system of regulations in place to preserve the integrity of the electoral process.

In dissent, Justice Craig Wright insisted that the majority had "minimize[d] the effect this statute has on the ability of individual citizens to freely express their views in writing on political issues."[45] Ballot issues, perhaps *especially* local propositions, are often controversial and thus identity disclosure requirements may inhibit speech in ways that are beyond our estimation.[46] Had the majority employed strict scrutiny as its standard of review, he suggested, it would have realized that the "incremental value in education which is gained in knowing the name of an individual who advocates a position" was not a sufficiently compelling state interest,[47] nor were the means employed those most narrowly tailored to achieve the objective at hand.

The United States Supreme Court

Justice Stevens's opinion for the Court definitively stated, "an author's decision to remain anonymous, like other decisions concerning omissions or additions to the content of a publication, is an aspect of the freedom of speech protected by the First Amendment."[48] Finding that the Ohio statute "does not control the mechanics of the electoral process," Stevens explained that it is actually "a regulation of 'pure speech' and 'the content of speech,' meaning that 'exacting scrutiny' was required."[49] Certainly, the prevention of fraud was a compelling governmental interest, but he rejected the state's "blunderbuss approach" as an excessive and overreaching effort to attack a problem that could already be addressed by other provisions.[50]

Tempering Stevens's tone a bit, Justice Ginsburg (joining in the Court's reasoning, but writing separately) offered that with respect to the issue of disclosure, "in for a calf is not always in for a cow";[51] that is, while disclosure might not be the prevailing interest in *this* case, the Court did not thereby "hold that the State may not in other, larger circumstances require the speaker to disclose its interest by disclosing its identity."[52] And in his separate concurrence, joining only the judgment of the Court, Justice Thomas insisted that what should be sought in this case was the "original understanding" of the Speech and Press Clauses[53]—focusing, in essence, on "whether the Framers in 1791 believed anonymous speech sufficiently valuable to deserve the protection of the Bill of Rights."[54] Because he found that "freedom of the press" in colonial times referred to small, independent publishing and leafleting outfits, and stressing the significance of anonymous and pseudonymous political debate between the Federalists and Anti-Federalists,[55] Thomas deemed the Ohio statute to be unconstitutional.

Dissenting in this case, Justice Scalia, joined by Chief Justice Rehnquist, focused on the lineage of statutes prohibiting anonymous expression in the course of political campaigns, stressing that such restrictions have been not only in place since the late nineteenth century, but that they exist in nearly every state, at the federal level, and even in various foreign countries because the interests in promoting "civil and dignified" campaign debate are understood to be best served—as the various legislatures in these jurisdictions have realized—by a policy requiring individuals to put their name behind that which they contribute for consideration in the political marketplace.[56] Why, he wondered, was an anonymous leaflet any more constitutionally protected "than an anonymous phone call or an anonymous letter," particularly given that both facilitate "wrong by eliminating accountability, which is ordinarily the very purpose of the anonymity."[57] To assume, as the majority did, "that all anonymous communication is in our society traditionally sacrosanct," he contended, was a "distortion of the past" certain to lead to a "coarsening of the future."[58]

THE CONSTITUTION OF MCINTYRE V. OHIO ELECTIONS COMMISSION

In many ways, *McIntyre v. Ohio Elections Commission* embodies the classic conception of the "marketplace of *ideas*" in the sense that while the "identity of the source is helpful in evaluating ideas,"[59] the principal focus for the Court in this case was "*ideas*"—from wherever they may come. Going so far as to directly refer to Justice Holmes's dissent in *Abrams* ("the 'best test of truth is the power of the thought to get itself accepted in the competition of the market'"),[60] Stevens reasoned that with "ideas" as the central commodity to be exchanged,[61] then the source of the message was "no different from other components of the document's *content* that the author chooses to include or exclude."[62] In this respect, then, anonymity may very well provide "a way for a writer who may be personally unpopular to ensure that readers will not prejudge her message simply because they do not like its proponent."[63] Indeed, to assume that individuals are incapable of evaluating competing claims absent the name of the author was to discount the discerning potential of voters. That is, as Mrs. McIntyre's counsel before the Ohio Supreme Court argued, the desire to know *who* is saying something is actually often a thinly veiled attempt to *dismiss*—not consider—their ideas or take them less seriously, representing an appeal to "prejudice," as opposed to "reason or logic."[64]

But while the classic vision of "free trade in ideas" controlled this case, *McIntyre* is significant at the same time for the particular emphasis on the quality of electoral speech and the character of political practices evident in Justice Scalia's dissenting emphasis on the state's custodial claims in this context. In an unquestionably normative tone, Scalia's principal concern was the state's interest in facilitating—not requiring, but surely promoting—a more refined manner of public deliberation, a more "civil and dignified" dialogue within the course of campaigns and elections,[65] so as to discourage "gutter politics." Conveying the process concerns central to the custodial perspective, in fact, he referred to "observers of the past few national elections" who had "expressed concern about the increase of character assassination—'mudslinging' is the colloquial term—engaged in by political candidates and their supporters *to the detriment of the democratic process.* Not all of this, in fact not much of it, consists of actionable untruth; most is innuendo, or demeaning characterization, or mere disclosure of items of personal life that have no bearing upon suitability for office."[66] Fundamentally, then, what the majority had failed to accept was that the enshrinement of the right to speak anonymously[67]—that is, that *method* of speech—brought with it the "increased potential for 'dirty tricks'" sure to arise in the electoral process given the Court's removal of that "principal impediment" (disclosure) which relies upon the "reluctance of most individuals and organizations to be publicly associated with uncharitable and uncivil expression" as a means of *improving* the democratic process.[68] This is significant in the sense that it resists the sort of self-congratulatory statement such as, "I find this practice quite offensive to democracy, but nevertheless must err on the side of individual liberty," or, "Were I a legislator I would vote for this, but as a judge I must rule against it"—type responses frequently seen in cases constituting dilemmas in the truest sense. Indeed, Scalia makes no effort to hide his sentiment that the state has the proprietary responsibility to protect the democratic process in this sense. But, on a more theoretical level, what is intriguing in Scalia's explication of the state's claim is the notion that at some point an individual's *electoral* speech offerings take the form of a *public* good, implying consequences for the political process, and hence necessitating state supervision.

Indeed, as the state had argued before the Ohio Supreme Court, compliance with the provision actually yielded an *increase* in the amount of information available for individuals to evaluate in a campaign, and thus was an "expression of the basic democratic principle that when voters are provided with more information, rather than less, and campaigns are conducted with honesty and integrity, the public interest is served."[69] More information in the marketplace of ideas meant more accountability for one's actions,[70] a more vigorous set of safeguards to preserve electoral integrity, an accurate account of the interests supporting particular persons or proposals, and less capacity for confusion or outright deception at crucial points during an election.[71] In essence, as Assistant Attorney General Andy Sutter put it to the U.S. Supreme Court, the state's position was simply that you first identify yourself "and then say whatever you want."[72] Put differently, a requirement such as this satisfied both the individual's interest in First Amendment protections and the public interest in disclosure because, as one state official put it, "it strikes a chord with the average person that if you can't stand behind what you say, then you shouldn't be saying it."[73]

As is frequently the case, the division over conceptual approaches maps onto a division in adopted rhetorical modes of argument. The dissenters, Scalia and Rehnquist, were clearly influenced by the state's precautionary logic, appealing as it did to *Bellotti* and *Buckley* to make the case for the prophylactic and generally "disinfecting" role, if you will, of "sunlight" in a democracy.[74] Wary of losing the *general* protection in the defense of the *particular* provision,[75] the state insisted that disclosure was essential to the electoral process—affording the state the regulatory room within which to protect the process and provide citizens with the requisite information necessary to make decisions about candidates and issues.[76]

While *McIntyre* might not be identical to the questions considered in campaign finance and other disclosure cases dealing with candidate elections, the state still urged that "the value of an informed voting public is equally compelling in the context of *issue* elections, for the results of either kind of election can have serious ramifications for the citizenry for years to come."[77] Indeed, in the course of such campaigns (like tax levies), "sometimes the only way to evaluate the biases of the spokesperson is to know who that spokesperson is," and thus the interest in "ensuring that the public at least knows who is making that statement," because, as one official involved in the state's defense reasoned, "people do rely on who is saying something as one important characteristic or component in deciding how they are going to vote or react—otherwise, nobody would care about endorsements."[78]

Such a precautionary approach is evident as well in Justice Scalia's repeated appeals to the state's role in "protecting" the democratic process. "The Court invalidates a species of *protection* for the election process," he offers first, continuing then to note that "our cases . . . suggest that no justification for regulation is more compelling than *protection* of the electoral process." "So significant have we found the interest in *protecting* the electoral process," he continued "that we have approved the prohibition of political speech *entirely* in areas that would impede the process," stressing again in conclusion that the "last question relevant to our decision is whether the prohibition of anonymous campaigning is effective in *protecting* and enhancing democratic elections"—all within the space of ten pages.[79] That a wordsmith like Scalia would contemplate the state's obligation as that of "protector" of campaigns and elections—and presumably those individuals and institutions that comprise and animate them—is a clear indication of the conceptual appeal of "custody" in cases where institutions are threatened by aggregate individual activities.

When comparing the above instances within the precautionary mode (disclosure, transparency, accountability) with the aspirational alternative employed by the majority, we have both the essence of the modes themselves *and* one of the starkest cases of competing invocations in the entire electoral speech domain. For one thing, the majority was not persuaded by the portrait of a flummoxed and enfeebled polity,[80] incapable of assessing "books" without their "covers," so to speak. Indeed, Justice Stevens resisted what he found to be the state's inclination to "underestimate the common man," proposing instead that "people are intelligent enough to evaluate the source of an anonymous writing," and can capably "evaluate its anonymity along with its message, as long as they are permitted, as they must be, to read that message."[81] Only under such conditions and once this has taken place then, it is for the *people* "to decide what is 'responsible,' what is valuable, and what is truth."[82]

The adoption of this mode is critical to his emphasis on the dissemination of ideas, as opposed to their digestion. "A written election-related document—particularly a leaflet—is often a personally crafted statement of a political viewpoint," he posited, and, "Mrs. McIntyre's handbills surely fit that description."[83] For analytical purposes, the key word here is *often*: the point is not that there *cannot* or *will not* be incidents of malfeasance, fraud, or scurrilousness; the point is that there will *tend* not to be, and thus rather than assuming less, electoral designs and practices have the capacity to aspire for *more* and anticipate *better*. Thus, Stevens argued, rather than being a "pernicious, fraudulent practice," anonymous pamphleteering is set forth here as an "honorable tradition of advocacy and dissent," with anonymity as a device integral to the very nature of and capacity for the "advocacy" and "dissent"—or, the "speaking of truth to power." Construed in this light, anonymous speech is akin to "a shield from the tyranny of the majority,"[84] and thus "exemplifies the purpose behind the Bill of Rights, and of the First Amendment in particular: to protect unpopular individuals from retaliation—and their ideas from suppression—at the hand of an intolerant society."[85] Certainly, the "right to remain anonymous *may* be abused when it shields fraudulent conduct," he conceded, "but political speech by its nature will sometimes have unpalatable consequences, and, in general, our society accords greater weight to the value of free speech than to the dangers of its misuse."[86]

The apparent explanation for the general lack of aspirational rhetoric of this sort as the case worked its way through the *state* courts, was suggested in the course of my interviews with government officials, jurists, and attorneys involved in the case. At the most basic level, it seems, the conflicting modes (precautionary concern in Ohio—aspirationalism in Washington, D.C.) were a function of the awareness that most *state* court judges have of the actual nature and operations of the electoral process—not as it exists in abstract, theoretical, normative, or academic terms, but as it is lived, or understood on an experiential level by those who must themselves run for election and who are thus especially familiar with the potential for the sorts of "artful misrepresentations of interested men" and the "vicious arts by which elections are too often carried."[87]

Consider, for example, the impressions of one state official active in preparing the case for the state supreme court, who explained that much of the oral argument before *these* justices centered on the potential for abuse, scurrilousness, and misrepresentation in electoral contests—especially those in which *they* (as opposed to their counterparts on the U.S. Supreme Court) had been candidates, and those in which they would continue to compete when seeking retention. As this official explained, the state was expecting to face sharp questioning on constitutional questions as it defended the law, but instead it appeared that "*the justices were more interested in the fact that this could happen to them.*" These judges, in other words, demonstrated a "personal interest," given their own "electoral connection" to the populace, and were clearly troubled by the fact that "*they* could be subject to the same kind of campaigning."[88]

One justice announced as much during the oral argument—telegraphing this very "interest"—by stating "I want to move it from the idea of obnoxious ideas and unpopular ideas to scurrilous material." "How," this justice wondered, "do we find out a person who has clearly abused the right [to free speech], who that person is, if the government does not have a right to say 'you ought to identify yourself before you start calling people names that aren't true.' Have you ever been a subject of one of these scurrilous things? Maybe some of us are coming from that perspective."[89] Such an intimate exposure to the less than honorable elements in a democracy would seem to put judges in the position—with legislators—of drawing on *their own* experience with the electoral process, which as we saw in Chapter 3, figures prominently in the logic of and urge toward precautions.

In this regard, as one official with the Ohio Elections Commission explained, the Ohio justices "probably had received experience in local races and elections similar to this one," noting, too, that as a general rule "you are going to get people that are more politically involved and active on the [Ohio] Supreme Court," and by extension they "are going to have more of a particular interest in that type of scenario."[90] More to the point, as another commission official recalled, "you had some people on the Court who had been through some very, very difficult races in the months before that [the hearing of the *McIntyre* case]."[91] Indeed, certain Ohio Supreme Court justices who heard the *McIntyre* case acknowledged that their personal experiences in running for election influenced the conclusions reached in this case—not in a deterministic manner per se, but surely in the sense that they were much more inclined to accept the state's frame for the issue.[92]

A distinction such as this—between the *elected* "protectors" of the *electoral* process and the *appointed* justices of the U.S. Supreme Court—was certainly on the mind of Justice Scalia as he chastised "the Justices of the majority" for "set[ting] their own views—on a practical matter that bears closely upon the real-life experience of elected politicians and not upon that of unelected judges—up against the views of 49 . . . state legislatures and the federal Congress."[93] "How is it," Scalia continued, "that all of these elected legislators, from around the country and around the world, could not see what six Justices of this Court see so clearly that they are willing to require the entire Nation to act upon it: that requiring identification of the source of campaign literature does not improve the quality of the campaign?"[94]

At a more theoretical level, though, what Stevens's rejection and Scalia's embrace of precautionary logic raises for our consideration is the question of the institutional independence of the judiciary in the review of electoral process cases generally. That is, consider that the election of judges in some sense shifts the balance and separation of powers in our political system, in the sense that jurists who must run for election are, one would think, almost surely more inclined to find persuasive the state's claims for the necessity of state supervision. By contrast, with appointed judges, provisions of an electoral code passed by elected legislators would be reviewed by a "neutral" court (at least in theory), with no "horse in the race," so to speak, as compared to their *elected* counterparts who would (or should), it seems, be subject to the same criticism that befalls legislators passing election "reform" legislation (i.e., that it is actually self- rather than system-interested).

Returning to the instant case to flesh out this point, one could certainly argue, following the path marked out by that U.S. Supreme Court, that anonymity does indeed have an "honorable tradition." But one could also argue that *having never run for office* (as was the case, for example, with all but one of the justices who heard this case—and all of the justices presently on the Court),[95] such individuals are actually ill-qualified to review electoral process law because they (perhaps) cannot or will not accept what the "real-life experience of elected politicians" has to teach.[96] Let me stress here that this is not to imply that the justices are somehow political "innocents"—or that they are in any way absolved, isolated, or otherwise removed from "political" interests, implications, or pursuits. Both academic and popular accounts of goings-on at the high Court have quite clearly demonstrated that the justices make innumerable political calculations in their chambers.[97]

Moreover, particularly in the era following Supreme Court nominee Robert Bork's confirmation hearings, the experience of any justice (or judge) going through the nomination and confirmation process clearly reinforces for them the intensely political position of their seat and the Bench that supports it. Still though, being *appointed* (however contentious the proceedings and however engaged the populace) is not the same as being *elected*, in that appointees do not themselves participate in the raising of money, the bookkeeping, the creation of advertisements, the reactions to the advertisements of opponents, the crafting of sound bites, the party building and "get-out-the-vote" efforts, the shaking of hands (beyond those of members of the U.S. Senate and other elites), and all the other "nuts and bolts" issues of waging a modern campaign. Whether or not this is a desirable phenomenon—and whether it is perhaps the very reason for an unelected federal judiciary—is not my concern. My interest is in understanding how the various constitutional elements coalesce and evolve within these episodes and thus the method of selection appears to be significant in this effort.

Beyond the tug-of-war between aspirational and precautionary postures, the rhetorical constitution of this case is equally compelling as it is shaped by the historical mode, a force of reasoning which, as we saw in *Burson*, can be harnessed and channeled to lead in any number of directions. Consider, for example, that both Justice Stevens's majority opinion *and* Justice Thomas's concurrence (recall that Thomas joined only the *judgment* of the Court, not its reasoning) are informed by their interpretation of historical *principles*, though their lines of reasoning appear to remain parallel as they continue on into jurisprudential space. For Justice Stevens and the majority, Margaret McIntyre's case was about more than just a politically active mother taking on the school board with anonymous leaflets; what her case involved were deeper, more significant, historically, and even philosophically rooted rights of authorial license[98]—or the freedom to employ the form appropriate to the expressive interests at stake (even though, again, she did not assert such an interest), and one broader than, though inclusive of, questions of political speech.[99] For the majority here, the sublime and transcendent principles of Western society acted as a complement to the theoretical and historical intentions of the Bill of Rights, meaning that Mrs. McIntyre simply found her place in the long line of advocates who brought their ideas to "market" under the cover of anonymity or pseudonymous monikers (e.g., "Publius").

For his part, Thomas urged at the outset that the analysis "focus on the practices and beliefs held by the Founders concerning anonymous political articles and pamphlets,[100] and then proceeded to conclude, after a long historical exposition on anonymity in the pre- and postrevolutionary eras, that while "loath to overturn a century of practice shared by almost all of the States," he believed "the historical evidence *from the framing* outweighs *recent tradition*."[101] And thus Thomas presents something of a twist in the historical mode: privileging the (inferred) antecedent practices of the founding generation over the (evident) accrued practices of succeeding generations. And yet, what stands out in the invocation of historical materials, as Thomas presents them, is the curiousness by which his historical account appears to hop-scotch from the founders to the present day, ignoring the two hundred years of documented and evolving historical alteration of whatever is presumed to have been the approach of that earlier founding generation.

Which presents us with an additional element of intrigue in the rhetorical constitution of this case, because Justice Scalia, relying, as well, on historical materials, conceded that anonymous electioneering "was not prohibited by law in 1791 or in 1868," and was, in fact, "widely practiced at the earlier date," and "an understandable legacy of the revolutionary era in which political dissent could produce governmental reprisal."[102] But, as he suggests in his dissent, the practices of the *framers* active in both "founding" eras (ratification and Reconstruction) could be trumped by the practices of those *following* the framers as these communities worked to govern in an increasingly complicated and expanding democratic system. The temporal and evidentiary prioritization then was spelled out: "Where the meaning of a constitutional text (such as 'the freedom of speech') is unclear,"[103] he contended, "the widespread and long-accepted *practices* of the American people are the best indication of what fundamental beliefs it was intended to enshrine."[104] And the roots of such "protection[s] for the election process"[105] were obvious in the policy that "exists, in a variety of forms, in every state except California, and that has a pedigree dating back to the end of the 19th century."[106] Thus, a governmental practice that "has become general throughout the United States, and particularly one that has the validation of long, accepted usage, bears a strong presumption of constitutionality."[107] With these competing constructions of history in mind, we turn now to the final constitutional element of this case: the *cognitive* contours of the plane sustaining the investigation.

What is most interesting in this pursuit is that the review and resolution of this case was associated, almost from the start, with that famous prototype of pseudonymous speech: "Publius," the adopted moniker of James Madison, Alexander Hamilton, and John Jay, in their collection of articles which we know as *The Federalist Papers*. Though alluded to by Justice Black in *Talley*,[108] this image—pervading this case as both a frame and a schema—took on particular resonance in *McIntyre* given the explicitly electoral intentions of the statute and its enforcement within the context of an issue campaign—akin to the debate over the ratification of the federal Constitution. As Justice Stevens noted at the outset, the "respected tradition of anonymity in the advocacy of political causes," "is most famously embodied in the Federalist Papers."[109] Or, as Justice Thomas added in concurrence, "There is little doubt that the Framers engaged in anonymous political writing," with the "essays in the Federalist Papers" as "only the most famous example of the outpouring of anonymous political writing that occurred during the ratification of the Constitution."[110]

And yet, while first introduced as a relevant consideration by Judge Whiteside in dissent at the Tenth Appellate District Court of Appeals, and noted by Ohio Supreme Court Justice Craig Wright (the lone dissenter),[111] this frame was not really developed as the case made its way through the lower courts. Still, as Ohio prepared for oral argument before the U.S. Supreme Court, individuals involved in developing the state's position were "very concerned about *The Federalist Papers* issue" because it was "an icon" and necessarily stood as a "big roadblock" in the state's path, despite the momentum from victories in the lower courts.[112] Indeed, in the opening statement of the brief submitted to the U.S. Supreme Court, counsel for McIntyre astutely set forth the *Federalist* frame and argued that the Ohio statute was so broad that "had it been in effect during the nonpartisan campaign to ratify the U.S. Constitution, it would have prohibited the publication and distribution of the Federalist Papers,"[113] because Publius's publications likewise lacked the name and residence of the person responsible for the literature. Or, in other words, as counsel explained—while offering another layer to this frame—the "ability to speak anonymously often provides safe haven for those who wish to express unpopular views," something which is "particularly true during moments of high political tension when the tolerance for robust debate is often overwhelmed by the impulse toward enforced political orthodoxy."[114]

Situating the case in its proper cognitive space, then, McIntyre's counsel underscored the fact that it was "not surprising" that "the tradition of anonymous literature reached its apogee in this country during the period immediately surrounding the Revolutionary War,"[115] thus forcing counsel for the state to negotiate the "roadblock" created by this image. Indeed, as Justice O'Connor asked in oral argument: "I mean, I guess you'd say that Ohio could require, had we been back in those days, the disclosure of the writers of all of the Federalist Papers?"[116] "No, Your Honor," Assistant Attorney General Andy Sutter replied, "We think this is a much more limited statute that addresses only campaign literature or broadcast media."[117] "Well, they were circulated in support of a referendum on whether the Constitution should be adopted or ratified. You would say it would have been perfectly okay to require disclosure?" she replied.[118] The "circumstances then were somewhat different," Sutter offered; for one thing, "the protections of the First Amendment make a difference."[119] Even so, he suggested, "if today the Federalist Papers were being circulated,"

> we would argue that the State had a compelling interest in requiring the speakers to place their name on the literature. There would be no difference, and that is our point here. There is no principled way to distinguish different types of campaign literature, distinguishing the well heeled, or those who are capable of communicating more effectively, with those who do so on a smaller level.[120]

And thus the cognitive capture in *McIntyre* likely occurred when *The Federalist Papers* came to stand *for* the case, as opposed to merely serving as an instructive historical analogy.

That is, while *Mrs. McIntyre* did not intend to withhold her identity (as the authors represented by "Publius" clearly did—a critical fact that could have easily distinguished the two situations in their own right), her case evolved into something more than the story of a mother distributing fliers to protest a tax increase. As the Court imagined this speech claim, then, "McIntyre" was tantamount to "Madison," such that to deny the anonymous speech rights of the "Mrs. McIntyres" of Ohio was to simultaneously dismiss "Publius" and in some sense the very Constitution (and later First Amendment) toward which his efforts were directed. In short, the state had been "framed": boxed into the almost impossible position of arguing against "Publius" in order to reach Mrs. McIntyre.

Consistent with, and likely encouraging of this adopted image of anonymous speech is Justice Stevens's evident preference for the particular dimension of speech implicated in *McIntyre*—that is, the "citizen"-oriented speech of an activist who hoped to persuade her neighbors with a homemade flier. In this respect, the calculus of constitutional elements Stevens brought to bear in this case (the classic conception, aspirational rhetoric, the images of the noble dissenter) is even more significant because as the senior associate justice in the majority, he accepted the opinion assignment and—while knowing that Mrs. McIntyre herself did not intend to withhold her identity—still proceeded to use the case as a vehicle for carving out a broad principle protecting "anonymous speech rights," saving the McIntyre estate a hundred dollars and establishing an important precedent for the future of electoral speech law in one fell swoop.

CONCLUSION

Though the state asserted its custodial interests in the policing of fraud and the discouragement of scurrilous political speech in the course of heated campaigns—while also extending its proprietary reach to the interests of the electorate (as opposed to simply the mechanics of the process) in defending the principle of disclosure and the public's right to have complete information—Justice Stevens reasoned that conditions such as these were quintessential instances where the "marketplace" really was properly directed at "*ideas.*" But *McIntyre* affords us the opportunity to examine in greater detail, as well, the marshaling of custodial logic toward the refinement of electoral speech—and, ultimately, American politics, as Justice Scalia vigorously urged in dissent. How, he wondered—merging a custodial entreaty with employed precautions—could the *un*elected members of the

Court purport to better understand the need for such information in the maintenance of a democracy? And yet, this was not enough to overcome the conflation in this case between Mrs. McIntyre's distribution of leaflets lacking a name and address and James Madison, Alexander Hamilton, and John Jay's collective use of the pseudonym "Publius" to disseminate their ideas comprising what would later become *The Federalist Papers*. It *is* hard to overcome an "icon."

CHAPTER 7

Buckley v. American Constitutional Law Foundation, Inc.

THE INSTITUTIONS of direct democracy allow both the interests who sponsor propositions and the members of the public who sign petitions to participate in the legislative process, affording an opportunity for democratic engagement all the more profound, given that 71 percent of Americans live in a city or state—or both—that allows for some manner of direct legislation.[1] But to see such propositions enacted—that is, to win a sufficient degree of support from the voters—advocates must first reach the ballot; which means garnering enough signatures from registered voters during the petition circulation phase to indicate plausible citizen support for the measure. And so the focus of this chapter is that phase of the initiative process when signatures are gathered: when campaigns typically rely on a combination of volunteers and paid circulators, who receive compensation based on the number of signatures collected, and who frequently are professionals that travel from state to state working for the highest "bidder."

The controversy that inspired this case, *Buckley v. American Constitutional Law Foundation, Inc.* (*ACLF*),[2] really began in the immediate wake of another Supreme Court decision, *Meyer v. Grant*,[3] where the Supreme Court found Colorado's ban on payments to petition circulators to be a violation of the First Amendment. Responding to an increase in reported incidents of fraud and corruption during the petition phase of the initiative process in the presidential election year following *Meyer*, the state passed Senate Bill 93-135, amending existing initiative statutes and requiring, among other things, that petition circulators wear badges indicating whether they were volunteers or whether they were being paid, as well as their name and the name and telephone number of the individual for whom they were working;[4] that those proponents making use of paid circulators disclose the name, payment rate per signature, and total amount paid to each circulator (on a monthly basis *and* upon filing the petition with the secretary of state); and that circulators be registered electors, eligible to vote on the measure (e.g., at last eighteen years of age, without a felony conviction, etc.).[5] Joined by a diverse coalition of groups and individuals from all points on the political spectrum,[6] Bill Orr, executive director of the American Constitutional Law Foundation (ACLF), challenged the statute (as well as the preexisting requirement that petitions be circulated within a six-month period of time), arguing that the state's regulations violated the First and Fourteenth Amendments of the federal Constitution.[7]

Following a trial wherein U.S. District Court Judge Richard Matsch struck down the badge requirement and elements of the disclosure provisions, but upheld the age, affidavit, registration, and six-month time limit, the Tenth Circuit Court of Appeals affirmed with respect to the age, affidavit, and time-limit restrictions, but reversed the lower court on the registration requirement. The appeals court also invalidated both the *monthly* and *final* disclosure provisions in that they required that proponents report the name and address of each *payee*, as well as how much was paid to each, though it let stand the requirement calling for the disclosure of *payors*, as well as the total amount spent to procure signatures. Affirming the Tenth Circuit's holding, the U.S. Supreme Court, in an opinion by Justice Ginsburg (joined by Justices Scalia, Kennedy, Souter, and Stevens, with Thomas joining in judgment only),[8] reasoned in essence that the state had planted too many obstacles in the way of would-be circulators and thereby had unconstitutionally diminished the number of message carriers and, significantly, the potential for both "political conversations and the exchange of ideas" and "interactive communication concerning political change" in the electoral speech marketplace.[9]

CONTEXT, CONCERNS, CONSIDERATIONS

Government by the People

Part populist and part progressive, a hybrid political spirit supporting the institutions of direct democracy in the forms of the initiative and referendum developed and began to transform American state politics in the early part of the twentieth century (see Table 7.1).[10] Inspired by the most republican of desires, the institutions and opportunities of direct democracy were appealing to a populace, especially in the western states,[11] that

TABLE 7.1 *The Initiative and Referendum Process in the States*[a]

		Direct Democracy Options		Initiative Varieties		Const. Amendments	State Laws
State	Year of Adoption	Initiative	Popular Referendum	Const. Amendment	Statute	Direct-D Indirect-I	Direct-D Indirect-I
[b]Alaska	1956	x	x		x		I
Arizona	1911	x	x	x	x	D	D
Arkansas	1910	x	x	x	x	D	D
California	1911	x	x	x	x	D	D
Colorado	1912	x	x	x	x	D	D
Florida	1972	x		x		D	
Idaho	1912	x	x		x		D
Illinois	1970	x		x		D	
Kentucky	1910		x				
Maine	1908	x	x		x		I
Maryland	1915		x				
Mass.	1918	x	x	x	x	I	I
Michigan	1908	x	x	x	x	D	I
Mississippi	1914/1992[c]	x		x		I	
Missouri	1908	x	x	x	x	D	D

Montana	1904/1972[d]	x	x	x	x	D	D
Nebraska	1912	x	x	x	x	D	D
Nevada	1905	x	x	x	x	D	I
New Mexico	1911		x				
North Dakota	1914	x	x	x	x	D	D
Ohio	1912	x	x	x	x	D	I
Oklahoma	1907	x	x	x	x	D	D
Oregon	1902	x	x	x	x	D	D
SouthDakota[e]	1898/1972/ 1988	x	x	x	x	D	D
Utah	1900/1917	x	x		x		D/I
Washington	1912	x	x		x		D/I
Wyoming	1968	x	x		x		I

a Table adapted from information and explanations provided by the Initiative and Referendum Institute. Available at: www.iandrinstitute.org/statewide_i&r.htm (accessed February 14, 2006).

b This list includes only those states that maintain some sort of initiative or popular referendum process. Every state has some form of legislative referendum process.

c Mississippi voters approved an initiative and referendum amendment in 1914, but the state supreme court removed the provision (on a technicality) from the state constitution in 1922. Voters once more approved the initiative in 1992.

d Montana adopted a provision that allows for directly initiated constitutional amendments in 1972.

e South Dakota, in 1972, adopted a provision that allows for directly initiated constitutional amendments; in 1988 it repealed the indirect initiative for statutes.

found "progress" too often impeded by feckless state legislatures,[12] and all too often beholden to "narrow interests."[13] At least in some sense then, the initiative process was intended to afford a representative "safety valve,"[14] an option that could be employed to address "things that the Legislature can't or won't deal with," because "they are too heavily invested," as one initiative activist put it.[15]

What is crucial here is that at least the ostensible purpose of direct democracy was to bring about a better political situation by diminishing the influence of corporate money and returning power to the people.[16] "Reform" efforts of this sort—policies and proposals intended to promote "good government"—found a welcoming audience in an environment rife with political corruption. New institutional mechanisms for direct legislation could, it was proposed, develop civic virtue, desist political anomie, and promote participation and accountability by establishing an additional "check" to preserve the political "balance" in that the *people* have at their disposal a device that can either prompt or punish the various branches of government.[17]

Commentators, and those interviewed during the course of this research, have painted drastically different pictures of the actual (as opposed to abstract) relationship between the mechanisms of direct legislation and various other governmental institutions, with some finding the association to be complementary[18]—something like a partnership[19]—and others finding it to be contradictory, with an inherent and potentially irreconcilable hostility or "institutional tension,"[20] in that two classes of individuals (legislators and the citizens who put them there) find themselves competing for lawmaking authority. Such a role for citizens is empowering, for some, in its implied faith in the people to engage in the project of self-government.[21] But for others it is *dangerous*, in that laws are written and evaluated by nonprofessionals,[22] those who not only lack expertise but who are equally susceptible to corruption, misrepresentation, fraud, manipulation, and ill-considered judgments.[23]

Government by the People—of Colorado

Keeping the Gate In 1910, Colorado voters approved an amendment to Section 1, Article V of the state constitution, establishing the initiative and referendum. The first paragraph of that amendment establishes the people as protolawmakers, stating that legislative power of the state shall be "vested in a General Assembly consisting of two houses—both to be elected by the people":

> but the people reserve to themselves the power to propose laws and amendments to the Constitution and to enact and reject the same at the polls independent of the General Assembly, and also reserve power at their own option to approve or reject at the polls any act, item, section or part of any act of the General Assembly.[24]

To implement such power, of course, "the people" must satisfy the terms (generally established by the assembly) for securing a spot on the ballot, meaning that the state acts as a critical gate keeper of sorts from the earliest phases of citizen-lawmaking efforts.

Some consideration of the state's role is thus appropriate. As one state elections official explained, proponents must first file with the legislative staff, accept review and comment on the text of their measure, and then take the measure to the secretary of state. "Title-setting" is the next stage, wherein a three-member board "sets" the official language that will appear on the ballot and on the petitions that are circulated. At this point, the state does not play much of a role until the proponents return within the allotted six-month window of time and have their petitions reviewed by the secretary of state's office. To gain a spot on the ballot, a measure must achieve a total number of *valid* signatures equal to 5 percent of the total number of votes cast for all candidates in the general election for the office of secretary of state, a number which can vary significantly depending on, for example, the competitiveness or contentiousness of other ballot matters.[25] In verifying the signatures, the secretary's office then uses random sampling techniques to check the names on the petitions against the registered voter rolls; and depending on the number of invalid signatures, the secretary certifies the petition, is forced to check every signature, or fails the petition.[26]

For practical purposes this standard is generally only met when proponents collect 30–40 percent more signatures than is required (given the typical "failure" rate for most petition drives),[27] and thus sponsors often turn to both volunteer and professional circulators,[28] usually paid a set amount per signature,[29] a practice that allows measures to meet the state burden, but one that also invites a tremendous infusion of money into this realm of the electoral process and raises concerns about the "buying" of access to the ballot.[30] Indeed, following the *Meyer* decision (finding unconstitutional Colorado's prohibition on paid petition circulation), proponents of initiatives were able to garner many more signatures and thus qualify many more issues for the ballot in subsequent elections. But as paid circulators became more involved in the petition process, allegations of fraud increased;[31] and so, Senate Bill 650 was proposed ostensibly to protect the initiative process and keep it true(r) to its democratic roots.[32]

As such, the Assembly appears to have been working under the impression that purely volunteer circulators were somehow better for the process (for the institutions and individuals who comprised it) because their involvement portrayed genuine citizen support and because robust engagement was still quite possible under such guidelines.[33] Paid circulators, by contrast, were seen as something like political mercenaries—acting out of self-interest rather than in the state's or public's interest—working not so much for the cause itself as for the financial gain to be realized by "speaking" for the cause. Colorado's concerns here were not entirely unwarranted: comprehensive academic studies have shown that, with enough time and money, well-funded initiative proponents can almost always get on the ballot,[34] though the data show that this translates in a less direct way to certain success on election day.[35]

Yet as one prominent initiative proponent and activist explains, it is actually the presence of moneyed interests that works to prevent fraud during the circulation phase, because the large financial stakes make the petition process more "self-regulating" in that wealthy sponsors would not want to waste money on fraudulent signatures that they had paid for on the front end but which were then disqualified on the back end.[36] As this individual reasoned, "Petition proponents die when they are found to have fraudulent signatures," because if it is discovered "they have got no time left and they are out of business and they have spent fifty thousand dollars, a hundred thousand dollars, or a half million dollars,"—so "they don't want it to happen," and are thus *themselves* "the best line of defense against circulator fraud."

When it *does* happen though, this activist offered, it "is usually one idiot who either wants the money or desperately believes in the measure and wants to help and does something really stupid or foolish"—though even in cases like that, she continued, such improprieties "tend to be obvious," because "you have got somebody who is maybe using three different pens," and "it just doesn't look right [because] you can see the regularity and that is not the way a petition is." *Real* petitions are, put simply, "random," with a "mishmash of marks in strange places," "written in different inks," and with "things off this way and leaning in this way." So the sponsor will simply say, "'I am not submitting this. This will get us in trouble,' [because] there are criminal penalties there."[37]

"Sign Here" While there is obviously some sort of interaction between a circulator and potential signatory, the actual nature of this encounter—as well as the larger question of whether or not the nature of the engagement is properly a matter of state concern in the first place—is much debated. Consider, for example, the following depiction of the "hoopla process" of gathering signatures. As veteran California petition circulator Ed Koupal (in)famously described his method, "First, you set up a table with six petitions taped to it and a sign in front that says,

> SIGN HERE. One person sits at the table. Another person stands in front. That's all you need—two people. While one person sits at the table, the other walks up to people and asks two questions. (We operate on the old selling maxim that two yeses make a sale.) First, we ask if they are a registered voter. If they say yes, we ask them if they are registered in that county. If they say yes to that, we immediately push them up to the table where the person sitting points to a petition and says "Sign this." By this time the person feels, "Oh, goodie, I get to play," and signs it.[38]

And, if a table using this method doesn't get *eighty signatures per hour*, Koupal added, it is moved to a new location the next day. Boastful of his fine-tuned method and its predictable yield, Koupal estimated that about "75 percent of the people sign when they're *told to*."[39] Note two things here for our consideration of the primary cognitive contours in the "constitution" section below: (1) eighty signatures per hour is the *minimum* amount necessary to stay put, implying that this is the standard for experienced circulators; and (2) calculated at this minimum rate, such a method yields an average of one signature *every forty-five seconds.*

But while Koupal's account of his "process" is intriguing as it bears on psychology, marketing, and manipulation, his frankness regarding the *content* of such exchanges is our central concern here. When asked whether people tend even to *read* the petitions they sign, Koupal responded, "Hell no," while adding that he and his associates "certainly don't offer" such an opportunity either. But most importantly, given the constitution of this case and the Court's conception of a "political conversation" taking place, he wondered: "Why try to educate the world when you're trying to get signatures?" The purpose was to "get things done, not to educate people," he stressed; and, you "can't get things done if you spend your time doing that." After all, "We're running a business and we're experts."[40]

Yet other experienced circulators and sponsors liken the process less to "hoopla" and more to "cold calls,"[41] in that the relationship between "buyer" and "seller" (signatory and circulator) must be quickly established, with the interest of the voters piqued, their resistance overcome, their attention held, and their expressed written support for your efforts gained by some persuasive means. Signature gathering is hard work, say those involved, because you are "always jumping from talking to idiots to engaging in graduate school discussions" and you "are constantly dealing with people rejecting you."[42] And so, as Paul Grant (the respondent in *Meyer v. Grant*) has explained, while a certain degree of "salesmanship" is necessary,[43] this may not differ in significant ways from much of our political discourse that is "packaged," as it were, in a simple and easily digestible form for public consumption (e.g., "sound *bites*"). More important, the collection of signatures is but one early phase in the process of direct legislation and is intended only to give measures a *chance* of being debated by the people once a proposition reaches the ballot.

THE DEVELOPMENT OF BUCKLEY V. AMERICAN CONSTITUTIONAL LAW FOUNDATION, INC.

Meyer v. Grant and Its Aftermath

To understand the state interests and First Amendment concerns at stake in *ACLF* requires a brief summary of *Meyer*, referenced above and in Chapters 2, 3, and 5. Writing for a unanimous Court, Justice Stevens reasoned that the state's burden in demonstrating the need for a ban on *paid* petition circulation was "well-nigh insurmountable,"[44] given that "the circulation of a petition involves the type of interactive communication concerning political change that is appropriately described as 'core political speech.'"[45] The proffered concern for encouraging "grassroots" support in the form of exclusively voluntary circulation was unpersuasive for the Court because the state had failed to provide evidence that professional (i.e., paid) circulators were more likely to denigrate the electoral process than their volunteer counterparts.[46] While the state certainly maintained a legitimate interest in preserving the integrity and order of the ballot, Stevens found that its chosen method "restricts access to the most effective, fundamental, and perhaps economical avenue of political discourse, direct one-on-one communication."[47]

In response to *Meyer* and the record number of initiative propositions that qualified for the ballot in 1992, the Colorado General Assembly passed the legislation described above with the ostensible intention of encouraging more "grassroots" participation in the political process.[48] Such was the legislature's motivation, according to one state elections official involved in drafting some of the legislation in question,[49] given its "frustration with the U.S. Supreme Court," and because the assembly thought the initiative was "supposed to be a grassroots, populist kind of idea" that "ought to be the people's process" rather than one that could be overtaken by wealthy interests capable of buying their way onto the ballot with enough paid petition circulators.[50] The legislature "struggled with trying to come up with something else that might be acceptable, that would still achieve similar purposes," and concluded that if people were required to wear badges announcing that they were a "paid circulator," then this would at least "tell the people out on the street that this is a person who doesn't believe in this cause, who is just being paid to do it"—something which was the "next best thing to prohibiting paid circulation."[51]

More specifically, another state official stressed, the legislature put forth the voter registration requirement to preserve direct democracy as a *citizens'* process, not just a people's process—and even more specifically, a *Colorado* citizens' process.[52] As a way of eliminating the overrun on its legislative process, wherein people are "bussed in from California" and "for a month at a time" are "put up at a little local motel," and where "their job is to go out and get as many signatures as they can," the assembly required that circulators be registered in Colorado if they wished to participate in the making of Colorado law or to engage in changes to the state's founding charter (i.e., its constitution).[53] In this sense, registration requirements were an essential mechanism supporting the enforcement of *other* components of the state's scheme of electoral regulations.[54] Construed in this light, circulators were "speakers" to some degree, but were also involved in "nominating" an issue or idea for the ballot—making them, in effect, "agents" of the state in the electoral process,[55] and meaning that the government was within its prerogative to enact measures to prevent fraud and abuse in the system. On another level, from the state's perspective, the reasoning of *Meyer* and similar approaches misperceived the historical purpose and procedural function of the initiative process which "really wasn't designed to *create* support," but rather "to measure *existing* support." That is, "the whole concept behind the initiative process was to address a legislature that was failing to consider the popular will," rather than *circumvent* the legislative process "when the popular will had not been formulated."[56]

And, as a factual matter, there *were* more reported incidents of abuse after the *Meyer* decision granted constitutional protection to paid petition circulation.[57] During the period from 1990 to 1992, in fact, "the Secretary of State referred some 15 to 20 cases of potential fraud involving initiatives to the Attorney General for prosecution," and nine arrest warrants were issued for "very flagrant abuse of the initiative process," though the state was only able to achieve three forgery convictions, mostly because the offenders could not be located.[58] At the same time, while overt fraud (e.g., forging signatures to collect more money) was a problem, so too were general deception and manipulation, in the form of blatant lies and also the more subtle misrepresentations as to the true nature of the proposition, machinations made possible and amplified by this central element of the state's frame: "As a practical matter, people don't have time to read the petition—and so, a lot of what is being said, a lot of what the public knows, is based upon what the circulators tell them."[59]

The Lower Courts

At the U.S. District Court level, Judge Richard Matsch found compelling the testimony from the trial suggesting that the identification badge requirement "burdens core political speech."[60] With respect to the requirement that circulators be registered voters who are eligible to vote on the measure that is the subject of the petition, Matsch found that because the source of the requirement was not the Senate bill in question, but rather a constitutional amendment adopted by the people in 1980—and because "there is nothing in the United States Constitution that requires that any state provide for the initiative and referendum" in the first place—it was acceptable to limit the pool of participants in this manner.[61] Regarding the disclosure provisions, Matsch found that the trial record supported the revelation of certain pieces of information,[62] though he concluded that "what is of interest is the payor, not the payees" and so the names and addresses of each individual circulator could not be compelled.[63] Consistent with this distinction, Matsch reasoned that by requiring a final report detailing all contributions and expenditures, and those responsible for them, the state could both provide information to the public *and* police fraud in the electoral process, though monthly disclosure requirements were overly burdensome and involved too much individual expense for proponents of initiatives and referendums.[64]

The Tenth Circuit Court of Appeals, in an opinion by Judge Mary Beck Briscoe,[65] declined to review each provision of the law as *necessarily* implicating "core political speech" concerns (the apparent operating assumption of the U.S. Supreme Court in *Meyer v. Grant*),[66] but at the same time, Briscoe determined that *Meyer* made it clear that the state's choice to reserve the initiative does not leave it "free to condition its use by impermissible restraints on First Amendment activity."[67] While the state argued it needed the requirement in order to ensure residency, the Court deemed a simple residency requirement to be a more narrowly tailored alternative. Further, by the time the Tenth Circuit heard this case, the U.S. Supreme Court had decided *McIntyre v. Ohio Elections Commission*,[68] and following Justice Stevens's reasoning in that case, the circuit court dismissed the state's efforts to reinstate the name badge requirements.[69] Finally, Briscoe found only a "temporary disability" in the age requirement,[70] and the Court affirmed Judge Matsch's conclusions regarding the disclosure provisions.

The United States Supreme Court

The U.S. Supreme Court, in an opinion authored by Justice Ruth Bader Ginsburg,[71] stressed first and foremost that while states have "considerable leeway to protect the integrity and reliability of the ballot-initiative process,"[72] the First Amendment "requires vigilance in making those judgments, to guard against undue hindrances to political conversations and the exchange of ideas."[73] And thus, the registration requirement was unconstitutional because it "drastically reduces the number of persons, both volunteer and paid, available to circulate petitions,"[74] and because the state's asserted interest in policing fraud could be served by other existing means. Further, the Court affirmed the district and appellate court's holdings against compelling the disclosure (in badge form) of the identity of the circulator, precisely at the "moment when the circulator's interest in anonymity is greatest,"[75] though the majority, like the lower court, expressed no opinion on the constitutionality of the additional requirement that the badge disclose whether the circulator is a volunteer or is being paid—and, if so, by whom. Finally, the justices accepted the distinction between the disclosure of *circulators* and *payors* in light of the state's "substantial interest" in informing voters of the "source and amount of money spent by proponents to get a measure on the ballot."[76]

Concurring in judgment only, Justice Thomas wrote separately to expand on his belief that the majority opinion appeared to depart from the "now-settled approach"[77] of applying strict scrutiny in such cases and he wished to reassert the primacy of this standard in cases when a state's election law "directly regulates core political speech."[78] Justice O'Connor, joined by Justice Breyer, concurred with the majority on the question of identification badge requirements (agreeing that the provision "directly regulates the core political speech of petition circulation"),[79] but dissented on the question of whether circulators must be registered voters, finding such a requirement to be a "neutral qualification for participation in the petitioning process,"[80] calling for a lower standard of review, such as that employed in *Burdick v. Takushi*,[81] given that the provision only "incidentally" and "indirectly" burdened the one-on-one communicative aspects of petition circulation.[82] But what was more "disturbing," she found, was the Court's determination that the state's *disclosure* framework was partly unconstitutional. The Tenth Circuit's ruling should be reversed on these grounds, she contended, because these provisions were reasonable in that they were "a step removed from the one-on-one, communicative aspects of petition circulation" and burdened this communication "in only an incidental manner" in the service of a legitimate governmental interest.[83]

Believing that Colorado could "constitutionally require that those who circulate initiative petitions to registered voters actually be registered voters themselves," and fearing the "wide-reaching implication[s] for state regulation of elections generally" resulting from the Court's opinion,[84] Chief Justice Rehnquist resisted the Court's conclusions. Though he agreed with the majority that "the badge requirement for petition circulators is unconstitutional" in light of *McIntyre*,[85] he disagreed with the Court's affirmation of the Tenth Circuit's invalidation of the requirement that the names, addresses, and amounts paid to each circulator be disclosed in a final report, because under Colorado law all petition circulators had already relinquished anonymity in abiding by affidavit requirements included on the petitions themselves.

THE CONSTITUTION OF BUCKLEY V. AMERICAN CONSTITUTIONAL LAW FOUNDATION, INC.

As the above discussion of its interests indicates, the state reasoned in custodial terms that the petition-circulation process was ongoing within the larger electoral speech marketplace, meaning that while citizens engaged in the opportunity for expression, so too was the signature-gathering stage designed to be a political barometer in the sense that measures with widespread public support would easily acquire enough signatures and gain access to the ballot for consideration by the voters, whereas those measures with less support would likely fail to clear this initial hurdle. Directly linked to this, as the interviews for this case study suggest, was the assumption (or hope) that volunteers (and their particular means for gathering signatures) were at least theoretically more likely to provide an accurate gauge of citizen-support for a proposition because, as previous studies have realized, "volunteers do not try to cheat as much as paid circulators because 'they're not there for the money, they're there for the cause,'"[86] implying that the incentives for volunteers are not so encouraging of "recklessness in pressing people to sign petitions."[87] Put differently, one might imagine this as an instance where, for the state, the equilibrium or balance achieved by the natural forces of the market would be disrupted by the infusion of vast sums of money, thus skewing public opinion, clouding the issues, and threatening the integrity of the process by which preferences are registered. The "root of all evil," if you will, had infested the soil where the "grassroots" had initially been planted—and so, as the custodian (or "gardener," with apologies), the state acted to . . . "weed" out the problem.[88]

Central to the state's custodial conception in this regard was the "deputization" that it presumed it could carry out, construing (and perhaps conscripting) petition circulators as "an integral *part of the process* by which Colorado law is added to or amended—a process usually resulting in changes to Colorado's Constitution." And thus, "As part of that process, "circulators assume obligations and responsibilities to all of the people in Colorado, not just themselves or those who support the viewpoint they are advancing. Opponents of their measures and the people of Colorado have an equally strong interest in insuring that the process by which proposed changes to Colorado's Constitution are made fair and free of abuse."[89] The argument here was that these citizen-*speakers* were also citizen-"functionaries" within the electoral process—having been pulled in by their chosen manner of political participation.[90] In this sense, the spokesperson for a ballot measure was thus bound by the same proprietary expectations as political parties or write-in candidates who desired a place on the ballot.[91]

One thing that the custodial claim makes especially clear in this case is that there is not—and cannot be—any such thing as "pure speech" (i.e., "pure" in the "unmixed" or "unadulterated" sense) when considering freedom of expression within the electoral process, because the form and function of such expression is necessarily and inextricably linked to the structures, institutions, and practices implicated in conducting elections. At the theoretical level then, the notion of "institutional speech" (recall the discussion in Chapter 2) invites an evaluation of the communication expressed within the arena wherein it as actualized. Put differently, political speech in the form of an antiabortion rally, held at a local park, and during an off-election year lacks the inherent connection to the institutions of democratic decision making, whereas electoral speech exists within the democratic process and thus necessarily implicates the state in a custodial supervision of the environs under its charge.

Further indices of "institutional" constraints on electoral speech are evident in the above "deputization" theory and its implicated imagery of enforcement and protection. As Chief Justice Rehnquist wrote of this in dissent, the Court today "invalidates a number of state laws designed to prevent fraud in the circulation of candidate petitions and to ensure that *local* issues of state law are decided by *local* voters, rather than by out-of-state interests."[92] Then, after noting that "ballot initiatives of this sort . . . were advanced as a means of limiting the control of wealthy special interests and restoring electoral power to *voters*,"[93] he again chastised the Court for striking down the state's attempt to allow its own voters "to decide what issues should go on the ballot to be decided by the State's registered voters."[94] The registration requirement was thus perfectly constitutional, and even sound governing policy, he suggested, in that it was "obviously intended to ensure that the people involved in getting a measure placed on the ballot are the same people who will ultimately vote on that measure—*the electors of the State*."[95] Rather than "implicat[ing] political thought and expression" as a form of protest, as the majority suggested, Rehnquist insisted that the failure to register was really an indication of one's status as a "political dropout."[96]

Significantly, then, if individuals made the "conscious decision not to register to vote on the grounds that they reject the democratic process, they should have no right to complain that they cannot circulate initiative petitions to people who *are* registered electors.[97] Here, we see the custodial energy transmitted by the defense of the registration requirement as a mechanism for the enforcement of antifraud legislation in a literal or applied sense, but also in metaphorical terms, as an affirmation of the notion of "investment" in a political community, whereby one formally becomes a "member," as it were, and bears the fruit (but also shares the burdens) of shareholding. And thus we see another shade in the normative cast that this conceptual framework can show, as the Chief Justice makes the case for a kind of populism,[98] in his emphasis on the requisite attachments to place that come from making oneself a part *of*, as opposed to relegating oneself apart *from*, the polity and its chosen indices of citizenship and conditions of self-government.

But for the Court majority, even those individuals that Chief Justice Rehnquist referred to as "dropouts," could be worthy purveyors—"speakers" with something legitimate to say—in the electoral marketplace of ideas. Developing this contention, with a specific appeal to the concern for "quantums" that we saw in Chapter 2's discussion of the classic conception of the marketplace, the badge requirement was problematic for Justice Ginsburg because it "'very definitely limited the number of people willing to work'" on certain initiative efforts.[99] Worse though was the registration requirement, because as the majority imagined it, such a policy "drastically reduces the *number* of persons, both volunteer and paid, available to circulate petitions,"[100] "decreases the *pool* of potential circulators,"[101] "reduces the voices available,"[102] limits "the *number* of voices who will convey [the initiative proponents'] message," which "cuts down the *number* of message carriers in the ballot-access arena without impelling cause,"[103] and consequently diminishes "'*size* of the audience [proponents] can reach.'"[104]

Moreover, the conditions of entry to the marketplace spelled out by the state and adopted by the dissent failed to recognize that the refusal to register may itself be an act of "political thought and expression,"[105] a "'form of . . . private and public protest,"[106] or as something rejected by many individuals because "'they don't believe that the political process is responsive to their needs.'"[107] As such, the majority found compelling the testimony of Paul Grant, describing the circulation of initiative petitions as an act of "drawing on people who are not involved in normal partisan politics for the most part"—large numbers of whom are the "natural support" for such initiatives, but who are not registered voters.[108]

One of the things that we can draw from the Court's reasoning here as it pertains to the concept of the marketplace is that it matters less, if at all, who the "message carriers" are, where the "goods" to be traded arrive from, who subsidized their entry, or whether they would or could survive "on their own," so to speak, absent some "interested" support. Central to this vision is the notion of a "market" in effect without a "place" in the sense that "ideas"—as opposed to communicators of ideas—are the actual "goods" to be traded, meaning that the "exchange" at the core of the concept may take place quite easily outside (above, beyond, or around) the system established by the state. Put differently, there is room within this particular classic conception of the marketplace to accept that *non*registration, while perhaps consistent with "dropping out" in some instances, may also or instead be a passionate political statement, act of resistance, or expression of dissent that is, *in itself*, as much a "commodity" in the political marketplace of ideas, even while it eschews—or is rejected by—that very market framework that sustains it.

In rhetorical terms, the most salient element of the constitution of *ACLF* pertains to the ongoing empirical imprecision with which the Court articulates the evidentiary standard (or lack thereof) required to sustain regulations aimed at diminishing fraud during the signature-gathering phase of the petition process. Though the Court accepted some restrictions on speech rights—such as the prohibition against petitioning by minors or the six-month time limit—without any evidence that such requirements were actually "necessary" (apparently accepting them as intuitively sensible), the more significant regulations designed to protect the public from fraudulent petitioners, to assist the state in prosecuting offenders, and to provide would-be signers and voters with information they might desire for making their decisions, were subject to the highest level of scrutiny (recall Justice Stevens's assertion that the state's burden in such cases and under such conditions was "well *nigh* insurmountable"),[109] and deemed an unconstitutional violation of First Amendment rights, even though the state provided evidence showing that, especially in the ten years subsequent to the *Meyer* decision, incidents of fraud had increased.[110]

Yet, Justice Ginsburg's majority ruling in *ACLF* concluded still, reiterating the conjecture at the heart of *Meyer*, that without "*evidence* to the contrary,"

> we are not prepared to assume that a professional circulator—whose qualifications for similar future assignments may well depend on a reputation for competence and integrity—is any more likely to accept false signatures than a volunteer who is motivated entirely by an interest in having the proposition placed on the ballot.[111]

Curiously though, she offered this restatement in the face of evidence that had been provided "to the contrary," making the recapitulation of the *Meyer* assumption harder to accept. As Justice O'Connor reminded the majority in the dissenting portion of her opinion, "An elections officer for the State of Colorado testified that only paid circulators have been involved in recent fraudulent activity," and an FBI agent also testified to recent investigation of fraud in which only paid circulators were being involved. Even William Orr, the executive director of ACLF, explained to the Court during the trial that, while volunteer organizations were "self-policing" and thus there was "not much likelihood of fraud," "paid circulators are perhaps different."[112]

And so, the Court's empirical mode in this case is perhaps most significant because it raises more questions than it answers. States do not tend to keep data bases of residents, nor do secretaries of state typically have the staff to go out and verify every address listed as a residence.[113] At the same time, successful prosecutions depend on *locating* offenders, and thus in a practical sense, one wonders how a state can find individuals suspected of fraud if they cannot track them through voter registration rolls. To be sure, circulators are still required to file affidavits with their relevant information, but without a master registry of officially eligible individuals, the state seems to be without the enforcement mechanisms to supervise its own system. Of greater concern, however, were the implications of the reiterated standard. On the one hand, there appears to be *some* potential to theoretically satisfy this burden (otherwise it would not be "well *nigh*"—it would be "not at all"); but on the other hand, even if possible, the *means* by which to accomplish this remain uncertain given that the requirements remain unrevealed and have an impressionistic—"we still do not think this is enough"—feel to them, as communicated by the Court.

Of course one could argue that courts are in the business of judging, and are thus not required to spell out in literal terms just how such a burden would (or could) be "surmounted." At the same time, though, with the *Meyer* Court finding unpersuasive the state's documented evidence of fraud connected to paid petition circulation, ruling the state's ban to be unconstitutional, and then reviewing the legislation enacted to deal with the repercussions of that very ruling, eleven years later in *ACLF*—wherein it still found Colorado's evidence of an upsurge in fraud wanting in some way, while once more speaking of "insurmountabil[ity]," it is unclear how exactly a state (not just Colorado, but any of the twenty-eight states that allow for some form of direct democracy) could meet such an ambiguous burden. Obviously case-by-case litigation is possible, perhaps even expected in a certain sense (the Court reviews a Colorado petition circulation case every eleven years until the unrevealed burden is finally, i.e., serendipitously met?), but short of some sort of direction in dicta (perhaps suggesting that a ten-fold increase in fraud must be demonstrated, or there must be a ratio of at least one fraudulent signature for every thousand legitimate ones), one would think that the implication of the Court's empirical constitution of this case is to encourage *more*, not less, legislation as the state tries other regulatory avenues and approaches to combat a problem that still exists, but which must be addressed in a scattershot, as opposed to selective, manner.

And as we have seen in the previous case studies, the contemplation of conceptual and rhetorical elements discussed above seem to be largely a function of the cognitive contours of this case, including as they did the schema of "conversation," as well as the ancillary schemata of "communication," "persuasion," and obviously "speech" (in its "spoken" form) as the Court portrayed its assumptions about the discursive nature of the exchange between circulators and signatories. From the outset of the opinion, in fact, the interpretive frame within which Justice Ginsburg was working and writing was apparent, particularly as she relied on *Meyer* to first stress that petition circulation is "'core political *speech*,' because it involves 'interactive *communication* concerning political change,'"[114] and then proceeded to assert that the First Amendment "requires us to be vigilant in making those judgments, to guard against undue hindrances to *political conversations* and the exchange of ideas,"[115] meaning that restrictions that "significantly inhibit communication with voters about proposed political change . . ."[116] are especially problematic.

The Court's vision of petition circulation is thus predicated on the notion that at its core, it is "one-on-one *communication*,"[117] wherein "the circulator must endeavor to persuade electors to sign the petition,"[118] an "endeavor" which, referring to the Court's equally evident schema in *Meyer*, "of necessity involves both the expression of a desire for political change and a *discussion* of the merits of the proposed change."[119] Or, as Justice Thomas put it, relying on the same images of the exchange, Senate Bill 650 was unconstitutional because it diminished the potential to communicate "political messages,"[120] and to engage in free "*discussions* about matters of public concern."[121]

But in light of the above discussion of "Hoopla," it is essential to explore this notion of "political conversations." Amici National Voter Outreach, Inc., for example, suggests something else, describing a typical "conversation" in its brief to the Court for this case: "Here, sign this. It will really [tick off California Governor] Pete Wilson."[122] More generally, the experiences of activists and the research of scholars raises serious questions about the Court's continued embrace of this schema. Whether because "petitioners report that they can gather several thousand signatures and have not one signer read the petition language,"[123] or because pollsters have boasted that they can "get people to sign a petition that was randomly worded or made up of nonsense sentences"—suggesting that those skilled in the art of manipulation "can talk people into signing almost anything"[124]—some investigation of the Court's constructs is necessary.

Such an inquiry is especially revealing because, in economic terms and at least for *paid* circulators, engaging in "political conversations" would, ironically, seem not to be the primary objective. Certainly some degree of substantive interaction is necessary, but it is important to bear in mind that what is desired, above all, is a *signature*. Given time and resource constraints, in fact, it seems that genuine deliberation of the merits of the initiative proposition, at least at this stage (which is the only stage under formal review here), is at least unlikely, and worse, undesirable, given that petition circulators—though they may also hope to persuade you of the merits of their proposition(s)—fundamentally desire to gather your signature: something which may very well need to be accomplished in less than forty-five seconds. In other words, why take the time to engage in "political conversations" of a substantive nature if the point is to gather as many as possible in a relatively short period of time (over 120,000 in less than six months in Colorado)?[125]

In other words, despite the Court's fixation on the "conversation" schema, the imagery of "transaction" (and certainly its attendant economic connotations) seems to better accord with the actual nature of circulator/signatory interactions, whereby the "rational" gatherer may not only prefer to avoid a "conversation" with would-be signers, but—especially if this is his or her primary source of income (as it is for many circulators who travel from state to state)—may in fact *need* to resist genuinely deliberative encounters because they detract from the paramount obligation which is to gather signatures, as opposed to garnering "support" per se. Indeed, it may very well be that the experienced circulator knows that any attempt to coax a signature from an individual is not "worth" more than a twenty-second investment of time—suggesting something like a "point of diminishing marginal returns" for the circulator's effort to carry such "conversations," after which the most efficient option would be to catch a different passerby in the stream of individuals coming in and out of the supermarket or making their way through the mall.

Considering the "conversation" from the other side, one might just as well rest an economic overlay on the signatory's involvement in this exchange. Most who have encountered petition circulators, particularly the more experienced ones, understand the basic psychology of the encounter, taking place, for purposes of this thought experiment, outside the local market: (1) walking into the store, shopper spots circulator, circulator spots shopper, and eye contact is established; (2) circulator approaches shopper and says, "Excuse me, sir, but would you like to pay lower taxes?" And from here, the interaction proceeds in one of two directions: (a) the inquiry is ignored, perhaps silently or possibly with an angry retort; (b) an exchange takes place, wherein a "conversation" may occur, leading to one of several possible results: (i) the shopper signs the petition as a function of his/her preexisting support (i.e., a "soft" sell); (ii) the shopper signs the petition because the circulator is sufficiently persuasive (or aggressive) and the shopper is sufficiently open-minded (or ignorant) to accept the circulator's necessarily biased depiction of the proposition; (iii) the shopper signs the petition because she or he sees no real "cost," so to speak, in simply offering a signature since such "support" serves only to help place an issue on the ballot (and thus has no immediate implication or binding effect on the shopper), at which time the proposition will still have to win the support of the majority of voters; or, (iv) the shopper signs the petition because she or he does not want to be bothered and can tell that an easy indication of support (a mere signature) will quickly appease the circulator and allow the shopper to head into the market—or out to the car—and, ironically, *avoid* any actual "conversation" about the issue.

With concerns such as these in mind, it was the overcoming of this "conversation" (circulation = "core political speech") schema that was essential to the state's effort to "get the justices to wake up from where they were in *Meyer v. Grant*," as one attorney involved in preparing the argument put the matter.[126] And so, the state's communicative frame was designed to "create an impression" that petition circulation is "is not such a lily white pure process," but rather is something "that has a very dark underbelly to it,"[127]—and the central "impression" that the state pursued was one stressing that individuals "push initiatives for sheer greed, economics, for retribution, for a host of reasons." In this vein, then, it was imperative to make clear that circulation "is not just the little old lady from Colorado PIRG [Ralph Nader's "Public Interest Research Group"] who is down pushing the bottle bill and volunteering her time at the supermarket saying, 'Do you realize this stuff is not recyclable?'"[128] The real problem, as this official explained, was that the Court had "not been able to shake that [vision of the] 'little old lady with her clipboard,'" out collecting signatures to support the bottle bill, even though such an image was an undoubtedly "idealized view" that failed to appreciate the business of signature collection wherein the "little old lady" would be up against the beverage industry and its hordes of paid circulators.[129]

A final thought on the cognitive constitution of this case takes us to a question asked by Justice Breyer during oral argument. Responding to the claim by another justice that petition circulation is one citizen trying to persuade another about a particular issue, Breyer openly wondered, "How much *do* we actually know about this [process], or how much did we know about it in Meyer?"[130] While I hesitate to make too much of this claim (for fear that it devolves to the hyper-behavioralist concern for "what the justices had for breakfast"), it *is* important to ask what the justices really do "know about this," in terms of their own experience, especially since one would encounter petition circulators in only about half of the states and primarily in the west. How many have been approached for their signature? Did they sign? Did they "*converse*"?

CONCLUSION

In conceptual terms, *ACLF* is instructive in several ways. First, we have from the majority a clear articulation of a subtheme of the classic conception, the concern for "quantums" of speech, whereby the assumption, as it was here, is that that more speakers is inherently better because it generates more overall speech in the process. What such an anticipation implies is a kind of law of averages within the telos of the market, where it is accepted that, over time, the *more* will yield the *better.* From an entirely different standpoint, Chief Justice Rehnquist's stress on one's investment in and responsibilities to the democratic process adds some nuance to the concept of "custody" as applied to this particular electoral realm (the direct democratic process), which is *itself* a citizen-construct supervised by the state.

As rhetorically constituted, perhaps the most salient feature in this case actually bridges two cases—and the eleven years of legislation and litigation between them. Specifically, as we saw in the above discussion, the Court once more cryptically contemplated the evidentiary requirements for demonstrating fraud, but—due to the cognitive fixation on the "conversations" imagined to occur in the exchange between circulators and voters—once more found the form and frequency of the instances insufficient to sanction such regulations. This burden is interesting to bear in mind as we transition into our final case study chapter, where evidentiary precision was also desired, but ultimately not required to sustain a restriction on the speech interests of those desiring to contribute money to candidates for office.

CHAPTER 8

Nixon v. Shrink Missouri Government PAC

IT IS OFTEN NOTED that money is the "mother's milk" of American politics.[1] While the increasing costs of campaigns at the federal level tend to receive the most attention, particularly in presidential election years,[2] campaigns for state office, too, have become vastly more expensive in the last generation. Indeed, candidates for state level offices (e.g., the legislature, the Supreme Court, governor) raised more than $1.4 billion during the 2003–4 election cycle, while the states' party committees and legislative caucuses added an additional $411 million to that amount.[3] That sums of money reach these levels obviously portends the changing characteristics and methods of political campaigning in the United States, such as the general necessity for television advertisements, the formidable "war chests" that are filled (to wage campaigns and to scare away challengers), and the diminishing potential for "retail" politics, owing to demographic shifts. With these changes in the operation of political campaigns has come at least the increased "appearance" that politicians are, or tend to be, "in the pocket" of "big money," "on the take," "bought and paid for," and any of the other idioms commonly invoked to bespeak the relationship—or *perceived* relationship, as we will consider in this chapter—between elected officials and the contributors who finance their campaigns.

While a fuller account of the genesis of the legislation under review in this case can be found below, in essence Missouri's 1994 effort to limit contributions to candidates for state office (Senate Bill 650) was a product of the general citizen angst of that election year—manifest throughout the nation in the form of term limits, for example, and taking shape at the state level as a reaction against an especially raucous and expensive race for governor in 1992.[4] As a response to the problems exposed in that race, Senate Bill 650 was passed, calling in relevant part for the introduction of contribution limits on candidates for state office, ranging from $250 to $1,000, depending on the office and size of the constituency and to be adjusted biennially for inflation.[5]

The state defended these limits by referring to its interest in preventing corruption—and, significantly, in a phrase with which campaign finance scholars are quite familiar, the "*appearance* of corruption"—in the political process. Pegged generally to the contribution limits deemed constitutional (at the federal level) in *Buckley v. Valeo*,[6] the state reasoned that its regulatory scheme was necessary to preserve the integrity of campaigns and elections by limiting the amount that candidates could receive, protecting them in effect from the felt necessity to render special treatment, and at the same time, discouraging the inference that may be drawn by a public that would assume improprieties in the close proximity of money to politics. But an important intention (or at least consequence) of the bill was also to facilitate increased opportunities for citizen participation in the process by both quieting the voice of "big money" and conveying the impression that the political system was in the hands of the people.

Shrink Missouri Government PAC (hereafter, Shrink), a political action committee established by Bevis Schock, and its preferred candidate in the 1998 Republican primary election for state auditor (Zev David Fredman), alleged that the limits violated their rights to free speech because the contribution amounts essentially foreclosed opportunities for less-established candidates and patrons who lacked broad support and institutional resources akin to those of the major parties, for example—and who therefore were dependent on *larger* contributions, from their necessarily *fewer* sources, in order to mount a serious campaign. As counsel for Shrink put it during oral argument before the U.S. Supreme Court, this effort of the Missouri legislature to reform "comes at a high cost to political outsiders, like Fredman, who lack the advantages of incumbency and party endorsement," on the one hand, while also restricting "small political action committees, like Shrink, which work outside mainstream party politics to promote their political goals," and to "promote the election of candidates committed to these goals," on the other hand.[7]

In the first challenge to this specific contribution-limit provision,[8] U.S. District Judge Catherine Perry found for the state, relying on, among other things, the potential for vote buying and the public perception of widespread corruption in the political process. Per Shrink's request, the U.S. Court of Appeals for the Eighth Circuit enjoined the law and then ultimately reversed the lower court's decision in a 2-1 opinion authored by Judge Pasco Bowman, who asserted that the state had failed to meet its evidentiary burden. The U.S. Supreme Court then reversed the appeals court, with Justice Souter writing for the majority (joined by Chief Justice Rehnquist and Justices Stevens, O'Connor, Ginsburg, and Breyer) and finding that given the way the Missouri limits tracked those deemed constitutional at the federal level in *Buckley v. Valeo* (discussed in more detail below), they properly served the state's interest in preventing "corruption" and its "appearance."

In a concurring opinion, Justice Stevens offered the more abrupt claim that contribution limits did not offend the Constitution because money was decidedly *not* "speech" (it was "property"), while Justice Breyer, in a separate concurrence (joined by Justice Ginsburg) welcomed the state's efforts to "level the playing field" and promote greater participatory parity in the form of political speech. Justices Kennedy and Thomas each dissented, with Justice Scalia joining the Thomas opinion, each emphasizing the numerous negative consequences that they continued to trace to the *Buckley* foundation and the subsequent structure that had been built upon it since the mid-1970s. Both saw the majority's determinations in *Shrink* as, fundamentally, an affront to individual liberty.

CONTEXT, CONCERNS, CONSIDERATIONS

Mother's Milk

Efforts to reform the American electoral process date back to the colonial era when some states attempted to limit the practice of providing voters with free food and drink.[9] As campaigning became increasingly party-oriented, and as candidates sought to reach a mass audience, in the early to mid-1800s, spending increased considerably, though campaigns were still financed by a small number of sources. By the election of 1896, already an election of dramatic political contrasts, total spending reached its peak to that point ($7 million), with William Jennings Bryan raising less than 20 percent of the amount amassed by William McKinley.[10] To address the perceived abuses of money in the political system, Congress passed a series of acts throughout the twentieth century, including the Tillman Act of 1907, the first federal effort to regulate campaign finance, banning corporate contributions to presidential campaigns;[11] the Federal Corrupt Practices Act, broadening the government's authority to compel disclosure of contributions and expenditures for House and Senate candidates; the Hatch Act of 1939, and as amended in 1940, prohibiting political contributions of more than $5,000 to federal candidates or campaign committees and extending the restrictions on political activities by civil service employees; and the Taft-Hartley Act of 1947, prohibiting direct contributions from unions to candidates.

The most consequential and, for purposes of this book, constitutive of these efforts has, however, been the Federal Election Campaign Act (FECA), passed by Congress in 1971, and as amended in 1974 and 1979, in the wake of the Watergate scandal and the general decline in public trust of elected officials.[12] This law, the focus of *Buckley*, called for the disclosure of the sources of campaign contributions and campaign expenditures; the public funding of presidential primaries and general elections; limits on campaign expenditures for those accepting public funding; limits on expenditures from individuals' personal funds; a $1,000 limitation on independent expenditures; the establishment of the Federal Election Commission (FEC); and a range of contribution limits for various individuals and organizations. And in its most recent major legislative effort along these lines—in many ways a response to the campaign finance practices (and evasions) that *Buckley* and its progeny wrought—Congress passed the Bipartisan Campaign Reform Act (BCRA, aka "McCain-Feingold"), which in its two most notable provisions called for a ban on "soft" money contributions to national political parties by corporations, unions, and individuals, and instituted a host of restrictions on electioneering communications within defined ("blackout") periods of time around election day.

Which Came First? . . .

Whether or not politicians are disproportionately influenced *by* or otherwise offer undue attention *to* the wishes, interests, or values of contributors—or whether individuals and organizations simply choose to offer financial support to those candidates with whom they already agree, is a classic "chicken-or-egg"-type question that is in many ways at the heart of the campaign finance debate. What constitutes "corruption" to some, in other words (e.g., a correlation between the "interests" of groups supporting a politician through financial contributions and the voting record for that individual), is simply "representation" for others. That is, politicians are *supposed* to respond to their constituents' and donors' interests, so it is no surprise—indeed, it is to be expected—that one would see reciprocal support. While a review of the literature examining these questions is beyond the scope of this chapter, a few observations are worth noting here. For one, research has demonstrated a de facto correlation between contributions and "access" to legislators, though this proximity is arguably just as much a function of the common concerns of interest groups and legislators.[13] Drawing similar conclusions as to mutual interests between donors and politicians, another study has examined the voting behavior of "lame-duck" office holders (i.e., those presumably no longer "beholden" to the wishes of contributors), and has found that these individuals maintained their voting patterns even in the absence of the contributions they had consistently received from various groups when running for reelection.[14]

And yet, other scholarship questions the general assumption sustaining most research inquiries on this topic—that "corruption" exists principally in the form of discernible quid pro quo relationships between contributors and candidates—by looking at the participation of House members in committee (as opposed to simple floor votes) and suggesting that "moneyed interests do affect the decision-making processes of Congress," though the effects are not so obvious as "vote-buying."[15] Indeed, as former Senator William Proxmire has suggested, the effort to locate *overt* examples of "corruption," whereby support was garnered through a financial lure, misses the more subtle, yet pervasive influence of money on the contours of our political process. The impact of a campaign contribution, for example, may not be felt in a "vote," per se, but may instead "come in a speech not delivered," a "colleague not influenced," the "calling off of a meeting that otherwise would result in advancing legislation," a "witness not invited to testify before a committee," the hiring of "a key staff member for a committee who is sympathetic to the PAC," or even the "laying off or transferring [of] a staff member who is unsympathetic to a PAC."[16]

Or, as one political organizer involved in pressing for campaign finance reform suggests, commenting specifically on the culture, practices, and widely perceived abuses in Missouri's political system that inspired the law under review in *Shrink* (an initiative which garnered the support of 74 percent of the public in its earlier form as a ballot proposition), "there are a great many people who believe that corruption is simply unevenness or imbalance in access to policymakers—that that is itself corruption and that it is not just bribe-taking."[17] Thus, at least from the standpoint of "appearances" and assumptions, which is the focal point for the cognitive constitution of this case, this activist added, "if you can so weight your ability to speak to your legislators, for example, such that the outcome of that weighted speech is that you always win, then it is irrelevant what goes on inside of the head of the legislator that finally casts that vote," because the perception "has already taken hold that it was the money that encouraged the decisions."[18]

"Do No Harm"

For critics of reform efforts, the proposed solution—that is the very idea of adding layers of regulation—is fundamentally flawed, self-defeating, and repeating,[19] in that such an agenda violates a central normative assumption of democracy (the notion that voters are civically competent),[20] but also that such efforts tend to yield a series of "unintended consequences,"[21] which are, in some cases, more disturbing than the problems they purport to fix.[22] Indeed, as one individual involved in Shrink's defense asserted, "The reason we are here is because of regulations," specifically those "changes to the FECA that led to Buckley v. Valeo." And so it is *regulations*, this individual stressed, that have "so distorted the process," in that "politicians that campaigned in the seventies and sixties . . . didn't have to do what they have to do now," because "their finance committees raised money." But now, "you have to be raising money full time" just to "fix the problem that was *caused by* regulation."[23]

On another level though, while "reform" may be the goal, it could be that a focus exclusively on one resource (i.e., money) is too narrow and may, in fact, increase inequality in the political system.[24] Considering the relationship between intentions and consequences in yet another way, it is worth noting that "reforms" are, by design, not neutral. That is, reforms seek to correct an "imbalance" purported to exist in the political marketplace,[25] meaning that they are addressed toward what the group in power perceives to be the problem;[26] or, in a more Machiavellian vein, what this group professes to be the problem, perhaps as a way of protecting its own interests while seeming to be acting in the "public interest."[27] Legislation might be enacted to "level the playing field," for example, though this act of "leveling" may clearly benefit one set of interests, even as it is couched in rhetoric that suggests such efforts are for the "*common* good,"[28] for example—perhaps even toward the "*common* cause,"[29] or in the "*public* interest."[30] Meanwhile, efforts to "enhance" speech,[31] ostensibly to improve the political process, typically call upon the state to provide the "counterbalances" necessary to compensate for the influence of private economic forces in the electoral marketplace of ideas, an invitation which of course introduces a host of additional complications in its own right.[32]

Buckley v. Valeo

Because of its precedential significance, it is important to review once more the issues and holding of *Buckley v. Valeo*. As we saw in Chapter 2, *Buckley* was a per curiam opinion of the eight justices sitting at the time (Stevens took no part),[33] which, for our purposes, held most importantly that a distinction of constitutional significance existed between political expenditures and contributions, with limits on the former found to violate the First Amendment, while restrictions on the latter were sustained in light of the state's legitimate interest in preventing both actual corruption and "the *appearance* of corruption."[34] Given the thrust of the Court's holding in *Shrink*, it is important to recall that in light of the recent abuses of public authority (i.e., Watergate), the Court, in *Buckley*, was more prepared to accept a defense of the FECA that relied on public perceptions—whether accurate or not. As the per curiam opinion explained, it was not necessary to look beyond the primary purpose of the act—limiting "the actuality and appearance of corruption resulting from large individual financial contributions"—to find a constitutional justification for the contribution limits. "Under a system of private financing of elections," the opinion continued, a "candidate lacking immense personal or family wealth must depend on financial contributions from others to provide the resources necessary to conduct a successful campaign."[35] The implication is that, "to the extent that large contributions are given to secure political quid pro quos from current and potential office holders, the integrity of our system of representative democracy is undermined."[36]

However, and of most significance for our inquiry into the constitution of *Shrink*, the Court also stressed that "of almost equal concern as the danger of actual quid pro quo arrangements is the impact of the appearance of corruption stemming from public awareness of the opportunities for abuse inherent in a regime of large individual financial contributions."[37] And thus, "Congress could legitimately conclude that the avoidance of the appearance of improper influence 'is also critical . . . if confidence in the system of representative Government is not to be eroded to a disastrous extent.'"[38] Focusing on appearances, then, was essential for the *Buckley* Court as it would be for the *Shrink* majority, because laws criminalizing bribery were directed at only the "most blatant and specific attempts of those with money to influence governmental action,"[39] and were thus insufficient to address the more subtle and systemic deficiencies flowing from the vast sums of money in politics.

THE DEVELOPMENT OF NIXON V. SHRINK MISSOURI GOVERNMENT PAC

"Show Me" the Money!

Seeking to diminish the influence of money in state elections, two initiative propositions were circulating simultaneously in 1994, one sponsored by Roy Blunt, then the Republican secretary of state and later a U.S. congressman, and another by the liberal populist group, Association of Community Organizations for Reform Now (ACORN). The two groups consolidated their efforts and the ACORN version made the ballot as "Proposition A," passing with 74 percent of the vote.[40] Perhaps wary of a citizen-written law, the General Assembly passed "Senate Bill 650," which called for: (1) a ceiling on expenditures; (2) a prohibition against contributions while legislators were in session; and (3) higher contribution limits, ranging from $250 to $1,000, depending on the office (and adjusted for inflation).

To determine the appropriate amounts for these limits, State Senator Wayne Goode, co-chair of the bipartisan Interim Joint Committee on Campaign Finance, and a legislator with a combined thirty-six years in the Assembly, explained that the "members of the Committee discussed among ourselves at length not only what it cost to run a campaign and deliver a message to the populace, but also at what point is there the potential for contributions to become unduly influential."[41] "I believed in 1993 and I believe today," Goode stressed in his affidavit prepared for the trial, "that contributions over those limits have the appearance of buying votes as well as the real potential to buy votes," meaning that the "greater the contribution, the greater the potential there is for the appearance of and the actual buying of votes."[42] And so it was the "consensus of the Committee," with which he concurred that "the limits we set forth in the bill balanced the need to run an effective campaign with the appearance of buying votes."[43]

Because Senate Bill 650 would have gone into place between the August primary and the November election, a provision was inserted to prevent the law from taking effect until January 1995. Thus, the contribution limits passed by the voters (Proposition A, in November of 1994) immediately, if only temporarily, became law. Given the contentiousness of campaign finance issues, the proposition's expenditure and contribution limits faced immediate court challenges. Figure 8.1 provides a description of the components of Senate Bill 650 and Proposition A and their respective paths through the courts. The focus of this chapter is the contribution limits case, "*Shrink* III," that eventually reached the United States Supreme Court.[44]

The Lower Courts

Accepting the (appearance of) "corruption" rationale as the state's principal justification for the law, Judge Catherine Perry determined that the affidavit of State Senator Wayne Goode, as well as a series of newspaper

FIGURE 8.1 *Missouri Campaign Finance Legislation and Challenges*[a]

Proposition A

▶ **Contribution limits:**
sliding scale ranging limits: sliding scale from $100 to $300 *per election cycle.*

▶ **War chests:**
prohibition against candidates carrying over amounts ranging from $1,000 to $3,000 from one election to another.

▶ **Expenditure limits:**
prohibition against candidates spending more than $100 to $300 of their personal resources in their campaign for office. (Interpreted as a limit on "contributions" to one's own campaign.)

Senate Bill 650

▶ **Contribution limits:**
sliding scale ranging from $250 to $1,000 *in any one election.*

▶ **Timing of Contributions:**
Prohibition against elected officials or candidates receiving contributions while the legislature is in session.

▶ **Expenditure limits:**
Limit on the total amount spent, ranging from $30,000 to $1,500,000.[b]

1995: *Carver v. Nixon,* 882 F.Supp. 901: Proposition A's contribution limits upheld; reversed by the 8th Circuit Court of Appeals, 72 F.3d 633 (1995); certiorari denied by the US Supreme Court, 116 S. Ct. 2579 (1996).

1995: *Shrink Missouri Government PAC v. Maupin* (Shrink I), 892 F.Supp. 1246: SB 650's limit on total expenditures, Prop. A's limits on expenditures from personal resources and "war-chest" provisions found unconstitutional; affirmed by the 8th Circuit, 71 F.3d 1422 (1995); certiorari denied, 116 S. Ct. 2579 (1996).

1996: *Shrink Missouri Government PAC v. Maupin* (Shrink II), 922 F.Supp. 1413: SB 650's prohibition against receiving contributions while the General Assembly is in session ruled unconstitutional.

1998: *Shrink Missouri Government PAC v. Adams* (Shrink III), 5 F.Supp. 2d 734 (1998): SB 650's contribution limits upheld; reversed by the 8th Circuit, 161 F.3d 519 (1998); reversed by the US Supreme Court, *Nixon v. Shrink Missouri Government PAC*, 528 U.S. 377 (2000).

a Missouri campaign finance legislation and challenges as of 2000, when Shrink was decided.

b Candidates who opted out of the expenditure limits faced two penalties: (1) They could receive contributions only from individuals, while opponents who complied with the limits could accept from parties, PACs, unions, etc.; and, (2) They were compelled to file daily reports, detailing contributions and expenditures, once their expenditures exceeded the limits. Failure to comply meant criminal sanctions.

editorials from that period,[45] were sufficient evidence that the legislature had enacted Senate Bill 650 in an attempt to minimize both the perception and real potential for vote buying. Moreover, she found that the limits were set at an amount presumably beyond the budget of the large majority of state residents and thus only applied to a small number of donors,[46] suggesting that "meaningful participation" was still possible, and there was "no reason to believe that Missouri's contribution limits have any 'dramatic adverse effect' on funding campaigns for state office," where candidates "are still able to amass impressive campaign war chests."[47]

Noting that there was a "strong likelihood that appellants will prevail when the case is heard on the merits," the Eighth Circuit Court of Appeals granted an injunction pending appeal.[48] Upon hearing the case, Chief Judge Pasco Bowman, joined by Judge Donald Ross,[49] determined that what was required in such cases was "some *demonstrable evidence* that there were genuine problems that resulted from contributions in amounts greater than the limits in place,"[50] and thus mere *conjecture* was insufficient to support such restrictions on speech rights. Judge Bowman's opinion also explained that, given the effects of inflation, in today's dollars, "the SB 650 limits [pegged to those upheld in *Buckley* in 1976] appear likely to 'have a severe impact on political dialogue' by preventing many candidates for public office 'from amassing the resources necessary for effective advocacy.'"[51] For his part, Judge John Gibson dissented, finding the majority's contemplation of economic implications to be a flawed approach,[52] and concluding that whatever may be "the pernicious effects of inflation, I am certain that the First Amendment's dictates do not depend upon the Consumer Price Index."[53]

The United States Supreme Court

Writing for a six-member majority,[54] Justice Souter concluded that the Missouri legislature had addressed itself to "answering" the "perception of impropriety" and "countering the cynical assumption that large donors call the tune" within its political system.[55] Thus, in finding that the evidence introduced into the record was "enough to show that the substantiation of the congressional concerns reflected in *Buckley* has its counterpart supporting the Missouri law,"—and, importantly concluding as we will see in the constitution section of this chapter, that absent any definitive demonstration that assumptions (whether accurate or not according to the data) had changed in the intervening years since *Buckley*—Souter reasoned that the limits in place here were not "so radical in effect as to render political association ineffective, drive the sound of a candidate's voice below the level of notice, and render contributions pointless,"[56] meaning that there was "no reason in logic or evidence to doubt the sufficiency of *Buckley* to govern this case in support of the Missouri statute."[57]

Offering "one simple point" in his brief concurring opinion, Justice Stevens wrote to state, that "money is property; it is not speech."[58] Constitutional law surely affords protections for property, and it protects the "right to use one's own money to hire gladiators," for example, but these property rights "are not entitled to the same protection as the right to say what one pleases."[59] Justice Breyer, meanwhile (joined by Justice Ginsburg), wrote separately "to address the critical question of how the Court ought to review this kind of problem" and to explain why "the Court's choice here is correct."[60] "On the one hand," he offered, "a decision to contribute money to a campaign is a matter of First Amendment concern—not because money *is* speech (it is not); but because it *enables* speech."[61] On the other hand, "restrictions upon the amount any one individual can contribute to a particular candidate seek to protect the integrity of the electoral process—the means through which a free society democratically translates political speech into concrete governmental action."[62] And where "competing constitutional interests" were at stake, he argued,[63] the Court has "balanced interests" and deferred to "empirical legislative judgments,"[64] something which should be done in this case as well, because "the legislature understands the problem—the threat to electoral integrity, the need for democratization—better than do we."[65]

Dissenting, Justice Kennedy wrote that upholding contribution limits of this sort "suppresses one of our most essential and prevalent forms of political speech."[66] Further, and especially because *Buckley* was once again used to justify a restriction on political speech, Kennedy argued that the "justifications for the case system and *stare decisis* must rest upon the Court's capacity, and responsibility, to acknowledge its missteps." Thus, it was the Court's "duty to face up to adverse, unintended consequences flowing from our own prior decisions," an "obligation" that the justices had not accepted in this case, choosing instead a course of action that "perpetuates and compounds a serious distortion of the First Amendment resulting from our own intervention in *Buckley*."[67] Perhaps the most serious such "consequence" for Kennedy was the growing prevalence of "covert speech,"[68] or the forcing of a "substantial amount of political speech underground, as contributors and candidates devise ever more elaborate methods of avoiding contribution limits, limits which take no account of rising campaign costs"[69]—a development which "mocks the First Amendment."[70]

In his dissent, Justice Thomas (joined by Justice Scalia) also indicated his willingness to overrule *Buckley* because it failed to respect the fact that "free exchange should receive the most protection when it matters the most—during campaigns for elective office."[71] Curiously, he noted, the majority in this case, "rather than going out of its way to *protect* political speech, goes out of its way to *avoid* protecting it,"[72] all the while failing to appreciate that "contributions to political campaigns generate essential political speech" perhaps primarily because citizens and donors realize that "the best advocate for a candidate (and the policy positions he supports) tends to be the candidate himself."[73] Finally, Thomas rejected the majority's "illiberal aggregate rights approach" because he reasoned that courts (and legislatures) "have no yardstick by which to judge the proper amount and effectiveness of campaign speech."[74] Such determinations, for Thomas, should be left to free citizens functioning in a free society.

THE CONSTITUTION OF NIXON V. SHRINK MISSOURI GOVERNMENT PAC

While Shrink encouraged a classic conception of the marketplace, whereby candidates could "say what they want and assume that over time our nation will reject poor ideas and gravitate to good ones"[75]—the preferred conceptual framework for the three dissenters, Kennedy,[76] Thomas,[77] and Scalia[78]—the justices comprising the majority drew on a hybrid of custodial and equality conceptions of the marketplace in sustaining the state's regulatory framework and the theory and values animating it. *Shrink* provides evidence, in addition to that which we saw at work in Chapters 6 and 7, of the normative valence orienting the custodial model, especially when money is the speech dimension under review.

In this vein, consider the response of the Missouri attorney general,

Jay Nixon, to the Court's request for more specific terms supporting the state's particular vision of the nature of the "corruption" to be deterred by such legislation. "Is it," Justice Scalia asked, "corruption for an official to mirror his views to the electorate just so that he can be reelected?" "No," Nixon replied, "a politician mirroring his views to the people he represents is not corruption"—it is "democracy," and only becomes "corruption" at the point "when he acts *contrary* to what his other—his position would be otherwise."[79] Nor would it be corruption, Nixon offered, for a candidate to respond affirmatively if a labor union tells him or her, as Justice Scalia posed in a hypothetical, "you know, we will go all out in working for you, getting out the vote, going door-to-door, ringing the doorbells, if you will support an increase in the minimum wage."[80] The significance of this distinction conceded by Missouri—between contributions of money and contributions in kind (manifest as labor, involvement, energy)—is quite telling of the way the state privileged *time* over *money* as a political commodity, but also in the implication that the dimension of speech *de*emphasized in this approach (money) is actually threatening to the democratic process, while an "equal," in-kind contribution of time embodies the democratic process.

But it is also important here to emphasize Missouri's evident concern for the people (as distinguished from the process), manifest here in the attempt to prevent the advantages accrued in the economic domain from being transferred to the electoral speech domain, and thus implicating the *equality* conception of the marketplace of ideas. To address this concern, the government pursued a more dispersed common denominator that might allow for greater parity in terms of opportunities for political speech and influence. Orienting this conception was the notion that there is, in fact, a "correct" amount of money that should be spent on politics,[81] a belief which, as one state official involved in campaign finance regulation surmised, had energized both Proposition A and Senate Bill 650 because the public was "deeply disturbed" by seeing the "large blocs of contribution money associated with specific and narrowly focused interest groups going to candidates."[82] Contributions of this size, though not necessarily this *scope*, concerned the average Missourian, this official assessed, "because people wondered, 'Why is my one vote not worth the same amount . . . simply because that person was able to contribute financial resources to the candidate?'"[83]

Underscoring the state interest in this case, another state official involved in crafting the state's defense of the statute stressed that the key "distinction between time and money," from the state's perspective, was that "no one has more than twenty-four hours a day." Thus, "everybody that is going to work on a campaign," is "going to contribute something of their *time*," drawn from "a finite amount that they can contribute." Such a scheme puts a premium on this sort of "contribution" as a means of "equalizing" the opportunity for participation and influence, because, this official reasoned, under such a plan "it makes no difference, if I am stuffing envelopes, if I am a sixteen-year-old coming in after high school, or a wealthy dowager."[84]

Fundamentally, then, "nearly everybody has the ability to contribute some of their time, but not everybody can contribute money, or at least not money in the amounts that in this day and age candidates are looking for."[85] The day consists of only so many hours, in other words, and so by tempering the influence of financial contributions the state could encourage in their place more "people"-oriented forms of political participation, if you will, such as door-to-door canvassing, rallies, "get out the vote" efforts, and other forms of involvement that required individuals to draw upon the resource of time, allocated as it was equally (or at least *more* equally) to all state residents—making such methods of electoral expression ostensibly more "democratic," if for no other reason than that a greater percentage of the "demos" could theoretically take part and have more of a stake in the outcome.[86]

Such a rationale appears to be the central thrust of the articulation offered up by Justice Breyer (and joined by Justice Ginsburg), addressed as it was more distinctly to the expansion of opportunity in the speech marketplace. Consider first, for example, his concern during oral argument (anticipating both his ruling in this case and the judicial philosophy he would eventually develop several years later in his "Madison Lecture" and in his book, *Active Liberty*),[87] "Why can't a State say, in our democracy . . . we believe the important democratic interests are furthered by not having very rich people own a candidate." Moreover, he wondered why Missouri was not properly qualified to say: "We want to *equalize the opportunity*, though we will never make it totally equal, but *we* want to *spread it around a bit*, so a person with $1,000, which means as much to him as $15 million to Ebenezer Scrooge, also has a *chance to participate* and is not drowned out by the $15 million. . . . Why can't a State decide that, if that's the *kind* of democracy that it *wants*?" he wondered.[88]

Note a few things here. First, contra *Buckley*, Breyer for one obviously accepts some modicum of "equalization" as a legitimate state goal—at least in terms of "opportunity" for political influence (i.e., the "it" that is to be "spread" around), as well as the "chance to participate" for John Q. Public and his contribution (up to $1,000) versus the $15 million offering of "Ebenezer Scrooge." Second, the "we" who would be "spread[ing] it around" refers, obviously, to the state as the entity charged with the responsibility for facilitating the "spread[ing]." More importantly, though, such logic is clearly analogous to policies of redistribution in the economic realm, which require—following the initial "spread"—consistent supervision of the newly apportioned distribution (i.e., to *keep* it "spread"), especially if—to stay with the analogy—there is as great a tendency for "it" (again, influence) to consolidate in the political sphere as there is for wealth to do so in the economic sphere. Third, in bringing the emphasis on equality back to merge with the majority's more general custodial emphasis, Breyer's final question is critical, emphasizing as it does the normative vision sustaining such an approach, and as it accepts that there are various "kind[s]" of democracy that could be adopted and that the state can properly (i.e., custodially) "want" one over another.

Such themes also appear quite clearly in Breyer's concurring opinion in this case, specifically as he reasons that the law represented a legitimate and much-needed effort both to "democratize the influence that money itself may bring to bear upon the electoral process," and to "build public confidence in that process and broaden the base of a candidate's meaningful financial support, encouraging the public participation and open discussion that the First Amendment itself presupposes"—the upshot of which, he stressed, was to "make the process fairer and more democratic."[89] The significance of this passage is in its implication that rendering more, not fewer, people capable of making financial contributions ("broaden[ing] the base of a candidate's meaningful financial support") benefits the electoral process by expanding and diversifying the points of input, the effect of which would be to "democratize" this influence in the interest of both the people and the process.[90]

In a manner affording some conceptual distance between his emphases on both equality and custody, Breyer's argument does not necessarily diminish the amount of money in politics per se, or even disfavor money as a commodity in the speech marketplace. Rather, it seeks to simply "democratize" it by keeping contributions under control and thus making it at least theoretically possible that more people could be involved (i.e., contribute) in this manner. One implication of this is that given the broadened base of potential support and with the signal sent that any individual's contribution could very nearly be matched by another's—such that each contributor's offering now matters that much more—there could actually be a larger quantity of money in the electoral process, albeit more evenly distributed. Note, too, the claim that state facilitation of this sort would serve to make the process "fairer," thus implying both some notion of initial "fairness" (to serve as a frame of reference) and some sense or value of measurement with which to approximate improvements—requiring in other words that we have some indication as to what "fair" means from the start, which would thus prepare us to recognize the specific "valued *added*" as the system becomes "fair*er*," implying an increased amount (or degree) of whatever commodity was accepted as the baseline measure for "fair" at the outset.

Furthermore, and perhaps of greatest precedential value for purposes of the campaign finance debate in the decades to come, Breyer openly questioned the assertions in *Buckley* that rejected the "concept that government may restrict the speech of some elements of our society in order to enhance the relative voice of others,"[91] noting that "those words cannot be taken literally."[92] Indeed, he observed, "The Constitution often permits *restrictions on the speech of some* in order to prevent a few from drowning out the many—in Congress, for example, where constitutionally protected debate, Art. I, § 6, is limited to provide every Member an *equal opportunity* to express his or her views."[93] "Or in elections," he continued, "where the Constitution tolerates numerous restrictions on ballot access, limiting the political rights of some so as to make effective the political rights of the entire electorate." "Regardless," he continued, "as the result in Buckley made clear, the statement does not automatically invalidate a statute that seeks a fairer electoral debate through contribution limits, nor should it forbid the Court to take account of the competing constitutional interests just mentioned."[94]

Indeed, such conceptual assumptions were quite clearly influenced by the particular empirical orientation of the Court in this case, receptive as it was to the argument that contribution limits were essential given the public perception of a problem. That is, if people believe that large contributions garner special favors or unequal treatment—or, perhaps more accurately, if those *in power* believe this, whether or not it is true—then it is just as much a state concern as demonstrable instances of fraud, bribery, or collusion.[95] Significantly, because these shadowy practices are by their nature hard to "prove" (or *dis*prove), they inspire a host of perceptions as to the influence of money in politics which then take on a life of their own, rendering them all the more difficult to dislodge from people's minds, precisely because they are assumed to take place in secret (making it difficult to know what we really know—or don't know, or cannot know) and because they are assumed to be so simultaneously and sufficiently pervasive that the "appearance" is effectively the reality—almost to the extent that to question the prevailing wisdom or request evidence is to appear naive as opposed to merely skeptical.

But it was just such a set of images, assumptions, and appearances that the state was attempting to "attack," in the words of one official involved in crafting the argument for Missouri on appeal, because "the perception of corruption, even if that perception is irrational," is a problem, because "even if it [the perception] exists, it harms the system, and so we ought to be able to do things to prevent it from existing."[96] Thus, a system that "permits unlimited, direct contributions to candidates creates a public perception that both the election process and the decisions of elected officials are corrupt," meaning that elected officials are "perceived to be in debt to large contributors, and to make decisions, either consciously or unconsciously, based on that indebtedness rather than the public interest they are sworn to promote."[97] Moreover, "The purse strings held by an elite group of wealthy contributors *appear* to voters as puppet strings, providing ultimate control and virtual invisibility."[98] "In addition, a regime of unlimited contributions creates a public *belief* that access to an elected official and control over the public agenda are for sale, and available for a price that only a few can pay."[99]

Furthermore, the state continued to stress in its reply brief, the public "*perceives* that large contributions purchase not only votes, but also access, attention and services for select constituents, and an ability to influence the government's agenda, including the power to keep certain items off that agenda."[100] Such a "pervasive appearance of corruption" was, according to amici secretaries of state, inspired in part by the "simple fact that the vast majority of Americans cannot afford to contribute substantial money to campaigns as their wealthy counterparts do."[101] Public perception, in other words, is shaped by the reality that, because most people cannot afford large contributions, those who can receive special treatment *must* receive it.

Such assumptions were critical to the consideration of the case at trial, wherein Judge Perry, responding to Shrink's request for some demonstration of "real harm," explained, "A *perception* of influence peddling is 'real harm' regardless of whether such peddling is actually afoot."[102] Indeed, she continued: "To the extent Citizen Smith thinks that an elected official is giving Citizen Jones preferential treatment based on the latter's largess in the most recent election, the confidence of Citizen Smith in the integrity of her government is diminished."[103] In fact, even for one "unschooled in politics," she insisted, "*no great deductive leap*" was necessary to "reach a conclusion that the contribution of substantial sums to a candidate for political office gives rise to a *perception* among the public that the contributor is trying to curry favor with the recipient."[104]

Yet, even with the ceiling on limitations pegged to the amount maintained at the federal level in *Buckley*, Chief Judge Pasco Bowman of the Eighth Circuit distinguished the instant case in an important way that tells us much about the essence of all cases that turn on "appearances." Acknowledging that the *Buckley* Court had assented to a certain degree of imprecision in the relationship between contributions and corruption, he explained that the appeals court was "unwilling to extrapolate from those examples that in Missouri at this time there is corruption or a perception of corruption from 'large' campaign contributions, without some *evidence* that such problems really exist." The state must, in other words, "prove that Missouri has a *real* problem with corruption or a *perception* thereof as a direct result of large campaign contributions."[105]

Such a colloquy through the lower courts is instructive, particularly because, as one elected state official involved in crafting the legislation put it, "more than anything else" $1,000 was the adopted limit because "the *impression* was that at some point above that amount legislators believed that they may start to *feel* beholden." "There certainly wasn't any scientific approach in coming up with that number," this legislator added; it was more a matter of trying to find a balance between "what the public would consider very large amounts of money—and a lot would consider a thousand dollars to be a lot of money"—and "what the lawmakers perceived as defensible under the law."[106] Rooting its arguments in these perceptions, then, the state proposed that "Missouri certainly is permitted to rely upon *common sense* and accepted tenets of human behavior in adopting rules governing its elections."[107]

Indeed, Justice Souter reasoned, apparently drawing on the logic of such "common sense," examples of corruption (or its "appearance") may not, in fact, be necessary, given that the "quantum of empirical evidence needed to satisfy heightened judicial scrutiny of legislative judgments will vary up or down with the novelty and plausibility of the justification raised."[108] While there may not be a discernible event (e.g., a Watergate scandal) to bear in mind when considering a restriction on political money of this sort, and as was the case with *Buckley*, there also was no evidence that public cynicism had dissipated in the intervening generation. Nor, given the fact that 98 percent of contributions to candidates in the state auditor's race were under $1,000,[109] did the limits appear to foreclose the potential to "amass the resources necessary for effective advocacy."[110]

Along the lines of what we saw in Chapter 5 (*Burson*), *Shrink*, too, appears to have been *rhetorically* constituted by evidence that cannot be provided (that which is not "known" per se), just as it was at the same time by the specific claims that could be empirically verified. In other words, in a manner consistent with the decision that electioneering radii must have been necessary—and must still be necessary—even without any empirical support for this claim (given the inherent difficulty in demonstrating such a need), contribution limits, too, were essential, directed as they were toward the cloud of "corruption" that exists (amorphously, indistinctly, and pervasively) *prior* to—and this is critical—the point where there *is* demonstrable proof of quid pro quo corruption, at which time such activities would be prosecutable under bribery statutes.[111] The upshot of this, then, as Richard Hasen has observed, is that "under the 'appearance of corruption' evidentiary standard, it will nearly always be possible for the state to point to public perceptions of corruption to justify contribution limits."[112]

As such, it bears looking in more detail at how and why appearances hold such sway over this realm of electoral speech law. Perhaps the most striking feature of the cognitive constitution of this case was the schematic window opened up by Justice Souter's concession of his own perceptions of money in politics and willingness to extrapolate from such conjecture. Specifically, Souter reasoned, the appearance of corruption likely meant a few different things. For example, he observed: "I think most people assume—I do, certainly—that someone making an extraordinarily large contribution is going to get some kind of extraordinary return for it. I think that is a pervasive assumption."[113]

A second assumption that he believed "most people" would make—including himself—was that "there is certainly an appearance of, call it an attenuated corruption, if you will, that large contributors are simply going to get better service, whatever that service may be, from a politician than the average contributor, let alone no contributor." Were these perceptions not "sound"? he wondered.[114] So compelling was the "appearance" schema for the justices in the majority, it seems—and by the rhetorical extension and projection, for the public—that even if scholars, generally political scientists, "may be reasonably sure that the money does *not* buy what most people think it buys," there does not appear to have been a refutation that "most people do *think* that it buys something that shouldn't be bought . . . ,"[115] which for cognitive constitutional purposes appears to have been controlling, whether accurate in "reality" (as opposed to "appearance") or not.

Moreover, the "constitutionally sufficient justification," Souter reminded us—as explained in *Buckley*—was the "prevention of corruption and the appearance of corruption."[116] Indeed, he wrote, "we spoke in *Buckley* of the perception of corruption 'inherent in a regime of large individual financial contributions' to candidates for public office as a source of concern 'almost equal' to *quid pro quo* improbity."[117] "The public interest in countering that perception was, indeed, the entire answer to the overbreadth claim raised" in *Buckley*, he continued; and this "made perfect sense" because in leaving "the perception of impropriety unanswered," you encourage the "cynical assumption that large donors call the tune could jeopardize the willingness of voters to take part in democratic governance."[118]

In discussing amendments to the Hatch Act in 1940, Senator John A. Bankhead captured the essence of the Court's cognition here, alluding to that which "we all know" regarding the role of money in politics. "We all know that money is the chief source of corruption," he offered, adding that "we all know that large contributions to political campaigns not only put the political party under obligation to the large contributors, who demand pay in the way of legislation, but we also know that large sums of money are used for the purpose of conducting expensive campaigns through the newspapers and over the radio."[119] Or, as Solicitor General Seth Waxman (who argued on behalf of the federal government in *Shrink*, intervening to preserve contribution limits at the federal level) put it: "We need not confront daily the demoralizing show of elected officials chasing immense contributions that everyone knows buy preferential access and influence."[120]

Research has, in fact, demonstrated that defenders of reform are correct in assuming the public does see "large campaign contributions as unduly influencing the official behavior of members of Congress"—though such perceptions "extend not only to givers of the large contributions banned by the Bipartisan Campaign Reform Act (BCRA) and earlier reforms but also to contributions made within the law's limits."[121] At the same time, for opponents of reform, those measures introduced to correct, debunk, or wash away such perceptions clearly have not met their objectives given that public opinion consistently indicates such sentiments irrespective of regulatory responses. The significance of all this is obviously found in the Court's equally amorphous discussion of "corruption," resting as it ultimately did on impressions about what people think: not what they know, what the data show, or what the evidence has proven, but simply what they nonetheless assume or perceive of the system and the relationship between contributions and candidates.

And thus, the repeated emphases on the schema of intuition, "common sense," and the problems we "perceive," even if we cannot prove them, are all the more essential to the constitution of this case, especially given their inherently subjective nature. In this sense, consider the argument of amici National Right to Life PAC State Fund (for respondents), which explained in its brief that relying on such impressions (absent corroborating empirical proof) was to essentially shield the state's (and the Court's) assertions from challenge by offering an "argument that was not 'open to disconfirmation' and [which] therefore contains within itself no limiting principle."[122] The problem with such contentions is that they "cannot be disproved except by proving that subjective perceptions of corruption are wrong"; and that "can only be done by proving the negative proposition that actual corruption does not exist."[123] The consequence of such logic is that "because it cannot be disproved, it must be assumed to be true, and therefore, can serve as the justification for even more severe restrictions on freedom."[124]

CONCLUSION

Shrink is a particularly intriguing case because, as we saw above, all three conceptions of the marketplace of ideas are represented in the majority, concurring, and dissenting opinions, which means that this, perhaps more than any of the previous three case studies, best portrays the manner in which and means by which "speech" interests are unequivocally evident in both the claims of "injured" speakers *and* the regulatory schemes constructed to facilitate the electoral process of exchange. Regarding the rhetorical constitution of *Shrink*, we see the significance of the limits of empiricism in capturing the degree—even the actual existence—of "corruption." Yet, contrary to cases where this may compel erring on the side of the party asserting a First Amendment violation (see Chapter 7), the majority here, once more, capitulates to the state's claims.

One would have to think this is a significant function of the cognitive constitution developed in this case, wherein the author of the majority opinion volunteered during oral argument that he "assumed" improprieties, even while the evidence was at best mixed at a general, systemic level, and rather limited (to newspaper editorials, for example) at the state level, in part because—in the wake of *Buckley*—it was less "novel" to draw such inferences in the first place. That *Shrink* was constituted along these lines, and with this particular composition of elements, will be especially important for the future of state campaign finance regulation, especially in light of the Supreme Court's ruling in *Randall v. Sorrell*,[125] finding unconstitutional Vermont's scheme of contribution and expenditure restrictions and pointing to the contribution limit amounts in *Shrink* as something of a model for other states. We will consider the implications of this development in the Conclusion.

CONCLUSION

A Constitution We Are Expounding

AS WE HAVE SEEN BY NOW, the constitution of electoral speech law is a function of the contributions and confluence of its primary conceptual constituents, the rhetorical modes that facilitate its analysis and articulation, and the cognitive contours that shape the means by and manner in which the particular dimension of expression is cast before, conceived by, and communicated to the Court. Such are the *elements* that constitute this domain—set forth in global terms in Chapters 1 through 4—and that have sustained our examination of the *episodes* in which these elements are established, and through which they evolve in effecting the constitution of the whole.

Thinking in terms of constitutional elements and episodes in this manner helps us to understand why, despite their surface similarities, *Burson* and *McIntyre* led to very different outcomes. Each involved a middle-aged mother attempting to communicate with voters at the point (or in the *place*) of greatest effect: at the polling place for Rebecca Freeman and outside the school board meeting for Margaret McIntyre. Both involved political speech, the variety of expression thought to warrant the greatest protection, and thus the most rigorous ("exacting" or "strict") form of scrutiny was applied in the review of both cases. The cases were heard three years apart, and in both there were at least forty-six state laws (prohibiting such expression to some degree) that hung in the balance of the Court's ruling, though neither controversy involved an incident with any immediate threat to citizens. Both cases percolated up through their state court systems, and in both the state supreme court ruling was reversed by the U.S. Supreme Court. In the end though, Rebecca Freeman was relegated to (remain at) the 101st foot—in some cases missing an opportunity to engage voters—and Margaret McIntyre, who never intended to distribute her fliers anonymously, emerged as the judicially conceived instantiation of a right to anonymous political speech. Why?

In the same spirit, if "political conversations" were so central to the Supreme Court's vision of the exchange between petition circulators and signatories in *ACLF*, then why would the same not hold true for advocates and voters outside the polling place? In the Colorado case, "speakers" wanted to communicate with the citizenry to qualify measures for the ballot; in Tennessee, activists desired to make a final case for their candidates and causes. Obviously the environment was significant for the Court, but if the value to be preserved—"strictly" and/or "exactingly"—is that of the potential for such "conversations," then why the distinction? Or, considering the same cases, why the emphasis on the fact that the circulation of petitions represents the most economical and effective means of communicating for would-be speakers (in *ACLF* and, before that, *Meyer*), without the corollary extension of the right to pursue the most efficient manner of expression at the polls? Or, for that matter, why not extend the principle in the direction of writing a check for an amount over $1,025, if such a manner of expression is thought to be the most economical, effective, and efficient way of expressing oneself in the political arena—as it might be for wealthier individuals who spend most of their *time* making money?

Obviously every case has its own unique facts; and certainly precedent plays an important role, as do judicial politics, doctrine, and so on. But no single contribution can satisfactorily explain the variance in outcomes and orientation within this universe of cases, given its distinct nexus of free speech and electoral process values, assumptions, and directives. What was necessary was an assessment of the entire domain, so as to pursue the parallels, pause at the intersections, tease out the ties that bind, and analyze not just analogically but comparatively, and to do so with a coordinated interest in both a distillation of the whole and a more organic exploration of its especially instructive episodes. What was necessary was an understanding of the *constitution* of electoral speech law.

A CONSTITUTION WE ARE EXPOUNDING

In *McCulloch v. Maryland*, Chief Justice John Marshall famously wrote that were the Constitution to detail all its powers, the manifestations that they might take, and the means by which they might be executed, it would thus "partake of the prolixity of a legal code," could "scarcely be embraced by the human mind," and would "probably never be understood by the public." And so, he reasoned, to understand its "nature" required only that "its great outlines should be marked," allowing for deduction and inference to be carried out by succeeding generations. In sum, "We must never forget that it is a Constitution we are expounding."[1]

In the spirit of this passage, the balance of this chapter will consider how the "constitution" of electoral speech law described in this book might continue to be "expounded," as it were, in its application and extension to various issues of impending constitutional concern. Specifically, I attend first to *evaluation*, or those factors that appear most likely to shape constitutional developments in terms of the particular inclinations of members of the Roberts Court. We then turn to *expansion*, to address some possibilities for an enlargement of the electoral speech domain, and conclude with an interest in *extension*, or a particular focus on controversies presently being considered, especially regarding how far and in what directions they may reach.

Evaluation

While the increasing number of cases that are reviewed in this domain is significant unto itself, so too is the palpable agitation evident in the Court's recent rulings. While an effort to operationalize such distaste would fail to capture its flavor, the controversy leading to, and the adjudication of *McConnell v. FEC* (which went on the fast track to the Supreme Court and promptly yielded an approximately three-hundred-page ruling, including eight opinions by six different authors), is, I think, a good indication of the contentiousness of electoral speech questions on the recent Court. In sum, positions appear to be entrenched, energies run high, and on such matters the Court is, as they say, quite "hot."

One might surmise that this is simply a function of the discontentment evident in the Court's recent jurisprudence on many fronts (e.g., the commerce clause, the establishment clause, the takings clause); indeed, some scholars would suggest that this division is simply a function of the variance in the justices' ideological "attitudes."[2] But, as we saw in Chapter 4, these assumptions about how "liberals" and "conservatives" should respond to asserted electoral speech claims are, if I may be so blunt, simply wrong. Certainly ideological elements are somehow manifest in the decisions of the modern Court,[3] but such labels—at least as presently conceived[4]—are rather facile in their failure to account for the competing "speech" interests that are at stake in virtually every case in this domain.

Indeed, as we saw in Chapter 4 (recall Table 4.2), the outcomes in electoral speech cases are almost exactly the opposite of what attitudinalism predicts. Justice Thomas, for one, actually evinces the highest percentage support for the asserted speech claim, though he should show the third lowest, followed by Justice Scalia, who should be the least, not the second most, supportive of First Amendment claims. Justice Ginsburg, meanwhile, who should be the second most "supportive" of "First Amendment freedoms," comes out tied for the lowest percentage (with Justice Breyer)—lower even than former Chief Justice Rehnquist.[5] To be clear, this is not to say that various political, policy, or ideological interests do not play a role in the Court's understanding of electoral speech; it is simply to urge a renewed and unrestricted attention to the myriad forms, values, and methods that could properly be construed as "political" influences and interests. Indeed, especially in light of the influence of money in politics—and the Court's own hand in establishing this (see *Buckley v. Valeo*)—it is essential to think in broader terms and to assess the conjunctive consequences of the Court's evaluation of expression *within* elections: weighing not simply freedom of speech and democracy, but considering free speech *in* a democracy.

Justice Stevens, for example, is coded in "attitudinal" terms as at least moderately "conservative" (his score is -.5), yet he is conventionally thought of as one of the "liberals" (and possibly even the most liberal), though, you will recall from Table 4.1, when *money* is the dimension of speech calling, he rarely listens.[6] In this sense, he does not vote to uphold the *asserted* speech interest (what a "liberal" would do), meaning that he is relegated to the "conservative" camp within such a dichotomy; though anyone who has paid heed to his reasoning would realize that this is an uneasy association to make. Indeed, Stevens (like Justices Souter, Ginsburg, and Breyer) clearly "supports" *speech*, but typically finds—again, when money is the form of speech in question—that it is through one or the other (equality or custodial) marketplace conceptions that expression interests can best be pursued in the spirit of and service to democracy. There is, to be sure, some variant on the seven commandments of animalism at work here ("All forms of speech may be 'equal,' but some are more equal than others"),[7] and such distinctions are certainly more particular than the absolutist inclinations of the "conservatives" on the Court (who are now the "liberals"),[8] but an analysis that fails to take seriously the differences between an *Active Liberty* "liberal" (i.e., Breyer) and a conservative-libertarian "liberal" (e.g., Thomas)—failing to appreciate that John Dewey is not John Locke, in other words—will neglect the nuance that is necessary to understand the constitution of this body of law.

Expansion

What Figure I.1 clearly indicated is that this domain has been consistently expanding since the early years of the Burger Court and is growing at its fastest rate ever in the first two terms of the Roberts Court. Recall that the present cohort of justices reviewed two such cases in the 2005 Term, with another scheduled for oral argument as this book goes to press during the 2006 Term. And while *money* is the speech dimension that has received the most attention in recent terms (Table I.1), eight of the fifteen cases considered by the Rehnquist Court (1986–2005) actually involved novel electoral speech questions[9]—that is, they were not simply revisitations of campaign finance concerns in a new context.

"Nudge, Nudge, Wink, Wink" The above-noted case scheduled for oral argument in late April of the 2006 Term, *Federal Election Commission v. Wisconsin Right to Life* (hereafter *WRTL* II) is the second time in as many years that the justices will, in some sense, be addressing a challenge to the provision (§ 203) of the BiPartisan Campaign Finance Reform Act (BCRA, or "McCain-Feingold") that prohibits corporations from using general treasury funds to finance "electioneering communications."[10] The first case, *Wisconsin Right to Life, Inc. v. Federal Election Commission,*[11] considered whether or not the corporation could bring an as-applied challenge to section 203 of the BCRA, an appeal which the district court had rejected, but that was vacated and remanded by the U.S. Supreme Court for consideration of WRTL's claims.[12]

In an opinion joined in full by Circuit Judge David Sentelle, District Judge Richard Leon found section 203 unconstitutional as applied to the three broadcast advertisements that were intended to be run by WRTL within thirty days of Wisconsin's 2004 federal primary and sixty days of the general election that year, as well as those "materially similar ads" that the group anticipated running in the future. Thus, because of the time sensitive nature of the issue in the buildup to the 2008 presidential election (§ 203 had operative effect on December 15, 2007—or thirty days before the scheduled January 14, 2008, Iowa Caucus), the U.S. Supreme Court accepted the case to consider whether the district court erred in its finding that the statutory prohibition was unconstitutional as applied to WRTL's particular advertisements.[13]

Central to Judge Leon's ruling in the reconsideration was the inference that, by virtue of its remand, "the Supreme Court, in essence, acknowledged the possibility that certain ads (i.e., "genuine issue ads"), that are neither express advocacy nor its functional equivalent could be unconstitutionally captured by BCRA's electioneering communications definition."[14] If the ads were found to be either "express advocacy," or its "functional equivalent," then *McConnell* would be controlling and the ads could be regulated; if, however, they were deemed "genuine issue ads," then the constitutionality of the provision would depend on whether or not the government had a compelling interest for such restrictions within the relevant "black-out" periods. For Leon (and Circuit Judge Sentelle), it did not.

For one thing, while there was a "call to action" at the end of the ads, there was no mention of the previous votes of either Senator Russell Feingold or Senator Herbert Kohl; nor was there mention of Feingold's race for reelection. Moreover, and in what I would suggest is the most critical posture for this case as it reaches the Supreme Court, Judge Leon rejected the FEC's invitation to render scrutiny beyond the "face" of the ads themselves—or beyond its "four corners,"[15] as the judge put it—and to also consider their actual "intent" to affect the election. If nothing else, he reasoned, "common sense . . . dictates that requiring such prerequisites to assessing whether a given ad is a 'sham ad' and therefore regulable under BCRA's electioneering communications definition is both practically and theoretically unacceptable."[16]

In practical terms, he explained, as-applied challenges would have to be "conducted during the expedited circumstances of the closing days of a campaign when litigating contextual framework issues and expert testimony analysis is simply not workable";[17] but such a charge assumed both that subjective intent to affect the election should negate otherwise genuine issue ads *and* that the conjecture of experts could project the "likely" impact of ads in the first place.[18] That is, for Leon, the judiciary "should not be in the business or trying to read any speaker's mind," because such an inquiry was "unprecedented and not properly a part of any First Amendment analysis."[19] WRTL's advertisements, having been found not to have "intended to influence the voters' decisions," were thus exempt from consideration as to "whether the ads *in fact* would have—or potentially could have—affected Senator Feingold's reelection,"[20] and in the end were therefore *not* the functional equivalent of express advocacy.

Judge Leon also found that the government's compelling interest in regulating express advocacy did not apply in this case to genuine issue ads, because these ads avoided connecting words and images to questions of the fitness of candidates and thus were not inclined to encourage the sort of political corruption and public cynicism associated with express advocacy or issue ads of the "sham" variety.[21] Genuine issue ads might somehow still encourage or discourage (subtly or subconsciously) support for a candidate, but for the district court, there was "no evidentiary or common sense basis to believe that such facially neutral ads were *necessarily* intended to affect an election, or will *necessarily* be viewed as such," and thus "Section 201's definition [of 'electioneering communications'] as applied through section 203 to WRTL's 2004 antifilibustering issue ads is unconstitutional."[22]

We pause to consider a few points in this ruling, especially as the case will be considered by the Supreme Court. For one thing, as Judge Richard Roberts pointed out in dissent in this case, in *McConnell* the Supreme Court—when evaluating whether section 201 was overly broad in its definition of "electioneering communications"—had "specifically examined both the purpose of the ads before it as well as their impact on the relevant election."[23] Thus, as Roberts put it, a "purpose-and effect-based inquiry" was necessary to determine if WRTL's ads were genuine or not, because as the Court had explained in *McConnell*, the "presence or absence of magic words cannot meaningfully distinguish electioneering speech from a true issue ad."[24] One would expect this to be a central issue in the high Court's consideration of this matter, though the replacements of Chief Justice Roberts (for Chief Justice Rehnquist) and Justice Alito (for Justice O'Connor) make it hard to predict just how much precedential force *McConnell* will muster on this front.

But in terms that have less to do with adherence to precedent and more to do with signals, note that the district court's ruling is suffuse with a sentiment that I will refer to—with apologies to Monty Python—as a "nudge, nudge, wink, wink" attitude toward campaign finance regulation and the realities of American politics.[25] The suggestion here is that the proper evaluative approach must limit itself to the literal words of the advertisement, with no consideration of the context surrounding the ad (i.e., the contentiousness of the filibuster issue that summer), or the subtext that may well speak volumes without an utterance. In this vein, Judge Leon's inferential lens—what he referred to as "the untutored viewer's eye"[26]—is significant for symbolic and substantive reasons, because in some sense it renders the constitutional question subject to what those "untutored" in politics might glean from seeing or hearing the broadcast.

This is considerably different than a "reasonable man" standard, for example—assuming prudence, diligence, and the ability to use *reason*—in that its analytical point of reference would be the "man" whose "eyes" remain "untutored," or to put the matter differently an individual apparently lacking in political skepticism and sensibilities. For example, compare this assessment to that of District Judge Perry (see Chapter 8), who reasoned that even for one "unschooled in politics," no great "deductive leap" was necessary to conclude that large contributions could lead to the perception of corruption in the political process.[27] This is *not* an example of "aspirationalism" in action (see Chapter 3), because that approach understands the negative *possibilities* of politics but aspires to the notion that the people and the process can surmount such challenges. Judge Leon's metaphor suggests something quite different.

Whether or not it would take a "tutored" eye to see what was at work in these ads (e.g., the fact that both senators were Democrats from a "blue" state, where it would be natural to assume that they at least opposed the nominees and most likely supported the filibuster), there is the separate issue of the coordination of media (and messages) ever more common as broadcast ads have become more regulated. In this case, WRTL used its advertisement to direct listeners and viewers to a Web site, created by the group, which featured "e-alerts" critical of Senator Feingold on the filibuster issue.[28] Such a maneuver—sending potentially regulable speech "off-shore," if you will (to the Internet), or alternatively "laundering" it back from the Web to the media of radio or television—would seem to indicate that the "broadcast" prong of the coordination was something of a ruse (a Trojan Horse?) to gain access to the airwaves during the black-out period with what would effectively be at least a *semi*-"sham" ad. Certainly Judge Leon could sincerely believe that WRTL's ads were "genuine" in their "issue" orientation, but this opinion also feels like an act of judicial civil disobedience, perhaps owing to a frustration with the entire regulatory enterprise of campaign finance—along the lines of that expressed by Justices Kennedy, Thomas, and Scalia in *Shrink*. But for whatever reason, it is hard to take seriously the assertion—let the "nudging" and "winking" begin—that the advertisements were not necessarily intended to communicate the "magic words" in code because, technically, insinuation and innuendo (however obvious their aims might be, or *should* be) were not tantamount to incantation.

Cyber Speech Voting over the Internet, should it ever catch on, will also have an important effect on electoral speech law, if for no other reason than that advocates—like Rebecca Burson and all those small, underfinanced campaigns she represents—will have even less of an opportunity to reach voters physically. Certainly, blogs have the capacity to function something like an agora, but in a critical sense they do not tend to be the "commons" that exists at the polling place, for example, because private choice drives individuals to one or another Web site, but *everyone* must (or everyone used to have to) proceed to the polls to vote. If more voting does shift to the Internet, will advocacy groups find ways to insinuate themselves into the Web paths of would-be voters? Will states be compelled to provide cyber-"space" for various parties, and allow for the equivalent of stickers, signs, pens, and sample ballots to appear on one's computer screen?

The Internet is poised to shape the future of electoral speech law in other ways as well. For example, political expression in the form of online petitions, automatic e-mail barrages to legislators, and so on, will likely draw upon the reasoning of *McIntyre* as officials attempt to enforce accountability in a world where "pamphleteering" can span the world in seconds. In the same spirit, the process of petition circulation is almost sure to be affected by technologies yet unrealized—those that may seek to recreate (or relocate) the grounds of "political conversation" engaged in between advocates and signatories. Must a "conversation" entail the *physical* presence of both parties, or may *virtual* alternatives present themselves as citizens and interests seek new ways to meet state thresholds? And with the anticipated ease that this would present in terms of reaching citizens all over the state, would not the government be expected to raise the bar in correspondence with the increased ease in circulation? That is, the sentiment of officials in states that allow for direct democracy seems to be that it is *supposed* to be difficult to make a law (or pass a constitutional amendment)—and thus, if technology simplifies things too much, will the state be inclined (or compelled) to institute new obstacles?

And with such cyber-politics in mind, one question that is almost certain to bear on electoral speech jurisprudence in the next generation is whether or not the increasing accessibility of the Internet makes resource distribution *more* or *less* of an issue in electoral speech jurisprudence. With more of the citizenry "wired," in other words—and with the increasing significance of this medium to the exchange of ideas and the flexing of political-coalitional muscle (e.g., networked organizations engaging in carefully orchestrated e-mail campaigns), it could be that money—though it will never be *un*important in American politics—might perhaps be displaced, or at least reconfigured, by the potential for "influence" literally at the fingertips of citizens with laptops and a lot to say.

"Deceptive Practices" *Burson*, if it stands for the principle that voters warrant protection from the (potentially) nefarious "speech" of others, has the potential to reach beyond the polling place. Consider, for example, the

bill introduced into the 110th Congress by Senators Barack Obama and Charles Schumer, entitled the "Deceptive Practices and Voter Intimidation Prevention Act of 2007."[29] Based on congressional findings that the "unimpeded exercise" of the right to vote is "essential to the functioning of our democracy," and intended to address "newer tactics aimed at suppressing voter turnout," including "the dissemination of false information intended to prevent voters from casting their ballots, intimidate the electorate, and undermine the integrity of the electoral process,"[30] the act seeks to hold accountable, through civil and criminal penalties, anyone who "seeks to keep voters away from the polls, confuse the electorate, and undermine the integrity of the electoral process by providing false information."[31]

Relying explicitly on *Burson* and the notion that government has a compelling interest in protecting both voters and the political process, the act also deflects the anticipated First Amendment retort, asserting in its fifteenth finding that the "First Amendment does not preclude the regulation of false speech, even if it is political in nature," with support for this claim drawn from the U.S. Supreme Court's assertion in *Garrison v. Louisiana* that the "use of the known lie as a tool is at once at odds with the premises of democratic government and with the orderly manner in which economic, social, or political change is to be effected"—which is to say, in essence, that "knowingly false statement[s] and the false statement made with reckless disregard of the truth, do not enjoy constitutional protection."[32]

As noted in the act's various findings, minorities (e.g., African Americans, Native Americans, and immigrants) have been the victims of some of the most notorious recent incidents whereby voters have received postcards providing false information about eligibility, where voters were turned away if they could not provide photo identification, where fliers were distributed that warned voters that they could be imprisoned if found guilty of even minor traffic violations, and where voters received automated phone messages telling them they were ineligible to vote and suggesting criminal penalties if they tried to cast a ballot on election day.[33] Certainly the above examples are troubling reminders of the machinations possible in American politics; and so it makes sense that the state would assert its proprietary authority to address such problems—in the same way and for the same reason that it might stake out a buffer zone on the grounds of the polling place, for example.

Whether or not the act will pass is unclear as this book goes to press—and whether or not it would be deemed constitutional by the present cohort on the Court is equally uncertain. The only current justices who sat on the *Burson* Court are Scalia, Kennedy, Stevens, and Souter (Thomas had yet to be confirmed), though the latter two were dissenters, while the former two each wrote separate concurring opinions distancing themselves to some degree from Justice Blackmun's plurality opinion. Should the act pass and face review, it may be significant that a violation requires first and foremost that a person "*know*[s] such information [e.g., a voter's eligibility, the time, place, or manner of an election, or a candidate's party affiliation] to be *false*,"[34] suggesting a fairly high burden of proof to be met at trial and paralleling in certain ways the legal standard for libel cases—a correlation suggested as well by the fact that *Garrison* (noted above and central to the rationale for the act) was announced on the same day as *New York Times v. Sullivan*,[35] the seminal freedom of the press case establishing the "actual malice" standard, or requiring (for purposes of proving defamation) that a statement was *known* to be false or that there was demonstrably "reckless disregard" for whether the statement was false or not.

Extension

Recall that campaign finance cases represent the modal dimension of speech (i.e., money) within this domain, comprising eighteen of the thirty-nine cases considered in this study, or nearly half of the entire body (see Table I.1). Like the money that finds its way into politics, campaign finance cases keep coming back to the Court and one would not expect that to change given the contentiousness in the resolution of these cases and considering that the 2008 presidential election is certain to be the most expensive in history (with 2012 sure to surpass that record, of course). That said, the Court's most recent foray, *Randall v. Sorrell*, suggests some important prospects and possibilities for the future of campaign finance.

I Know It When I See It Justice Potter Stewart famously shrugged at the Court's repeated attempts to define "hard core pornography" in the 1960s and conceded that while descriptive precision might not be possible, he "knew it when he saw it."[36] One sees something like this in the Court's ruling in *Sorrell*, involving a challenge to Vermont's Act 64, which imposed stringent limits on both the amount that candidates for state office may spend on their campaigns and the amount that various interests (parties, individuals, organizations) may contribute to those campaigns. As Justice Breyer wrote for the Court, in addressing the "contributions" component of the act, some "lower bound" must exist for such limits—in light of the "constitutional risks to the democratic electoral process"—and thus the rationale for preserving the integrity of elections did "not simply mean 'the lower the limit, the better.'"[37] Of course, where that "bound" might be located—and *how* one might justify that placement in some principled manner—is the rub. Justice Thomas has previously stressed that courts have no "yardstick" for making such determinations (see Chapter 8); and while Justice Breyer would likely agree to this in principle (though he would still prefer to defer to the legislature, for the most part), in *this* case he seems to suggest that the Court—while obviously informed by briefs, the trial record, oral argument, and so on—could still essentially "eye-ball" the amounts and divine from this that the state's scheme was amiss.

One of the reasons that the state's contribution limits could be "seen" as unconstitutionally low in this case was that they were the lowest in the nation,[38] "substantially lower,"[39] in fact, than those upheld in *Nixon v. Shrink Missouri Government PAC*.[40] (Indeed, they were not even indexed for inflation, as was the case with the limits in *Shrink*, meaning that the distance between Vermont and other states would only increase over time.) Two observations can be made about this. First, the Missouri limits—themselves rather imprecisely constructed (recall the discussion in Chapter 8)—were the benchmark used by Justice Breyer in evaluating the Vermont scheme and appear now to be the unannounced model for other states interested in at least regulating contributions to candidates for state office. (Restrictions on expenditures appear to be off-limits in light of *Sorrell*—and, before that, *Buckley*.) Second, in light of the first point, one could imagine state campaign finance *regulation* beginning to portray the typical effects of *de*regulation, in that a "race" to what was (pre-*Sorrell*) the "middle," would now be the more traditional "race to the bottom," as Missouri's spot in the rankings, while actually only near the bottom, appears to be effectively the new "bottom" (or floor), given the suspicion cast upon the constitutionality of those schemes in states falling in between the unconstitutional amounts in Vermont and their constitutional counterparts in Missouri.[41] The relativity of all this was not lost on Justice Thomas, who observed in his concurrence (in judgment) that "the relative limits of other States cannot be the key factor, for such considerations are nothing more than a moving target."[42]

Another function of the "it" that the Court "saw" in this case involves the threshold—albeit rather undertheorized—for determining whether pluralistic political contests (i.e., competition) are possible under financial constraints. As he reasoned for the Court, Breyer explained that the critical question "concerns not simply the *average* effect of contribution limits on fundraising but, more importantly, the ability of a candidate running against an incumbent officeholder to mount an *effective* challenge."[43] Thus, he continued in this seemingly structuralist vein, attention to average races was much less relevant than attention to *competitive* races because the latter cost much more money to muster. Considering the amounts in question, then, and the evidence provided by the petitioner, Breyer concluded that the effect was to "raise a reasonable inference that the contribution limits are so low that they may pose a significant obstacle to candidates in competitive elections."[44] Indeed, he went on to point out (and this may be one of the few times pastries have been alluded to in a Supreme Court opinion), the limits were so low—and granting of no exceptions—that a volunteer "who offers a campaign the use of her house along with coffee and doughnuts for a few dozen neighbors to meet the candidate" a few times during the campaign would find that she was soon over the limit.[45]

Which is to take us to one final question of significance raised by *Sorrell*: what is the relationship between contribution limits and campaign participation? Recall from Chapter 8 that in *Shrink* the Court accepted the state's argument that the limits were high enough to allow for financial participation by the wealthy, but not so high as to foreclose the sort of "in kind" contributions in the form of stuffing envelopes, "get out the vote" efforts, or various other man-powered versions of participation for those of more modest means. In short, the roughly $1,000 limit for contributions to candidates for statewide office was not beyond being "matched" by the will of organized and energized citizens. But the limits in *Sorrell*, by contrast, presented something very different in that they were so low that they hampered—rather than encouraged—participation because, as noted above, they ironically impeded precisely the sort of campaign activities (e.g., gatherings for coffee and donuts) that those giving primarily of their time, energy, and skills might be inclined to pursue, because even contributions of this variety still tend to require some initial (financial) "ante" to render themselves useful to a campaign. In other words, someone still has to buy the envelopes to be stuffed and someone has to buy dinner for the college students knocking on doors to "get out the vote."

Et Tu, Buckley? While the Court's consideration of *Shrink* was shielded in some sense by *Buckley* (in that finding the state limits unconstitutional would seem to undermine the federal equivalents to which they were pegged),[46] the ruling in *Sorrell* had the effect of opening another front in the assault on the paradigm, this time in the form of Justice Stevens's dissent. It is quite significant that Chief Justice Roberts (the replacement for Rehnquist, who had been the only recent justice to have been a part of the consideration of *Buckley*) was the only justice to join *in full* Justice Breyer's opinion for the Court in *Sorrell*. Breyer (and, by extension, Roberts), reasoned that overruling *Buckley* would "dramatically undermine this reliance on our settled precedent."[47]

Meanwhile, Justice Alito (the replacement for O'Connor), while joining in most of Breyer's opinion, conspicuously resisted sections II-B-1 and II-B-2 (involving the Court's "decline" of the "respondents' invitation to reconsider *Buckley*"), stressing instead that whether or not *Buckley* should be reexamined "in whole or in part," the respondents had not set forth that argument with sufficient care and thus it was, for Alito, "unnecessary to reach the issue."[48] Justices Ginsburg and Souter, for their part, have routinely relied on *Buckley* as the standard for campaign finance cases and so we would have to count this as four votes in its favor (Breyer, Roberts, Souter, and Ginsburg) and one vote for both adopting an approach informed by *Buckley*, and also avoiding the award of any stamp of approval (Alito).

But on the other side of the equation, the discontent is growing. Justices Thomas, Kennedy, and Scalia have repeatedly stressed their inclination to overturn *Buckley*—and, as of *Sorrell*, so too has Justice Stevens. To be sure, Stevens has for some time insisted that money is "conduct," not "speech"; but in *Sorrell* he adopted the language and reasoning of Justice White to call for *Buckley* to be overturned—at least with regard to its protection for unlimited individual expenditures—which is, of course, the key. Because *Buckley* distinguished between contributions and expenditures, "overturning" it for one may not be overturning it for another; that is, while Justices Thomas, Kennedy, and Scalia intend to remove the government from the regulation of campaign finance entirely (except for disclosure requirements, one would think), Justice Stevens's dissatisfaction with the current state of campaign finance leads him to reverse *Buckley* in the other direction: allowing for even greater regulation of the role of money in politics, particularly with regard to allowing for caps on expenditures as a way of encouraging more emphasis on "speech" of the vocal, as opposed to the checkbook variety.[49]

What much of this is building toward is perhaps obvious, but still worth stating: as of early 2007, the next appointment to the Supreme Court will have a profound influence on the future of electoral speech law—how, when, where, and in what way its "constitution" will be "expounded." But another appointment by George W. Bush may not necessarily change all that much. Indeed, Chief Justice Roberts appears to be in the camp for upholding *Buckley* (if one accepts as evidence of this his joining of Breyer's opinion in *Sorrell*), and Justice Alito is on record with something of a "no comment" on the matter (or, in the parlance of our time: "Don't go there!"), though both were appointed by Bush. Certainly part of this is due to the fact that, relative to *Roe v. Wade*, for example, campaign finance cases do not figure as prominently into judiciary committee hearings, and thus the matter gets some cover by virtue of the attention directed toward more hot-button Supreme Court precedents (or "super"-precedents). But if a movement to deregulate the entire money-as-speech dimension begins to build—perhaps on the heels of the U.S. Supreme Court's forthcoming decision in *WRTL* II—and if a Republican wins the White House in 2008, then *Buckley* may be in jeopardy.

CONCLUSION

There is an acknowledged immodesty—even "chutzpah," depending on one's cultural geography—in any study purporting to explain "*the* constitution" of *anything*, let alone something as complicated as an entire body of law. My hope is that scholars will have found this book valuable, in terms of its questions, methods, arguments, and ambitions. But it is also my hope that concerned citizens will find value in this work—dense and abstract as it may be in places (ironically, with the "prolixity of a . . ."), but still attentive to what are, if you will, the human elements and real life implications realized in the four case-study explorations. Indeed, what this investigation of elements and episodes has demonstrated (to the author as much as the reader, I hope) is just how profoundly significant electoral speech law is to the organization and operations of American politics—structuring the rules of the game, surveying the field of play, setting the length of quarters, and establishing the salary caps—which is to emphasize in the end precisely *why* its constitution warrants expounding.

Reference Matter

APPENDIX

Interview Methods and Protocol

BECAUSE OF MY INTEREST in understanding how cases were constituted—that is, how they came to be what they were in the end, how they changed along the way, and what the factors and forces were that influenced these developments—I arranged to conduct interviews with those individuals who figured prominently in each of the four case studies, from the roots of the controversy through the U.S. Supreme Court's review of the case. By scrutinizing briefs, newspaper articles, reports, lower court opinions, and various other archival sources, I was able to populate a list of those eight to twelve individuals central to the constitution of each case. I wrote to each person, following up with phone calls, and eventually scheduled interviews (mostly on-site and in person, though a few were conducted by phone) with thirty-three people during the period of May 28–July 6, 2001.

I traveled first to Ohio, then to Tennessee, then to Missouri, and finished with Colorado. Being in the "field" in this sense allowed me to concretize many of the particular problems discussed in the cases and afforded me, as well, the opportunity to add another nine individuals to my schedule (referred, as I was, by my original sources—for a grand total of forty-two). Several of these people were subjects that I had attempted to contact, unsuccessfully, and thus as with many research methods, there was some measure of serendipity in just "hanging around," as some practitioners of qualitative methods are inclined to say. Most interviews lasted about an hour and a half, with the shortest taking only thirty minutes and the longest going past the three-hour mark. With a few exceptions (where it seemed imprudent or where chaos reigned—such as in a few judicial chambers!), I audiotaped the interview and then immediately transcribed it. When taping was not an option, I took copious notes and drafted a report on the interview immediately thereafter. These transcriptions and reconstructions were essential to my analysis of the interview data, particularly in teasing out themes in various arguments and the strategic approaches to each case before the Supreme Court.

I have not included the names of those interviewed, choosing instead to refer to them as "state officials," "judges," "election officials," "activists," "advocates," "counsel," and so on. In those passages where the above are antecedents, I have opted for "she" as the third-person pronoun. In the notes I refer to them by number (#1–42). Certainly each individual interviewed was—by her or his involvement in this case or by her or his career choice—a "public figure," but I have chosen to preserve anonymity for purposes of candor and in the interest of discretion. Suffice to say that those I spoke with are people one would need to speak with to understand the nuances of these cases. I am grateful to each of them for sharing their time and insights.

Notes

PREFACE

1. Wilson Carey McWilliams, *The Idea of Fraternity in America* (Berkeley and Los Angeles: University of California Press, 1973), ix. Moreover, he noted in a characteristically self-deprecatory tone, "This book began as a doctoral dissertation, which is warning enough for the experienced. To the usual faults of dissertations I have added other defects, nurtured in the intervening years and perfected by revision." His assessment of the manner by which problems are "perfected" in the transformation from dissertation to book manuscript is spot-on; but, of course, as two generations of admirers would attest, his "revisions" were—and will remain—unmatched. His candor, wit, wisdom, and presence are surely missed—though, thankfully, his truth is marching on.

INTRODUCTION: THE CONSTITUTION OF ELECTORAL SPEECH LAW

1. See *Bush v. Gore*, 531 U.S. 98 (2000).

2. See, e.g., Richard Posner, "Florida 2000: A Legal and Statistical Analysis of the Deadlock and the Ensuing Litigation," *Supreme Court Review* (Chicago: University of Chicago Press, 2001), 1–60; and Posner, *Breaking the Deadlock: The 2000 Election, the Constitution, and the Courts* (Princeton, N.J.: Princeton University Press, 2001). Cf. Richard Hasen, "A 'Tincture of Justice': Judge Posner's Failed Rehabilitation of *Bush v. Gore*," *Texas Law Review* 80 (2001): 137–54.

3. *Bush*, 109 (per curiam) ("Our consideration is limited to the present circumstances, for the problem of equal protection in election processes generally presents many complexities").

4. The notion of a "political thicket"—or a field of inquiry and determination into which courts should not intrude—was famously articulated by Justice Felix Frankfurter in *Colegrove v. Green*, 328 U.S. 549, 552–53, 556 (1946) (noting that while the Court was being asked to revise the state's congressional representative districts "in order to reflect great changes," "no court can affirmatively re-map the Illinois districts so as to bring them more in conformity with the standards of fairness for a representative system"; and concluding: "To sustain this action would cut very deep into the very being of Congress. Courts ought not to enter this political thicket").

5. A necessarily abbreviated listing of these works would include Bruce Ackerman, ed., *"Bush v. Gore": The Question of Legitimacy* (New Haven, Conn.: Yale University Press, 2002); Jack M. Balkin, "*Bush v. Gore* and the Line Between Law and Politics," *Yale Law Journal* 110 (June 2001): 1407; Howard Gillman, *The Votes That Counted: How the Court Decided the 2000 Presidential Election* (Chicago: University of Chicago Press, 2001); Samuel Issacharoff, Pamela Karlan, and Richard Pildes, eds., *When Elections Go Bad: The Law of Democracy and the Presidential Election of 2000*, 2nd ed. (New York:

Foundation Press, 2001); and Cass Sunstein and Richard Epstein, eds., *The Vote: Bush, Gore, and the Supreme Court* (Chicago: University of Chicago Press, 2001).

6. On the impact of the decision, at least with respect to public opinion, see Elizabeth Garrett, "The Impact of *Bush v. Gore* on Future Democratic Politics," and Milton Heumann and Lance Cassak, "The Supreme Court and *Bush v. Gore*: Resolving Electoral Disputes in a Democracy," in *The Future of American Democratic Politics: Principles and Practices*, ed. Gerald Pomper and Marc Weiner (New Brunswick, N.J.: Rutgers University Press, 2003), 141, 161.

7. See, e.g., Robert G. Dixon, Jr., *Democratic Representation: Reapportionment in Law and Politics* (New York: Oxford University Press, 1968); and Dixon, "The Warren Court Crusade for the Holy Grail of 'One Man-One Vote,'" *Supreme Court Review* (Chicago: University of Chicago Press, 1969), 219–70.

8. See, e.g., John Aldrich, *Why Parties?* (Chicago: University of Chicago Press, 1995).

9. See, e.g., Richard Franklin Bensel, *The American Ballot Box in the Mid-Nineteenth Century* (New York: Cambridge University Press, 2005).

10. See, e.g., Keith J. Bybee, *Mistaken Identity: The Supreme Court and the Politics of Minority Representation* (Princeton, N.J.: Princeton University Press, 1998).

11. See, e.g., Douglas J. Amy, *Real Choices/New Voices: The Case for Proportional Representation Elections in the United States* (New York: Columbia University Press, 1993).

12. See, e.g., Richard Hasen, *The Supreme Court and Election Law: Judging Equality from* Baker v. Carr *to* Bush v. Gore (New York: New York University Press, 2003).

13. Nancy Maveety, *Representation Rights and the Burger Years* (Ann Arbor: University of Michigan Press, 1991), 221.

14. See, e.g., Ward E. Y. Elliot, *The Rise of Guardian Democracy: The Supreme Court's Role in Voting Rights Disputes, 1845–1969* (Cambridge, Mass.: Harvard University Press, 1974).

15. *Monitor Patriot Co. v. Roy*, 401 U.S. 265, 272 (1971).

16. See, e.g., *Mills v. Alabama*, 384 U.S. 214, 218 (1966) ("Whatever differences may exist about interpretations of the First Amendment, there is practically universal agreement that a major purpose of that Amendment was to protect the *free discussion of governmental affairs*," which "of course includes discussions of candidates, structures and forms of government, the manner in which government is operated or should be operated, and all such matters relating to political processes [emphasis added]").

17. *Reynolds v. Sims*, 377 U.S. 533, 562 (1964).

18. See, e.g., *Storer v. Brown*, 415 U.S. 724, 730 (1974) (stressing that "as a practical matter, there must be a substantial regulation of elections if they are to be fair and honest and if some sort of order, rather than chaos, is to accompany the democratic processes").

19. See *Brown v. Hartlage*, 456 U.S. 45, 52 (1982) ("Just as a state may take steps to ensure that its governing political institutions and officials properly discharge public responsibilities and maintain public trust and confidence, a State has a legitimate interest in upholding the integrity of the electoral process itself"); and *Timmons v. Twin Cities Area New Party*, 520 U.S. 351, 364–65 (1997) ("States certainly have an interest in protecting the integrity, fairness, and efficiency of their ballots and election processes as means for electing public officials").

20. See, e.g., the Reapportionment cases generally (*Baker v. Carr*, 369 U.S. 186 [1962], *Reynolds v. Sims*, 377 U.S. 533 [1964], etc.) (aggregating to the constitutional equation of "one person" and "one vote" for purposes of representation), but also the Court's supervision of party nominating practices in the "White Primary" cases (e.g., *Nixon v. Herndon*, 273 U.S. 536 [1927], *Smith v. Allwright*, 321 U.S. 649 [1944], and *Terry v. Adams*, 345 U.S. 461 [1953]).

21. James Farr, "Understanding Conceptual Change Politically," in *Political Innovation and Conceptual Change*, ed. Terence Ball, James Farr, and Russell Hanson (New York: Cambridge University Press, 1989), 29.

22. To more vividly portray the particularly constitutive significance of election law, contrast a statute governing, for example campaign contributions with a *non*election law such as the "Violence Against Women Act." In reviewing the latter, if the justices deem the law or some part of it to be unconstitutional, as a five-member majority did in *U.S. v. Morrison*, 529 U.S. 598 (2000) (finding that Congress lacked authority under the Commerce Clause or Section 5 of the Fourteenth Amendment to provide federal civil remedies for victims of gender-motivated violence), it is invalidated—allowing the legislature to perhaps consider an alternative constitutional basis—though, significantly, there is no *necessary* impact on social or political institutions themselves or the process by which these institutions are designed and populated.

By contrast, when reviewing an election law, the Supreme Court's evaluation has an inherent and immediate influence on the nature of campaigns and elections, thus influencing who runs, how they run, who supports them (and how), who wins office, and ultimately who is put in the position to create, execute, and, at least in the thirty-nine states that elect their judges, review laws in the first place.

23. On the power of law to "constitute" institutions—or, in this case, ideals and identities—see Rogers Smith, *Civic Ideals* (New Haven, Conn.: Yale University Press, 1997), 31 (noting that citizenship laws "literally constitute—they create with legal words—a collective civic identity," and "proclaim the existence of a political 'people,'" in the sense that they "designate who those persons are as a people, in ways that often become integral to individuals' senses of personal identity as well").

24. While *constitutes* is the more apt verb for the purposes of this project, my understanding of these processes, phenomena, and outcomes is influenced by the concept of *structure* as that term is used in both the nominative and transitive verbal sense in sociology and related fields. See, e.g., William Sewell, Jr., "A Theory of Structure: Duality, Agency, and Transformation," *American Journal of Sociology* 91 (1992): 2 ("Whatever aspect of social life we designate as structure is posited as 'structuring' some other aspect of social existence—whether it is class that structures politics, gender that structures employment opportunities, rhetorical conventions that structure texts or utterances, or modes of production that structure social formations").

25. Samuel Issacharoff, Richard Pildes, and Pamela Karlan, *The Law of Democracy: Legal Structure of the Political Process* (Westbury, NY: Foundation Press, 1998), 1. See also, Samuel Issacharoff and Richard Pildes, "Politics as Markets: Partisan Lockups of the Democratic Process," *Stanford Law Review* 50 (February 1998): 644 ("The democratic politics we experience is not an autonomous realm of parties, public opinion, and elections, but a product of specific institutional structures and legal rules. Democracy is as much the creation of these structures as it is an organic expression of any preexistent 'popular will'").

26. For other works stressing the underappreciated structural significance of election laws and the constitutive consequences of courts' constructions of these statutes, see, e.g., Douglas Rae, *The Political Consequences of Electoral Laws* (New Haven, Conn.: Yale University Press, 1971) (focusing on how election laws shape nations' political party systems and concluding that such laws work to the advantage of strong parties and to the disadvantage of weak ones); Bernard Grofman and Arend Lijphart, eds., *Electoral Laws and Their Political Consequences* (New York: Agathon, 1986), 15 (stressing that "institutions can constrain and structure political choices in a fundamental way"); David Ryden, *Representation in Crisis* (Albany: State University of New York Press, 1996) (focusing on the fact that "political parties provide a set of structures that are integral to the attainment of effective representation," but lamenting the fact that "they are consistently overlooked or disparaged by the Court"); Robert Dudley and Alan Gitelson, *American Elections: The Rules Matter* (Boston: Longman, 2001) (analyzing the election of 2000 through institutional lenses); Louis Massicotte et al., *Establishing the Rules of the Game* (Toronto: University of Toronto Press, 2004) (providing a comparative analysis of voting rights, rules, theories, and traditions); Matthew Streb, ed., *Law and Election Politics: The Rules of the Game* (Boulder, Colo.: Lynne Rienner, 2004) (providing essays emphasizing the significance of particular laws and court rulings for the operations of electoral politics); and Pippa Norris, *Electoral Engineering: Voting Rules and Political Behavior* (New York: Cambridge University Press, 2004) (offering comparative research linking electoral systems to political strategies).

27. David Ryden, ed., *The U.S. Supreme Court and the Electoral Process* (Washington, D.C.: Georgetown University Press, 1999), 1–2, 267–84 (discussing the many ways in which the U.S. Supreme Court structures the "rules of the game" of electoral politics, including cases dealing with the nature and organization of primaries, ballot access, the actions and structure of parties, the concepts of representation and association, etc.).

28. Ibid., 2.

29. See ibid., 5, 171 ("The Supreme Court often lacks the requisite theoretical footing in which to anchor its decisions," because "its decisions rely on contradictory assumptions about the workings of politics, and they often work at cross-purposes" and on occasion have "serious deleterious consequences for practical politics").

30. See Paul S. Edwards and Nelson W. Polsby, "The Judicial Regulation of Political Processes: In Praise of Multiple Criteria," *Yale Law and Policy Review* 9, no. 2 (Spring–Summer 1991): 193 ("There is no theoretical consensus regarding electoral structures from which to derive a single principle or criterion for regulating elections").

31. See Samuel Issacharoff, "Oversight of Regulated Political Markets," *Harvard Journal of Law and Public Policy* 24 (Fall 2000): 100 ("Without inquiring into the robustness of democratic competition, the Court does not have the tools to assess the regulatory structure that must inevitably accompany democratic politics").

32. See Bradley Smith, "Faulty Assumptions and Undemocratic Consequences of Campaign Finance Reform," *Yale Law Journal* 105 (1996): 1049.

33. See Pamela Karlan, "Just Politics? Five Not So Easy Pieces of the 1995 Term," *Houston Law Review* 34 (1997): 313 (urging the Court to be more "self conscious about the extent to which its decisions in fact depend on an *unexamined* political theory—a theory that sometimes ignores history and community in favor of an abstract individualism that entrenches existing distributions of power even as it purports to make us free [emphasis added]").

34. See Daniel Lowenstein, "The Supreme Court Has No Theory of Politics—And Be Thankful for Small Favors," in *U.S. Supreme Court and the Electoral Process*, ed. Ryden, 245–66, 264 (arguing, as the title would suggest, that the Supreme Court "should not select a political theory and impose it on the nation any more than it should impose an economic theory").

35. See *Lucas v. Forty-Fourth General Assembly of the State of Colorado*, 377 U.S. 713, 748–49 (1964) (Justice Potter Stewart, dissenting) (asserting that he could not "join in the fabrication of a constitutional mandate which imports and forever freezes one theory of political thought into our Constitution . . .").

36. *Hartlage*, 52–53.

37. My attention to "elements" draws upon the conceptualization of Walter Murphy who explicated those that might comprise "judicial strategy," as well as the notion of "vectors," which Michael Kent Curtis has suggested can shape our understanding of the development of freedom of speech outside the courts. See *Elements of Judicial Strategy* (Chicago: University of Chicago Press, 1964) and *Free Speech, "The People's Darling Privilege"* (Durham, N.C.: Duke University Press, 2000), 15.

38. See *Luther v. Borden*, 48 U.S. (7 How.) 1 (1849).

39. As this book goes to press, one additional case, *Federal Election Commission v. Wisconsin Right to Life* (*WRTL* II) has not yet been decided.

40. 106 U.S. 371 (1882) (upholding a federal statute that prohibited all executive officers and employees of the United States not appointed by the president with "advice and consent" of the Senate from "requesting, giving to, or receiving from, any other officer or employee of the government, any money or property or other thing of value for *political purposes* . . . [emphasis added]"). While the language in the statute under review in *Curtis* suggests a possible application to political campaigns, this does not seem to have been the situation according to the facts of this case.

41. 290 U.S. 534 (1934) (finding it within the power of Congress to pass the Federal Corrupt Practices Act of 1925, establishing a series of regulations to be enforced against political committees accepting contributions and making expenditures for the purpose of influencing the election of presidential or vice-presidential electors in two or more states). *Burroughs* is not included in my review, because while it does deal with "political money," as it were—which, forty years later, *would be* construed as "speech"—this particular case dealt with an Article II challenge to the power of the federal government to set such terms regarding the "appointment" of electors.

42. 347 U.S. 612 (1954) (finding the disclosure provisions of the Federal Lobbying Act to be neither unconstitutionally vague, nor a violation of the freedoms of speech, press, or petition). *Harriss* involved federal regulations on money in politics, but it was directed specifically at lobbying and direct efforts to influence *legislation*, as opposed to elections.

43. 407 U.S. 385 (1972) (finding that convictions at the District Court level for conspiracy to violate 18 USCS 610—essentially regarding the required or voluntary nature of contributions to a union's political fund—were based on erroneous jury instructions). *Pipefitters* was not included within the domain of electoral speech cases for at least three reasons: (1) the Court focuses exclusively on the statutory interpretation of USCS 610 (i.e., Does it also imply voluntary contributions?) and the case record (i.e., jury instructions, facts) from the lower court and does *not* reach the question of whether or not the provision offends the federal constitution; (2) nor is the Court even *asked* to consider the constitutional

questions that may be posed by such legislation; it is simply asked to find that the law does not apply to the facts of this case; (3) given the year (1972) and the fact that this case comes pre-*Buckley*, we do not as of yet even have what might be the *assumed* constitutional linkage: the equation of money to speech.

44. 418 U.S. 241 (1974) (finding unconstitutional Florida's "right of reply" law granting political candidates a right to equal space to reply to criticism made by a newspaper). Clearly, a case involving the compulsion of a newspaper to "speak" in print implicates the First Amendment, but the first line of Chief Justice Burger's opinion for the Court gives some sense for why this case was not included: "The issue in this case is whether a state statute granting a political candidate a right to equal space to reply to criticism and attacks on his record by a newspaper *violates the guarantees of a free press* [emphasis added]." *Tornillo*, 243.

45. 459 U.S. 87, 91–92 (1982) (involving a small political party challenging the constitutionality of the disclosure provisions of an Ohio statute requiring that all candidates file a statement identifying their contributors and each recipient of allocated campaign funds, as well as the disclosure of the object of each purpose). As Justice Marshall explained for the Court in the first lines of reasoning following the description of the facts, "The Constitution protects against the compelled disclosure of political *associations* and beliefs. Such disclosures 'can seriously infringe on privacy of *association* and belief guaranteed by the First Amendment.' . . . [citations omitted; emphasis added]."

By contrast, *Eu v. San Francisco Democratic Committee*, 489 U.S. 214 (1989) *was* included because, as the Court announced in its ruling, the primary holding was that the provision of the California Elections Code calling for a ban on primary endorsements violated the First Amendment by "preventing a party's governing body from *stating* whether a candidate adheres to the party's tenets or whether party officials believe that the candidate is qualified for the position sought," and thus "directly hampers the party's ability to *spread its message* and hamstrings voters seeking to inform themselves about the candidates and issues, and thereby burdens the core right to *free political speech* of the party and its members." *Eu*, 223 (emphasis added).

46. *The Supreme Court and Election Law*, 1.

47. See note 39.

48. Mark DeWolfe Howe, ed., *The Common Law* (Boston: Little, Brown, 1881; reprint, Cambridge, Mass.: Harvard University Press, 1963), 5.

49. See Jerome Frank, *Courts on Trial* (Princeton, N.J.: Princeton University Press, 1949), 147; and Karl Llewellyn, "Some Realism About Realism—Responding to Dean Pound," *Harvard Law Review* 44 (1931): 1237.

50. Gregg Ivers and Kevin McGuire, eds., *Creating Constitutional Change* (Charlottesville: University of Virginia Press, 2004), 1.

51. For a methodologically and substantively broad range of studies dedicated to understanding both internal and external elements in this sense, see, e.g., C. Herman Pritchett, *The Roosevelt Court* (New York: Macmillan, 1948); Robert Dahl, "Decision-Making in a Democracy: The Supreme Court as a National Policy Maker," *Journal of Public Law* 6 (1958): 279; Martin Shapiro, *Law and Politics in the Supreme Court* (New York: Free Press, 1964); Walter Murphy, *Elements of Judicial Strategy* (Chicago: University of Chicago Press, 1964); Glendon Schubert, *The Judicial Mind* (Evanston, Ill.: Northwestern University Press, 1965); Lee Epstein and Tracy George, "On the Nature of Supreme Court Decision Making," *American Political Science Review* 86 (June 1992): 324;

Lee Epstein and Jack Knight, *The Choices Justices Make* (Washington, D.C.: CQ Press, 1998); Cornell Clayton and Howard Gillman, eds., *Supreme Court Decision-Making: New Institutionalist Approaches* (Chicago: University of Chicago Press, 1999); Howard Gillman, "How Political Parties Can Use the Courts to Advance Their Agendas: Federal Courts in the United States, 1875–1891," *American Political Science Review* 96, no. 3 (September 2002): 511–24; and, Jeffrey Segal and Harold Spaeth, *The Supreme Court and the Attitudinal Model Revisited* (New York: Cambridge University Press, 2003).

52. See, e.g., Vincent Blasi, "Holmes and the Marketplace of Ideas," *Supreme Court Review* (Chicago: University of Chicago Press, 2004), 2.

53. 250 U.S. 616 (1919) (involving the prosecution of dissenters who had urged resistance to the war effort in America and abroad).

54. *Abrams*, 630 (emphasis added).

55. For one well-known example of this distinction between "concepts" and "conceptions," see Ronald Dworkin, *Law's Empire* (Cambridge: Belknap Press, 1986), 71 ("The contrast between concept and conception is here a contrast between levels of abstractions at which the interpretation of the practice can be studied").

56. Paul Pierson and Theda Skocpol, "Historical Institutionalism in Contemporary Political Science," in *Political Science: State of the Discipline*, ed. Ira Katznelson and Helen Milner (New York: W. W. Norton, 2002) (conjunctures refer to "interaction effects between distinct causal sequences that become joined at particular points in time"). See also, Karen Orren and Stephen Skowronek, "Beyond the Iconography of Order: Notes for a 'New' Institutionalism," in *The Dynamics of American Politics*, ed. L. C. Dodd and C. Jillson (Boulder, Colo.: Westview Press, 1994).

57. See, e.g., Ken Kersch, *Constructing Civil Liberties: Discontinuities in the Development of American Constitutional Law* (New York: Cambridge, 2004), 11, n. 17 (the "study of constitutional development may be an empirical study, but it is also inevitably a study of ideas").

58. Another image might be helpful here: that of "moving pictures" rather than "snapshots" as a way of understanding the course and development of political phenomena, practices, policies, and institutions. On this distinction, see Paul Pierson, "Not Just What, but *When*: Timing and Sequence in Political Processes," *Studies in American Political Development* 14 (Spring 2000): 72.

59. Daniel Polsby, "*Buckley v. Valeo*: The Special Nature of Political Speech," *Supreme Court Review* (Chicago: University of Chicago Press, 1976), 41–42 (arguing that *Buckley v. Valeo* "makes the clearest acknowledgement that has yet been given by the courts of the multivalency of the First Amendment," and observing that in this case "free speech interests of the highest and most hallowed sort were on the line—and individual interest in unlimited speech on political topics, and a collective interest in keeping the poison of selfish interest out of the wellspring of democracy").

60. Jack Balkin, "Ideological Drift and the Struggle over Meaning," *Connecticut Law Review* 25 (1993): 871.

61. *See* R. H. Coase, "The Market for Goods and the Market for Ideas," *American Economic Review* 64, no. 2 (May 1974): 389 ("Economists usually call for governmental intervention, which may include direct governmental regulation, when the market does not operate properly").

62. See, e.g., F. A. Hayek, *The Road to Serfdom* (Chicago: University of Chicago Press, 1944); Ludwig von Mises, *Human Action: A Treatise on Economics* (New Haven, Conn.:

Yale University Press, 1949); and Milton Friedman (with Rose Friedman), *Capitalism and Freedom* (Chicago: University of Chicago Press, 1962).

63. Regarding "market failures," *See* Jerome Barron, "Access to the Press—A New First Amendment Right, *Harvard Law Review* 80, no. 8 (1967): 1641–78.

64. Stephen Breyer, *Active Liberty: Interpreting Our Democratic Constitution* (New York: Alfred A. Knopf, 2005), 48 (emphasis added).

65. Owen Fiss, "Why the State?" *Harvard Law Review* 100 (February 1987): 788.

66. Philip Bobbitt, *Constitutional Fate: Theory of the Constitution* (New York: Oxford University Press, 1982); Erwin Chemerinsky, "The Rhetoric of Constitutional Law," *Michigan Law Review* 100 (August 2002): 2008, 2035 (Such a "rhetorical enterprise," he notes as well, "profoundly influences much of what the Court does and how the Court's decisions should be evaluated").

67. Farr, "Understanding Conceptual Change Politically," 3 (emphasis added).

68. For a critical perspective on the "images" that underlie the Court's rulings on democratic politics, generally, see Issacharoff and Pildes, "Politics as Markets," 646 (arguing that "the Court's electoral jurisprudence lacks any underlying vision of democratic politics that is normatively robust or realistically sophisticated about actual political practices," and that instead "the images of democratic politics that underlie the Court's decisions," increasingly seem "ad hoc," with "different views of the point of politics emerg[ing] almost at random as the Court confronts questions that range from patronage to redistricting to restructurings of the political process through voter initiatives").

69. *A Clearing in the Forest: Law, Life, and Mind* (Chicago: University of Chicago Press, 2001), xiii (emphasis added).

70. As the civil rights attorney Anthony Amsterdam and the psychologist Jerome Bruner have recently argued in their discussion of "rhetorics," there are "various linguistic processes by which a speaker can create, address, avoid, or shape issues that the speaker wishes or is called upon to contest, or that a speaker suspects (at some level of awareness) may become contested." *Minding the Law* (Cambridge, Mass.: Harvard University Press, 2000), 165.

71. See Lee Epstein and Joseph Kobylka, *The Supreme Court and Legal Change* (Chapel Hill: University of North Carolina Press, 1992), 310 (arguing that "beneath the Court-based and environmental factors that stimulate doctrinal change by the Supreme Court lurk the arguments made by the attorneys and interests that sponsor and support constitutional litigation").

72. William Gamson, "News as Framing," *American Behavioral Scientist* 33, no. 2 (November–December 1989): 157.

73. Robert Entman, "Framing: Toward Clarification of a Fractured Paradigm," *Journal of Communication* 43, no. 4 (Autumn 1993): 51. For the most thorough discussion of "frameworks," see Erving Goffman, *Frame Analysis* (New York: Harper Colophon Books, 1974).

74. Mary John Smith, *Persuasion and Human Action* (Belmont, Calif.: Wadsworth, 1982), 29.

75. See, e.g., Louis Fisher, *Constitutional Dialogues: Interpretation as Political Process* (Princeton, N.J.: Princeton University Press, 1988), 231–74; Keith Whittington, *Constitutional Construction* (Cambridge, Mass.: Harvard University Press, 1999); Kevin McMahon, *Reconsidering Roosevelt on Race: How the Presidency Paved the Way to Brown* (Chicago: University of Chicago Press, 2004); Neal Devins and Louis Fisher, *The Democratic Constitution* (New York: Oxford University Press, 2004); and Ronald Kahn and Ken Kersch, eds., *The Supreme Court and American Political Development* (Lawrence:

University Press of Kansas, 2006).

76. As Walter Murphy has wisely observed, "It is always difficult—and usually impossible—to know that A does x *because* of B's activity." *Elements of Judicial Strategy*, 8. Also see Lawrence Baum's apt realization that judicial behavior remains a "puzzle." *The Puzzle of Judicial Behavior* (Ann Arbor: University of Michigan Press, 1998).

77. See Mark Tushnet, *A Court Divided: The Rehnquist Court and the Future of Constitutional Law* (New York: W. W. Norton, 2005), 67 (noting that one has to "go back to the years from 1811 to 1823 to find a longer period with no changes in personnel on the Court").

78. 504 U.S. 191 (1992).

79. 514 U.S. 334 (1995).

80. 525 U.S. 182 (1999).

81. 486 U.S. 414 (1988).

82. 528 U.S. 337 (2000).

83. *McCulloch v. Maryland*, 17 U. S. (4 Wheat.) 316, 407 (1819).

CHAPTER 1: CONSTITUENT CONCEPTS

1. For the more general notion of superintending democracy, see Christopher Banks and John Green, eds., *Superintending Democracy: The Courts and the Political Process* (Akron, Ohio: University of Akron Press, 2001), 2 (arguing that "the judiciary oversees democratic institutions and does so with the goal of furthering democratic purposes").

2. Pamela Karlan, "Just Politics? Five Not So Easy Pieces of the 1995 Term," *Houston Law Review* 34 (Summer 1997): 290.

3. *Baker v. Carr* 369 U.S. 186 (1962) (finding the Tennessee General Assembly had violated the equal protection rights of its citizens "by virtue of the debasement of their votes" because it had failed to reapportion the assembly since 1901 when the state had a very different population distribution).

4. Samuel Issacharoff and Richard Pildes, "Politics as Markets: Partisan Lockups of the Democratic Process," *Stanford Law Review* 50 (February 1998): 644–45.

5. *Nixon v. Herndon*, 273 U.S. 536, 540 (1927) (finding as an unconstitutional violation of the Fourteenth Amendment a Texas statute regulating primary elections such that "in no event shall a negro be eligible to participate in a Democratic party primary election held in the State of Texas"); *Nixon v. Condon* 286 U.S. 73, 82 (1932) (finding unconstitutional the statute passed in the wake of *Herndon*, whereby Texas now provided that "every political party in this State through its State Executive Committee shall have the power to prescribe the qualifications of its own members and shall in its own way determine who shall be qualified to vote or otherwise participate in such political party"); *Grovey v. Townsend* 295 U.S. 45 (1935) (*upholding* the exclusion of a black voter who sued after being denied an absentee ballot for participation in the Democratic primary because, as the unanimous Court explained, the party's action did not constitute state action and thus did not fall within reach of the Fourteenth Amendment).

6. 304 U.S. 144 (1938) (involving a due process challenge to a federal prohibition on the interstate shipment of "filled milk" [skimmed milk mixed with nonmilk fats]).

7. Ibid., 152, n. 4. For early commentary on the extension and implications of *Carolene*, see, e.g., Robert Cover, "The Origins of Judicial Activism in the Protection of Minorities," *Yale Law Journal* 91, no. 7 (June 1982): 1287; and Bruce Ackerman, "Beyond Carolene Products," *Harvard Law Review* 98, no. 4 (February 1985): 713.

8. 313 U.S. 299 (1941) (*upholding* the convictions of various Louisiana officials who had committed acts of fraud in the primary election, based on statutes making it a felony to conspire to interfere with a federally protected right, and acknowledging most significantly that in the overwhelmingly Democratic South, the primary election was, in effect, the general election and thus federal protected voting rights were necessarily compromised).

9. 321 U.S. 649, 664–65 (1944) (reversing course from *Grovey* and finding that primary elections *were* part of the "machinery for choosing officials" and concluding that when the privilege of membership in a party is also the essential qualification for voting in a primary to select nominees for a general election, "the state makes the action of the party the action of the state").

10. 345 U.S. 461, 469 (1953) (reviewing the constitutionality of a "self-governing voluntary" club's policy of not admitting blacks for membership and finding that because the "Jaybird [Democratic Association's] primary has become an integral part, indeed the only effective part, of the elective process that determines who shall rule and govern in the county, [t]he effect of the whole procedure, Jaybird primary plus Democratic primary plus general election, is to do precisely that which the Fifteenth Amendment forbids—strip Negroes of every vestige of influence in selecting the officials who control the local county matters that intimately touch the daily lives of citizens").

11. John Hart Ely, *Democracy and Distrust: A Theory of Judicial Review* (Cambridge, Mass.: Harvard University Press, 1980), 87, 73–105 (outlining a "participation-oriented, representation-reinforcing approach to judicial review" predicated on the notion of the Supreme Court as the "Referee" [the subtitle of chapter 4], responsible for "policing the process of representation"). For an early criticism of this theory, see Laurence Tribe, "The Puzzling Persistence of Process-Based Constitutional Theories" (reviewing *Democracy and Distrust*), *Yale Law Journal* 89 (1980): 1063; and for a more recent challenge, see Daniel Lowenstein, "Political Reform Is Political," in *The U.S. House of Representatives: Reform or Rebuild?* ed. Joseph Zimmerman and Wilma Rule (Westport, Conn.: Praeger, 2000), 200.

12. See Issacharoff and Pildes, "Politics as Markets," *passim.*

13. Ely, *Democracy and Distrust*, 102–3.

14. "Politics as Markets," 648.

15. Ibid.

16. Richard Hasen, *The Supreme Court and Election Law: Judging Equality from* Baker v. Carr *to* Bush v. Gore (New York: New York University Press, 2003), 4–8 (emphasis added).

17. Ibid., 4–8.

18. Ibid., 76–77.

19. See Samuel Estreicher, "Platonic Guardians of Democracy" (review of *Democracy and Distrust*, by John Hart Ely) *New York University Law Review* 56 (1981): 551 ("Technical virtuosity and a compelling style cannot mask the fact that Ely's Supreme Court is "a bevy of Platonic Guardians" imposing its own ideal conception of the requirements of 'true democracy'"). See, too, Justice Clarence Thomas's concurrence in *Holder v. Hall*, 512 U.S. 874, 913 (1994) ("We would be mighty Platonic guardians indeed if Congress had granted us the authority to determinate the best form of local government for every country, city, village, and town in America").

20. See *Richardson v. Ramirez*, 418 U.S. 24 (1974) (relying on the "other crime" clause of Section 2 of the Fourteenth Amendment to the federal Constitution to uphold a California law denying convicted felons the right to vote).

21. See, e.g., Brian Pinaire, Milton Heumann, and Laura Bilotta, "Barred from the Vote: Public Attitudes Toward the Disenfranchisement of Felons," *Fordham Urban Law Journal* 30, no. 5 (2003): 1519; Milton Heumann, Brian Pinaire, and Thomas Clark, "Beyond the Sentence: Public Perceptions of Collateral Consequences for Felony Offenders," *Criminal Law Bulletin* 41, no. 1 (2005): 24; Jeff Manza, Clem Brooks, and Christopher Uggen, "Public Attitudes Toward Felon Disenfranchisement in the United States," *Public Opinion Quarterly* 68 (2004): 276; and Marc Mauer and Tushar Kansal, "Barred for Life: Voting Rights Restoration in Permanent Disenfranchisement States," a report prepared by the Sentencing Project, Washington, D.C. (February 2005).

22. Richard Pildes, The Supreme Court 2003 Term, "Foreword: The Constitutionalization of Democratic Politics," *Harvard Law Review* 118 (2004): 28–154, 31, n. 6 (arguing that *Bush v. Gore* was a "quintessential example of judicialized politics" that typifies the "constitutionalization" of democratic politics).

23. "Constitutionalization of Democratic Politics," 31.

24. Ibid., 31.

25. Ibid.

26. Ibid., 31–32.

27. Ibid., 35.

28. Ibid., 39 (noting that even as courts—and *the* Court, specifically—interject themselves ever more into the democratic process, "constitutional law currently lacks a general structure that would properly organize the emerging 'law of politics,'" for example).

29. Hasen, *Supreme Court and Election Law*, 13. See, too, Thomas Keck, *The Most Activist Court in History: The Road to Modern Judicial Conservatism* (Chicago: University of Chicago Press, 2004), 208 (noting that "the later Rehnquist Court recognizes no 'political thickets' in which it is unwilling to exercise its power"); and Pamela Karlan, "Exit Strategies in Constitutional Law: Lessons for Getting the Least Dangerous Branch out of the Political Thicket," *Boston University Law Review* 82 (June 2002): 671, 672, 698 (observing that with the current Court "embroiled in the very heart of the political thicket," the future might be forecast by the recent history revealing "a Court that seems willing to head even deeper into the woods" because it is "deeply distrustful of the political branches and ambitious for its own power").

30. See, e.g., Mark Graber, *Transforming Free Speech: The Ambiguous Legacy of Civil Libertarianism* (Berkeley and Los Angeles: University of California Press, 1991) (arguing that the justification for or defense of free speech was "transformed" in important ways from the pre– to post–World War I conceptions, changing not so much in terms of *what* speech was protected, but rather *why* it was protected [from *individual* liberty to the *social* good], and who was expected to do the protecting [judges vs. elected officials]); David Rabban, *Free Speech in Its Forgotten Years* (New York: Cambridge University Press, 1997) (focusing on the "forgotten years" in free speech history—principally the nineteenth century); Michael Kent Curtis, *Free Speech, the People's "Darling Privilege": Struggles for Freedom of Expression in American History* (Durham, N.C.: Duke University Press, 2000) (addressing the speech claims and interests put forth by Abolitionists as they challenged the institution of slavery in America); and Geoffrey Stone, *Perilous Times* (New York: W. W. Norton, 2004) (discussing, e.g., freedom of speech debates during a range of periods in American history, including the revolutionary era and the Civil War).

31. See Curtis, *Free Speech*, 8–9, 12, 18 (noting that "from the Sedition Act through the Civil War and continuing through the first quarter of the twentieth century, courts

were too often hostile to dissenting speech when it was under attack"; reviewing such cases with a "stunted and crabbed view," if at all; and observing, as well, that "when free speech battles were fought and won in the political arena, courts were simply not involved").

32. See *Stromberg v. California*, 283 U.S. 359 (1931) (reversing the conviction of a woman who had violated a California law that prohibited the display of a red flag "as a sign, symbol, or emblem of opposition to organized government").

33. *United Public Workers of America v. Mitchell*, 333 U.S. 75 (1947).

34. 250 U.S. 616 (1919).

35. Of this opinion, and its rhetorical power, Justice Frankfurter noted: "It is not reckless prophecy to assume that his [Holmes's] famous dissenting opinion in the Abrams case will live so long as English prose retains its power to move." Quoted in Alexander Meiklejohn, *Political Freedom* (New York: Oxford University Press, 1965), 71. Another scholar has called Holmes's dissent in this case "the greatest utterance on intellectual freedom by an American, ranking in the English tongue with Milton and Mill." Max Lerner, *The Mind and Faith of Justice Holmes* (Boston: Little, Brown, 1943), 306.

36. *Abrams*, 630.

37. Aristotle, *The Politics*, trans. T. A. Sinclair, rev. Trevor J. Saunders (New York: Penguin Books, 1982), book 4, chap. 14, 276–80.

38. Indeed, it is important to stress here that Milton was writing in an era of mercantilism when the market was tightly regulated by the Crown and the guilds, as opposed to the more laissez-faire capitalist environment of Holmes's day. See Steven K. Winter, *A Clearing in the Forest: Law, Life, and Mind* (Chicago: University of Chicago Press, 2003), 272. See *Areopagitica and Other Political Writings* (Indianapolis: Liberty Fund, 1999), 45 ("And though all the windes of doctrin were let loose to play upon the earth, so Truth be in the field, we do injurious by licensing and prohibiting to misdoubt her strength. Let her and Falshood grapple; who ever knew Truth put to the wors, in a free and open encounter").

39. But see David Cole, "Agon at Agora," *Yale Law Journal* 95 (April 1986): 857, 876 (arguing that the value of Milton's impassioned pleas may be largely rhetorical, as he was a censor for Cromwell's regime and was generally concerned with the search for an objective, divine Truth, a foundation that no longer animates free speech theory).

40. And "even if they are restrained," they continue, "common Sense will often get the better: but to give one Side Liberty to say what they will, and not suffer the other to say any thing, even in their own Defence, is comprehensive of all the Evils that any Nation can groan under, and must soon extinguish every Seed of Religion, Liberty, Virtue, or Knowledge." "Discourse on Libels," in *The English Libertarian Heritage*, ed. David L. Jacobson (Indianapolis: Bobbs-Merrill, 1965), 232–33.

41. See, e.g., his *Chapters on Socialism*, in *On Liberty and Other Writings*, ed. Stefan Collini (Cambridge: Cambridge University Press, 1989), 221–79.

42. See *On Liberty*, 19 ("No argument . . . can now be needed, against permitting a legislature or an executive, not identified in interest with the people, to prescribe opinions to them, and determine what doctrines or what arguments they shall be allowed to hear").

43. See ibid., 20 ("If all mankind minus one, were of one opinion, and only one person were of the contrary opinion, mankind would be no more justified in silencing that one person, than he, if he had the power, would be justified in silencing mankind").

44. See ibid., 20 (noting that the "peculiar evil of silencing the expression of an opinion" is that "if the opinion is right," the people are "deprived of the opportunity of

exchanging error for truth," whereas if the opinion is wrong, "they lose, what is almost as great a benefit, the clearer perception and livelier impression of truth, produced by its collision with error").

45. See ibid., 21 ("To refuse a hearing to an opinion, because they are sure that it is false, is to assume that *their* certainty is the same thing as *absolute* certainty").

46. See ibid., 21, 26 (noting that the "silencing of discussion is an assumption of infallibility," and observing that "it is not the feeling sure of a doctrine [be it what it may]," which is "an assumption of infallibility"; it is "the undertaking to decide that question *for others*, without allowing them to hear what can be said on the contrary side." And this "pretension," he "denounce[d] and reprobate[d]" "not the less" if put forth on the side of his own "most solemn convictions").

47. See ibid., 44 ("The fatal tendency of mankind to leave off thinking about a thing when it is no longer doubtful, is the cause of half their errors").

48. See ibid., 23 ("There must be discussion, to show how experience is to be interpreted. Wrong opinions and practices gradually yield to fact and argument: but facts and arguments, to produce any effect on the mind, must be brought before it").

49. See ibid., 24, 37 ("The steady habit of correcting and completing his own opinion by collating it with those of others, so far from causing doubt and hesitation in carrying it into practice, is the only stable foundation for a just reliance on it"; and, "However unwillingly a person who has a strong opinion may admit the possibility that his opinion may be false, he ought to be moved by the consideration that however true it may be, if it is not fully, frequently, and fearlessly discussed, it will be held as a dead dogma, not a living truth").

50. C. Edwin Baker, *Human Liberty and Freedom of Speech* (New York: Oxford University Press, 1989), 286, n. 5. But see too David Lowenthal, *No Liberty for License: The Forgotten Logic of the First Amendment* (Dallas: Spence Publishing, 1997), 44 (arguing that "Mill was never so vulgar as to think that the truth of an idea depended on its marketability or that it could be identified, at any given time, with what prevails in some so-called 'marketplace of ideas'").

51. On such linkages, see Haig Bosmajian, *Metaphor and Reason in Judicial Opinions* (Carbondale, Ill.: Southern Illinois University Press, 1992), 54–58; and Cole, "Agon at Agora," *passim* (both arguing that each subsequent author misread and misunderstood the assumptions of his predecessor).

52. A cottage industry of Holmes scholarship exists. For general and recent discussions, see Louis Menand, *The Metaphysical Club: A Story of Ideas in America* (New York: Farrar, Straus & Giroux, 2002); and Albert Alschuler, *Law Without Values: The Life, Work, and Legacy of Justice Holmes* (Chicago: University of Chicago Press, 2002). On Holmes's views on freedom of speech, specifically, see David S. Bogen, "The Free Speech Metamorphosis of Mr. Justice Holmes," *Hofstra Law Review* 11 (1982): 97, 120, 188. On the particular influence of William James, see Thomas Grey, "Holmes and Legal Pragmatism," *Stanford Law Review* 41 (1989): 788.

53. *Debs v. United States* 249 U.S. 211 (1919) (upholding the conviction of Eugene V. Debs for giving a speech perceived to be intended to obstruct the war effort); *Schenck v. United States* 249 U.S. 47 (1919) (upholding the conspiracy conviction of a prominent member of the Socialist Party who had distributed leaflets urging resistance to conscription).

54. Rabban, *Free Speech in its Forgotten Years*, 342–43, 350.

55. See Zechariah Chafee, *Free Speech in the United States* (Cambridge, Mass.: Harvard University Press, 1941), 86.

56. See Stone, *Perilous Times*, 200; and Bradley C. Bobertz, "The Brandeis Gambit: The Making of America's 'First Freedom,' 1909–1931," *William and Mary Law Review* 40 (1999): 587–607.

57. See Richard Polenberg, *Fighting Faiths: The "Abrams" Case, the Supreme Court, and the First Amendment* (New York: Viking Press, 1987) (drawing upon the research that Holmes is believed to have done during the summer of 1919, including studying President Abraham Lincoln's wartime suppression of speech and reading John Locke's *Second Treatise on Civil Government*); and Anthony Lewis, *Make No Law: The Sullivan Case and the First Amendment* (New York: Vintage Books, 1992), 81 (drawing on Polenberg's work to make the same claim).

58. See Menand, *Metaphysical Club*, 60–65 (attributing much of Holmes's perspective to his experiences during the Civil War where his views were shaped by seeing the consequences of certainty and parties willing to fight to the death to prove it).

59. As both Graber (*Transforming Free Speech*, 221) and Rabban (*Free Speech in Its Forgotten Years*, 3–5) have noted, in the era following World War I prominent progressive thinkers such as John Dewey, Zechariah Chafee, and Roscoe Pound reconceived the philosophical justification for what we think of as civil liberties and thus presented a new orientation toward, conception of, and rationale for freedom of speech.

60. See *Free Speech: A Philosophical Enquiry* (Cambridge: Cambridge University Press, 1982), 15, 16; and Schauer, "First Amendment Opportunism," in *Eternally Vigilant*, ed. Lee Bollinger and Geoffrey Stone (Chicago: University of Chicago Press), 194, n. 73 ("Although the marketplace theory has not fared well in the academic literature . . . it is still a staple of popular free-speech rhetoric [citations omitted]").

61. See *The Tolerant Society* (New York: Oxford University Press, 1986), 45.

62. See *Freedom of Expression and Partisan Politics* (Columbia: University of South Carolina, 1989), 215 (arguing that a "free marketplace of ideas is not only an aspect of democratic theory, it is a presupposition of American constitutionalism").

63. See *Human Liberty and Freedom of Speech*, 3, 7, 12, 131 (acknowledging the marketplace theory as "the dominant rationale given for freedom of speech"; finding that "marketplace imagery ('competition of ideas,' the value of 'robust debate') pervades judicial opinions"; and concluding that the marketplace theory "surely dominates both rhetorically and conceptually" and "has dominated scholarly and judicial thinking about the first amendment").

64. See *Free Speech in an Open Society* (New York: Alfred A. Knopf, 1992), 7–8.

65. See *Democracy and the Problem of Free Speech* (New York: Basic Books, 1993), 4, 17, 34, and 251 (observing that the "most striking development in free speech law is that marketplace thinking has become so dominant . . ." and contending that in the current period, "Holmes's view is clearly ascendant").

66. See "Do Not Go Gently into That Good Right: The First Amendment in the High Court of Australia," in *Supreme Court Review* (1997) (Chicago: University of Chicago Press, 1998), 441 (observing that the "prevalent U.S. notion" is "that political communication is best understood as a 'free market' of ideas").

67. See *The Law of Democracy: Legal Structure of the Political Process* (Westbury, N.Y.: Foundation Press, 1998), 617 (observing the "long tradition" of viewing political speech from the vantage point of a marketplace of ideas).

68. See *First Amendment Law* (St. Paul: West Publishing, 2000), 7 ("The instrumental approach to the First Amendment which has won the most favor with the courts has been

the marketplace of ideas theory").

69. Winter, *Clearing in the Forest*, 259, 271, 88–89 (" . . . Holmes's formulation of the 'marketplace of ideas' concept . . . has served as the organizing metaphor for much of modern free speech law").

70. Using the Lexis database (February 25–26, 2006), searches were conducted of U.S. Supreme Court opinions for evidence of *explicit* invocations of the "marketplace of ideas" in its various iterations and as alluded to in its most commonly synonymous forms, including: "marketplace of ideas"; "market place of ideas"; "marketplace" w/3 "ideas"; "free trade in ideas"; "free trade" w/3 "ideas"; "free market" w/3 "ideas"; "competition" w/3 "ideas"; "exchange" w/3 "ideas"; *and* "interchange" w/3 "ideas."

71. 310 U.S. 88, 105 (1940) ("Abridgment of the liberty of such discussion can be justified only where the clear danger of substantive evils arises under circumstances affording no opportunity to test the merits of ideas by competition for acceptance in the market of public opinion").

72. 314 U.S. 252, 283 (1941) ("A trial is not a 'free trade in ideas,' nor is the best test of truth in a courtroom 'the power of the thought to get itself accepted in the competition of the market'").

73. But see Blasi, "Holmes and the Marketplace of Ideas," 13, n. 41, finding that the first translation of the competition of the market into the "marketplace of ideas" seems to have been in a letter to the *New York Times* (December 28, 1935), discussing "men and ideas competing in the market place of ideas where public opinion is formed."

74. 337 U.S. 1 (1949) (emphasis added) (referring to the opinion by Chief Justice Hughes in *De Jonge v. Oregon*, but summarizing it as follows: It is "only through free debate and free exchange of ideas that government remains responsive to the will of the people and peaceful change is effected. The right to speak freely and to promote diversity of ideas and programs is therefore one of the chief distinctions that sets us apart from totalitarian regimes").

75. 345 U.S. 41, 56 (1953) ("We have here a publisher who through books and pamphlets seeks to reach the minds and hearts of the American people. He is different in some respects from other publishers. But the differences are minor. Like the publishers of newspapers, magazines, or books, this publisher bids for the minds of men in the market *place* of ideas") (emphasis added).

76. 381 U.S. 301, 308 (1965) ("The dissemination of ideas can accomplish nothing if otherwise willing addressees are not free to receive and consider them. It would be a barren marketplace of ideas that had only sellers and no buyers").

77. See, e.g., W. Wat Hopkins, "The Supreme Court Defines the Marketplace of Ideas," *Journalism and Mass Communication Quarterly* 73, no. 1 (Spring 1996): 41 (noting that twenty-four of the forty-nine justices who served on the Supreme Court for at least one term between the years of 1919 and 1995 used the metaphor at least once).

78. See Winter, *Clearing in the Forest*, 19, note (reminding us, in this respect, of the conventional expressions of "that idea isn't *worth* much" and "with the right *packaging* that idea just might *sell*").

79. 337 U.S. 1, 4 (1949) (Chief Justice Hughes, for the Court) (It is only "through free debate and free exchange of ideas that government remains responsive to the will of the people and peaceful change is effected").

80. 343 U.S. 250, 285 (1951) (Justice Douglas, dissenting) ("The free trade in ideas which the Framers of the Constitution visualized disappears. In its place there is substituted

a new orthodoxy—an orthodoxy that changes with the whims of the age or the day, an orthodoxy which the majority by solemn judgment proclaims to be essential to the safety, welfare, security, morality, or health of society").

81. 341 U.S. 494, 557 (1951) (Justice Frankfurter, concurring—appendix, quoting *Thornhill*, 105) ("Abridgment of the liberty of such discussion can be justified only where the clear danger of substantive evils arises under circumstances affording no opportunity to test the merits of ideas by competition for acceptance in the market of public opinion").

82. 393 U.S. 503, 512 (1969) (Justice Fortas, for the Court) ("The classroom is peculiarly the 'marketplace of ideas.' The Nation's future depends upon leaders trained through wide exposure to that robust exchange of ideas which discovers truth 'out of a multitude of tongues, [rather] than through any kind of authoritative selection'").

83. 413 U.S. 15, 47 (1973) (Justice Douglas, dissenting) ("Perhaps the people will decide that the path towards a mature, integrated society requires that all ideas competing for acceptance must have no censor. Perhaps they will decide otherwise. Whatever the choice, the courts will have some guidelines. Now we have none except our own predilections").

84. 354 U.S. 476, 484 (1957) (Justice Brennan, for the Court) ("The protection given speech and press was fashioned to assure unfettered interchange of ideas for the bringing about of political and social changes desired by the people").

85. 427 U.S. 50, 88 (1976) (Justice Stewart, dissenting) ("Much speech that seems to be of little or no value will enter the marketplace of ideas, threatening the quality of our social discourse and, more generally, the serenity of our lives. But that is the price to be paid for constitutional freedom").

86. 424 U.S. 1 (1976) (per curiam opinion) ("The public interest also suffers if that result comes to pass, for there is a consequent reduction in the free circulation of ideas both within and without the political arena [citations omitted]").

87. 435 U.S. 765, 809 (1978) (Justice White, dissenting) ("Such expenditures may be viewed as seriously threatening the role of the First Amendment as a guarantor of a free marketplace of ideas").

88. 421 U.S. 809, 826 (1975) (Justice Blackmun, for the Court) ("The relationship of speech to the marketplace of products or of services does not make it valueless in the marketplace of ideas").

89. 425 U.S. 748, 781 (1976) (Justice Rehnquist, dissenting) ("The logical consequences of the Court's decision in this case, a decision which elevates commercial intercourse between a seller hawking his wares and a buyer seeking to strike a bargain to the same plane as has been previously reserved for the free marketplace of ideas, are far reaching indeed").

90. 438 U.S. 726, 745, 772 (1978) (Justice Stevens, for the Court) ("For it is a central tenet of the First Amendment that the government must remain neutral in the marketplace of ideas"); and Justice Brennan (dissenting) ("I would place the responsibility and the right to weed worthless and offensive communications from the public airways where it belongs and where, until today, it resided: in a public free to choose those communications worthy of its attention from a marketplace unsullied by the censor's hand").

91. 454 U.S. 290, 295 (1981) (Chief Justice Burger, for the Court) ("The Court has long viewed the First Amendment as protecting a marketplace for the clash of different views and conflicting ideas," a concept, he continued, which "has been stated and restated almost since the Constitution was drafted").

92. 447 U.S. 74, 97 (1980) (Justice Powell, concurring in part and in the judgment) ("The State may not compel a person to affirm a belief he does not hold. . . . This principle

on its face protects a person who refuses to allow use of his property as a marketplace for the ideas of others").

93. 447 U.S. 530, 538 (1980) (Justice Powell, for the Court) ("If the marketplace of ideas is to remain free and open, governments must not be allowed to choose 'which issues are worth discussing or debating'" [citations omitted]).

94. 453 U.S. 490, 549, 550 (1981) (Justice Stevens, dissenting in part) ("This ordinance cannot, therefore, be sustained on the assumption that the remaining channels of communication will be just as effective for all persons as a communications marketplace which includes a thousand or more large billboards available for hire. . . . If the First Amendment categorically protected the marketplace of ideas from any quantitative restraint, a municipality could not outlaw graffiti").

95. 460 U.S. 37, 71–72 (1983) (Justice Brennan, dissenting) ("In order to secure the First Amendment's guarantee of freedom of speech and to prevent distortions of 'the marketplace of ideas,' governments generally are prohibited from discriminating among viewpoints on issues within the realm of protected speech [citation omitted]").

96. 485 U.S. 46, 52 (1988) (Chief Justice Rehnquist, for the Court) ("False statements of fact are particularly valueless; they interfere with the truth-seeking function of the marketplace of ideas [citations omitted]").

97. 491 U.S. 397, 429 (1989) (Chief Justice Rehnquist, dissenting) (rejecting the notion that the flag is simply "another 'idea' or 'point of view' competing for recognition in the marketplace of ideas").

98. 505 U.S. 377, 387–88 (1992) (Justice Scalia, for the Court) ("The rationale of the general prohibition, after all, is that content discrimination 'raise[s] the specter that the Government may effectively drive certain ideas or viewpoints from the marketplace'" [citations omitted]).

99. *RAV*, 401 (Justice White, concurring in part) ("A ban on all fighting words or on a subset of the fighting words category would restrict only the social evil of hate speech, without creating the danger of driving viewpoints from the marketplace [citations omitted]").

100. 505 U.S. 672 (1992) (Justice Kennedy, concurring in part) ("The effect of a rule of law distinguishing between sales and distribution [of literature] would be to close the marketplace of ideas to less affluent organizations and speakers, leaving speech as the preserve of those who are able to fund themselves").

101. 514 U.S. 334, 341, 341–42 (1995) (Justice Stevens, for the Court) ("The State does not suggest that all anonymous publications are pernicious or that a statute totally excluding them from the marketplace of ideas would be valid." And: "Whatever the motivation may be, at least in the field of literary endeavor, the interest in having anonymous works enter the marketplace of ideas unquestionably outweighs any public interest in requiring disclosure as a condition of entry").

102. 515 U.S. 819, 831, 847, 850 (1995) (Justice Kennedy, for the Court) ("Our understanding of the complex and multifaceted nature of public discourse has not embraced such a contrived description of the marketplace of ideas").

103. *Rosenberger*, 850 (Justice O'Connor, concurring) ("This safeguard accompanying the University's financial assistance, when provided to a publication with a religious viewpoint such as Wide Awake, ensures that the funds are used only to further the University's purpose in maintaining a free and robust marketplace of ideas, from whatever perspective").

104. 517 U.S. 484, 523, n. 4 (1996) (Justice Scalia, concurring in part) (stressing

that neither of the government's rationales "provides any basis for permitting government to keep citizens ignorant as a means of manipulating their choices in the commercial or political marketplace").

105. 521 U.S. 844, 885 (1997) (Justice Stevens, for the Court) ("The dramatic expansion of this new marketplace of ideas [the Internet] contradicts the factual basis of this contention. . . . As a matter of constitutional tradition, in the absence of evidence to the contrary, we presume that governmental regulation of the content of speech is more likely to interfere with the free exchange of ideas than to encourage it").

106. 528 U.S. 377, 411 (2000) (Justice Thomas, dissenting) ("The Founders sought to protect the rights of individuals to engage in political speech because a self-governing people depends upon the free exchange of political information. And that free exchange should receive the most protection when it matters the most—during campaigns for elective office").

107. 535 U.S. 564, 573 (2002) (Justice Thomas, for the Court) ("The First Amendment states that 'Congress shall make no law . . . abridging the freedom of speech.' This provision embodies 'our profound national commitment to the free exchange of ideas'").

108. 540 U.S. 93, 265 (2003) (Justice Thomas, concurring in part and dissenting in part) ("In response to this assault on the free exchange of ideas and with only the slightest consideration of the appropriate standard of review or of the Court's traditional role of protecting First Amendment freedoms, the Court has placed its *imprimatur* on these unprecedented restrictions").

109. 538 U.S. 343, 358 (2003) (Justice O'Connor, for the Court) ("The hallmark of the protection of free speech is to allow 'free trade in ideas'—even ideas that the overwhelming majority of people might find distasteful or discomforting").

110. 393 U.S. 23, 32 (1968) (Justice Black, for the Court) ("Competition in ideas and governmental policies is at the core of our electoral process and of the First Amendment freedoms").

111. 460 U.S. 780, 794 (1983) (Justice Stevens, for the Court) ("By limiting the opportunities of independent-minded voters to associate in the electoral arena to enhance their political effectiveness as a group, such restrictions threaten to reduce diversity and competition in the marketplace of ideas").

112. 438 U.S. 1, 32, n. 22 (1978) (Justice Stevens, dissenting) ("'Dissemination of ideas can accomplish nothing if otherwise willing addressees are not free to receive and consider them. It would be a barren marketplace of ideas that had only sellers and no buyers.' . . . It would be an even more barren marketplace that had willing buyers and sellers and no meaningful information to exchange [citations omitted]").

113. 385 U.S. 374, 407 (1967) (Justice Harlan, dissenting) ("First, we cannot avoid recognizing that we have entered an area where the 'marketplace of ideas' does not function and where conclusions premised on the existence of that exchange are apt to be suspect").

114. 418 U.S. 323, 339–40 (1974) (Justice Powell, for the Court) ("However pernicious an opinion may seem, we depend for its correction not on the conscience of judges and juries but on the competition of other ideas").

115. 310 U.S. 88, 105 (1940) ("Abridgment of the liberty of such discussion can be justified only where the clear danger of substantive evils arises under circumstances affording no opportunity to test the merits of ideas by competition for acceptance in the market of public opinion").

116. 371 U.S. 415, 437 (1963) (Justice Brennan, for the Court) ("'Free trade in ideas' means free trade in the opportunity to persuade to action, not merely to describe facts [citations omitted]").

117. 468 U.S. 609, 636 (1984) (Justice O'Connor, concurring) ("An association must choose its market. Once it enters the marketplace of commerce in any substantial degree it loses the complete control over its membership that it would otherwise enjoy if it confined its affairs to the marketplace of ideas").

118. 520 U.S. 351, 382 (1997) (Justice Stevens, dissenting) ("It is a central theme of our jurisprudence that the entire electorate, which necessarily includes the members of the major parties, will benefit from robust competition in ideas and governmental policies that is at the core of our electoral process and of the First Amendment freedoms [citations omitted]").

119. 421 U.S. 7, 15 (1975) (Justice Blackmun, for the Court) ("No longer is the female destined solely for the home and the rearing of the family, and only the male for the marketplace and the world of ideas"). See, too, *Craig v. Boren*, 429 U.S. 190 (1976), and *J.E.B. v. Ala. ex rel. T.B.*, 511 U.S. 127 (1994), both referring to this passage and its dismissal of this "outmoded misconception."

120. 125 S. Ct. 2722, 2747 (2005) (Justice O'Connor, concurring) ("In the marketplace of ideas, the government has vast resources and special status. Government religious expression therefore risks crowding out private observance and distorting the natural interplay between competing beliefs").

121. One of the earliest critical evaluations was offered up by John Wigmore who noted, soon after the *Abrams* ruling was announced, that "simply as a matter of 'free trade in ideas,' is there not in Anglo-America today an irrevocably established free trade in every blasphemous, scurrilous, shocking, iconoclastic, or lunatic idea that any fanatical or unbalanced brain can conceive?" "*Abrams vs U.S.*: Freedom of Speech and Freedom of Thuggery in War-Time and Peace-Time," *Illinois Law Review* 14 (1920): 558. Thus, from the start, critics equated the predicates of the marketplace metaphor with a kind of reification of the perceived relativism and licentiousness pervasive in American society at the end of World War I. For a more recent critical assessment of the logic of protecting "falsehoods" in the quest for the "truth," see Dale Herbeck, "*New York Times v. Sullivan*: Justice Brennan's Beautiful Lie," *Free Speech Yearbook* 28 (1990): 40.

122. Zechariah Chafee, Jr., was the first to offer a sustained argument for the connection between "unlimited discussion" and the "discovery and spread of truth." *Free Speech in the United States*, 31–33. For a modern defense of truth-potential, see Smolla, *Free Speech in an Open Society.*

123. See Kathleen M. Sullivan, "Free Speech and Unfree Markets," *UCLA Law Review* 42 (April 1995): 959–64.

124. David Strauss, "Persuasion, Autonomy, and Freedom of Expression," *Columbia Law Review* 91 (March 1991): 334, 349.

125. Vincent Blasi, "Holmes and the Marketplace of Ideas," *Supreme Court Review* (Chicago: University of Chicago Press, 2004), 13.

126. On this note, see Jerome Frank, *Courts on Trial: Myth and Reality in American Justice* (Princeton, N.J.: Princeton University Press, 1949), 92–93.

127. See Jerome Barron, "Access to the Press—A New First Amendment Right," *Harvard Law Review* 80, no. 8 (1967): 1641. Also see Paul Brietzke, "How and Why the Marketplace of Ideas Fails," *Valparaiso Law Review* 31 (Summer 1997): 951, 963.

128. See Kathleen Hall Jamieson, *Dirty Politics* (New York: Oxford University Press, 1992), 60. Cf. Richard Lau and David Redlawsk, "Voting Correctly," *American Political Science Review* 91, no. 3 (September 1997): 585–98.

129. See Herbert Marcuse, "Repressive Tolerance," in *A Critique of Pure Tolerance*, ed. R. P. Wolff et al. (Boston: Beacon Press, 1968), 92, 98, and 110.

130. See Richard Schwarzlose, "The Marketplace of Ideas: A Measure of Free Expression," *Journalism and Mass Communication* (1989): 28–30; and Robert Entman and Steven Wildman, "Reconciling Economic and Non-Economic Perspectives on Media Policy: Transcending the 'Marketplace of Ideas,'" *Journal of Communication* 42, no. 1 (Winter 1992): 11.

131. See Noah Zatz, "Sidewalks in Cyberspace: Making Space for Public Forums in the Electronic Environment," *Harvard Journal of Law and Technology* 12 (Fall 1998): 149, 152.

132. See Robert Putnam, *Bowling Alone* (New York: Simon and Schuster, 2000).

133. See, e.g., Diana Mutz, "Cross-Cutting Social Networks: Testing Democratic Theory in Practice," *American Political Science Review* 96, no. 1 (March 2002): 111–26.

134. See, e.g., Pamela Johnston, Ivor Crewe, and Donald Searing, "The Nature of Citizenship in the United States and Great Britain: Empirical Comments on Theoretical Themes," *Journal of Politics* 53, no. 3 (August 1991): 805; Jenny Kitzinger, "Introducing Focus Groups," *British Medical Journal*, 311, no. 7000 (July 29, 1995): 299; and Alan Johnson, "'It's Good to Talk': The Focus Group and the Sociological Imagination," *Sociological Review* 44, no. 3 (August 1996): 516.

135. See Cass Sunstein, "Deliberative Trouble? Why Groups Go to Extremes," *Yale Law Journal* 110, no. 1 (October 2000): 71–119; and Sunstein, *Republic.com* (Princeton, N.J.: Princeton University Press, 2002).

136. See Note, "The Constitutional Right to Anonymity: Free Speech, Disclosure, and the Devil," *Yale Law Journal* 70 (1960): 1084; and "Free Communication of Ideas and the Quest for Truth: Toward a Teleological Approach to First Amendment Adjudication," *George Washington Law Review* 41, no. 2 (December 1972): 161.

137. See Owen Fiss, "Why the State?" *Harvard Law Review* 100 (February 1987): 787–88.

138. *There Is No Such Thing as Free Speech* (New York: Oxford University Press, 1994), 16–17.

139. Walter Berns, *The First Amendment and the Future of American Democracy* (New York: Basic Books, 1976), 156. See, too, Paul Chevigny, *More Speech: Dialogue Rights and Modern Liberty* (Philadelphia: Temple University Press, 1988), 7; and Alexander Bickel, *The Morality of Consent* (New Haven, Conn.: Yale University Press, 1975), 77.

140. See Schauer, *Free Speech*, 21 (criticizing the "survival theory of truth," and noting that if we "define moral truth as what in fact survives, then we are committed to saying that Nazism was 'right' in Germany in the 1930s, and that slavery was equally 'correct' or 'wise' in parts of the United States prior to the Civil War"). Also see Harry Wellington, "On Freedom of Expression," *Yale Law Journal* 88 (1979): 1105 ("In the long run, true ideas do tend to drive out false ones. The problem is that the short run may be very long").

141. See Schauer, *Free Speech*, 35–36 (arguing that the argument from democracy "views freedom of speech as a necessary component of a society premised on the assumption that the population at large is sovereign").

142. Schauer, *Free Speech*, 35–46.

143. Jack Balkin refers to the "democracy-based" theoretical approach to freedom of speech as the "republican" or "progressivist" model because of its "focus on democratic deliberation rather than individual autonomy." "Digital Speech and Democratic Culture: A Theory of Freedom of Expression for the Information Society," *New York University Law Review* 79, no. 1 (April 2004): 29.

144. See Cass Sunstein, *One Case at a Time: Judicial Minimalism on the Supreme Court* (Cambridge, Mass.: Harvard University Press, 1999), 177–78; Sunstein, *Democracy and the Problem of Free Speech*, xvii, xx; and, Sunstein, *The Partial Constitution* (Cambridge, Mass.: Harvard University Press, 1993), 164. As the moniker would suggest, Sunstein's intention here is to locate this conception of free speech in James Madison's political theory, because as he argues, for this founder the First Amendment is linked to "the American revision of sovereignty and to a particular conception of democracy" and the free speech principles of the American constitutional tradition should therefore be understood in light of the commitments to political equality and public deliberation. *Democracy and the Problem of Free Speech*, xvii. For a different perspective on Madison, see Richard Matthews, *If Men Were Angels: James Madison and the Heartless Empire of Reason* (Lawrence: University Press of Kansas, 1995), 22, 85.

145. In her biography of Justice Brandeis, Philippa Strum noted that his favorite book, *The Greek Commonwealth*, praises Pericles' funeral oration as the highest point of democracy. See Lewis, *Make No Law*, 87.

146. 274 U.S. 357 (1927). More famous for its dissenting spirit, Brandeis concurred in the judgment of the Court because he felt that Whitney's attorneys had failed to rest the argument on the appropriate legal grounds. See Zechariah Chafee, Jr., *Free Speech in the United States* (Cambridge, Mass.: Harvard University Press, 1967), 347.

147. *Whitney*, 375.

148. For a view of Brandeis's vision that departs from Holmes's marketplace test for "truth" and that resists the conflation with the work of Alexander Meiklejohn and the "antipathy to individualism and to commercial endeavor that informs" the philosopher's thought, see Vincent Blasi, "The First Amendment and the Ideal of Civic Courage: The Brandeis Opinion in *Whitney v. California*," *William and Mary Law Review* 29 (Summer 1988): 685, 686.

149. See Pnina Lahav, "Holmes and Brandeis: Libertarian and Republican Justifications for Free Speech," *Journal of Law and Politics* 4 (1987): 451.

150. See Alexander Meiklejohn, "The First Amendment Is an Absolute," in *Supreme Court Review*, ed. Philip Kurland (Chicago: University of Chicago Press, 1961), 252.

151. Meiklejohn, *Political Freedom*, 55.

152. See Alexander Meiklejohn, *Free Speech and its Relation to Self-Government* (New York: Harper and Row, 1948). Of course, the question of what constitutes appropriately "public" speech has been the source of some debate and, after initially being pressed on the terms of his argument (see Zechariah Chafee, "Book Review," *Harvard Law Review* 62, no. 5 [March 1949]: 891), Meiklejohn went on to concede that art, science and literature, for example, could be legitimately included as "public" speech (see "The First Amendment Is an Absolute," 252), drawing challenges from some prominent thinkers. See, e.g., Robert Bork, "Neutral Principles and Some First Amendment Problems," *Indiana Law Journal* 47 (Fall 1971): 1–35; and Lillian BeVier, "The First Amendment and Political Speech: An Inquiry into the Substance and Limits of Principle," *Stanford Law Review* 30 (January 1978): 299–358 (seeking a broader set of theoretical parameters for "political speech").

153. See Thomas Emerson, *Toward a General Theory of the First Amendment* (New York: Random House, 1966); and Emerson, "Toward a General Theory of the First Amendment," *Yale Law Journal* 72, no. 5 (April 1963): 878–79.

154. "Toward a General Theory of the First Amendment," 878–79.

155. Baker, *Human Liberty and Free Speech*, 47–48.

156. Sunstein, *One Case at a Time*, 177–78.

157. See Schauer, *Free Speech*, 67–72.

158. Thomas Scanlon, "A Theory of Freedom of Expression," *Philosophy and Public Affairs* 1, no. 2 (Winter 1972): 204–26. But see Scanlon's mild revision of this argument in "Freedom of Expression and Categories of Expression," *University of Pittsburgh Law Review* 40, no. 4 (Summer 1979): 532.

159. See Martin Redish, "The Value of Free Speech," *University of Pennsylvania Law Review* 130 (1982): 646.

160. Baker, *Human Liberty and Freedom of Speech*, 51.

161. See Vincent Blasi, "The Checking Value in First Amendment Theory," *American Bar Foundation Research Journal*, no. 3 (1977): 521. See "Free Speech and Good Character: From Milton to Brandeis to the Present," in *Eternally Vigilant*, ed. Bollinger and Stone, 60–95 (tracing the concept of "character" as a precondition for citizenship in society from John Milton to today). See too Blasi, "Holmes and the Marketplace of Ideas," 2.

162. See Lee Bollinger, *The Tolerant Society* (New York: Oxford University Press, 1988).

163. See Steven Shiffrin, *The First Amendment, Democracy, and Romance* (Cambridge, Mass.: Harvard University Press, 1990).

164. Ronald Collins and David Skover, *The Death of Discourse* (Boulder, Colo.: Westview Press, 1996).

165. See Fish, *There Is No Such Thing as Free Speech*, 102–19.

166. This argument, as Baker writes, can generally be classified as fitting into one of four frameworks: (1) correct failures of economic markets to the extent possible without restricting anyone's speech freedom; (2) guarantee all viewpoints adequate, but not necessarily equal, access to the marketplace of ideas; (3) guarantee all viewpoints equal access to the marketplace of ideas (e.g., equal time for each candidate); or (4) guarantee all individuals equal access. *Human Liberty and Freedom of Speech*, 37–46.

167. Ibid., 37.

168. Jerome Barron, "Access to the Press—A New First Amendment Right," 1641.

169. As Baker implies in his discussion of this approach, the "market failures" critique maintains the predicates of the marketplace itself, but merely observes the necessary regulations and supervision required to preserve *freer* and *fairer* competition. *Human Liberty and Freedom of Speech*, 3.

170. "Developments: Election Law," *Harvard Law Review* 88, no. 6 (April 1975): 1236.

171. Herbert Alexander, *Financing Politics*, 4th ed. (Washington, D.C.: CQ Press, 1992), 163.

172. Ibid.

173. See, e.g., Robert Post, "Reconciling Theory and Doctrine in First Amendment Jurisprudence," in *Eternally Vigilant*, ed. Bollinger and Stone, 160. Also noting this exaggerated contrast, Frederick Schauer suggests that while the advocates of the "democracy" (or "self-government") model for free speech imagine a kind of theoretical impasse between

their proffered justification and the marketplace-quest-for-truth approach, "the arguments are not nearly so distinct." In fact, a closer examination of the "paradoxes and other weaknesses of the argument from democracy reveals that much of its strength derives not from its independent force, but from the extent to which it is a discrete and important *subset* of the argument from truth." *Free Speech*, 45, 46.

174. Sunstein, *Democracy and the Problem of Free Speech*, 243 (emphasis added).

175. Ibid., 51. For more on the "New Deal for Speech" argument, see the more extended discussion in *The Partial Constitution*, 197–231.

176. Sunstein seems to realize as much as he then shifts his emphasis from "markets" to "free markets" and concludes: "*Free* markets in expression are incompletely adapted to the American conception of sovereignty and to the commitment to government by discussion," meaning that "if we are to promote our founding ideals, we need to rethink our free speech principles." *Democracy and the Problem of Free Speech*, 119 (emphasis added).

CHAPTER 2: CONCEPTUAL CONFLUENCE

1. James Mahoney, "Path Dependence and Historical Sociology," *Theory and Society* 29, no. 4 (December 2000): 507.

2. Paul Pierson, "Not Just What, but *When*: Timing and Sequence in Political Processes," *Studies in American Political Development* 14 (Spring 2000): 76.

3. Ibid., 83. See, too, Paul Pierson and Theda Skocpol, "Historical Institutionalism in Contemporary Political Science," in *Political Science: State of the Discipline*, ed. Ira Katznelson and Helen Milner (New York: W. W. Norton, 2002), 700 (noting that "arguments about path dependence can thus help us to understand the powerful inertial 'stickiness' that characterizes many aspects of political development").

4. Pierson, "Not Just What, but *When*," 83.

5. Thomas Keck, "Activism and Restraint on the Rehnquist Court: Timing, Sequence, and Conjuncture in Constitutional Development," *Polity* 35, no. 1 (Fall 2002): 130.

6. In this sense, my argument is predicated on the notion that, as Mark Graber has suggested, "doctrinal evolution resembles institutional development," in the sense that "broader ideological environment[s]" can restrict both the possible and preferred arguments one is able to make. *Transforming Free Speech* (Berkeley and Los Angeles: University of California Press, 1991), 220. See, too, Howard Gillman and Cornell Clayton, "Beyond Judicial Attitudes: Institutional Approaches to Supreme Court Decision-Making," in *Supreme Court Decision-Making: New Institutionalist Approaches*, ed. Howard Gillman and Cornell Clayton (Chicago: University of Chicago Press, 1999), 3 (observing that institutional settings are an "omnipresent feature of our attempts to pursue a preferred course of action" and arguing that it is "not possible to imagine political behavior—or, for that matter, any purposeful human behavior—proceeding without some overt or tacit reference to the institutional arrangements and cultural contexts that give it shape, direction, and meaning").

7. See Pierson and Skocpol, "Historical Institutionalism," 709 (stressing that institutions are "remade over time" and "often have a highly 'layered' quality [citations omitted]").

8. To be clear here, the point in using descriptors like "downstream" is not intended as teleological code for "progress," but simply to stress that in ontological terms the particular concoction created at, and *through* the confluence of constitutional concepts simultaneously constructs the legal domain and constitutes it in such a way that: (1) none of the ingredients can be separated from the mix; and (2) the mix itself becomes a *re*constituted composition of its initial constituents.

9. The development of competing conceptual frameworks within which the Court understands the place, purpose, and potential of freedom of speech during campaigns and elections, is informed by—but distinct from—Philip Bobbitt's notion of "reconceptualization," whereby change comes to the Constitution in its most frequent manner as the "incremental corrections in course that courts make as they confront unanticipated fact-situations and must apply old rules reconsidered in the light of new cases." See *Constitutional Fate: Theory of the Constitution* (New York: Oxford University Press, 1982), 224.

10. For one of the earliest and most thorough inquiries into the question of the appropriate role for the state in regulating political campaign activities, see "Developments: Election Law," *Harvard Law Review* 88, no. 6 (April 1975): 1233–98.

11. See Julian Eule, "Promoting Speaker Diversity: *Austin* and *Metro Broadcasting*," in *Supreme Court Review* (1990) (Chicago: University of Chicago Press, 1991), 105–32.

12. See the per curiam Court's famous pronouncement in *Buckley v. Valeo*, 424 U.S. 1, 48–49 (1976) ("The concept that government may restrict the speech of some elements of our society in order to enhance the relative voice of others is wholly foreign to the First Amendment").

13. 250 U.S. 616, 630 (1919).

14. 540 U.S. 93, 259 (2003). Here the Court upheld, most importantly in a 5–4 ruling, Titles I and II of the BCRA, pertaining to soft money and electioneering restrictions.

15. 424 U.S. 1 (1976).

16. The opinion, however, was quite fractured, with all the justices joining only the "case or controversy" section of the decision. Three justices (Brennan, Stewart, and Powell) joined all parts of the decision; Justice Marshall joined all except for the finding that limitations on expenditures by candidates from personal or family resources were unconstitutional; and Justice Blackmun joined all parts except for the finding that contribution limits were constitutional. Justice Rehnquist joined all parts except for the holding that public financing was constitutional with respect to the financing of nominating conventions, while Chief Justice Burger joined only the sections explaining that the interest in preventing corruption was insufficient to justify expenditure limits and the section pertaining to the scope of the FEC's authority, and Justice White joined only in the holding that public financing was constitutional, though he indicated his agreement with the restrictions on contributions.

17. Limitations were placed at $1,000 for individuals and groups; $5,000 for Political Committees; and, $25,000 in total contributions during any calendar year.

18. *Buckley*, 19 (emphasis added).

19. *Buckley*, 19 (emphasis added).

20. *Buckley*, 20–21 (emphasis added).

21. 454 U.S. 290 (1981) (hereafter, *CARC*).

22. *CARC*, 296.

23. *CARC*, 296.

24. *CARC*, 296 (emphasis added).

25. *CARC*, 299. Significantly, the Court also construed the speech environment here as the purest form of speech marketplace in the sense that initiative campaigns are by definition about ideas and proposals, rather than candidates, and thus there was less concern that amassed wealth could distort or sully the process, as one might expect when elected officials are involved.

26. 486 U.S. 414 (1988).

27. *Meyer*, 422.

28. *Meyer*, 425.

29. See Chapter 7 for more on this facet of the case.

30. As the state argued during Paul Grant's initial trial, the prohibition on payments to circulators hardly amounted to a serious diminution of political speech, because even when allowing *only* volunteer circulators, Colorado still ranked fourth out of twenty-three states (plus the District of Columbia) in terms of the total number of measures placed on the ballot. *Paul K. Grant v. Natalie Meyer* et al., civil action no. 84-JM-1207 (1984): 7.

31. *Meyer*, 422 (emphasis added).

32. *Meyer*, 422–24 (emphasis added).

33. 425 U.S. 610 (1976).

34. *Hynes*, 626.

35. *Hynes*, 628.

36. See *McConnell*, 288 (Justice Scalia, dissenting) ("Our precedents teach, above all, that Government cannot be trusted to moderate its rules for suppression of speech"). See, too, Frederick Schauer, *Free Speech: A Philosophical Enquiry* (New York: Cambridge University Press, 1982), 128 ("The issue is not whether newspapers should or should not be fair. Rather it is whether any governmental agency should be entrusted with the power to decide whether they are fair or not").

37. This attitude was first expressed (in this body of cases) by Justice Black, rejecting the premises of the Hatch Act, legislation which prohibited federal employees from taking "any active part in political management or in political campaigns":

> It [the Act] makes honest participation in essential political activities an offense punishable by proscription from public employment. It endows a governmental board with the awesome power to censor the thoughts, expressions, and activities of law-abiding citizens in the field of free expression, from which no person should be barred by a government which boasts that it is a government of, for, and by the people—all the people. (*United Public Workers of America v. Mitchell*, 330 U.S. 75, 115 [1947])

38. *Buckley*, 248. See also, Schauer, *Free Speech*, *passim*; and David Rabban, *Free Speech in its Forgotten Years* (New York: Cambridge University Press, 1997), 21 ("Government regulation of speech, however, well intentioned initially, can easily lead to repression of merely unpopular views").

39. 352 U.S. 567 (1957).

40. *Auto Workers*, 593.

41. 435 U.S. 765, 777 (1978).

42. *Bellotti*, 791 (emphasis added).

43. 456 U.S. 45 (1982).

44. *Hartlage*, 59.

45. *Hartlage*, 59.

46. See, e.g., *FEC v. National Conservative PAC*, 470 U.S. 480 (1985) (hereafter, *NCPAC*) (invalidating a provision of the Presidential Election Campaign Fund Act that prohibited independent PAC expenditures of more than $1000 on behalf of a presidential candidate who had accepted public financing).

47. See, e.g., *FEC v. Massachusetts Citizens for Life, Inc.*, 479 U.S. 238, 257 (1986) (hereafter, *MCFL*) (acknowledging that direct corporate spending on political activity "raises the prospect that resources amassed in the economic marketplace may be used to provide an unfair advantage in the political marketplace," but also reasoning that corporations created expressly for political purposes, as opposed to those which operate in the economic

sphere, should be exempt from the rule requiring corporations to create and maintain a segregated, independently-funded fund for political contributions).

48. 494 U.S. 652 (1990).

49. *Austin*, 679.

50. *Austin*, 680.

51. *Austin*, 706.

52. *Austin*, 713.

53. *Austin*, 706, 713.

54. 518 U.S. 604 (1996).

55. *Colorado* I, 644. Five years later, however, in *FEC v. Colorado Republican Federal Campaign Committee* 533 U.S. 431 (2001), generally known as "*Colorado* II," the Court found that while "independent" expenditures by parties do not constitute contributions, party expenditures made "in coordination" with candidates are, for practical purposes, "contributions."

56. See Warren Richey, "Speech Limits Weighed for Judicial Candidates," *Christian Science Monitor*, March 26, 2002, 2.

57. *Republican Party of Minnesota v. White*, 536 U.S. 765, 768 (2002).

58. *White*, 782.

59. *White*, 794.

60. *White*, 794.

61. *White*, 795 (emphasis added).

62. *White*, 795.

63. *White*, 795.

64. *St. Amant v. Thompson* 390 U.S. 727 (1968); *New York Times v. Sullivan* 376 U.S. 254, 270 (1964) (reversing the lower Alabama courts in a seminal libel case stemming from statements included in an advertisement in the newspaper and outlining a rigorous set of principles designed to protect the freedom of the press, while famously announcing that the Court would "consider this case against the background of a profound national commitment to the principle that debate on public issues should be uninhibited, robust, and wide-open").

65. *St. Amant*, 732 (emphasis added).

66. 401 U.S. 295 (1971).

67. Damron brought suit against the newspaper because it falsely reported that he had been charged in a federal court with perjury in a civil rights suit, when the article should have instead referred to the candidate's brother.

68. *Ocala Star-Banner*, 301 (emphasis added). See too *Monitor Patriot Co. v. Roy*, 401 U.S. 265 (1971), decided on the same day as *Ocala* and involving similar facts, though *Monitor* pertained to a libel action brought against a New Hampshire paper that had run a column referring to a candidate for the U.S. Senate as a "former smalltime bootlegger." Reversing the lower court, a unanimous Supreme Court ruled that a public official (including candidates for political office) could not recover damages unless it could be proven that the statement was made with "actual malice" or "reckless disregard of the truth"—the basic standard set forth in *Sullivan*.

69. The literature on the Warren Court is vast, but for recent works treating the Warren Court's egalitarian tendencies, see Lucas A. Powe, *The Warren Court and American Politics* (Cambridge, Mass.: Harvard University Press, 2000); and Morton Horwitz, *The Warren Court and the Pursuit of Justice* (New York: Hill and Wang, 1999). For an earlier critical

perspective, see Philip Kurland, "Egalitarianism and the Warren Court," *Michigan Law Review* 69 (1970): 634 (arguing that the Warren Court's "egalitarian bent" cannot "find specific justification in the language or history of the Constitution as originally framed"; nor can it find assistance in the "history and purpose of the equal protection clause of the fourteenth amendment, the place at which the doctrine of equality specifically entered constitutional language").

70. *Baker v. Carr* 369 U.S. 186 (1962). See Richard Hasen, *The Supreme Court and Election Law: Judging Equality from* Baker v. Carr *to* Bush v. Gore (New York: New York University Press, 2003), 21 ("After *Baker*, the trend in Warren Court formal equality cases pointed almost uniformly toward an expansive notion of political equality"); and Robert Dixon, *Democratic Representation* (New York: Oxford University Press, 1968), 6 ("The rigidity with which the equality idea is being applied in reshaping legislative districts, coupled with possible applications to such governmental areas as the electoral college, judgeship elections, voting practices inside legislatures, and local government, is a major event in America's long romance with the principle of egalitarianism").

71. Dixon, *Democratic Representation*, 4.

72. Ibid., 3. See, too, Thomas M. Keck, *The Most Activist Court in History: The Road to Modern Judicial Conservatism* (Chicago: University of Chicago Press, 2004), 67, 83 ("The Warren Court's abandonment of restraint in the reapportionment context was one of a dramatic series of doctrinal innovations expanding the scope of constitutional rights during the 1960s," though, of course, the members of this Court "fundamentally disagreed whether they were authorized to police the democratic process in this way"); and Samuel Issacharoff, Richard Pildes, and Pamela Karlan, *The Law of Democracy* (New York: Foundation Press, 1998), 134 ("*Baker* was perhaps the most profoundly destabilizing opinion in the Supreme Court's history").

73. See *Colegrove v. Green*, 328 U.S. 549 (1946).

74. See John Moeller, "The Supreme Court's Quest for Fair Politics," *Constitutional Commentary* 1 (1984): 210 ("The search for fairness blossomed in the reapportionment cases, beginning with *Baker v. Carr*"—cases that demonstrated that while "equality is the means, fairness is the end." Such a "pursuit of fairness has led the Court into a quagmire," Moeller finds, because "what began as a quest for the equal weighting of votes by population, then evolved to evaluating the quality of access to the political system, and finally matured into a call for equal success in the political system"). For the stress on "fair" competition as extended into the era of the Burger Court, see *Gaffney v. Cummings*, 412 U.S. 735, 753 (1973) (stating that the very essence of districting was to produce "politically fair" results).

75. Dixon, *Democratic Representation*, 8.

76. Samuel Issacharoff, "Oversight of Regulated Political Markets," *Harvard Journal of Law and Public Policy* 24 (Fall 2000): 91.

77. 372 U.S. 368 (1963).

78. *Gray*, 381. As Lucas Powe notes in his comprehensive study of this era, it was Robert Kennedy (in oral argument as amicus for the federal government) who "became the first person in the Courtroom to utter the magic words 'one man, one vote,' which Douglas immediately changed to 'one person, one vote.'" *Warren Court and American Politics*, 242.

79. 377 U.S. 533 (1964).

80. *Reynolds*, 562.

81. *Reynolds*, 565 (emphasis added).

82. *Reynolds*, 565 (emphasis added).

83. *Reynolds*, 566 (emphasis added).

84. 377 U.S. 713, 736 (1964) (emphasis added).

85. In other words, the value of exchange within such a framework resides not just with the newly (or re-) enfranchised communicants, but with *society*, which benefits from the consideration of those ideas that might not have been introduced in an entirely "free" marketplace context, absent affirmative state efforts, subsidies, or facilitation. Consider, for example, the rationale behind "public" television and radio programs: both were established on the fact that there are some programs, interests, problems, and views that benefit the *public* by being aired, but that would likely not be available in a purely economically driven market framework; that is, because they would likely not generate profits, they tend not to be introduced even though they offer some putative value to the polity.

86. 383 U.S. 663 (1966).

87. *Harper*, 666.

88. *Harper*, 668.

89. Hasen, *Supreme Court and Election Law*, 86.

90. See, e.g., Martin Shapiro, *Law and Politics in the Supreme Court* (New York: Free Press, 1964), 218, 248 (contending that it is "impossible to construct a single *a priori* theory, model, or definition of democracy that will command universal support," and criticizing the Court for hiding behind the "neutral principle of 'one man, one vote,' a ringing Constitutional principle that exempts it from the hard political work of actually increasing the degree of equality in our political system").

91. See Robert G. Dixon, Jr., "The Warren Court Crusade for the Holy Grail of 'One Man-One Vote,'" *Supreme Court Review* (Chicago: University of Chicago Press, 1969), 219.

92. See Ward Elliott, *The Rise of Guardian Democracy: The Supreme Court's Role in Voting Rights Disputes, 1845–1969* (Cambridge, Mass.: Harvard University Press, 1974), 2 (critically assessing the "bureaucratic, elitist ideology of action-minded intellectuals" portrayed by the Warren Court voting and civil rights decisions and discussing that Court's "Guardian Ethic" which was "democratic in its stress on equality," but which was "antidemocratic in its stress on administration and intellectual elitism" and which "tended to extend equality in form while debasing it in substance," granting equal access to representative institutions, but treating those institutions "as though they were unfit to decide the main questions").

93. For more on the theoretical overlap of these two domains, see Kenneth Karst, "Equality as a Central Principle in the First Amendment," *University of Chicago Law Review* 43, no. 1 (Autumn 1975): 53 (arguing that informed choices by the citizenry, the search for truth, and self-development depend on the realization of the "equality principle" inherent in the First Amendment and stressing that, because "part of the 'central meaning' of the first amendment is the guarantee of equal liberty of expression," the "first amendment demands an even greater degree of equality in the electoral process than does the equal protection clause").

94. Morton Horwitz, Supreme Court 1992 Term, "Foreword: The Constitution of Change: Legal Fundamentality without Fundamentalism," *Harvard Law Review* 107 (November 1993): 109–10 ("During the last twenty-five years, free speech doctrine has taken a surprising turn," in that since the late 1960s, the "generalization and universalization of

freedom of speech, and the Court's concomitant devotion to its abstract doctrine of 'content neutrality,' . . . have combined to produce a Lochnerization of the First Amendment"). See, too, Cass Sunstein, *Free Markets and Social Justice* (New York: Oxford University Press, 1997), 229 (arguing that *Buckley v. Valeo* "might well be seen as the modern-day analogue of the infamous and discredited case of *Lochner v. New York*").

95. See, e.g., Mark Tushnet, "An Essay on Rights," *Texas Law Review* (May 1984): 1387 (observing a generation ago that the "first amendment has replaced the due process clause as the primary guarantor of the privileged" and arguing that it now "protects the privileged more perniciously than the due process clause ever did," and "stands as a general obstruction to all progressive legislative efforts"). Also see, Catherine MacKinnon, *Only Words* (Cambridge, Mass.: Harvard University Press, 1993), 71 (arguing that the "law of equality and the law of freedom of speech are on a collision course in this country").

96. See Chapter 1 for more on "market failures."

97. For a recent version of this argument, see Cass Sunstein, *The Partial Constitution* (Cambridge, Mass.: Harvard University Press, 1993), 40–67. For a theoretical overview of such phenomena, generally, see Jack Balkin, "Ideological Drift and the Struggle over Meaning," *Connecticut Law Review* 25 (Spring 1993): 871; and see, Rabban, *Free Speech in Its Forgotten Years*, 20–21 (rejecting such claims of First Amendment misappropriation).

98. See Fred Wertheimer and Susan Weiss Manes, "Campaign Finance Reform: A Key to Restoring the Health of Our Democracy," *Columbia Law Review* 94 (May 1994): 1126–59 (arguing that the current system of campaign finance undermines our system of equal political representation); and Sidney Verba, "Would the Dream of Political Equality Turn Out to Be a Nightmare?" *Perspectives on Politics* 1, no. 4 (December 2003): 665–66 (noting that for "equal *consideration*" [as opposed to "equal treatment"] to exist, "equal *capacity* to express political voice and equal *expression* of that voice are key [emphasis added]").

99. See, e.g., R. H. Coase, "The Market for Goods and the Market for Ideas," *American Economic Review* 64, no. 2 (May 1974): 384–91 (arguing that there should be consistency, in terms of regulation, between the economic marketplace and the marketplace of ideas); Lillian BeVier, "Campaign Finance Reform: Specious Arguments, Intractable Dilemmas, *Columbia Law Review* 94, no. 4 (May 1994): 1279 (arguing that "only reforms that are practically guaranteed to achieve a clearly specified and unquestionably legitimate corruption-prevention goal are worth the sacrifice of political freedom that their enforcement inevitably entails"); and Sanford Levinson, "Politics, Government, and Public Affairs: Regulating Campaign Activity—the New Road to Contradiction?"review of *Politics and Money: The New Road to Corruption*, by Elizabeth Drew, *Michigan Law Review* 83 (February 1985): 939–52 (explaining the difficulties inherent to all regulative efforts, especially the distinction between money and political activities, for example).

100. On the role of the state as a "promoter" *of* (as opposed to "participant" *in*) expression, see Thomas Emerson, "The Affirmative Side of the First Amendment," *Georgia Law Review* 15, no. 4 (Summer 1981): 799 ("Governmental *promotion* occurs when the government undertakes to facilitate use of the system by private [or nongovernmental] persons or groups. . . . Governmental *participation* occurs when the communication emanates from the government itself, through a government official, a government agency, or an institution controlled by the government [emphasis added]").

101. What such involvement seeks to ensure, as Ronald Dworkin has written, is that "each citizen" has a "fair and equal opportunity not only to hear the views of others, as

these are published or broadcast, but to command attention for his own views, either as a candidate for office or as a member of a politically active group committed to some program or convictions." "The Curse of American Politics," *New York Review of Books* (October 17, 1996), 23.

102. Owen Fiss, "Free Speech and Social Structure," *Iowa Law Review* 71 (July 1986): 1416. See, too, Fiss, "Why the State?" *Harvard Law Review* 100 (February 1987): 783 ("We should be able to start at the other end—to begin with the fact of state intervention in economic matters, and then use that historical experience to understand why the state might have a role to play in furthering free speech values"); Fiss, *Liberalism Divided* (Boulder, Colo.: Westview Press, 1996), 31–46; and, Fiss, *The Irony of Free Speech* (Cambridge, Mass.: Harvard University Press, 1996), 1–26.

103. *Free Speech, "The People's Darling Privilege"* (Durham, N.C.: Duke University Press, 2000), 424.

104. 395 U.S. 367 (1969).

105. What *Red Lion* wrought, as Lucas Powe has observed, was an "entirely new free speech jurisprudence," on account of the unique nature of the medium and its distinct potential for distortion as compared to other forms of communication. *Warren Court and American Politics*, 333. Thus was the line drawn as well between speech and property in that the *New York Times* could rely on its own resources, while broadcasters looked to *public* property to disseminate information, which heightened the state's interest in maintaining the open channels for the distribution of ideas. But at the same time, Powe reasons, the case could be read as a "vote of no confidence in *Sullivan* and the ability of a free press to provide the needed information" to the public, were it not for state supervision and/or facilitation. Ibid., 334.

106. *Red Lion*, 390 ("viewers and listeners" emphasized in the original; subsequent emphases are added). For a thorough analysis of the implications of this "right to receive" expression, see William E. Lee, "The Supreme Court and the Right to Receive Expression," *Supreme Court Review* (Chicago: University of Chicago Press, 1987), 331–32. Note, however, that the Court refused to apply this rationale to newspapers, five years later in *Miami Herald Co. v. Tornillo*, 418 U.S. 241 (1974). Finally, in *Arkansas Educational Television Commission v. Forbes*, 523 U.S. 666 (1998), the Court explained that the reasoning in *Red Lion* did not apply to televised political debates sponsored by public broadcasters, as this kind of forum was inherently "nonpublic."

107. 453 U.S. 367 (1981).

108. *CBS, Inc. v. FCC*, 453 U.S. 367, 396 (1981) (emphasis added).

109. 466 U.S. 789 (1984). The "public forum doctrine," in the Court's jurisprudence, as Mark Tushnet has explained, essentially posits that "governments must make some public spaces available to people who want to use them for speech purposes, such as demonstrations and protest marches," spaces which are still, despite the passage of time since the New Deal–era establishment of this concept, thought to primarily implicate "traditional venues" such as "public streets and parks." *The New Constitutional Order* (Princeton, N.J.: Princeton University Press, 2003), 70–71.

110. *Taxpayers for Vincent*, 820.

111. *Taxpayers for Vincent*, 820 ("signs posted on public property are doubtless 'essential to the poorly financed causes of little people' . . .").

112. *Taxpayers for Vincent*, 818.

113. *Taxpayers for Vincent*, 819.

114. *Free Speech in the United States*, 406.

115. Consider here Brennan's observation that "common sense" would suggest that, at least regarding speakers with messages "generally unpopular or simply unpopular among property owners," it is "hardly likely" that a group "advocating an increase in the rate of a property tax would succeed in persuading private property owners to accept its signs," meaning that if forced to rely on *private* property for the dissemination of ideas, then groups with *alternative* views effectively have no "alternative avenues." Moreover, even as compared with "handbills," which are oftentimes the adopted means of communication for groups with less funding, Brennan wrote that "a message on a sign will typically reach far more people" than the leaflet option, because a "message on a posted sign remains to be seen by passersby as long as it is posted, while a handbill is typically read by a single reader and discarded." Furthermore, "not only must handbills be printed in large quantity, but many hours must be spent distributing them," and thus the "average cost of communicating by handbill is therefore likely to be far higher than the average cost of communicating by poster." See *Taxpayers for Vincent*, 820.

116. *Taxpayers for Vincent*, 819.

117. "Fora Americana: Speech in Public Places," *Supreme Court Review* (1974) (Chicago: University of Chicago Press, 1975), 245 (emphasis added).

118. *Buckley*, 49.

119. *Buckley*, 49.

120. See D.C. Circuit Court Judge Skelly Wright, "Politics and the Constitution: Is Money Speech?" *Yale Law Journal* 85 (July 1976): 1004.

121. *FEC v. National Right to Work Committee*, 459 U.S. 197 (1982) (involving a FECA prohibition on corporate expenditures in connection with federal elections, unless an organization has established a separate, segregated fund for purely "political" expenditures; and requiring that corporations without capital stock only solicit contributions to the separate fund from "members" of the corporation).

During the 1976 election NRWC had solicited 267,000 contributions from persons who were not "members," and thus the FEC brought suit. Writing for a unanimous Court, Justice Rehnquist found that the regulatory interests of Congress outweighed the First Amendment claims of the corporation and added, in an important statement about the particular problems stemming from the corporate form, that "the first purpose of 441b [the provision under review] is to ensure that substantial aggregations of wealth amassed by the special advantages which go with the corporate form of organization should not be converted into political 'war chests' which could be used to incur political debts from legislators who are aided by the contributions." *NRWC*, 207.

122. *Austin*, 660.

123. *Austin*, 666.

124. The irony of Justice Marshall's finding of "apparent" corruption in this case, is that this language came back to haunt him one year later in *Renne v. Geary*, 501 U.S. 312 (1991), when the Court, over his animated dissent, co-opted the rationale in *Austin* and reasoned that California's restrictions on political endorsements were legitimate state efforts to prevent voter confusion and corruption in the electoral process because, given their considerable influence, parties should be treated like corporations.

125. *Austin*, 669 (emphasis added).

126. Of course, this notion represented something of an about-face from *Bellotti*, where the Court had reasoned that if legislative findings indicated "that corporate advocacy

threatened imminently to undermine democratic processes, thereby denigrating rather than serving First Amendment interests, these arguments would merit our consideration," but concluding that "there has been no showing that the relative voice of corporations has been overwhelming or even significant in influencing referenda in Massachusetts, or that there has been any threat to the confidence of the citizenry in government." *Bellotti*, 789.

127. *Colorado* I, 650 (emphasis added). For an earlier argument along the same lines, see Justice Byron White (part dissent/part concurrence), *Buckley*, 265 ("There is nothing objectionable—indeed it seems to me a weighty interest in favor of the provision—in the attempt to insulate the political expression of federal candidates from the influence inevitably exerted by the endless job of raising increasingly large sums of money. I regret that the Court has returned them all to the treadmill").

128. U.S. Constitution, Art. I, § 4, cl. 1.

129. *Burdick v. Takushi*, 504 U.S. 428, 433 (1992) (citing *Storer v. Brown*, 415 U.S. 724, 730 [1974]).

130. *Burdick*, 433.

131. See *Cox v. Louisiana*, 379 U.S. 536, 554 (1965) (emphasizing that while both are "fundamental in our democratic society," the rights to free speech and assembly "still do not mean that everyone with opinions or beliefs to express may address a group at any public place and at any time." "The constitutional guarantee of liberty implies the existence of an *organized* society maintaining public *order*," in other words, "without which liberty itself would be lost in the excesses of anarchy [emphasis added].")

132. See *Timmons v. Twin Cities Area New Party*, 520 U.S. 351, 367 (1997) (accepting the state's contention that "political *stability* is best served through a healthy two-party system" and that "party splintering and excessive factionalism" could be tempered by the maintenance of the duopoly [emphasis added]").

133. *MCFL*, 257 (noting that "concern over the corrosive influence of concentrated corporate wealth reflects the conviction that it is important to protect the *integrity* of the marketplace of political ideas [emphasis added]").

134. Frederick Schauer and Richard Pildes, "Electoral Exceptionalism and the First Amendment," *Texas Law Review* 77, no. 7 (June 1999): 1818.

135. Ibid., 1805.

136. Supreme Court 2003 Term, "Foreword: The Constitutionalization of Democratic Politics," *Harvard Law Review* 118 (2004): 52.

137. "Constitutionalization of Democratic Politics," 148.

138. Vested in such a concern for the *process*, the *custodial* approach to discerning the place, parameters, and purchase of free expression in a democracy hearkens back in some respects to the work of the philosopher John Dewey, who, after World War I, increasingly came to base his "concern about free speech on its contribution to democracy rather than on its status as a natural right of autonomous individuals." Rabban, *Free Speech in its Forgotten Years*, 4.

Or, for a modern "Deweyan" in this respect, see Justice Stephen Breyer, who urges that "courts should take greater account of the Constitution's democratic nature when they interpret constitutional and statutory texts," and who stresses that the First Amendment should be read "not in isolation but as seeking to maintain a system of free expression designed to further a basic constitutional purpose: creating and maintaining democratic decision-making institutions." Stephen Breyer, *Active Liberty* (New York: Alfred A. Knopf, 2005), 5, 39, 47. See, too, Breyer, "Madison Lecture: Our Democratic Constitution," *New*

York University Law Review 77, no. 2 (May 2002): 245; and Owen Fiss, "The Censorship of Television," in *Eternally Vigilant: Free Speech in the Modern Era*, ed. Lee C. Bollinger and Geoffrey Stone (Chicago: University of Chicago Press, 2002), 283 (drawing specifically on Justice Breyer's reasoning in *Turner* II to argue that his approach should be viewed as "a movement away from the libertarian doctrine that has so dominated the Court for the last twenty-five years," and that it "constitutes an important first step toward the recovery of a jurisprudence that sees the First Amendment more as a protection of the democratic system than as a protection of the expressive interests of the individual speaker").

139. C. Edwin Baker, "Campaign Expenditures and Free Speech," *Harvard Civil Rights-Civil Liberties Law Review* 33 (Winter 1998): 19.

140. Ibid., 19.

141. Ibid., 2.

142. Ibid., 3. Further developing this claim, Baker reasons that elections are "legally structured institutions designed to further the governing process"—which, in their most overt sense, "are designed to choose office holders, especially legislators and chief executives"; but which in a more general sense are structured to "further various institutional goals: most centrally, to choose good office holders, but also to respect the equal right of various people to be involved in the process; to make the process efficacious and workable; to create and justify the belief that the process is fair; and, according to some theorists, to stimulate deliberation and reflection about the public good." "Campaign Expenditures and Free Speech," 25.

143. *Auto Workers*, 570.

144. See *St. Amant*, 736 (Justice Fortas, dissenting) ("The First Amendment is not so fragile that it requires us to immunize this kind of reckless, destructive invasion of the life, even of public officials, heedless of their interests and sensitivities. The First Amendment is not a shelter for the character assassinator, whether his action is heedless and reckless or deliberate. The First Amendment does not require that we license shotgun attacks on public officials in virtually unlimited open season. The occupation of public officeholder does not forfeit one's membership in the human race. The public official should be subject to severe scrutiny and to free and open criticism. But if he is needlessly, heedlessly, falsely accused of a crime, he should have a remedy in law. *New York Times* does not preclude this minimal standard of civilized living").

145. See the discussion of *Burson v. Freeman* in Chapter 5.

146. See, e.g., Hadley Arkes, "Civility and the Restriction of Speech: Rediscovering the Defamation of Groups," in *Free Speech and Association*, ed. Philip Kurland (Chicago: University of Chicago Press, 1975), 391 ("When we speak of civility we speak, really, about the fostering of moral codes and about the kind of life, the manners, even the modes of making a living that we hold up for emulation—about the occupations that are more or less respectable for people suited to live in civil society. And not the least of the elements of civility, giving some insight into ourselves and our standards, are the things we regard as respectable to say in public"); and Alexander Bickel, *The Morality of Consent* (New Haven, Conn.: Yale University Press, 1975), 76–77 (wondering "whether our experience has not taught us that . . . a marketplace without rules of civil discourse is no marketplace of ideas, but a bullring").

147. See the discussion of *Nixon v. Shrink Missouri Government PAC* in Chapter 8.

148. See the discussion of *McIntyre v. Ohio Elections Commission* in Chapter 6.

149. As Justice Stephen Breyer has recently argued, for example, "Participation is most

forceful when it is direct, involving, for example, voting, town meetings, political party membership, or issue-or interest-related activities," though it is "weak," he continues, while still existing "minimally," when "it is vicarious, reflected, say, in the understanding that each individual belongs to the political community with the right to participate should he or she choose to do so." *Active Liberty,* 15–16.

150. See Schauer and Pildes, "Electoral Exceptionalism," 1806.

151. On this general notion, see, e.g., the assessment of the democratic theorist Robert Putnam, whose diagnostic report on American politics and society in the 1990s called for campaign reforms to be "aimed at increasing the importance of social capital—and decreasing the importance of financial capital—in our elections, federal, state, and local." *Bowling Alone* (New York: Simon and Schuster, 2000), 412 (emphasis added).

152. *Active Liberty*, 47.

153. See Bruce Cain, "Moralism and Realism in Campaign Finance Reform," *University of Chicago Legal Forum* (1995): 111 (noting that recent discussions of campaign finance reform rely on "moralistic terms such as 'corruption,' 'unfairness,' and 'trusteeship,'" but criticizing the "moral idealism" of such reformers for trying to regulate the motives of elected officials or encouraging deliberative democracy, for example).

154. See Daniel Ortiz, "The Democratic Paradox of Campaign Finance Reform," *Stanford Law Review* 50 (1998): 901–5 (arguing among other things that campaign finance reform efforts imply an ironic distrust of the citizenry).

155. On the nature of such "harm," see *White*, 797 (Justice Stevens, dissenting) (criticizing the majority for finding unconstitutional a canon of judicial conduct prohibiting candidates for judicial office from "announcing" their views on "disputed legal or political issues" in the course of a campaign and referring to such judicial campaign speech as "harmful," while begrudgingly accepting ["so be it," he conceded] the Court's holding that the "solution" to such problem-speech would have to be "more speech"). On the notion of "corrosive influence," see *MCFL*, 257.

156. "Corruption," in *Political Innovation and Conceptual Change*, ed. Terence Ball, James Farr, and Russell Hanson (New York: Cambridge University Press, 1989), 222–23.

157. "In these terms," Euben continues, "political corruption involves the altering of the foundations or constitution of something (or someone) in a manner which lowers it (or them) in dignity, quality, character or value . . . and has less to do with individual malfeasance than with systematic and systemic degeneration of those practices and commitments that provide the terms of collective self-understanding and shared purposes." "Corruption," in *Political Innovation and Conceptual Change*, 222–23.

158. See Samuel Issacharoff and Richard Pildes, "Campaign Finance Hydraulics," *Texas Law Review* 77 (1999): 1718 (arguing that "corruption" and "distortion" are "dependent on some notion of what a 'pure' or 'clean' or 'accurate' process would produce").

159. For excellent introductions to the politics driving the establishment—and *entrenchment*—of university speech codes, see Milton J. Heumann and Thomas Church, eds., *Hate Speech on Campus* (Boston: Northeastern University Press, 1997); and Jon Gould, *Speak No Evil: The Triumph of Hate Speech Regulation* (Chicago: University of Chicago Press, 2005).

160. See, e.g., Richard Delgado, "Words That Wound: A Tort Action for Racial Insults, Epithets, and Name-Calling," *Harvard Civil Rights-Civil Liberties Law Review* 17 (1982): 133.

161. For the "liberal" position on such matters, see ACLU president and law professor

Nadine Strossen's essay in Heumann and Church, eds., *Hate Speech on Campus*, and "Frontiers of Legal Thought II, the New First Amendment: Regulating Racist Speech on Campus; A Modest Proposal?" *Duke Law Journal* (June 1990): 484.

162. See, e.g., Catherine MacKinnon, *Only Words* (Cambridge, Mass.: Harvard University Press, 1993); Andrea Dworkin, *Pornography: Men Possessing Women* (New York: E. P. Dutton, 1989); and, the discussion by Judge Frank Easterbrook of the Indianapolis statute informed by MacKinnon's arguments in *American Booksellers Association, Inc. v. Hudnut*, 771 F.2d 323 (1985).

163. See Robert George, *Making Men Moral* (New York: Oxford University Press, 1995).

164. 330 U.S. 75 (1947).

165. *Mitchell*, 94–95.

166. *Mitchell*, 111.

167. *Mitchell*, 99. The Court revisited the Hatch Act in *United States Civil Service Commission v. National Association of Letter Carriers, AFL-CIO*, 413 U.S. 548, 575 (1973) (involving a challenge brought by several federal employees' unions and certain local Democratic and Republican political committees to section 9 of the Hatch Act which prohibits federal employees from taking "an active part in political management or in political campaigns"). Affirming the holding in *Mitchell*, Justice White and the majority stressed that the statute was justified because forbidding activities like these "will *reduce the hazards to fair and effective government* [emphasis added]," a distinction that the Court drew to contrast the restriction with a bar on free speech or the right to vote. Most importantly, this provision of the act was meant to maintain the integrity of the marketplace (as well as the public's perception of it), by merely prohibiting partisan political activities by federal employees, rather than the right to vote, speak, or engage in nonpartisan political activities.

168. 418 U.S. 298 (1974).

169. *Shaker Heights*, 299.

170. *Shaker Heights*, 304 (emphasis added).

171. *Shaker Heights*, 302.

172. *Shaker Heights*, 303, 305, 303.

173. *Shaker Heights*, 304, 304.

174. *Shaker Heights*, 304.

175. *Shaker Heights*, 304.

176. *Shaker Heights*, 307 (emphasis added).

177. *Shaker Heights*, 304.

178. 424 U.S. 828 (1976).

179. *Greer*, 839, 847.

180. See *Bellotti*, 809 ("Such expenditures may be viewed as seriously threatening the role of the First Amendment as a guarantor of a free marketplace of ideas").

181. *CARC*, 311 (emphasis added).

182. *CARC*, 311.

183. *White*, 804.

184. *White*, 806. One would like more discussion of this point, to be sure, given the decades of research in political science demonstrating that politics necessarily influences judicial decision making. My sense is that, for Ginsburg, "politics" in essence means "partisan," or a politics of the "low" variety as Jack Balkin and Sanford Levinson have

argued. See "Understanding the Constitutional Revolution," *Virginia Law Review* 87, no. 6 (October 2001): 1045, 1062–63.

185. *White*, 807, n. 1. Further along in her opinion, Justice Ginsburg took her colleague, Justice Scalia, to task for apparently failing to recall *his own* reticence when asked his views on certain policies during his confirmation hearings: "The author of the Court's opinion," she noted before quoting from the transcript of Justice Scalia's confirmation hearing, "declined on precisely these grounds to tell the Senate whether he would overrule a particular case." "Let us assume that I have people arguing before me to do it or not to do it," Scalia stated at his hearing, continuing with:

> I think it is quite a thing to be arguing to somebody who you know has made a representation in the course of his confirmation hearings, and that is, by way of condition to his being confirmed, that he will do this or that. I think I would be in a very bad position to adjudicate the case without being accused of having a less than impartial view on the matter [quoting Justice Scalia]." (*White*, 819, n. 4)

186. *White*, 818.
187. *White*, 798.
188. *White*, 798.
189. *White*, 801.
190. 548 U.S. ____ (2006) (slip opinion).
191. *Sorrell*, slip op. (Stevens, dissenting), 5.
192. *Sorrell*, slip op. (Stevens, dissenting), 5.
193. *Sorrell*, slip op. (Stevens, dissenting), 5.
194. *Sorrell*, slip op. (Stevens, dissenting), 6 (emphasis added).

CHAPTER 3: RHETORICAL MODES

1. Robert J. Hume, "The Use of Rhetorical Sources by the U.S. Supreme Court," *Law & Society Review* 40, no. 4 (2006): 818.

2. This focus on the nature and form of argument is informed by the earlier work of Philip Bobbitt, *Constitutional Fate* (New York: Oxford University Press, 1982), 6–8, and (with respect to a typological assessment of argument) by the work of Mark Tushnet, *Red, White, and Blue* (Cambridge, Mass.: Harvard University Press, 1988) (especially his discussions of the "Jurisprudence of History," the "Jurisprudence of Democracy," and the "Jurisprudence of Philosophy"). See, too, Bobbitt, "Is Law Politics?" review of *Red, White, and Blue*, by Mark Tushnet, *Stanford Law Review* 41 (May 1989): 1233.

3. See, e.g., Martin Flaherty, "History 'Lite' in Modern American Constitutionalism," *Columbia Law Review* 95 (April 1995): 523.

4. Alfred Kelley, "Clio and the Court: An Illicit Love Affair," *Supreme Court Review* (Chicago: University of Chicago Press, 1965), 155.

5. Ibid., 155.

6. That is, while certain members of the Court tend to assert that their reading of specific historical texts somehow represents the definitive historical *truth*, it is essential to bear in mind that this is, itself, a function of the justice's rhetorical endeavor to win over other justices, to convince the public that they are right, perhaps to demean their colleagues, or simply to write what they think. One could and should, of course, extend Kelley's critique in a different direction and stress the equally significant implications of "law office empiricism," "law office sociology," "law office statistics," or, the gravest sin of all, "law office political science."

7. On "original intent," see Bobbitt, *Constitutional Fate*, 9–25; Tushnet, *Red, White, and Blue*, 21–69; Edwin Meese, III, "Toward a Jurisprudence of Original Intent," *Harvard Journal of Law and Public Policy* 11 (Winter 1988): 5–12; and Keith Whittington, *Constitutional Interpretation: Textual Meaning, Original Intent, and Judicial Review* (Lawrence: University Press of Kansas, 2001). For the justice's argument in favor of determining the historic meaning of particular words, concepts, or practices, as opposed to the purported "intentions" of their designers, see Antonin Scalia's essay in *A Matter of Interpretation*, ed. Amy Guttman (Princeton, N.J.: Princeton University Press, 1997).

8. 424 U.S. 828 (1976).

9. *Greer*, 839.

10. *Greer*, 841.

11. *Greer*, 842. Indeed, Burger continued, it was only slightly more than a century before that "some officers of the Armed Forces, then in combat, sought to exercise undue influence either for President Lincoln or for his opponent, General McClellan, in the election of 1864." *Greer*, 842.

12. 536 U.S. 765 (2002).

13. *White*, 785.

14. *White*, 785.

15. *White*, 785.

16. 514 U.S. 334 (1995).

17. *Greer*, 856.

18. *Greer*, 873.

19. *Greer*, 873.

20. 548 U.S. ____ (2006) (slip opinion).

21. *Sorrell*, 8 (slip op.).

22. *Sorrell*, 8 (slip op.).

23. On this strain, see Bernard Bailyn, *The Origins of American Politics* (New York: Vintage Books, 1967); and Gordon Wood, *The Creation of the American Republic, 1776–1787* (New York: W. W. Norton, 1969).

24. Consider Louis Brandeis's famous brief in *Muller v. Oregon*, 208 U.S. 412 (1908); the modern "authority" of Kenneth Clark's research in *Brown v. Board of Education*, 347 U.S. 483 (1954); and the famous "Baldus Study" in *McCleskey v. Kemp*, 481 U.S. 279 (1987).

25. See Donald Horowitz, *The Courts and Social Policy* (Washington, D.C.: Brookings Institution Press, 1977), 25, 277 ("The fit between law and social science is not a comfortable one and will not be for some time").

26. See Martin Shapiro, *Law and Politics in the Supreme Court* (New York: Free Press, 1964), 248–50 (criticizing the Court for failing to analyze the "actual political conditions in each state" when contemplating issues of representation).

27. See David Ryden, "The Supreme Court as Architect of Election Law: Summing Up, Looking Ahead," in *The U.S. Supreme Court and the Electoral Process*, ed. David Ryden (Washington, D.C.: Georgetown University Press, 2000), 278. See, too, Elizabeth Garrett, "Leaving the Decision to Congress," in *The Vote: Bush, Gore, and the Supreme Court*, ed. Cass Sunstein and Richard Epstein (Chicago: University of Chicago Press, 2001), 43.

28. 528 U.S. 337 (2000); *McConnell v. FEC* 540 U.S. 93, 259 (2003).

29. See *Munro v. Socialist Workers Party*, 479 U.S. 189, 195–96 (1986) (Justice White, for the majority) (upholding against a free association challenge a ballot access restriction

while noting: "To require States to prove *actual* voter confusion, ballot overcrowding, or the presence of frivolous candidacies as a predicate to the imposition of reasonable ballot access restrictions would invariably lead to endless court battles over the sufficiency of the 'evidence' marshaled by a State to prove the predicate. Such a requirement would necessitate that a State's political system sustain some level of damage before a legislature could take corrective action").

30. 486 U.S. 414 (1988).

31. 525 U.S. 182 (1999) (hereafter, *ACLF*).

32. *Meyer*, 425.

33. 533 U.S. 431 (2001) (hereafter, *Colorado* II).

34. *Colorado* II, 458 (emphasis added) (citing the declaration by Robert Hickmott, former Democratic fundraiser and national finance director for Timothy Wirth's Senate campaign ["We . . . told contributors who had made the maximum allowable contribution to the Wirth campaign but who wanted to do more that they could raise money for the DSCC so that we could get our maximum (Party Expenditure Provision) allocation from the DSCC"]; the Declaration of Timothy Wirth ["I understood that when I raised funds for the DSCC, the donors expected that I would receive the amount of their donations multiplied by a certain number that the DSCC had determined in advance, assuming the DSCC has raised other funds"]; and the declaration of Leon G. Billings, former Executive Director of the Democratic Senatorial Campaign Committee [DSCC] ["People often contribute to party committees because they have given the maximum amount to a candidate, and want to help the candidate indirectly by contributing to the party"]).

35. *Colorado* II, 459 (citing Hickmott's declaration that "[The tally system] is an informal agreement between the DSCC and the candidates' campaigns that if you help the DSCC raise contributions, we will turn around and help your campaign").

36. *Colorado* II, 459 (emphasis added).

37. Meanwhile, Thomas rejected the assumption that the other two passages demonstrated "corruption"-by-circumvention, because they were "made by Timothy Wirth, who was the object of the negative advertisements giving rise to this lawsuit, and by his national finance director," and because they do not describe "how donations were actually treated by the DSCC, either in general or in Wirth's particular case," but instead simply reflect the "understandings of how the money would be used in Wirth's election." *Colorado* II, 480, n. 10.

38. 523 U.S. 666 (1998) (hereafter, *AETC*).

39. See Bertrand de Jouvenel, "Seminar Exercise: The Chairman's Problem," *American Political Science Review* 55, no. 2 (1961): 368–72.

40. *AETC*, 681.

41. *AETC*, 681.

42. *AETC*, 692 (emphasis added).

43. "Democracy and Disorder," in *The Vote*, ed. Sunstein and Epstein, 142, 151.

44. See Peter Shane, "Rights, Remedies, and Restraint," *Chicago-Kent Law Review* 64 (1988): 531, 550, and to a slightly lesser extent, Lon Fuller, *The Morality of Law*, rev. ed. (1964; reprint, New Haven, Conn.: Yale University Press, 1977), 5–13, on the "morality of aspiration."

45. *Watchtower Bible and Tract Society of New York, Inc. v. Village of Stratton*, 536 U.S. 150, 167 (2002).

46. *Watchtower Bible*, 167 (emphasis added).

47. *Watchtower Bible*, 171.

48. *Watchtower Bible*, 171 (emphasis added).

49. 330 U.S. 75 (1947).

50. *Mitchell*, 113.

51. *Mitchell*, 113 (emphasis added).

52. *Mitchell*, 113–14 (emphasis added).

53. 494 U.S. 652 (1990).

54. *Austin*, 695 ("As conceded in Lincoln's aphorism about fooling 'all of the people some of the time,'" Scalia continued, "that premise will not invariably accord with reality; but it will assuredly do so much more frequently than the premise the Court today embraces: that a healthy democratic system can survive the legislative power to prescribe how much political speech is too much, who may speak, and who may not").

55. *McConnell v. FEC*, 540 U.S. 93, 258 (2003).

56. *McConnell*, 259.

57. 435 U.S. 765 (1978).

58. *Bellotti*, 790.

59. *Bellotti*, 790. See, too, William E. Lee, "The Supreme Court and the Right to Receive Expression," *Supreme Court Review* (Chicago: University of Chicago Press, 1987), 327. Along similar lines, as Chief Justice Burger wrote for the Court in *CARC*, 299: "Whatever may be the state interest or degree of that interest in regulating and limiting contributions to or expenditures of a candidate or a candidate's committees there is no significant state or public interest in curtailing debate and discussion of a ballot measure." This was, Burger added, because the "integrity of the political system will be adequately protected if contributors are identified in a public filing revealing the amounts contributed" (299).

60. 489 U.S. 214 (1989).

61. *Eu*, 223.

62. *Eu*, 223–24.

63. *Eu*, 223–24. Marshall continued this line of reasoning (dissenting) in *Renne v. Geary*, 501 U.S. 312, 349 (1991) ("The prospect that voters might be persuaded by party endorsements is not a *corruption* of the democratic political process; it *is* the democratic political process"; and, "The greater power to dispense with elections altogether does not include the lesser power to conduct elections under conditions of state-imposed voter ignorance. If the State chooses to tap the energy and the legitimizing power of the democratic process, it must accord the participants in that process—voters, candidates, *and* parties—the First Amendment rights that attach to their roles").

64. 536 U.S. 765 (2002).

65. *White*, 795.

66. See Oliver Wendell Holmes, Jr., "The Path of the Law," *Harvard Law Review* 10 (1897): 457 ("If you want to know the law and nothing else, you must look at it as a bad man").

67. *The Federalist Papers*, ed. Clinton Rossiter (New York: Penguin Books, 1961), 322.

68. Ibid.

69. See James Gardner, "Neutralizing the Incompetent Voter: A Comment on *Cook v. Gralike*, *Election Law Journal* 1, no. 1 (2002): 49 (attributing to the Court the perception that voters may "venture into public to cast their votes" and "become unsure, easily flummoxed, and susceptible to suggestion—in a word, incompetent").

70. In this sense, the precautionary mode accepts that the institution vested with the authority to oversee, regulate, and reform electoral practices (specifically *Congress* in the following passage) has "both wisdom and experience in these matters that is far superior" to that of the Court and thus "special deference to its judgment" is appropriate. See *Colorado Republican Federal Campaign Committee v. Federal Election Commission* (*Colorado* I), 518 U.S. (1996) 604, 650.

71. For example, while the precautionary mode would accept the legislature's determination that limits on contributions to state political candidates are necessary to discourage corruption and the "appearance of corruption" in state-wide campaigns (based on the relationship presumed to exist between candidates and contributors), a "realist" might *also* or *instead* assume that elected officials (who are not "angels") will pass laws (like contribution limits) to protect themselves—not the process—and essentially attempt to lock out challengers and preserve the status quo.

72. Consider, e.g., Justice Scalia's dissenting opinion in *McConnell*, 263 (concluding his opinion by reminding the majority that the "first instinct of power is the retention of power").

73. Problems addressed may very well return, as Justice Souter indicated in his majority opinion in *McConnell v. FEC*: "We are under no illusion that B.C.R.A. will be the last Congressional statement on the matter. Money, like water, will always find an outlet. What problems will arise, and how Congress will respond, are concerns for another day." *McConnell*, 118.

74. See Daniel Lowenstein, "Political Reform Is Political," in *The U.S. House of Representatives: Reform or Rebuild?* ed. Joseph Zimmerman and Wilma Rule (Westport, Conn.: Praeger, 2000), 194.

75. As Justice White explained in *Buckley v. Valeo*, 424 U.S. 1, 265 (1976), "It is also important to restore and maintain public confidence in federal elections," and to "obviate or dispel the impression that federal elections are purely and simply a function of money."

76. *Buckley*, 27.

77. *Buckley*, 27.

78. *Buckley*, 27–28 (emphasis added).

79. *Colorado Republican Federal Campaign Committee v. FEC* 518 U.S. 604 (1996).

80. *Colorado* II, 450.

81. *Colorado* II, 450 (emphasis added).

82. *Colorado* II, 450–51 (emphasis added).

CHAPTER 4: COGNITIVE CONTOURS

1. On the significance of what people "think" (i.e., what they "have in mind"), see George Lakoff, *Moral Politics: How Liberals and Conservatives Think*, 2nd ed. (Chicago: University of Chicago Press, 2002), 17.

2. Robert Entman, "Framing: Toward Clarification of a Fractured Paradigm," *Journal of Communication* (Autumn 1993): 53.

3. Mary John Smith, *Persuasion and Human Action* (Belmont, Calif.: Wadsworth, 1982), 29.

4. On the process of activating "mental constructs," see D. Domke, D. V. Shah, and D. B. Wackman, "Media Priming Effects: Accessibility, Association, and Activation," *International Journal of Public Opinion Research* 10, no. 1 (Spring 1998): 51–74.

5. Introduction to *Conceptual Change and the Constitution*, ed. Terence Ball and J. G. A. Pocock (Lawrence: University Press of Kansas, 1988), 4.

6. Murray Edelman, "Contestable Categories and Public Opinion," *Political Communication* 10, no. 3 (1993): 239 ("People readily express different, even contradictory, beliefs when focusing on different images or linguistic cues because they then compartmentalize their thinking and their opinions," Edelman continues, and "the person who believes nations should not 'interfere with other nations' internal affairs' may support a military invasion of Panama or of Iraq when the leaders of those countries are depicted as 'aggressive,' 'corrupt,' 'a madman,' or 'a Hitler'").

7. Ibid., 239.

8. See Timothy Brock and Melanie Green, eds. *Persuasion: Psychological Insights and Perspectives*, 2nd ed. (Thousand Oaks, Calif.: Sage Publications, 2005), 314.

9. See Steven K. Winter, *A Clearing in the Forest: Law, Life, and Mind* (Chicago: University of Chicago Press, 2001), 36 (noting that "some of our greatest minds have attested to the central role of images in reason," including Einstein, for example, who "attributed his genius not to his facility in mathematics, but to his ability to visualize," and indeed, his "first insights into the theory of relativity . . . occurred when he imagined himself riding on a beam of light looking back at a frozen clock tower or imagined himself chasing after and, then, matching the speed of a beam of light").

10. William Rivers, *Issues and Images* (Fort Worth: Harcourt, Brace, Jovanovich, 1992), xi.

11. Ibid., xi.

12. Winter, *Clearing in the Forest*, 6.

13. 521 U.S. 844 (1997).

14. Winter, *Clearing in the Forest*, 268–69 (emphasis added; citations omitted).

15. On this notion, see Edelman, "Contestable Categories and Public Opinion," 239 ("It is the expression of ideas that makes it possible to hold them, think about them, react to them, and spread them to others." And thus, "there must be an image as articulated in art, in words, or in other symbols").

16. See *Feiner v. New York*, 340 U.S. 315 (1951).

17. See *Lovell v. Griffin*, 303 U.S. 444 (1938).

18. See *Cohen v. California*, 403 U.S. 15 (1971).

19. See *Tinker v. Des Moines Independent Community School District*, 393 U.S. 503 (1969).

20. See *Buckley v. Valeo*, 424 U.S. 1 (1976).

21. See *Paris Adult Theatre I v. Slaton*, 413 U.S. 49 (1973).

22. *Metaphors We Live By* (Chicago: University of Chicago Press, 1980), 115 (emphasis added).

23. Lakoff, *Moral Politics*, 10.

24. Ibid., 10.

25. Winter, *Clearing in the Forest*, 212.

26. Ibid.

27. Ibid.

28. "On the Use of Metaphor in Political Analysis," *Social Research* 28 (Autumn 1961): 331 (quoting William Embler).

29. "Fire, Snakes, and Poisons: Metaphors and Analogues in Some Landmark Free Speech Cases," *Free Speech Yearbook* 20 (1982): 22.

30. Chief Justice Earl Warren, for example, heard only four cases—each coming, obviously, within the years comprising the Warren Court era.

31. 413 U.S. 548 (1973).

32. 470 U.S. 480 (1985).

33. 455 U.S. 129 (1982).

34. 540 U.S. 93 (2003).

35. 424 U.S. 1 (1976).

36. 352 U.S. 567 (1957).

37. 501 U.S. 312 (1991).

38. 466 U.S. 789 (1984); 523 U.S. 666 (1998); 504 U.S. 191 (1992).

39. *Greer v. Spock* 424 U.S. 828 (1976).

40. 456 U.S. 45 (1982).

41. 494 U.S. 652 (1990); 528 U.S. 337 (2000).

42. 395 U.S. 367 (1969).

43. 418 U.S. 298 (1974).

44. 401 U.S. 295 (1971); 401 U.S. 265 (1971).

45. 453 U.S. 367 (1981).

46. See, e.g., Rehnquist (dissenting), *First National Bank of Boston v. Bellotti*, 435 U.S. 765, 825, n. 4 (1978) ("It does not necessarily follow that such a corporation would be entitled to all the rights of free expression enjoyed by natural persons"). See, too, *MCFL*, *Austin*, and *Beaumont*.

47. See, e.g., Stevens (concurring), *Nixon v. Shrink Missouri Government PAC*, 528 U.S. 377, 398 (2000) ("Money is property; it is not speech. Speech has the power to inspire volunteers to perform a multitude of tasks on a campaign trail, on a battleground, or even on a football field. Money, meanwhile, has the power to pay hired laborers to perform the same tasks. It does not follow, however, that the First Amendment provides the same measure of protection to the use of money to accomplish such goals as it provides to the use of ideas to achieve the same results [asterisk citation omitted]"). See Chapter 8 for much more on this case.

48. 454 U.S. 290 (1981).

49. 514 U.S. 334 (1995).

50. *Colorado Republican Federal Campaign Committee v. FEC* 518 U.S. 604 (1996).

51. See Jeffery Segal and Harold Spaeth, *The Supreme Court and the Attitudinal Model* (New York: Cambridge University Press, 1993) (hereafter, *SCAM*); *and* Segal and Spaeth, *The Supreme Court and the Attitudinal Model Revisited* (New York: Cambridge University Press, 2002).

52. *SCAM*, 65.

53. It is important to note that *SCAM* looks to the more "hot-button," or "politically charged" areas of law (e.g., criminal justice issues) for evidence to support the assertion that policy preferences are the explanatory variable in decision making. But, as H. W. Perry reminds us, "All too often we tend to think of the Court's work as involving mostly major issues of societal importance for which justices have strong preferences for a desired outcome. For every Brown v. Board, however, there is a Brown v. Allen." *Deciding to Decide* (Cambridge, Mass.: Harvard University Press, 1991), 40.

54. *SCAM*, 243.

55. *SCAM-R*, 322 (updating the study done by Jeffrey Segal and Albert Cover,

"Ideological Values and the Votes of U.S. Supreme Court Justices," *American Political Science Review* 83, no. 2 [June 1989]: 557).

56. This high percentage within the particular domain of *electoral* speech law is consistent with Thomas Keck's finding that among the current justices, "Justice Kennedy has been the Court's strongest supporter of free speech, wherever it leads." *The Most Activist Supreme Court in History: The Road to Modern Judicial Conservatism* (Chicago: University of Chicago Press, 2004), 250.

57. Such calculations comport with those findings of Eugene Volokh who concluded that, considering the *entire* realm of free speech cases between 1994–2000, the two Democratic appointees on the Court (Ginsburg and Breyer) are ranked *fourth* and *ninth*, respectively, in terms of their voting support for the *asserted* free speech claims—for an average rate of support of 49 percent, while the average for Republican appointees was 57.1 percent. See "How the Justices Voted in Free Speech Cases, 1994–2000," *UCLA Law Review* 48 (June 2001): 1193.

58. On this, see Keck, *Most Activist Supreme Court in History, passim*, for the most definitive analysis of the various strands and implications of conservatism on the current Court; and Mark Tushnet, *A Court Divided: The Rehnquist Court and the Future of Constitutional Law* (New York: W. W. Norton, 2005), 9.

59. Recent federalism jurisprudence, for example, could be construed as consistent with this framework, at least in the sense that "states rights" has been "conservative" mantra since the aftermath of *Brown v. Board of Education* (in terms of compliance with a federal mandate) and perhaps most prominently since the candidacy of George Wallace for president in 1968 in terms of electoral politics, specifically.

60. To be clear, this discussion is *not* to suggest that decision making in this domain is not "political"—of course it is, as all things are. But it is *invested in* politics, more than *infested by* it, and portrays something more akin to politics in its "higher" form, involving, for example, the "promotion of certain core political principles," as opposed to the "low" variety, which is directed more at "which group or party will hold power." Jack Balkin and Sanford Levinson, "Understanding the Constitutional Revolution," *Virginia Law Review* 87, no. 6 (October 2001): 1045, 1062–63.

61. See the briefs submitted by the "left"-liberal ACLU as compared to the "left"-liberal groups, Common Cause, the Public Interest Research Groups, and, on *this* issue, the American Association of Retired Persons.

62. See "CRP Statement on McCain-Feingold Decision," at opensecrets.org Web site: www.opensecrets.org/pressreleases/2003/SCtDecision.asp (accessed December 15, 2006) (asserting that the GOP presently has a "significant advantage" over the Democrats in raising "hard money").

63. Volokh, "How the Justices Voted in Free Speech Cases," 1195, n. 7.

64. See, e.g., Diana C. Mutz et al., Political Persuasion: The Birth of a Field of Study," in *Political Persuasion and Attitude Change*, ed. Diana C. Mutz et al. (Ann Arbor: University of Michigan Press, 1996), 1. On "persuasion" as an "artistic" process, holding much in common with "effective selling" in fact, see Lief Carter, *Contemporary Constitutional Lawmaking: The Supreme Court and the Art of Politics* (New York: Pergamon, 1985), 16.

65. Herbert W. Simons, with Joanne Morreale and Bruce Gronbeck, *Persuasion in Society* (Thousand Oaks, Calif.: Sage Publications, 2001), 7 (emphasis in the original).

66. Smith, *Persuasion and Human Action*, 7. And thus, my use does *not* require that

persuasion necessarily "*change* an attitude in response to a message advocating a particular position or point of view." Joanne Miller and Jon A Krosnick, "News Media Impact on the Ingredients of Presidential Evaluations: A Program of Research on the Priming Hypothesis," in *Political Persuasion and Attitude Change*, ed. Mutz et al., 79.

67. See Alfred H. Kelly, "Clio and the Court: An Illicit Love Affair," *Supreme Court Review* (Chicago: University of Chicago Press, 1965), 155.

68. Steven Lubet, "The Trial as a Persuasive Story," *American Journal of Trial Advocacy* 14 (1990): 78. See, too, William Riker, *The Strategy of Rhetoric* (New Haven, Conn.: Yale University Press, 1996), 9 (coining and elaborating on the notion of "heresthetic" to describe "the art of setting up situations—composing of alternatives among which political actors must choose—in such a way that even those who do not wish to do so are compelled by the structure of the situation to support the heresthetician's purpose. . . . The line between heresthetic (manipulation) and rhetoric (persuasion) is wavy and uncertain"). See also the earlier version of this argument in Riker, *The Art of Political Manipulation* (New Haven, Conn.: Yale University Press, 1986).

69. See W. Lance Bennett and Martha Feldman, eds., *Reconstructing Reality in the Courtroom: Justice and Judgment in American Culture* (New Brunswick, N.J.: Rutgers University Press, 1981), 7 ("Stories are everyday communication devices that create interpretive contexts for social action"); ibid., 8 ("The interpretive power of stories take on special significance in the courtroom").

70. Cultivating an image then, or the construction and mutual reconstruction of images in society and political discourse, is something that can shape agendas, as Deborah Stone among others has argued. "Problem definition is a process of image making," she writes, "where the images have to do fundamentally with attributing cause, blame, and responsibility." Moreover, "conditions, difficulties, or issues thus do not have inherent properties that make them more or less likely to be seen as problems or to be expanded"; rather, "political actors *deliberately portray* them in ways calculated to gain support for their side," they "compose stories that describe harms and difficulties," and they "use narrative story lines and symbolic devices to manipulate so-called issue characteristics, all the while making it seem as though they are simply describing facts." "Causal Stories and the Formation of Policy Agendas," *Political Science Quarterly* 104, no. 2 (Summer 1989): 282 (emphasis added). See, too, Deborah Tannen, *Talking Voices: Repetition, Dialogue, and Imagery in Conversational Discourse* (New York: Cambridge University Press, 1989), 135. ("A major form of mutual participation in sensemaking is creating images," involving "both the speaker who describes or suggests an image in words, and the hearer or reader who creates an image based on that description or suggestion").

71. *Human Liberty and Freedom of Speech* (New York: Oxford University Press, 1989), 135.

72. Ibid.

73. Ibid. (emphasis added).

74. See Erving Goffman, *Frame Analysis* (Cambridge, Mass.: Harvard University Press, 1974), 10–11.

75. See Todd Gitlin, *The Whole World Is Watching: Mass Media in the Making and Unmaking of the New Left* (Berkeley and Los Angeles: University of California Press, 1980), 6 ("Frames are principles of selection, emphasis, and presentation composed of little tacit theories about what exists, what happens, and what matters").

76. See, e.g., Robert Benford and David Snow, "Framing Processes and Social

Movements: An Overview and Assessment," *Annual Review of Sociology* 26 (August 2000): 614 (Frames in communication "help to render events or occurrences meaningful and thereby function to organize experience and guide action").

77. See Bennett and Feldman, *Reconstructing Reality in the Courtroom, passim*; and Neal Feigenson, "The Rhetoric of Torts: How Advocates Help Jurors Think About Causation, Reasonableness, and Responsibility," *Hastings Law Journal* 47 (November 1995): 61.

78. See James Druckman, "The Implications of Framing Effects for Citizen Competence," *Political Behavior* 23, no. 3 (September 2001): 228.

79. On the distinction between "frames in communication" and "frames in thought," see Karen Callaghan and Franke Schnell, "Framing Political Issues in American Politics," in *Framing American Politics*, ed. Karen Callaghan and Franke Schnell (Pittsburgh: University of Pittsburgh Press, 2005), 3–4. For purposes of clarity, it is important to note here that there remains some terminological imprecision in the literature spanning various disciplines, resulting in a tendency to refer to "frames" as the interpretive processes and mechanisms that are elsewhere referred to as "schemas" or "schemata." See, e.g., Donald Schon and Martin Rein, *Frame Reflection* (New York: Basic Books, 1995), 23 ("We see policy positions as resting on underlying structures of belief, perception, and appreciation, which we call 'frames.' We see policy controversies as disputes in which the contending parties hold conflicting frames. Such disputes are resistant to resolution by appeal to facts or reasoned arguments because the parties' conflicting frames determine what counts as a fact and what arguments are taken to be relevant and compelling").

80. "Democratic Discussion," in *Reconsidering the Democratic Public*, ed. George E. Marcus and Russell L. Hanson (University Park: Pennsylvania State University Press, 1993), 362.

81. Entman, "Framing: Toward Clarification," 52 (emphasis in original). See, too, Benford and Snow, "Framing Processes and Social Movements," 614 ("In essence, [framing] denotes an active, processual phenomenon that implies agency and contention at the level of reality construction").

82. W. A. Gamson and A. Modigliani, "The Changing Culture of Affirmative Action," in *Research in Political Sociology* 3, ed. R. D. Braungart (Greenwich, Conn.: JAI Press, 1987), 143.

83. See William Gamson and Katherine Lasch, "The Political Culture of Social Welfare Policy," in *Evaluating the Welfare State*, ed. Shimon Spiro and Ephraim Yuchtman-Yaar (New York: Academic Press, 1983), 399.

84. Thomas Nelson and Zoe Oxley, "Issue Framing and Belief Importance and Opinion," *Journal of Politics* 61, no. 4 (1999): 1041, 1059. See, too, Donald Kinder and Thomas Nelson, "Domestic Debate and Real Opinions," in *Framing American Politics*, 118.

85. Entman, "Framing: Toward Clarification," 53. Also see Schon and Rein, *Frame Reflection*, 26 (The process of naming and framing "select for attention a few salient features and elations from what would otherwise be an overwhelmingly complex reality").

86. Nelson and Oxley, "Issue Framing," 1059. See, too, Thomas Nelson, Rosalee Clawson, and Zoe Oxley, "Media Framing of a Civil Liberties Conflict and Its Effect on Tolerance," *American Political Science Review* 91, no. 3 (September 1997): 568 (Frames can have "significant consequences for how viewers perceive and understand an issue, and they can direct the formulation of individual opinions about the controversy").

87. Entman, "Framing: Toward Clarification," 53. Also see, Benford and Snow,

"Framing and Social Movements," 623 (discussing the process of "frame amplification," which "involves accenting and highlighting some issues, events, or beliefs as being more salient than others" and allows for the provision of a "conceptual handle or peg for linking together various events and issues"); and James H. Kuklinski and Norman L. Hurley, "It's a Matter of Interpretation," in *Political Persuasion and Attitude Change*, ed. Mutz et al., 125 ("Political elites—elected officials, activists, or members of the media—can define the dimensions of political issues . . . and increase the salience of some issues vis-à-vis others").

88. See "Choice, Values, and Frames," *American Psychologist* 39, no. 4 (1984): 334–50, 343. See, too, Amos Tversky and Daniel Kahneman, "The Framing of Decisions and the Psychology of Choice," *Science* 211, no. 4481 (January 30, 1981): 453–58; and, Tversky and Kahneman, "Rational Choice and the Framing of Decisions," *Journal of Business* 86 (October 1986): S273 ("The framing of decisions depends on the language of presentation, on the context of choice, and on the nature of the display"). This work owes a debt to earlier work by Richard Thaler, who demonstrated that the effect of labeling a difference between prices as a "surcharge" rather than a "discount" was that it was easier for study participants to *forego* the discount than it was to *pay* the surcharge because the price difference is valued as a *gain* in one sense and as a *loss* in the other. See "Towards a Positive Theory of Consumer Choice," *Journal of Economic Behavior and Organization* 1 (1980): 39–60.

89. Shanto Iyengar, *Is Anyone Responsible?* (Chicago: University of Chicago Press, 1993), 11.

90. Entman, "Framing: Toward Clarification," 54. See, too, Donald Kinder, "Communication and Opinion," *Annual Review of Political Science* 1 (June 1998): 172 ("Frames seek to . . . define what the problem is and how to think about it; often they suggest what, if anything, should be done to remedy it").

91. Entman, "Framing: Toward Clarification," 54 (emphasis added).

92. James Druckman, "On the Limits of Framing Effects: Who Can Frame?" *Journal of Politics* 63, no. 4 (November 2001): 1042.

93. Thomas Nelson, Zoe Oxley, and Rosalee Clawson, "Toward a Psychology of Framing Effects," *Political Behavior* 19, no. 3 (1997): 228.

94. Druckman, "Implications of Framing Effects," 230.

95. Ibid.

96. See G. T. Fairhurst and R. A. Sarr, *The Art of Framing: Managing the Language of Leadership* (San Francisco: Jossey-Bass, 1996), xi.

97. See William Gardner and Bruce Avolio, "The Charismatic Relationship: A Dramaturgical Perspective," *Academy of Management Review* 23, no. 1 (January 1998): 41; and Callaghan and Schnell, preface to *Framing American Politics*, ed. Callaghan and Schnell, xi (Framing refers to the way that elites "define the political space" and "construct the boundaries or shape the contours within which issues will be considered").

98. See William Jacoby, "Issue Framing and Public Opinion on Government Spending," *American Journal of Political Science* 44, no. 4 (2000): 751 (noting that "framing effects occur when different presentations of an issue generate different reactions among those who are exposed to that issue").

99. Murray Edelman, "Contestable Categories and Public Opinion," *Political Communication* 10, no. 3 (1993): 232. Or, as he suggested earlier in his classic study of symbols in political life: "The terms in which we name or speak or anything do more than

designate it; they place it in a class of objects, thereby suggest with what it is to be judged and compared, and define the perspective from which it will be viewed and evaluated." *The Symbolic Uses of Politics* (Urbana: University of Illinois Press, 1967), 131.

100. Thomas Kuhn, *The Structure of Scientific Revolutions*, 3rd ed. (Chicago: University of Chicago Press, 1962, 1996), 113.

101. Hadley Cantril, "Perception and Interpersonal Relations," *American Journal of Psychiatry* 114 (1957): 119. Quoted in Walter Murphy, *Elements of Judicial Strategy* (Chicago: University of Chicago Press, 1964), 160, note.

102. Ibid., 119.

103. Ibid., 160–61, note (emphasis added).

104. See A. Tesser and C. Leone, "Cognitive Schemas and Thought as Determinants of Attitude Change," *Journal of Experimental Social Psychology* 13, no. 4 (July 1977): 340–56.

105. Smith, *Persuasion and Human Action*, 29.

106. Albert J. Moore, "Trial by Schema: Cognitive Filters in the Courtroom," *UCLA Law Review* 37 (December 1989): 279. See, too, Sandra Marshall, *Schemas in Problem Solving* (New York: Cambridge University Press, 1995), 34.

107. Smith, *Persuasion and Human Action*, 29; also, Susan Fiske and Shelley Taylor, *Social Cognition*, 2nd ed. (New York: McGraw-Hill, 1991), 15 ("A schema may be defined as a cognitive structure that represents one's general knowledge about a given concept or stimulus domain").

108. Moore, "Trial by Schema," 279–80. Moreover, Daniel Linz and Steven Penrod add, schemata "determine what we will attend to in a message and what we encode in memory," while also helping us to "draw inferences about what 'must' have happened even though we were not specifically given the information." "Increasing Attorney Persuasiveness in the Courtroom," *Law and Psychology Review* 8 (1984): 5.

109. Mark Johnson, *The Body in the Mind* (Chicago: University of Chicago Press, 1987), xiv.

110. Foreword to *Framing American Politics*, ed. Callaghan and Schnell, viii.

111. Fiske and Taylor, *Social Cognition*, 99.

112. Ibid., 122.

113. Entman, "Framing: Toward Clarification," 53.

114. Feigenson, "The Rhetoric of Torts," 88–89.

115. Callaghan and Schnell, "Framing Political Issues in American Politics," 14.

116. S. J. Sherman, D. M. Mackie, and D. M. Driscoll, "Priming and the Differential Use of Dimensions in Evaluation," *Personality and Social Psychology Bulletin* 16, no. 3 (1990): 405. See, too, Matthew Mendelsohn, "The Media and Interpersonal Communications: The Priming of Issues, Leaders, and Party Identification," *Journal of Politics* 58, no. 1 (1996): 112–25; Nicholas Valentino, "Crime News and the Priming of Racial Attitudes," *Public Opinion Quarterly* 63 (1999): 293–320; and, Donald Kinder and Thomas Nelson, "Domestic Debate and Real Opinions," in *Framing American Politics*, ed. Callaghan and Schnell, 117 (Frames "'prime' certain considerations, giving them a privileged position in memory among all possible thoughts that relate to an issue").

117. Miller and Krosnick, "News Media Impact," 80; and Druckman, "On the Limits of Framing Effects," 1043.

118. Shanto Iyengar and Donald Kinder, *News That Matters: Television and American Opinion* (Chicago: University of Chicago Press, 1987), 69 (emphasis in original).

119. Sherman, Mackie, and Driscoll, "Priming and the Differential Use of Dimensions," 406. Earlier work on "priming" stressed, for example, that the practice or repetitively locating targets in an array of stimuli could lead to the "automatization of attention"—wherein "primed" targets "jump out" and are thus perceived and processed in a preferential way. See R. M. Shiffrin and W. Schneider, "Controlled and Automatic Information Processing, II: Perceptual Learning, Automatic Attending, and a General Theory," *Psychological Review* 84, no. 2 (March 1977): 127–91.

120. See George Lakoff, *Don't Think of an Elephant* (White River, Vt.: Chelsea Green Publishing, 2004), 3 (arguing that the act of negating a frame still involves *evoking* that frame and so when you are arguing against the other side, "do not use their language," because, "their language picks out a frame—and it won't be the frame you want").

121. The effect here is similar to the problem with "conspiracy theories." See Brian K. Pinaire, "Internet Conspiracies," *Skeptic* 12, no. 1 (2005): 26 (noting that conspiracy theories portray a "grand irony," in that they "seem to work within the confines of an altered epistemology," in the sense that "less proof garners greater belief," and "paradoxically, the absence of evidence is taken as confirmation of the correctness of the claim, meaning that logically there is no way that such a proposition could be disproven").

CHAPTER 5: BURSON V. FREEMAN

1. See *Freeman v. Burson*, 802 S.W.2d 210, 211 (1990). Various interviewees (#1, 2, 3, 5, and 6) each confirmed and elaborated on Ms. Freeman's long-time political activism and reliance on polling place solicitation, especially for state and local races. See the Appendix for interview methods and protocol.

2. Interviewees #1, 2, and 6.

3. Interviewee #2.

4. See Robert Brett Dunham, "Defoliating the Grassroots: Election Day Restrictions on Political Speech," *Georgetown Law Journal* 77 (August 1989): 2137.

5. The "campaign-free zone" section of the election code of the State of Tennessee, reads, in pertinent part:

> Within the appropriate boundary as established in subsection (a) [one hundred feet from the entrances], and the building in which the polling place is located, the display of campaign posters, signs or other campaign materials, distribution of campaign materials, and solicitation of votes for or against any person or political party or position on a question are prohibited. (Tenn. Code Ann. 2–7111[b] [Supp. 1990])

6. *Charles W. Burson v. Mary Rebecca Freeman*, 504 U.S. 191 (1992) (hereafter, *Burson*), 205.

7. The first relevant portion of the reform legislation was passed in 1890, providing that only those voting or those officials working the election could be either in the room where the election was being held or within fifty feet of the entrance, though there were no penalties for violations and the law applied only to the more populated counties and cities. The second relevant provision, passed in 1901, was an amendment of the Tennessee Election Reform Act of 1897—with the act of 1897 classifying as a misdemeanor the use of bribery, intimidation, violence, or other efforts to induce or restrain the capacity or options of individual voters and with the amendment making it a misdemeanor as well for an individual (except for election officers) to come within thirty feet of a voter or ballot box. With these laws relatively unaltered until 1967, the state then further amended the secret ballot law, this time prohibiting the distribution of "campaign literature on the same floor

of a building, or within one hundred (100) feet thereof, where an election is in progress." Finally, in 1972, the state enacted a comprehensive series of election regulations, including the proscription of the display/distribution of campaign materials and the solicitation of votes within a hundred feet of the entrance to the polling place—that space comprising the "campaign free zone" being challenged by Rebecca Freeman. *Burson*, 205–6.

8. *Burson*, 198.

9. Justice Thomas took no part in the consideration of this case.

10. See the discussion in Chapters 2 and 3.

11. See Richard Bensel, *The American Ballot Box in the Mid-Nineteenth Century* (New York: Cambridge University Press, 2005), x. (noting that such environments were "richly endowed with ethno-cultural themes of identity, manhood, and mutual recognition of community standing"); and Bensel, "The American Ballot Box: Law, Identity, and the Polling Place in the Mid-Nineteenth Century," *Studies in American Political Development* 17, no. 3 (Spring 2003): 1–27.

On the notion of a polling place as a gathering spot for social life, see William E. Gienapp, "'Politics Seem to Enter into Everything': Political Culture in the North, 1840–1860," in William Gienapp et al., *Essays on American Antebellum Politics, 1840–1860* (College Station: Texas A&M University Press, 1982), 46–47.

12. Others were likely there as "floaters," Bensel notes—a term used to describe those men who arrived and waited for one of the parties to offer them something in return for their vote. *The American Ballot Box*, x (citing Mark W. Summers, *The Plundering Generation: Corruption and the Crisis of the Union, 1849–1861* [New York: Oxford University Press, 1987], 57).

13. The issue of bribery in this context mirrors that of campaign finance dilemmas: is the exchange of money sufficient (absent some quid pro quo) to establish harm; or, do such activities portray deeper and more complicated relationships between citizens and political actors? Consider, in this regard, Richard Bensel's argument that such interactions, between party agents and would-be voters in the mid-nineteenth century, "had become expectations in which, for instance, men came to think of themselves as Democrats because they were given things by men who worked for the Democratic party." And thus, "the men who were given things had become Democrats precisely because they had come to expect to be given things by Democratic agents at the polls," meaning that they "were not so much bribed as *rewarded* for their votes." Whatever the motivation and reciprocation, it seems that one dollar was the "going rate" for most votes in the mid-1800s; short of that, voters might receive "a pair of shoes, pants, or bushels of corn." *American Ballot Box*, ix, 59 (emphasis added).

14. Ibid., x.

15. *The Right to Vote: The Contested History of Democracy in the United States* (New York: Basic Books, 2000), 28.

16. Kentucky was the last state to abandon this method of voting, in 1891. See Paul Bourke and Donald DeBats, *Washington County: Politics and Community in Antebellum America* (Baltimore: Johns Hopkins University Press, 1995), 3–4, 6–13; Robert Dinkin, *Election Day* (Westport, Conn.: Greenwood Press, 2002), 16; and Kate Kelly, *Election Day* (New York: Facts on File, 1991).

17. See Bensel, *American Ballot Box*, 54–57. One of the main reasons for this transition, Bensel points out, was that voters had a hard time remembering the names of all the candidates for office.

18. See Keyssar, *The Right to Vote*, chap. 2.

19. For purposes of providing some context and orientation, this public/private distinction should be mapped onto the differences between urban and rural settings. In larger cities the polling places would be much closer together and anonymity was more of an option in such environments, as opposed to rural settings wherein the locales were more spread out but where individuals tended to know one another.

20. "Party hawkers," Dinkin writes, worked the polls and distributed often fraudulent ballots, for example slipping Democratic candidates' names onto what were ostensible Republican Party ballots. *Election Day*, 16. See ibid., 19 ("In the early years, when campaigns were brief, part of the vote-getting enterprise went on *around* polling places *after* the balloting had commenced [emphasis added]").

21. Bensel, *American Ballot Box*, 20 ("The polls on election day were frequently places in which liquor was both freely available and consumed to excess. The parties often provided, either as a courtesy or as bribe, free drinks to prospective voters, challengers, and election officials. As a result, the street or square outside the voting window frequently became a kind of alcoholic festival in which many men were clearly and spectacularly drunk").

22. Bensel, *American Ballot Box*, 21 ("Violence and intimidation were usually restricted to the immediate vicinity of the polling place; otherwise, potential voters were free to go about their business. It was only when men approached the polls that partisans began to construct them as allies or enemies").

23. A journal entry by Henry B. Miller, a young man describing the Missouri election of 1838 (with Thomas Hart Benton running for reelection to the U.S. Senate as a Jacksonian) explains that "the Whigs were down with a strong force and had possession of the Polls; when we came down there was great excitement, the Whigs collecting round the Polls and crying out 'Whigs Stick to the Polls, don't let the damned Democrats vote.'" "The Journal of Henry B. Miller," *Missouri Historical Society Collection* 6 (1931): 261–65; reprinted in Dinkin, *Election Day*, 68–70.

24. Bensel, *American Ballot Box*, 13.

25. Ibid., 21, n. 36, 22. Here, it is interesting to note that during legal proceedings for contested elections, it was standard procedure to have individuals testify as to their height, age, and weight as a way of gauging, apparently, their degree of membership in the "ordinary courage" club. Indeed, it was precisely such a standard that offered the typical justification for the claim that the polls were "no place for a woman."

26. Bensel, *American Ballot Box*, 172. See, too, Dinkin, *Election Day*, 9, 78–80 (noting that parties would hire "toughs" to "prevent voters favoring the other side from reaching polling places" and discussing the practice of "cooping"—common in cities like Baltimore, Philadelphia, and New York—whereby members of one party would kidnap members of another party (usually new immigrants or rural voters) and hold them in the neighborhood "coop" (the gang's local hangout) while drugging them with opiates and abating them with whiskey until the election had ceased for the day . . . a practice which, legend has it, led to the death of Edgar Allan Poe, a Whig who had been "cooped" by the Democrats in Baltimore and later died of complications stemming from the episode).

27. "If it was the American ticket [the party in power at that time in Baltimore]," he continues, the "crowd would part ranks, making an open path to the window. If it was the Democratic or 'reform' ticket . . . ,"

> a cry would go out, alerting other club members that a member of the opposition was attempting to vote. At one precinct, a Democratic clerk of election reported that the

"watchword" used by the club members was "ink-pink, I spy" followed by a whistle. A general (and clearly insincere) shout would ensue: "Make way for the voters!" This was the signal prompting a general movement of members, in mass, outward into the street. The would-be voter was thus physically moved away from the window by the sheer bulk of the crowd. (Bensel, *American Ballot Box*, 172)

28. Ibid., 290 (emphasis added).

29. See, e.g., Keyssar, *The Right to Vote*, 142–43; V. O. Key, *Politics, Parties, and Pressure Groups*, 5th ed. (New York: Crowell, 1964); and Lionel Fredman, *The Australian Ballot: The Story of American Reform* (East Lansing: Michigan State University Press, 1968). Eventually, as voting machines became more prevalent in the early to mid-twentieth century, they were thought to extend the privacy interest at the heart of this "reform" and serve as, in effect, "mechanical Australian ballots." See Jerrold Rusk, "Ballot," *Dictionary of American History*, rev. ed. (New York: Scribner, 1976).

30. See Keyssar, *Right to Vote*, 142–43; J. Morgan Kousser, *The Shaping of Southern Politics* (New Haven, Conn.: Yale University Press, 1974), 51–52; and Bensel, *American Ballot Box*, 14–15.

31. Massachusetts, however, was the first to adopt the secret ballot on a statewide level. See Richard A. Schurr, "*Burson v. Freeman*: Where the Right to Vote Intersects with the Freedom to Speak," *Whittier Law Review* 15 (1994): 890.

32. Interviewees #3 and 6.

33. Indeed, as the brief before the U.S. Supreme Court offered, "This statute was enacted two years after the Voting Rights Act of 1965 and five years after *Baker v. Carr*, 369 U.S. 186 (1962), the Tennessee case that ushered in a new era of electoral apportionment." Brief of Petitioner at 18, n. 7, *Burson v. Freeman*, 504 U.S. 191 (1992) (no. 90–1056).

34. *Meyer v. Grant*, 486 U.S. 414, 424 (1988) (citations omitted; emphasis added).

35. Interviewee #2.

36. In her own experience, Freeman testified that she had "received political communication at the polling place, and that in some cases her vote had been swayed by information she had received at the polls." Brief of Respondent at 4, *Burson v. Freeman*, 504 U.S. 191 (1992) (no. 90–1056).

37. In the words of the political consultant Kevin Igoe, in high visibility races, "people are more inclined to know ahead of time who they'll vote for. But in many local races, a well-organized campaign can still sway reluctant or undecided voters at the last minute." Dunham, "Defoliating the Grassroots," 2158. See, too, Dinkin, *Election Day*, 20 ("Although most voters have probably made up their minds about which candidates to choose for major offices, these last minute campaign ploys clearly affect decision making for minor offices and referendum measures"); and Abraham Ribicoff and Jon Newman, *Politics: The American Way* (Boston: Allyn and Bacon, 1967), 130–31.

38. *Burson*, 218.

39. Brief of the plaintiff-appellant at 15, *Freeman v. Burson*, 802 S.W.2d 210, 212 (1990) (no. 89-46-I).

40. Brief of the plaintiff-appellant at 15–16, *Freeman v. Burson*.

41. Interviewees #1, 2, 4, and 6.

42. This, however, appears to have been a misunderstanding; as the state explained in its petition for writ of certiorari to the Tennessee Supreme Court, Freeman filed suit due to "her misperception as to the Tennessee attorney general's interpretation" of the law, which centered around the question of who or what was allowed "on the grounds," regardless of

the hundred-foot barrier. Petition for writ of certiorari to the Tennessee Supreme Court at 2–3, n. 2, *Burson v. Freeman*, 504 U.S. 191 (1992) (no. 90–1056).

43. See brief of respondent at 8 ("Even a cursory reading of Tenn. Code Ann. § 2-7-111 reveals that this statute does violence to established First Amendment principles because it restricts one and only one category of speech—that directly relating to elections for public office and to other measures that appear on the election day ballot. A content-based restriction on political speech in a public forum must be subjected to the most exacting scrutiny").

44. Brief of plaintiff-appellant, 16 (discussing Ms. Alexander's testimony that "if a person were wearing a lapel badge with a picture of a donkey on it, that would be considered literature in a primary election, but not in a nonpartisan election unless the badge had someone's name on it," as well as her examples that "if a person were distributing handbills that say abortion is murder, this would not be considered campaign literature unless there was a question on the ballot specifically for that," and that "if someone were distributing handbills on behalf of a political figure who was not on the ballot that day, or distributing pamphlets with the message, 'Jesus Saves,' that person would be permitted to do so inside the 100-foot boundary if he did not create any interference"). Brief of plaintiff-appellant, 16

45. Brief of plaintiff-appellant, 15.

46. Brief of plaintiff-appellant, 6a.

47. *Freeman v. Burson*, 802 S.W.2d 210, 212 (1990) (citations omitted).

48. The state may enforce reasonable time, place, and manner regulations of expressive conduct as long as the restrictions "are content neutral, are narrowly tailored to serve a significant government interest, and leave open ample alternative channels of communication." *United States v. Grace*, 461 U.S. 171, 177 (1983) (quoting *Perry Education Assn. v. Perry Local Educators' Association*, 460 U.S. 37, 45 [1983]).

49. See *City of Renton v. Playtime Theatres, Inc.*, 475 U.S. 41 (1986) (upholding an ordinance prohibiting any "adult motion picture theatre" from locating within a thousand feet of any residential zone, single or multiple family dwelling, church, park, or school, because it was deemed to be content-neutral and because its aim was principally the minimization of the "secondary effects" that can surround such theaters).

50. See *Freeman v. Burson*, 212 (noting that the U.S. Supreme Court, in *City of Renton*, "limited its opinion to businesses that purvey sexually explicit materials and distinguished that type of expression as one for which society's interest is of a different and lesser magnitude than society's interest in protecting the kind of political expression at issue in the instant case," and distinguishing between the two because "in contrast to the restrictive zoning of pornography outlets, the statutes challenged in this case limit political expression," which "is at the core of our electoral process . . . [citations omitted]").

51. *Freeman v. Burson*, 213.

52. *Freeman v. Burson*, 214.

53. *Freeman v. Burson*, 214–15.

54. Recall that the plurality opinion was joined by Chief Justice Rehnquist, and Justices White, Kennedy, and Scalia (in judgment only), while those dissenting were Justices Stevens, O'Connor, and Souter.

55. *Burson*, 198.

56. *Burson*, 198.

57. *Burson*, 198. Stating in a more formal way the common quip that "strict" in

theory is "fatal" in *fact*, Blackmun "readily acknowledge[d] that a law rarely survives such scrutiny," but deemed the state's interests *and* methods sufficiently "compelling" and "narrowly tailored," respectively, to let the law stand. *Burson*, 200.

58. *Burson*, 208. For Blackmun, the state had successfully demonstrated that its interests met the necessary standard: case law supported the notion that the "right to vote freely for the candidate of one's choice is the essence of a democratic society." Along the same lines, the Court's opinion noted that "no right is more precious in a free country than that of having a voice in the election of those who make the laws under which, as good citizens, we must live. Other rights, even the most basic, are illusory if the right to vote is undermined." *Burson*, 199.

59. *Burson*, 209 (citing *Munro v. Socialist Workers Party*, 479 U.S. 189, 195–96 [1986]; emphasis in original).

60. *Burson*, 210.

61. *Burson*, 211.

62. *Burson*, 214.

63. *Burson*, 212.

64. 502 U.S. 105 (1991).

65. *Burson*, 212.

66. *Burson*, 213.

67. *Burson*, 214 (emphasis in original).

68. *Burson*, 214–15.

69. As the state explained, the "sole purpose of the use of the land within the 100 foot boundary, including its sidewalks, is the conduct of elections. . . . Since such land is a nonpublic forum, the standard for its constitutionality is one of reasonableness and § 2-7-111 meets that standard because of the governmental interests in preventing confusion, congestion, delay and interference in and around the polling place on election day." Brief of petitioner, 10.

70. 384 U.S. 214 (1966). In *Mills*, a unanimous Supreme Court set aside the conviction of a newspaper editor who violated Alabama's ban on election-day editorial endorsements. Applying this holding to the *Burson* case, Justice Stevens deemed that "*Mills* stands for the simple proposition that . . . the State does not have a legitimate interest in insulating voters from election-day campaigning." *Burson*, 227.

71. *Burson*, 218.

72. *Burson*, 218.

73. *Burson*, 218.

74. *Burson*, 228.

75. *Burson*, 217.

76. As Justice Stevens argued in dissent, "Tennessee's content-based discrimination is particularly problematic because such a regulation will inevitably favor certain groups of candidates," because those "with fewer resources, candidates for lower visibility offices, and 'grassroots' candidates benefit disproportionately from last-minute campaigning near the polling place." *Burson*, 224.

77. In this respect, then, the state preferred to refer to the area in question as a "politically neutral zone" rather than a "campaign-free zone," in order to emphasize the fact that this law was not so much singling out (or "criminalizing") political speech as much as it was objectively preserving an arena for the free and open participation of the people. Brief of petitioner, *passim*.

78. As the state stressed to the Court, "the ability of states to regulate speech activities around the polling place on election day is a serious question of national importance." Petition for writ of certiorari, 16. Containing the inquiry to the facts considered at the trial—whether there were or tended to be problems at polling places such as the firehouse where Ms. Freeman attempted to assemble—was too limited and thus the state sought to extend the geographic reach and deepen the historical roots of the instant controversy. Because forty-seven other states had similar buffer zones, the state framed the question in such a way that the Court's answer would necessarily and instantaneously constitute election law for nearly *every* community in the nation. Interviewees #3 and 6.

79. *Burson*, 198–211. See, too, I. Sandy Maisel, *Political Parties and Elections in the United States* (Lanham, Md.: Rowman and Littlefield, 2004), 642.

80. *Burson*, 207–8 (emphasis in original).

81. As we will see in more detail below, Blackmun's opinion begins with a discussion of the "viva voce" method of voting, popular in the colonial period, and then proceeds through a review of the transformation to the paper ballot, the parties' creation of their own ballots, the similar problems that foreign countries faced in their elections, and the eventual (near) universal adoption of the Australian ballot in the United States. *Burson*, 200–207.

82. Eldon Cobb Evans, *A History of the Australian Ballot System in the United States* (Chicago: University of Chicago Press, 1917).

83. *Burson* 202 (quoting Evans, *A History of the Australian Ballot System*, 10). Again primarily relying on Evans, Blackmun finds that the reforms of Australian ballot were well received, according to a commentator writing in *1892* in the *Annals of the American Academy of Political and Social Science*, an entire century before the Court considered the claims of Rebecca Burson. *Burson*, 204.

84. The efforts of the plurality to construct the argument around—or constitute the case in accord with—such reasoning and rhetoric was "deeply flawed" for Justice Stevens, writing in dissent, because it "confuses history with necessity, and mistakes the traditional for the indispensable." *Burson*, 220. Tradition has never been taken as a proxy for necessity when necessity must be shown, he explained; to the contrary, in fact, the Court's election law jurisprudence is "rich with examples of traditions that, though longstanding, were later held to be unnecessary," such as poll taxes, petition requirements, property-ownership requirements, and filing fees, which "were all longstanding features of the electoral labyrinth," for example, but which were later reviewed and found to either unconstitutional, unnecessary, or both. *Burson*, 221. As but one example, see *Dunn v. Blumstein*, 405 U.S. 330 (1972) (finding unconstitutional a "traditional" requirement [on the books since 1870] that residents live in the state of Tennessee for one year before being eligible to vote).

85. Notes 6 and 7 of the plurality opinion, for example, offer long passages quoted in Evans, which discuss episodes of bribery and intimidation occurring in the State of Indiana in the 1880s.

86. *Burson*, 207 (quoting J. Wigmore, *The Australian Ballot System as Embodied in the Legislation of Various Countries* [Boston: Charles Soule, 1889]) (emphasis added).

87. See, e.g., Wilson Carey McWilliams, "Democracy and the Citizen," in *How Democratic is the Constitution?* ed. William Goldwin and Joseph Schambra (Washington, D.C.: American Enterprise Institute, 1980); McWilliams, "Politics," *American Quarterly* 35, nos. 1–2, (1983): 19–38; and McWilliams, "Television and Political Speech," *Media Studies Journal* (Winter 2000): 110–15.

88. Interviewee #2.

89. *Burson*, 208.

90. *Burson*, 208.

91. *Burson*, 208.

92. *Burson*, 209, n. 11.

93. On such logic, see *Socialist Workers Party*, 195 (Justice White, for the Court) (stressing that to "require States to prove *actual* voter confusion, ballot overcrowding, or the presence of frivolous candidacies as a predicate to the imposition of reasonable ballot access restrictions would invariably lead to endless court battles over the sufficiency of the 'evidence' marshaled by a State to prove the predicate," and concluding that this "would necessitate that a State's political system sustain some level of damage before the legislature could take corrective action").

94. As Justice Stevens described the matter in dissent: "This analysis contradicts a core premise of strict scrutiny—namely that the heavy burden of justification is *on the State* [emphasis in original]. The plurality has effectively shifted the burden of proving the necessity of content discrimination from the State to the plaintiff." *Burson*, 226.

95. Several lower courts, Stevens noted, had "without exception, found such zones unnecessary." *Burson*, 222–23.

96. *Burson*, 223.

97. *Burson*, 223.

98. *Burson*, 228. Indeed, he reasoned, "The fact that campaign-free zones cover such a large area in some States unmistakably identifies censorship of election-day campaigning as an animating force behind these restrictions. That some States have no problem maintaining order with zones of 50 feet or less strongly suggests that the more expansive prohibitions are not necessary to maintain access and order." *Burson*, 218 (citations omitted).

Consider too, as one Florida district court did when addressing a similarly stated governmental interest in preventing voter harassment, that a voter could simply decline the contact with advocates. "If the quality of this interest is merely the offense suffered by a voter who approaches the polls only to be approached by a petitioner," this Court offered, then "this brief exposure to grassroots democratic process, however unpalatable to some individuals, cannot justify a restriction on speech when the offensive activity can be avoided readily by communicating a declination of interest to the petitioner." *Florida Committee for Liability Reform v. McMillan*, 682 F. Supp. 1536, 1542 (M.D. Fla. 1988) (involving a 150–foot distance from the entrance to the polling place).

99. Transcript of oral argument at 14, *Burson*.

100. As Burson explained, "It's our position, once you acknowledge the interest outside the polling place, then it's the legislature that is in the best position, through experience and the studies they're able to do, to determine what that appropriate distance would be." Transcript of oral argument at 16, *Burson*.

101. Interviewee #6.

102. Interviewee #6.

103. *Burson*, 207.

104. Interviewee #4.

105. Interviewee #4.

106. Interviewee #6.

107. Transcript of oral argument at 3, *Burson*.

108. Interviewees #3, 5, and 6.

109. Brief of petitioner, 12.
110. Interviewee #4.
111. Transcript of oral argument at 27, *Burson*.
112. Brief of petitioner, 12, 14 (emphasis added). See, too, transcript of oral argument at 27, *Burson*.
113. Transcript of oral argument at 5, *Burson* (emphasis added).
114. Brief of petitioner, 7 (emphasis added).
115. Transcript of oral argument at 6, *Burson* (emphasis added).
116. Interviewee #5.
117. Interviewee #5.
118. Transcript of oral argument at 27, *Burson* (emphasis added).
119. Interviewee #4.

CHAPTER 6: MCINTYRE V. OHIO ELECTIONS COMMISSION

1. Interviewee #7.
2. *Joseph McIntyre, Executor of the Estate of Margaret McIntyre, Deceased, v. Ohio Elections Commission*, 514 U.S. 334, 342 (1995) (hereafter, *McIntyre*). Mrs. McIntyre passed away from cancer in May 1994. The state then filed a motion to have the case dismissed as moot, but counsel for McIntryre saved the case by locating a U.S. Supreme Court case involving an Ohio law stating that criminal cases were not mooted by the death of the defendant.
3. § 3599.09 states, in pertinent part:

> (A) No person shall write, print, post, or distribute, or cause to be written, printed, posted, or distributed, a notice, placard, dodger, advertisement, sample ballot, or any other form of general publication which is designed to promote the nomination or election or defeat of a candidate, or to promote the adoption or defeat of any issue, or to influence the voters in any election, or make an expenditure for the purpose of financing political communications through newspapers, magazines, outdoor advertising facilities, direct mailings, or other similar types of general public political advertising, or through flyers, handbills, or other non-periodical printed matter, unless there appears on such form of publication in a conspicuous place or is contained within said statement the name and residence or business address of the chairman, treasurer, or secretary of the organization issuing the same, or the person who issues, makes, or is responsible therefore. . . . This section does not apply to the transmittal of personal correspondence that is not reproduced by machine for general distribution. (B) . . . No person shall use or cause to be used a false, fictitious, or fraudulent name or address in communication included within the provisions of this section.

4. 362 U.S. 60 (1960) (involving a challenge brought by distributors of unsigned handbills to a Los Angeles ordinance that prohibited the distribution of such leaflets unless they included the name and address of the individual or organization responsible for preparing, distributing, or sponsoring the material).
5. As counsel put it, the state's identity requirement was unconstitutional because the "First Amendment does not permit the state to regulate the content of political speech in such a broad or undifferentiated fashion, even if the state's goal is to assure a better informed electorate or tone down the hyperbole of political debate." Brief of petitioner at 18, *McIntyre v. Ohio Elections Commission*, 514 U.S. 334 (1995) (no. 93–986).
6. "As a practical matter," the petitioner explained, "what this [statute] means is that

leaflets distributed by established political organizations can be identified by means that do not require the responsible party officials to publicly disclose their home addresses. In contrast, private citizens like Mrs. McIntyre who cannot shield themselves behind a business address must be willing to give their home addresses as well as their names and thereby run the risk of hostile responses directed at their homes." Reply brief of petitioner at 8, *McIntyre v. Ohio Elections Commission*, 514 U.S. 334 (1995) (no. 93–986).

7. 319 U.S. 624 (1943).

8. *Barnette*, 642. Of course, *Barnette* was an about-face from the Court's determination, only three years before in *Minersville v. Gobitis*, 310 U.S. 586 (1940) (finding that a Minersville, Pennsylvania, mandatory flag salute requirement *was* constitutional).

9. 430 U.S. 705 (1977).

10. *Wooley*, 715.

11. *Wooley*, 715.

12. 357 U.S. 449 (1958).

13. *NAACP v. Alabama*, 462.

14. *NAACP v. Alabama*, 462.

15. 424 U.S. 1 (1976).

16. *Buckley*, 66.

17. *Buckley*, 66–68. See too *First National Bank of Boston v. Bellotti*, 435 U.S. 765, 791–92, n. 32 (1978): "Corporate advertising, unlike some methods of participation in political campaigns is likely to be highly visible. Identification of the source of advertising may be required as a means of disclosure, so that the people will be able to evaluate the arguments to which they are being subjected [emphasis in original; citations omitted]."

18. See *Brown v. Socialist Workers '74 Campaign Committee*, 459 U.S. 87 (1982) (unanimous determination that the Socialist Workers Party in Ohio had sufficiently demonstrated a "reasonable probability of threats, harassment, or reprisals" and thus was absolved of the contribution and identity disclosure requirement).

19. *Buckley*, 237.

20. Kathleen Hall Jamieson, *Dirty Politics* (New York: Oxford University Press, 1992), 233.

21. Robert Putnam, *Bowling Alone* (New York: Simon and Schuster, 2000), 341–42.

22. Ibid. (emphasis added).

23. Interviewee #38.

24. Interviewee #37.

25. Interviewee #37.

26. One elections commission official referred to the ongoing battles between the group—but particularly Mrs. McIntyre—and school officials as "your ultimate pissing contest" (interviewee #37), while one of Mrs. McIntyre's advocates explained that it was the perceived abuse of power that "kept her fighting" all the way from the initial incident in 1988 through the Supreme Court's review of the case in the 1994–95 term, just before she passed away. Interviewee #8.

27. *Columbus Dispatch* (February 27, 1994). To give some sense of the tension in the community at this time, it is worth noting here that the various confrontations met by "Citizens Against Tax Waste" led to the filing of a $1.77 million lawsuit against the Westerville School Board, in response to an altercation that occurred during the school board meeting of September 12, 1988. See *Columbus Dispatch* (July 26, 1989).

28. McIntyre's letter to McTigue explained, "The literature in question and presented

as Exhibit A and B was distributed in error. Due to some necessary changes, a few copies were run through with incomplete information. We thought all of those had been destroyed but apparently a few were missed and mixed in with the good fliers."

In a separate letter, Mrs. McIntyre included a testimonial from the printer, contending that "the documents that were shown to me could have been very easily altered to suit the person who is insisting on legal action against her. With today's high tech copiers anything is possible." The printer knew her to be a "law-abiding concerned taxpayer," moreover, and offered that the "whole thing" smelled like "sour grapes" to him. Both letters on file with author.

29. McIntyre's letter to McTigue.

30. The commission was scheduled to hear the complaint on July 17, 1989, but Hayfied failed to appear and thus the complaint was dismissed. Jennifer Brunner, assistant superintendent for the Westerville City School District Board of Education, then filed a motion to reconsider the dismissal and successfully arranged a new hearing. Appeal from the Court of Appeals of Ohio, Tenth Appellate District—Memorandum in Support of Jurisdiction, at 1, *McIntyre v. Ohio Elections Commission* (1992) (no. 92–1147).

31. As Mrs. McIntyre explained it, "I was working as an individual citizen, not as a committee, not as a group; therefore, I didn't need to file anything." "Except you didn't identify yourself as an *individual*; you identified yourself as a group," replied Michael Igoe, chairman of the commission. Excerpt of the proceedings before the Ohio Elections Commission, at 17, no. 89A–9 (March 19, 1990).

32. Excerpt of the proceedings before the Ohio Elections Commission, at 15, no. 89A-9 (March 19, 1990).

33. Excerpt of the proceedings, at 17. If Mrs. McIntyre did indeed *intend* to include her name and address on the fliers, it was still the case, according to Superintendent Hayfield, that most of the distributed fliers did *not* in fact contain the necessary information. "After the meeting we found most of the fliers were distributed in a wastepaper can, and I had the custodian in each meeting go through to see if we could find any piece of literature that had the names affixed to it. We found none, and I saw no good reason to submit boxes of literature to you." Excerpt of the proceedings at 19.

34. *Margaret McIntyre v. Ohio Elections Commission*, no. 90CVF 04 2835 (1990) (hereafter, *McIntyre* [1990]).

35. 677 F. Supp. 543 (S.D., 1988) (declaring section 3599.09 invalid as a prior restraint on First Amendment–protected freedom of speech).

36. *McIntyre* (1990); reprinted in "Memorandum in Support of Jurisdiction" (1992), exhibit B.

37. 104 Ohio St. 167 (1922).

38. RC 3599.09 required that a political publication contain the name and address of the person responsible for the document, whereas the statute at issue in *Babst* required that such a publication include the name and address of the voter responsible.

39. *McIntyre v. Ohio Elections Commission*, no. 90 AP-1221 (1992), 6–7 (hereafter, *McIntyre* [1992]).

40. *McIntyre* (1992), 9 (emphasis added).

41. Dissenting in this case, Judge Whiteside essentially found that the statute did not *apply* to Mrs. McIntyre. Because the "views were those of the person handing out the paper who had composed the message on the paper," he argued, "there was no anonymous communication." This was a "personal communication," which he pointed out was not

for "general" distribution, and thus he believed the judgment of the Franklin County Common Pleas Court should have been affirmed. *McIntyre* (1992), 25.

42. *McIntyre v. Ohio Elections Commission*, 67 Ohio St. 3d 391, 396 (1993) (hereafter, *McIntyre* [1993]).

43. *McIntyre* (1993), 396.

44. The ordinance at issue in *Talley*, the Ohio majority explained, "apparently had as its only purpose the identification of the author of the handbills." *McIntyre* (1993), 394. The U.S. Supreme Court, the Ohio Court explained, clearly distinguished the ordinance in question from other provisions intended to prevent the dissemination of falsehoods, and it made this clear in the following passage from the *Talley* decision:

> Counsel has urged that this ordinance is aimed at providing a way to identify those responsible for fraud, false advertising and libel. Yet the ordinance is in no manner so limited, nor have we been referred to any legislative history indicating such a purpose. *Therefore we do not pass on the validity of an ordinance limited to prevent these or any other supposed evils.* This ordinance simply bars all handbills under all circumstances anywhere that do not have the names and addresses printed on them in the place the ordinance requires [emphasis added]. (*McIntyre* [1993], 394)

"In contrast to the ordinance at issue in *Talley*," the Ohio justices offered, "appellee can legitimately claim that R.C. 3599.09 has as its purpose the identification of persons who distribute materials containing false statements. . . . Accordingly, unlike *Talley*, the disclosure requirement is clearly meant to "identify those responsible for fraud, false advertising and libel." *McIntyre* (1993), 394. In other words, for the Ohio Supreme Court, *Talley* did not prevent states from prohibiting particular types of anonymous speech; it simply proscribed *general* bans on such expression.

45. *McIntyre* (1993), 398.

46. See, e.g., *NAACP v. Alabama*.

47. *McIntyre* (1993), 400. Justice Wright pointed out that an individual could still be charged with a violation of the "false speech" statute, even without considering the element of anonymity. Furthermore, Wright offered, "the present case clearly shows that the omission of a name on a leaflet does not prevent the discovery of the author." *McIntyre* (1993), 400.

48. Justices O'Connor, Souter, Kennedy, Ginsburg, and Breyer joined the opinion, with Justice Thomas joining in judgment only. Justice Scalia dissented and was joined by Chief Justice Rehnquist. *McIntyre*, 342.

49. *McIntyre*, 345.

50. *McIntyre*, 357. With respect to these "other provisions," which criminalized "false" statements made during political campaigns, Stevens wrote "we need not, of course, evaluate the constitutionality of these provisions." *McIntyre*, 351.

51. *McIntyre*, 358.

52. *McIntyre*, 358. Ginsburg also argued that the Ohio statute was unconstitutional in light of the Court's recent precedent involving political speech, specifically *City of Ladue v. Gilleo*, 512 U.S. 43 (1994) (holding unconstitutional a law prohibiting homeowners from displaying signs, in the lawn or window, opposing the war in the Persian Gulf) and *United States v. Grace*, 461 U.S. 171 (1983) (holding unconstitutional a total ban on all leafleting and picketing on sidewalks adjoining the U.S. Supreme Court).

53. *McIntyre*, 359.

54. *McIntyre*, 370.

55. See *McIntyre*, 367 ("Both the Anti-Federalists and Federalists believed that the freedom of the press included the right to publish without revealing the author's name"). But see Saul Cornell, *The Other Founders* (Chapel Hill: University of North Carolina Press, 1999), 37–38, 76, 105–6 (arguing that the practice of publishing anonymous pamphlets was criticized even during even the debates over ratification).

56. Quote from *McIntyre*, 382.

57. *McIntyre*, 385.

58. *McIntyre*, 385.

59. *McIntyre*, 349 (quoting *New York v. Duryea*, 351 N.Y.S. 2d 978, 996 [1974]).

60. *McIntyre*, 348, n. 11 (1995). See, too, Stevens's argument later in the opinion, citing *Abrams v. United States* to make the argument that "in general, our society accords greater weight to the value of free speech than to the dangers of its misuse." *McIntyre*, 357 (1995).

61. Indeed, a theme stressed by counsel for Mrs. McIntyre at both the Ohio and U.S. Supreme Courts, was that marketplaces are "about arguments and ideas, not people or identities." Interviewee #8.

62. *McIntyre*, 342.

63. *McIntyre*, 342.

64. Appeal from the Court of Appeals of Ohio, Tenth Appellate District—reply brief of appellant at 5, *McIntyre v. Ohio Elections Commission*, no. 92–1147 (1993).

65. *McIntyre*, 382 (The usefulness of compelled identity disclosure "is seen in promoting a civil and dignified level of campaign debate—which the State has no power to command, but ample power to encourage by such undemanding measures as a signature requirement").

66. *McIntyre*, 382 (emphasis added).

67. "Imagine how much all of this would increase if it could be done anonymously," he concluded, noting as well that it "may take decades to work out the shape of this newly expanded right-to-speak incognito, even in the elections field." And in other areas, he predicted "a whole new boutique of wonderful First Amendment litigation opens its doors." "Must a parade permit," he continued, be issued to a group that refuses to provide its identity, or that agrees to do so only under assurance that the identity will not be made public?

> Must a municipally owned theater that is leased for private productions book anonymously sponsored presentations? Must a government periodical that has a "letters to the editor" column disavow the policy that most newspapers have against the publication of anonymous letters? Must a public university that makes its facilities available for a speech by Louis Farrakhan or David Duke refuse to disclose the on-campus or off-campus group that has sponsored or paid for the speech? Must a municipal "public access" cable channel permit anonymous (and masked) performers? The silliness that follows upon a generalized right to anonymous speech has no end. (*McIntyre*, 381)

68. *McIntyre*, 382.

69. Appeal from the Court of Appeals of Ohio, Tenth Appellate District—appellee's brief at 2, *McIntyre v. Ohio Elections Commission*, no. 92–1147 (1993).

70. In the words of one elections commission official, the emphasis on identity disclosure is to provide the citizens of Ohio some direction "if they want more information from that person, or from that campaign/candidate, whatever the case may be." "Having that name down there allows the citizens to know who is responsible for it," this official continued,

"so, if they want to go there, they can go to a place where they know they can get more information." Interviewee #37.

71. To emphasize this point, amici states point out: "Surveys have shown that voters are more likely to change their minds in referenda elections than candidate elections. . . . With 53% of the voters in referenda elections making a significant change in their voting intentions as the campaign proceeds, there is no doubt that last minute leaflets handed out to voters at the polling place may have a significant impact on a voter's decision." Brief for the States of Tennessee et al. as amici curiae supporting respondents at 19, *McIntyre v. Ohio Elections Commission*, 514 U.S. 334 (1995) (no. 93–986).

72. Transcript of oral argument at 50, *McIntyre*, 514 U.S. 334 (no. 93–986).

73. Interviewee #10. As this individual continued, "It was just a question of placing [her name] on her literature, taking responsibility for her statement. It wasn't what she said; it wasn't how she said it. It wasn't the context in which she said it; it was the fact that she failed to identify herself."

74. Brief of respondent at 9, 20, and 43. See Louis Brandeis, *Other People's Money and How the Bankers Use It* (New York: Frederick A. Stokes, 1933), 92 ("Publicity is justly commended as a remedy for social and industrial diseases. Sunlight is said to be the best of disinfectants").

75. As one member of the attorney general's office explained of the state's concerns in this case, the primary focus was that the "baby didn't go out with the bath water," meaning that "somebody like Margaret McIntyre who prints out one hundred copies of her own drafted material on a school levy was not the problem." The problem "was General Motors pumping millions of dollars [into a campaign]." Interviewee #10.

Various "friends of the Court" underscored this concern, arguing that a reversal of the lower court decision in the McIntyre case could set a dangerous, perhaps insurmountable, precedent for the regulations of elections: "The invalidation of Ohio's source identification requirement could not only jeopardize source identification laws in many other states, but could also call into question other election disclosure laws which limit anonymity in campaign contributions, expenditures, and communications." Brief of the Council of State Governments et al. as amici curiae supporting respondents at 3, *McIntyre v. Ohio Elections Commission*, 514 U.S. 334 (1995) (no. 93–986).

76. It was the significance of *voter* education and the necessary role for disclosure in a democracy that the state emphasized most and thus Ohio opened its brief by stating that "the right to *vote* is as important to our democratic system of government as any protected by the First Amendment." Brief of respondent at 3. Moreover, drawing upon the recently decided *Burson v. Freeman*, the state asserted its equally compelling interest in "ensuring that an individual's right to vote is not undermined by fraud in the electoral process." 504 U.S. 191, 199 (1992).

Were such essential information *not* to be disclosed, in fact, "an uninformed or misinformed vote cast in a candidate election may result in the election of a less deserving candidate, which might indirectly affect the shaping of public policy on particular issues," such as the "level of taxation of real property," and so "disclosure is as necessary in issue elections as in candidate elections." And in the end, the "disclosure of the identity of those whose distribution of printed materials or sponsorship of media advertising makes them principal supporters or opponents may send a clarion call to the public that closer attention is warranted." Brief of respondent at 29.

77. Brief of respondent at 13 (emphasis added).

78. Interviewee #10.

79. *McIntyre*, 371, 379, 381 (emphasis added).

80. A central component of the state's frame was the assertion that "the electorate comes in varying degrees of sophistication and just like fancy advertising, sophisticated advertising has a way of influencing the reader." Interviewee #10.

81. *McIntyre*, 348, n. 11 (quoting *New York v. Duryea*, 76 Misc. 2d 948, 966–67 [1974]).

82. *McIntyre*, 348, n. 11.

83. "As such," he continued, "identification of the author against her will is particularly intrusive; it reveals unmistakably the content of her thoughts on a controversial issue." By contrast, the "disclosure of an expenditure and its use, without more, reveals far less information":

> It may be information that a person prefers to keep secret, and undoubtedly it often gives away something about the spender's political views. Nonetheless, even though money may "talk," its speech is less specific, less personal, and less provocative than a handbill—and as a result, when money supports an unpopular viewpoint it is less likely to precipitate retaliation. (*McIntyre*, 355)

84. *McIntyre*, 357.

85. *McIntyre*, 357.

86. *McIntyre*, 357 (emphasis added).

87. *The Federalist Papers*, ed. Clinton Rossiter (New York: Penguin Books, 1961), 82, 384.

88. Interviewee #9.

89. Tape recording of oral argument before the Supreme Court of Ohio, *McIntyre v. Ohio Elections Commission*, 67 Ohio St. 3d 391 (1993) (no. 92–1147).

90. Interviewee #37.

91. Interviewee #36.

92. Interviewees #7, 11, and 13.

93. *McIntyre*, 381.

94. *McIntyre*, 381–82.

95. Justice Sandra Day O'Connor had been a member of the Arizona state legislature, but she is no longer on the Court. Justice David Souter had been the attorney general for the state of New Hampshire, but he was appointed to the position of assistant attorney general by Warren Rudman and was then appointed by Governor Meldrin Thompson to succeed Rudman as attorney general when Rudman entered the U.S. Senate.

96. *McIntyre*, 381 (Scalia, dissenting).

97. For academic accounts, see Forrest Maltzman, Thomas Spriggs, II, and Paul Wahlbeck, *Crafting Law on the Supreme Court: The Collegial Game* (New York: Cambridge University Press, 2000) and H. W. Perry, Jr., *Deciding to Decide: Agenda Setting in the United States Supreme Court* (Cambridge, Mass.: Harvard University Press, 1990). For journalistic and/or popular accounts, see Linda Greenhouse, *Becoming Justice Blackmun* (New York: Times Books, 2005), and Bob Woodward and Scott Armstrong, *The Brethren* (New York: Simon and Schuster, 1979).

98. *McIntyre*, 341, n. 4: "Great works of literature have frequently been produced by authors writing under assumed names," including Mark Twain, O. Henry, Voltaire, Charles Dickens, and so on.

99. *McIntyre*, 341–42 ("The decision in favor of anonymity may be motivated by

fear of economic or official retaliation, by concern about social ostracism, or merely by a desire to preserve as much of one's privacy as possible").

100. *McIntyre*, 360, 367 ("The understanding described above . . . when viewed in light of the Framers' universal practice of publishing anonymous articles and pamphlets, indicates that the Framers shared the belief that such activity was firmly part of the freedom of the press. It is only an innovation of modern times that has permitted the regulation of anonymous speech").

101. *McIntyre*, 370 (emphasis added).

102. *McIntyre*, 372.

103. See *McIntyre*, 375 ("In the present case, *absent other indication*, I would be inclined to agree with the concurrence that a society which used anonymous political debate so regularly would not regard as constitutional even moderate restrictions made the improve the election process. But there *is* other indication, of the most weighty sort: the widespread and longstanding traditions of our people [emphasis in original]").

104. *McIntyre*, 378 (emphasis added).

105. *McIntyre*, 371. See too *McIntyre*, 375–76 ("The earliest statute of this sort was adopted by Massachusetts in 1890, little more than 20 years after the Fourteenth Amendment was ratified. No less than 24 States had similar laws by the end of World War I, and today every State of the Union except for California has one, as does the District of Columbia . . . and as does the Federal Government . . . [citations omitted]").

106. *McIntyre*, 371. And thus, "Such a universal and long-established American legislative *practice* must be given precedence, I think, over historical and academic *speculation* regarding a restriction that assuredly does not go to the heart of free speech [citations omitted; emphasis added]"). *McIntyre*, 377.

107. *McIntyre*, 376.

108. *Talley*, 64–65.

109. *McIntyre*, 343, n. 6.

110. *McIntyre*, 360.

111. Wright expressed his dismay at the court's conclusions and was "sure that Publius and Cato would have strenuously disagreed with the majority as well." *McIntyre* (1993), 397.

112. Interviewee #10.

113. Brief of petitioner at 7.

114. Brief of petitioner at 8 (emphasis added).

115. Brief of petitioner at 8.

116. Transcript of oral argument at 30, *McIntyre*.

117. Transcript of oral argument at 30, *McIntyre*.

118. Transcript of oral argument at 31, *McIntyre*.

119. Transcript of oral argument at 31, *McIntyre*.

120. Transcript of oral argument at 31, *McIntyre*.

CHAPTER 7: BUCKLEY V. AMERICAN CONSTITUTIONAL LAW FOUNDATION, INC.

1. See John Matsusaka, *For the Many or the Few: The Initiative Process, Public Policy, and American Democracy* (Chicago: University of Chicago Press, 2004), 8.

2. *Victoria Buckley, Secretary of State of Colorado, v. American Constitutional Law Foundation, Inc.*, 525 U.S. 182, 192 (1999) (hereafter, *ACLF*).

3. 486 U.S. 414 (1988).

4. Colo. Rev. Stat., § 1-40-112(2) (providing that (a) "All circulators who are not to be paid for circulating petitions concerning ballot issues shall display an identification badge that includes the words 'VOLUNTEER CIRCULATOR' in bold-faced type which is clearly legible and the circulator's name"; and (b) "All circulators who are to be paid for circulating petitions concerning ballot issues shall display an identification badge that includes the words 'PAID CIRCULATOR' in bold-faced type which is clearly legible, the circulator's name, and the name and telephone number of the individual employing the circulator."

5. Colo. Rev. Stat., § 1-40-121.

6. Orr, a libertarian, and his son (a minor who desired to circulate petitions) were allied with Neil O'Toole, a labor lawyer, and political activists of all stripes for the purpose of strengthening the process of direct legislation in Colorado. Orr brought the case and O'Toole joined forces to form a coalition of advocates committed to protecting speech rights at the petition circulation phase of the initiative process.

7. ACLF and others had hoped to repeal the Senate bill by referendum, but the secretary of state informed them that they were precluded from doing so because the legislation contained a "safety clause," a common practice whereby the assembly makes exempt "laws necessary for the immediate preservation of the public peace, health or safety" from popular review. *American Constitutional Law Foundation v. Meyer* (1994), 998.

Orr desired to challenge the law on other grounds, specifically the "petition" clause of the First Amendment, but aside from his "pro se" brief (*see* pro se respondent Bill Orr's brief, *Buckley v. American Constitutional Law Foundation*, 525 U.S. 182 [1999] [no. 97–930] [tracing the right to petition through historical examples from the Book of Genesis to the English Book of Rights and linking this right to the implied right to self-government reserved by the people through the Ninth Amendment]), the primary legal strategy, and certainly each courts' review, focused instead on "speech" concerns—and thus I do as well.

8. As we will see in more detail below, the vote in this case was 6–3 on certain provisions and 8–1 on others, with the above named justices comprising the majority, with Justices O'Connor and Breyer concurring in part and dissenting in part, and with Chief Justice Rehnquist dissenting.

9. *ACLF*, 192, 186.

10. A review of terms seems appropriate at this point: The *initiative*, in its "direct" form, gives citizens the power to place a legislative measure (either a statutory provision or a constitutional amendment, depending on the state) directly on the ballot, so long as their "petitions" receive a certain number of valid signatures (an amount that varies by state), while the "indirect" initiative directs proposals to the legislature. A *referendum*, by contrast, in its "popular" form, allows the proponents—through a petition—to refer specific measures enacted by the legislature to the people, for acceptance or rejection. The "legislative" referendum allows the legislature to submit propositions to the people for their approval or rejection.

For an overview of the central theoretical and empirical questions that confront this form of governance, see, e.g., Austin Ranney and David Butler, eds., *Referendums: A Comparative Study of Practice of Theory* (Washington, D.C.: American Enterprise Institute, 1978), 3–37, 67–122; David Magleby, *Direct Legislation* (Baltimore: Johns Hopkins University Press, 1984), *passim*; Thomas Cronin, *Direct Democracy* (Cambridge, Mass.:

Harvard University Press, 1989), 1–59, 157–251; David Broder, *Democracy Derailed* (New York: Harcourt Press, 2000), chaps. 1–5, *passim*; Matsusaka, *For the Many or the Few*, *passim*; Daniel Smith and Caroline Tolbert, *Educated by Initiative* (Ann Arbor: University of Michigan Press, 2004), chap. 1.

11. See Nathaniel Persily, "The Peculiar Geography of Direct Democracy: Why the Initiative, Referendum, and Recall Developed in the American West," *Michigan Law and Policy Review* 2 (1997): 18. Direct democracy was growing in popularity as western states were in their relative infancy. Today Oregon has the largest number of initiatives proposed and adopted. See M. Dane Waters, *Initiative and Referendum Almanac* (Durham, N.C.: Carolina Academic Press, 2003), 8 (including data from the inception of direct democracy through the year 2000).

12. For a discussion of the "defects" of state legislatures at this time, see Cronin, *Direct Democracy*, 54–59.

13. See Elizabeth Garrett, "Democracy in the Wake of the California Recall," *University of Pennsylvania Law Review* 153, no. 1 (November 2004): 243 ("The goal of direct democracy . . . is to allow the people to circumvent the traditional legislative process when it is dominated by powerful narrow interests . . . which can, while representing only a minority disproportionately affect the legislative process either by taking advantage of vetogates to block change or by gaining benefits through logrolling").

14. The irony of this is that voters often gravitate toward the initiative because they view the government as unaccountable; yet measures that are passed (antitax efforts, for example) often put even more serious constraints on lawmakers and thus render them even more incapable of addressing the state's needs—thus angering the public and increasing the perception of aloofness and even arrogance. See Peter Schrag, *Paradise Lost* (Berkeley and Los Angeles: University of California Press, 1999), 19, 216.

15. Interviewee #21. Consider, e.g., the debate over a state lottery in California. Between the 1960s and 1970s, 70–75 percent of state residents supported a state lottery with money earmarked for education, but every year that a bill was introduced, as Barry Fadem explains, "the bill would be killed by the racetracks and the other folks who felt it would be competing for their dollar." Broder, *Democracy Derailed*, 83–84.

16. Despite the efforts of reformers, corporate interests have *also* made use of this method of lawmaking. See Daniel A. Smith and Joseph Lubinski, "Direct Democracy During the Progressive Era: A Crack in the Populist Veneer?" *Journal of Policy History* 14, no. 4 (2002): 360–61.

17. See Schrag, *Paradise Lost*, 9–14, 188 (arguing that the "new civics" of the initiative works "not merely as a check on irresponsible government, but as a driving engine for major policy initiatives on everything from taxes and environment regulation to control of illegal immigration and the death penalty").

18. See, e.g., Elizabeth Garrett, "Hybrid Democracy," *George Washington Law Review* 73, nos. 5–6 (August 2005): 1096.

19. President Woodrow Wilson, for one, suggested that the nature of the initiative was to "restore, not destroy, representative government." Cronin, *Direct Democracy*, 2.

20. Interviewee #24. One prominent critic writing during the Progressive era, offered that "such a fundamental principle and tradition as that of representation should not be thrown away, unless the change can be justified by a specific, comprehensive, and conclusive analysis of the causes of the failure of the state governments." Herbert Croly, *The Promise of American Life* (Indianapolis: Bobbs-Merrill, 1965), 320.

21. See Benjamin Barber, *Strong Democracy: Participatory Politics for a New Age* (1984; reprint, Berkeley and Los Angeles: University of California Press, 2004), 281–89.

22. See Hans A. Linde, "When Initiative Lawmaking Is Not 'Republican Government': The Campaign Against Homosexuality," *Oregon Law Review* 72 (1993): 34 ("Lawmaking by popular vote on an initiated proposal of course bypasses the committee study, hearings, amendments, and compromises of legislative deliberation: that was and is its purpose").

23. See Schrag, *Paradise Lost*, 191–92 (noting the Progressive era position of the editors of the *New York Times*: "While pretending to give greater right to the voters [the initiative] deprives them of the opportunity effectively and intelligently to use their powers").

24. *American Constitutional Law Foundation v. Meyer*, 870 F. Supp. 995, 998 (U.S. Dist. 1994) (hereafter, *ACLF* [1994]).

25. For example, the requirement for the 2001–2 and 2002–3 election cycles was derived from the special election held in 2000, a presidential election year, which resulted in a higher-than-normal threshold of 80,571 signatures as compared to 67,829 for 2005–6 and 62,438 for 1999–2000. See "Colorado Secretary of State Elections Center," available at Colorado Secretary of State Election Center Web site, www.elections.colorado.gov/DDefault.aspx?tid=192/ (accessed January 7, 2007).

26. Interviewee #15.

27. Interviewees #15, 16, and 17. But note that another initiative activist and attorney involved in the case had previously had as many as 48 percent of her collected signatures rejected by the secretary of state's office. Interviewee #20.

28. Rick Arnold, the owner of Nevada's "National Voter Outreach" firm, claims that "the growing professionalization" of signature-gathering firms is responsible for "at least 90 percent" of successful petitions. David Broder, "Ballot Battle: Collecting Signatures for a Price," *Washington Post*, April 12, 1998, A1.

29. Market conditions determine how much signature gatherers make. Fifty cents seems to be about the norm, but as David Broder discovered, "in Florida, in 1994, when gaming interests were paying $2.50 per name, some people were earning $750 a day." *Democracy Derailed*, 63. The state of California allows for direct mail solicitation of signatures, and as Peter Schrag explains, in 1996 the auto industry paid over "$12 per signature, or $5 million for 400,000 signatures." *Paradise Lost*, 208.

Given the inherent flux in the pricing system—considering the pressures of a fixed window of time, media coverage of the status of the effort, and the need for a surplus of signatures above the standard—it is not surprising that a common tactic of some circulators is to withhold their collected signatures from the sponsor in an effort to inflate the "going rate." Or, a more extreme machination occurs when one side of an issue pays the gatherers on the *other* side to destroy their signatures, or when the opposition "buys up" as many circulators as possible in order to deplete the labor pool and hopefully prevent a measure from reaching the ballot. See Motion for Leave to File Brief and Brief for the Council of State Governments et al., as amici curiae supporting petitioner at 3–6, *Buckley v. American Constitutional Law Foundation*, 525 U.S. 182 (1999) (no. 97–930).

30. David Broder alerts us to the startling sums involved: during the 1997–98 election cycle, "total spending for and against statewide initiatives reached $257,053,852, according to figures collected from the secretary of state offices in the initiative states." The single most expensive initiative campaign of that year pitted the California Indian tribes against the Las Vegas casinos and set a new state record of $92 million. *Democracy Derailed*, 163–64. Between the 2000 and 2004 primary campaigns nearly $500 million was spent *in*

California alone. See Thomas Stratmann, "Symposium on the Impact of Direct Democracy: Article: 'The Effectiveness of Money in Ballot Measure Campaigns,'" *Southern California Law Review* 78 (May 2005): 1041, 1045.

31. Indeed, in preparation for the trial and appeals culminating in *Meyer*, the state provided evidence of abuse and fraud linked to the paying of circulators going back at least to the 1940s, when the law was enacted. Interviewee #17.

32. Several parties interviewed for this book seriously questioned this as a genuine legislative intention. In the words of one activist, the legislature's actions were actually motivated more by suspicion and resentment in that they "have tried to put more bureaucratic hurdles in place to make it that much more of a pain in the ass for people to collect signatures and to just discourage people that much more," thereby preserving *their own* power. Interviewee #21.

33. As the state argued during Paul Grant's initial trial, the prohibition on payments to circulators hardly amounted to a serious diminution of political speech, because even allowing *only volunteer circulators*, Colorado still ranked fourth out of twenty-three states (plus the District of Columbia) in terms of the total number of measures placed on the ballot. *Paul K. Grant v. Natalie Meyer*, civil action no. 84-JM-1207 (1984), 7.

34. Mike Arno, owner of American Petition Consultants, a major California firm, boasts: "Yeah, I think that if you have enough money, you can get on the ballot. Yeah, no question." Daniel Lowenstein and Robert Stern. "The First Amendment and Paid Initiative Petition Circulators: Dissenting View and a Proposal," *Hastings Constitutional Law Quarterly* 17 (Fall 1989): 175, epigraph.

35. See Daniel Lowenstein, "Campaign Spending and Ballot Propositions: Recent Experience, Public Choice Theory, and the First Amendment," *UCLA Law Review* 29 (1982): 511, 608 (concluding that while more money does not always guarantee victory, "one-sided spending" [defined as "spending on either the affirmative or the negative side that exceeds $250,000 and that is at least twice as high as the spending of the opposite side"] is noticeably more successful), and Elisabeth Gerber, *The Populist Paradox* (Princeton, N.J.: Princeton University Press, 1999), esp. 1–20, 137–46 (finding that "citizen groups," which rely on personnel resources [i.e., "manpower"], and direct their attention toward mobilizing broad-based electoral support tend to enjoy "direct influence" in direct democracy, while economic interest groups exert considerable "indirect influence" over direct democracy, such as pressuring the legislature or spending large sums of money on "opposition" efforts and campaigns [i.e. "Vote NO! on [fill in the blank]"]).

36. Interviewee #18.

37. Interviewee #18.

38. Carla Lazzareschi Duscha, "The Koupals' Petition Factory," *California Journal* (March 1975): 83.

39. Ibid. (emphasis added). Another infamous method involves "a solicitor simultaneously soliciting signatures for 13 petitions from an ironing board." Motion for leave to file brief and brief of the Council of State Governments et al. at 8, *ACLF*.

40. Duscha, "Koupals' Petition Factory," 83 (emphasis added).

41. Interviewee #18.

42. Motion for leave to file and proposed amicus curiae brief of National Voter Outreach, Inc., in support of respondents at 2, n. 4 (quoting circulator Christopher Dunn), *Buckley v. American Constitutional Law Foundation*, 525 U.S. 182 (1999) (no. 97–930).

43. *Meyer v. Grant*, 486 U.S. 414 (1988). See joint appendix at 38, *Meyer v. Grant*,

486 U.S. 414 (1988) (no. 87–920) ("You go up to someone who is not familiar with you, doesn't know you, is not really interested in what you have to say, so my experience in the sales end of it has allowed me to know what kind of responses you can get and what kind of rejection rate you do get from that").

44. *Meyer*, 425.

45. *Meyer*, 421–22.

46. "No evidence," Stevens wrote, "has been offered to support the speculation, however, and we are not prepared to assume that a professional circulator—whose qualifications for similar future assignments may well depend on a reputation for competence and integrity—is any more likely to accept false signatures than a volunteer who is motivated entirely by an interest in having the proposition placed on the ballot." *Meyer*, 426. Stevens's assertion seems to suggest that the restrictions would be justified if the state managed to provide such "evidence," though considering the evidence offered by the state in *ACLF*, it is not apparent how much proof the Court requires.

47. *Meyer*, 424. The other provisions of the statute—prohibiting false claims on petitions, forbidding payments to signatories, and criminalizing forgery on petitions—were, for the Court, sufficient tools with which to police the electoral process. *Meyer*, 426–27.

48. Interviewee #17.

49. Interviewee #15.

50. Interviewee #15.

51. Interviewee #15. But consider, too, the experiences of one initiative activist and official with a third party in Colorado who had previously testified before the legislature and had perceived outright hostility toward the process(es) of direct democracy—even to the point where lawmakers blamed activists for requiring the new regulations. Interviewee #22. Or, as the head of one prominent and active interest group put it, the legislature was really just "pissed about what the voters have passed," and "pissed even about the things that have lost—that they have had to deal with." Interviewee #21.

52. Interviewee #17.

53. Interviewee #16.

54. See petitioner's brief at 32, *Buckley v. American Constitutional Law Foundation*, 525 U.S. 182 (1999) (no. 97–930) ("Registration helps insure that circulators are in fact subject to the jurisdiction of the Secretary of State and Colorado courts. Registration also helps proponents of initiatives and the entities that hire circulators. The registration requirement permits them to determine readily if circulators are Colorado residents by checking voter registration roles").

55. Given that "petitions are nothing more than primary election ballots for initiatives," explained an official involved in making the state's case, "you really have to look at it in that [electoral] context." And so, from "a technical point of view," she continued, "the circulators are the agents of the people who sign—and the people who sign ought to know who their agents are." Interviewee #17.

See, too, brief for the states of Washington et al., as amici curiae supporting petitioner at 8, *Buckley v. American Constitutional Law Foundation, Inc.*, 525 U.S. 182 (1999) (no. 97–930) ("There is no doubt that petition circulators do exercise core political speech when they explain and advocate a proposed ballot measure. However, petition circulators *also serve an important function in the election process*. The gathering of signatures to place an initiative on the ballot is analogous to gathering signatures to place a candidate on the ballot. The purpose is to determine if there is enough support for the measure to hold an election on it. Petition circulators are entrusted with obtaining valid signatures from registered voters [citations omitted; emphasis added]").

56. Interviewee #17.

57. See Richard Collins and Dale Oesterle, "Structuring the Ballot Initiative: Procedures That Do and Don't Work," *University of Colorado Law Review* 66 (Winter 1995): 74; and David Magleby, "Let the Voters Decide? An Assessment of the Initiative and Referendum Process," *University of Colorado Law Review* 66 (Winter 1995): 23 (both detailing evidence of increased fraud in the wake of *Meyer*).

58. Petitioner's brief at 4–8, *ACLF*.

59. Interviewee #17. "In fact," as this state official who worked on the case stressed to me, "we actually had some administrative hearings where people got up and testified that 'such and such a circulator, on such and such petition, told me that it was really about taxes, when in fact it was about gambling'—because there were a number of gambling initiatives place on the ballot in the early '90s. So, the legislature passed the identification and disclosure requirements, in response to some of those complaints."

60. *ACLF* (1994), 1002. While the state did have an interest in "honesty in public discussion of governmental issues," this interest, as well as the desire that a proposal have genuine grassroots support, could be met by other, narrower means that did not so substantially affect the number of potential circulators. *ACLF* (1994), 1002. Several plaintiffs testified to the fact that the badge requirement, especially on controversial issues, "made it more difficult to find circulators because of a fear of recrimination, retaliation and harassment." *ACLF* (1994), 1002. It should be noted, however, that one of the examples raised during the trial was that of a hemp proponent who was harassed while circulating his initiative at a DARE rally at a local park—a venue where he was not likely to receive a favorable reception given the connotations that attach to hemp advocacy. See brief for respondents American Constitutional Law Foundation, Inc., et al. at 19, *Buckley v. American Constitutional Law Foundation, Inc.*, 525 U.S. 182 (1999) (no. 97–930).

61. *ACLF* (1994), 1002. The record from the trial did indicate that this requirement, like the badge requirement, would exclude certain available petitioners and signatories (such as the unregistered Bill Orr and his son, a minor) from participating in the political process, but "the people are the source of the power [of direct democracy] and they may exercise their sovereign authority to limit the scope of that power so long as there is no discriminatory classification." And so, "this decision is not subject to any level of scrutiny by this court in the context of this case." *ACLF* (1994), 1002.

62. Given the business of circulation for hire, there is an interest in compelling disclosure by the proponents of the persons or entities being hired, not only to prevent fraud but to give the public information concerning who the principal proponents are and what kind of financial resources may be available to them. What may appear to be grassroots support might in actuality be well-financed special interests with a hidden agenda. *ACLF* (1994), 1003.

63. *ACLF* (1994), 1002.

64. Matsch explained "monthly reports affect the circulation process and therefore the amount of core political speech." For this reason they, too, were unconstitutional. *ACLF* (1994), 1002. Regarding the remaining provisions, Matsch found constitutional the six-month window of time allowed for the circulation of petitions, once the title had been set, and the state's requirement that circulators execute an affidavit that included the name and address of the circulator, among other things, but that also certified that that

circulator was a registered voter, that each signature was affixed in her presence, and a host of other assertions meant to preserve the integrity of the process. Such a requirement, he observed, "is a recognition of the central function of the circulator in preventing fraud and insuring accuracy in the petition signing process." *ACLF* (1994), 1004.

The state required this information because it may need to summon circulators to provide testimony at a hearing on challenges to the validity of some signatures. Anonymity concerns were not implicated here, as they were in the case of the identification badge requirement, Matsch explained, because there was a "qualitative difference" between the two—a difference that turned on "access." Those interested in retaliation, in other words, "will have considerably greater difficulty in finding these names and addresses in the masses of papers filed with the petitions as compared with the monthly reports and the identification badges." *ACLF* (1994), 1004.

65. *American Constitutional Law Foundation, Inc., v. Meyer*, et al., 120 F.3d 1092 (10th Cir. 1997) (hereafter, *ACLF* [1997]). Judge Carlos Lucero joined the decision, though Judge Oliver Seth, who heard oral argument in this case, passed away before the rendering of the final decision.

66. "We do not read *Meyer* to require that Colorado maintain a petition process that, in essence, allows unregulated access to the ballot," because such a reading "would conflict with the general rule that states have the power to regulate their elections and access to their ballots," and because "to subject every petition regulation to exacting scrutiny would tie Colorado's hands in seeking to assure equitable and efficient elections on ballot issues." *ACLF* (1997), 1097–98.

67. *ACLF* (1997), 1100.

68. 514 U.S. 334 (1995).

69. The circuit court distinguished the name badges from the name and address components of the affidavit requirement. "The badge requirement," Briscoe wrote, "operates when the reaction to their message may be the most intense, emotional, and unreasoned," as opposed to the identification affixed to affidavits which are held in files at the secretary of state's office. *ACLF* (1997), 1102. But Briscoe's conclusion was limited to the identification requirements, and as he explained, "we express no opinion regarding whether the additional requirements that the badge disclose whether the circulator is paid or a volunteer, and if paid, by whom, would pass constitutional muster standing alone." *ACLF* (1997), 1104.

70. *ACLF* (1997), 1101.

71. Recall that Justices Scalia, Kennedy, Souter, Stevens joined in the opinion, with Justice Thomas concurring in the judgment. Justice O'Connor (joined by Justice Breyer) concurred in part and dissented in part. Chief Justice Rehnquist dissented.

72. *ACLF*, 191.

73. *ACLF*, 192.

74. *ACLF*, 193.

75. *ACLF*, 199.

76. *ACLF*, 203.

77. *ACLF*, 206.

78. *ACLF*, 207 ("When core political speech is at issue, we have ordinarily applied strict scrutiny without first determining that the State's law severely burdens speech").

79. *ACLF*, 217.

80. *ACLF*, 218.

81. 504 U.S. 428 (1992) (setting out the following important standard for distinction: "When [First and Fourteenth Amendment] rights are subjected to severe restrictions, the regulation must be narrowly drawn to advance a state interest of compelling importance. But when a state election law provision imposes only reasonable, nondiscriminatory restrictions upon the First and Fourteenth Amendment rights of voters, the State's important regulatory interests are generally sufficient to justify the restrictions").

82. *ACLF*, 218.

83. *ACLF*, 221.

84. *ACLF*, 226 (emphasis added).

85. *ACLF*, 232. Given the parallel nature of the O'Connor and Rehnquist opinions (agreeing with the Court on the badge requirement, but disagreeing on the registration and disclosure requirements), it seems reasonable to conclude that *both* opinions are part concurrence and part dissent. For whatever reason though, the syllabus lists Rehnquist as "filing a dissenting opinion," with no indication of his agreement with the majority on the badge provision.

86. Lowenstein and Stern, "First Amendment and Paid Initiative Petition Circulators," 188. See too *ACLF*, 226 (noting an admission by Bill Orr, the executive director of ACLF, that "volunteer organizations" are "self-policing [and thus] there's not much likelihood of fraud," though "paid circulators are perhaps different").

87. Motion for leave to file a brief and brief for the Council of State Governments at 7, *ACLF* (discussing California Commission on Campaign Finance, *Democracy by Initiative: Shaping California's Fourth Branch of Government* [Los Angeles: Center for Responsive Politics, 1992]).

88. But consider one initiative advocate's reminder that "we pay folks to do all sorts of political work. We pay people to make phone calls for candidates. . . . We pay people to deliver literature to someone's door that says 'Vote for Joe.' Sometime that's a volunteer and sometimes they are paying a campaign worker. What's wrong with that? Nothing." Interviewee #21.

89. Reply brief of petitioner, 2 (emphasis added).

90. As Colorado Attorney General Gale Norton emphasized during oral argument, the voter registration requirement was essential because those engaged in debating the merits of a measure also perform "administrative election judge-type functions," in the sense that they ensure that "those who are signing the petition are who they say they are," among other things. Transcript of oral argument at 8, *ACLF*, 525 U.S. 182 (no. 97–930).

91. *Meyer*, by contrast, "focused on the *communicative* aspects of petition circulation and dealt with prohibiting an entire class of speakers—paid circulators—from engaging in a form of political speech," whereas this case, the petitioner contended, dealt more with the *procedural* aspects of the initiative process (emphasis added). Petitioner's brief at 8.

92. *ACLF*, 226.

93. *ACLF*, 226–27 (emphasis added).

94. *ACLF*, 227 (emphasis added). Moreover, he noted, while prohibiting states from limiting participation in this arena to registered voters, the Court had maintained a "sphinx-like silence" as to whether circulation may even be limited to state *residents*. *ACLF*, 228.

95. *ACLF*, 228 (emphasis added).

96. *ACLF*, 230.

97. *ACLF*, 231.

98. See *ACLF*, 226–27.

99. *ACLF*, 198 (quoting testimony of Paul Grant; emphasis added).

100. *ACLF*, 193 (emphasis added). At the time of trial, there were approximately 1.9 million registered voters in Colorado, though there were at least 400,000 individuals who were eligible to vote, but not registered. *ACLF*, 193.

101. *ACLF*, 194 (emphasis added).

102. *ACLF*, 210.

103. *ACLF*, 197 (emphasis added).

104. *ACLF*, 194–95 (citing *Meyer v. Grant*; brackets in original; emphasis added).

105. *ACLF*, 195 (testimony of Jack Hawkins). But see Justice O'Connor's dissent, questioning the veracity of this assumption by referring to Hawkins's next few statements where he explained that those who fail to engage the process in this traditional way "have interesting views of why they don't want to register to vote. *They're under a misconception that they won't be called for jury duty if they're not registered to vote and they're really concerned about being a jurist*, but in Colorado you can be a jurist if you drive a car or pay taxes or anything else" (*ACLF*, 219 [emphasis in original]).

106. *ACLF*, 196 (testimony of William Orr, executive director of ACLF).

107. *ACLF*, 196 (testimony of Jon Baraga). But see Justice O'Connor's observation that Baraga went on to say that many of those who found the political process unresponsive *would* register in there were an initiative on that the ballot that they wanted to support. *ACLF*, 220.

108. *ACLF*, 194.

109. *Meyer*, 425.

110. And yet, "The mention of fraud is a talismanic incantation in these cases," Neil O'Toole explained to the Court in oral argument, "and the long and short of it is, we don't see it." The most the state had presented, O'Toole stressed to the justices, was evidence of 2,000 fraudulent signatures out of 1,200,000 in 1992, suggesting that between nine and fifteen circulators had engaged in fraud, while only three were actually convicted of forgery. Transcript of oral argument, *ACLF*, 43.

111. *ACLF*, 203–4 (quoting *Meyer*, 426; emphasis added).

112. *ACLF*, 226.

113. Interviewees #15 and 16.

114. *ACLF*, 186 (emphasis added).

115. *ACLF*, 192 (emphasis added).

116. *ACLF*, 192 (emphasis added).

117. *ACLF*, 199 (emphasis added).

118. *ACLF*, 199 (emphasis added). Or, as another justice forecast this frame in oral argument, "signature gathering," is "perhaps primarily one citizen trying to *persuade* another citizen about the merits of a particular legislature [*sic*] proposal." Transcript of oral argument, *ACLF*, 6 (emphasis added).

119. *ACLF*, 199 (emphasis added).

120. *ACLF*, 210 (emphasis added).

121. *ACLF*, 211 (emphasis added). *Total* anonymity during the course of such an exchange was not compelled by the First Amendment, she conceded, and thus for example the affidavit requirement was an acceptable regulation—post *McIntyre*—because the burden could be met "after circulators have completed their *conversations* with electors." *ACLF*, 200 (emphasis added).

122. Quoted in Justice Thomas's concurring opinion: *ACLF*, 211, n. 3.

123. "Governing by Initiative," 21, 40 (emphasis added).

124. Cronin, *Direct Democracy*, 64 (emphasis added).

125. At the time of this research, the threshold for qualifying a proposition for the ballot was about 81,000 signatures, meaning that most proponents would need to realistically collect a minimum of about 120,000 (expecting a 30 percent rejection rate) in a span of less than six months.

126. Interviewee #24. Daniel Lowenstein and Robert Stern, for example, have suggested that the Court failed to see that the Colorado statute "did not prohibit any form of speech . . . but [rather] the *access to the ballot* of those with financial resources, to the detriment of those without such resources [emphasis added]." More significantly, they offered, "initiative proponents in Colorado were not barred from any means of speech," because advocates "were free to spend as much as they liked to hire individuals to go around *communicating* [but not *circulating*] one-on-one." "Paid Initiative Petition Circulators," 176, 211.

127. Interviewee #24.

128. Interviewee #24. A "bottle bill," of course, is officially a "law that requires a minimum refundable deposit on beer, soft drink and other beverage containers in order to insure a high rate of recycling or reuse." See the Container Recycling Institute's description, available at www.bottlebill.org/about_bb/whatis.htm (accessed February 8, 2006).

129. Interviewee #24.

130. Transcript of oral argument, *ACLF*, 17 (emphasis added).

CHAPTER 8: NIXON V. SHRINK MISSOURI GOVERNMENT PAC

1. See Herbert Alexander, *Financing Politics* (Washington, D.C.: CQ Press, 1992), 1 (attributed to the California Legislature's "Big Daddy" Jesse Unruh).

2. According to the Federal Election Commission's "Presidential Finance Summary Report," financial activity of 2004 presidential candidates and national conventions "totaled more than $1 billion, 56% more than comparable activity during the 2000 campaign." See www.fec.gov/press/press2005/20050203pressum/20050203pressum.html (accessed January 21, 2007).

3. See the Institute on Money in State Politics, "State Elections Overview, 2004." Available at www.followthemoney.org/press/Reports/200601041.pdf (accessed February 20, 2006).

4. As one state campaign finance official explained of the context for the state's limits, there was genuine public "outrage" driving the charge to reform state politics after the governor's race in 1992, an election wherein almost $6 million was spent to win the seat being vacated by the term-limited John Ashcroft. Interviewee #33.

5. The particular portion of the law under review in this case stated that "to elect an individual to the office of governor, lieutenant governor, secretary of state, state treasurer, state auditor or attorney general," $1,000 was the maximum amount for contributions made or accepted by individuals other than the candidate—an amount to serve as the baseline "for an adjustment each even-numbered year, to be made 'by multiplying the base year amount by the cumulative consumer price index . . . and rounded to the nearest twenty-five dollar amount, for all years since January 1, 1995.'" Mo. Rev. Stat. § 130.032.1(1) (1998 Cum. Supp.); quoted in *Nixon v. Shrink Missouri Government PAC*, 528 U.S. 377, 382–83 (2000) (hereafter, *Shrink*) (brackets in original).

6. 424 U.S. 1 (1976).

7. Transcript of oral argument at 23, *Shrink*, 528 U.S. 377 (2000) (no. 98–963) (emphasis added).

8. As Figure 8.1 indicates, there were several different legal challenges ongoing at the same time, each taking aim at different versions of the same general effort to establish contribution limits.

9. Bradley Smith, *Unfree Speech* (Princeton, N.J.: Princeton University Press, 2001), 18 (providing a thorough history of reform efforts in chapter 2). Other overviews of the history of reform can be found in Herbert Alexander, *Money in Politics* (Washington, D.C.: Public Affairs Press, 1972), 199–229; Alexander, *Financing Politics*, 23–47; and Herbert Alexander and Brian Haggerty, *The Federal Election Campaign Act* (Los Angeles: Citizens' Research Foundation), 13–35.

10. Alexander and Haggerty, *Federal Election Campaign Act*, 13.

11. Upon taking office in 1905, President Theodore Roosevelt recommended in his annual message to Congress that "all contributions by corporations to any political committee or for any political purpose should be forbidden by law; directors should not be permitted to use stockholders' money for such purposes." Quoted in: *U.S. v. Auto Workers*, 352 U.S. 567, 572 (1957).

12. See, e.g., Smith, *Unfree Speech*, chap. 2; Alexander, *Financing Politics, passim*; and, Christopher Banks and John Green, eds., *Superintending Democracy: The Courts and the Political Process* (Akron: University of Akron Press, 2001), 23–38.

13. See David Austen-Smith, "Campaign Contributions and Access," *American Political Science Review* 89, no. 3 (September 1995): 566–81.

14. See Stephen Bronars and John Lott, Jr., "Do Campaign Donations Alter How a Politician Votes? or, Do Donors Support Candidates Who Value the Same Things That They Do?" *Journal of Law and Economics* 40 (October 1997): 317.

15. See Richard Hall and Frank Wayman, "Buying Time: Moneyed Interests and the Mobilization of Bias in Congressional Committees," *American Political Science Review* 84, no. 3 (September 1990): 797–820, 814.

16. Quoted in Philip M. Stern, *Still the Best Congress Money Can Buy* (Washington, D.C.: Regnery Gateway, 1992), 49.

17. Interviewee #31.

18. Interviewee #31.

19. See brief for the First Amendment Project of the Americans Back in Charge Foundation and Representatives John T. Doolittle and Tom DeLay as amici curiae supporting respondents at 13, *Shrink* ("Petitioners have established that regulations already in place have done nothing to ameliorate the purported problem. Amazingly, they cite the failure of the regulations as justification to ratchet up the level of restrictions to new heights").

20. See Daniel Ortiz, "The Democratic Paradox of Campaign Finance Reform," *Stanford Law Review* 50, no. 3 (February 1998): 895 (arguing that reform legislation implies a lack of faith in the democratic competence of the citizenry).

21. Indeed, as some commentators have suggested "ironically, the laws of the 1970s led to an institutionalization of the special interests political reformers sought to eliminate." Alexander and Haggerty, *Federal Election Campaign Act*, 58.

22. For several examples of such consequences, see Cass Sunstein, *Free Markets and Social Justice* (New York: Oxford University Press, 1997), 223–41.

23. Interviewee #25. See, too, Stern, *Still the Best Congress Money Can Buy*, 119

(quoting former Congressman Bob Edgar as saying: "Eighty percent of my time, 80 percent of my staff's time, 80 percent of my events and meetings were fundraisers. Rather than go to a senior center, I would go to a party where I could raise $3,000 or $4,000").

24. See Nelson W. Polsby, "Moving Toward Equality in Campaign Finance? Another Equivocal Encounter Between Theory and Practice," in *Power, Inequality, and Democratic Politics: Essays in Honor of Robert Dahl*, ed. Ian Shapiro and Grant Reeher (Boulder, Colo.: Westview Press, 1988), 272.

25. See Sanford Levinson, "Politics, Government, and Public Affairs: Regulating Campaign Activity: The New Road to Contradiction" (review of *Politics and Money*, by Elizabeth Drew), *Michigan Law Review* 83 (February 1985): 945 ("If both political views and the propensity to spend money on politics were distributed randomly among the entire populace, it is hard to see why anyone would be very excited about the whole issue of campaign finance. It is only because we know there is no such randomization that we are concerned about spending by the rich").

26. See Smith, *Unfree Speech, passim.*

27. See amicus curiae brief of Gun Owners of America at 13, *Shrink* (no. 98–963) ("The results of recent national elections and statewide elections in Missouri confirm that the true beneficiaries of so-called campaign reforms are incumbent office holders, who are able to use such 'reform' to their advantage").

28. See Jonathan Macey, "Promoting Public-Regarding Legislation Through Statutory Interpretation: An Interest Group Model," *Columbia Law Review* 86, no. 2 (March 1986): 251 ("The reason special interest legislation is so often drafted with a public-regarding gloss is because this gloss raises the costs to the public and to rival groups of discovering the true effect of the legislation"). For a comprehensive discussion of potential approaches to equalization, and an endorsement of raising the "floor" rather than lowering the "ceiling" on campaign expenditures, see Joel Fleischman and Pope McCorkle, "Level-Up Rather Than Level-Down: Toward a New Theory of Campaign Finance Reform," *Journal of Law and Politics* 1 (Spring 1984): 211.

29. See Common Cause Web site, www.commoncause.org/.

30. See U.S. PIRG Web site, www.pirg.org/. This is not to disparage the name or mission of either group, but simply to underscore the rhetorical significance in seizing the ground of what is "common" or for the "public."

31. See Smith, *Unfree Speech*, 140 (arguing that the "enhancement" rationale "mistakes an effect of the First Amendment—uninhibited, robust debate of political matters—for the substance and principle of the First Amendment, which is liberty of expression"). See Fleischman and McCorkle, "Level-Up Rather Than Level-Down," 211.

32. See David Cole, "First Amendment Antitrust: The End of Laissez-Faire in Campaign Finance," *Yale Law and Policy Review* 9 (1991): 236, 245 ("Campaign finance issues present a classic Scylla and Charybdis scenario: in order to respond to the danger of private monopolization, we must empower government, the other pole of the peril"); Frederick Schauer, *Free Speech: A Philosophical Enquiry* (New York: Cambridge University Press, 1982), 128 ("Every enforced right of access involves the decision concerning to whom to grant the access, what ideas need additional exposure, and whether a presentation is fair or accurate"); and Bradley Smith, "Faulty Assumptions and Undemocratic Consequences of Campaign Finance Reform," *Yale Law Journal* 105, no. 4 (1996): 1049.

33. Recall from Chapter 2 that this opinion was quite fractured, with all the justices

joining only the "case or controversy" section of the decision. See the notes therein for the specific voting breakdown.

34. As such, the Court determined that federal candidate contribution limits of $1,000 (for individuals and groups), $5,000 (for political committees), and $25,000 (in total, during any calendar year) were constitutional.

35. *Buckley*, 26.

36. *Buckley*, 26–27.

37. *Buckley*, 27.

38. *Buckley*, 27 (citations omitted).

39. *Buckley*, 28.

40. The ACORN version imposed expenditure limits on candidates (including "contributions" to their own campaign funds); placed restrictions on the amount of money carried over from campaign to campaign ("war chests"); and placed severe limits of $100, $200, and $300 on contributions to state candidates, depending on the office.

41. Affidavit of Senator Wayne Goode. Produced as evidence in *Shrink Missouri Government PAC v. Richard Adams*, in the United States District Court for the Eastern District of Missouri, no. 4: 98CV357CDP, 1–2.

42. Affidavit of Senator Wayne Goode.

43. Ibid.

44. Once the Proposition A limits were ruled unconstitutional by the district court and Eighth Circuit Court of Appeals in *Carver v. Nixon*, the state reverted to those outlined in Senate Bill 650.

45. Specifically, Perry cited an article discussing contributions as high as $40,000 from a corporation to a candidate for state auditor in 1994, an article mentioning Governor Carnahan's desire for democratic institutions that "care as much about John Doe and Jane Doe as they do about any big company or any wealthy individual," and an editorial suggesting improper influence and favoritism in the state's banking relationships. *Shrink Missouri Government PAC v. Adams*, 5 F.Supp. 2d 734, 738, n. 6 (1998) (hereafter, *Shrink* [1998]). See, e.g., "The Central Issue Is Trust," editorial, *St. Louis Post-Dispatch*, December 31, 1993, 6C; and J. Mannies, "Auditor Race May Get Too Noisy to Be Ignored," *St. Louis Post-Dispatch*, September 11, 1994, 4B.

46. To assess the potential impact of the bill, Judge Perry considered how many donors made contributions exceeding the limits before the passage of the statute. "According to the data produced by defendants," she concluded, "of the 1,973 contributors to candidates for state auditor in the 1994 general election, 1,926 (or 97.62 percent) made aggregate contributions of $2,000 or less. Only forty-seven of the 1,973 (or 2.38%) made aggregate contributions of more than $2,000." Similarly, she added, "in the 1992 general election for secretary of state, less than 1.5% of the contributors made aggregate contributions exceeding $2,000." *Shrink* (1998), 738.

47. *Shrink* (1998), 741.

48. *Shrink Missouri Government PAC v. Adams*, 151 F.3d 763, 764 (1998, 8th Circ.)

49. Judge Ross joined only in the section of the majority opinion dealing with the state's failure to produce demonstrable evidence, differing with the Chief on the second argument regarding inflation.

50. *Shrink Missouri Government PAC v. Adams*, 161 F.3d 519, 521 (1998, 8th Circ.) (hereafter, *Shrink* [1998, 8th Circ.]) (emphasis added).

51. *Shrink* (1998, 8th Circ.), 523 (quoting *Buckley*, 21).

52. *Shrink* (1998, 8th Circ.), 525. In fact, he offered, comparison between the two periods was inappropriate because even expert economic analysis could not account for the "costs" of the new communications media. Perhaps the dollar was not "worth" as much, in other words, but perhaps speech was "cheaper" due to technological advances and thus the majority was really asking the wrong question.

53. *Shrink* (1998, 8th Circ.), 525. As Gibson suggested, there was considerable irony in Judge Bowman's proposition: "If Buckley's holding must wax and wane with inflation, as Part III B [of the decision] seems to argue, then the very statute that Buckley upheld would now be unconstitutional, for inflation alone would render the $1,000 limit 'different in kind' from when the Supreme Court upheld it." *Shrink* (1998, 8th Circ.), 525.

54. Recall that Chief Justice Rehnquist, and Justices Stevens, O'Connor, Breyer, and Ginsburg joined in the Court's opinion. Justice Kennedy dissented, as did Justice Thomas (joined by Justice Scalia).

55. *Shrink*, 390.

56. *Shrink*, 397.

57. *Shrink*, 397–98.

58. *Shrink*, 398. Volunteers can become active in politics, he continued, and can be inspired to their activism by the power of speech, while hired hands can be contracted to the do the same things by the power of money. "It does not follow, however," he was careful to note, "that the First Amendment provides the same measure of protection to the use of money to accomplish such goals as it provides to the use of ideas to achieve the same results."

59. *Shrink*, 399.

60. *Shrink*, 399–400.

61. *Shrink*, 400.

62. *Shrink*, 401.

63. *Shrink*, 402.

64. *Shrink*, 402.

65. *Shrink*, 403.

66. *Shrink*, 405.

67. *Shrink*, 406.

68. *Shrink*, 406.

69. *Shrink*, 406.

70. *Shrink*, 407. See, too, Justice Kennedy's concurrence (in judgment only) in *Randall v. Sorrell*, 548 U.S. ____ (2006) (slip opinion), 2 ("The universe of campaign finance regulation is one this Court has in part created and in part permitted by its course of decisions. That new order may cause more problems than it solves").

71. *Shrink*, 411.

72. *Shrink*, 412 (emphasis in original).

73. *Shrink*, 416.

74. *Shrink*, 427.

75. *St. Louis Post-Dispatch*, July 14, 1995.

76. See *Shrink*, 409 ("There are no easy answers, but the Constitution relies on one: open, robust, honest, unfettered speech that the voters can examine and assess in an ever-changing and more complex environment").

77. See *Shrink*, 420 ("In my view, the Constitution leaves it entirely up to citizens

and candidates to determine who shall speak, the means they will use, and the amount of speech sufficient to inform and persuade").

78. See *Austin v. Michigan Chamber of Commerce*, 494 U.S. 652, 680 (stressing that the "central truth of the First Amendment" is that "government cannot be trusted to assure, through censorship, the 'fairness' of political debate").

79. Transcript of oral argument at 10, *Shrink* (emphasis added). See, too, transcript of oral argument at 24, *Shrink* (Solicitor General Seth Waxman, intervening to preserve *federal* contribution limits, stressing, "Corruption is a subversion of the political process. Elected officials are influenced to act contrary to their obligations of office by the prospect of financial gain to themselves or the infusion of money into their campaigns").

80. Transcript of oral argument at 11, *Shrink*.

81. As one individual associated with Shrink's candidate insisted in a succinct statement of the respondent's position, "There *is* no correct amount of money that should be spent on politics," because "the amount that should be spent is the amount that people choose to spend on their own free will." Interviewee #26.

82. Interviewee #33. For similar sentiments from one of the country's more distinguished federal judges, see Skelly Wright, "Money and the Pollution of Politics: Is the First Amendment an Obstacle to Political Equality?" *Columbia Law Review* 82 (May 1982): 609 ("The voices of individual citizens are being drowned out in election campaigns—the forum for the political deliberations of our people. If the ideal of equality is trampled there, the principle of 'one person, one vote,' the cornerstone of our democracy, becomes a hollow mockery").

83. Interviewee #33.

84. Interviewee #27.

85. Interviewee #27.

86. On this point, see Robert Putnam, *Bowling Alone* (New York: Simon and Schuster, 2000), 40 (lamenting that "participation in politics is increasingly based on the checkbook, as money replaces time").

87. "Madison Lecture: Our Democratic Constitution," *New York University Law Review* 77, no. 2 (May 2002): 245; *Active Liberty* (New York: Alfred A. Knopf, 2005).

88. Transcript of oral argument at 42–43, *Shrink*. On the way Justice Breyer's reasoning is consistent here with "functionalist" theory, see Richard Pildes, The Supreme Court 2003 Term, "Foreword: The Constitutionalization of Democratic Politics," *Harvard Law Review* 118, no. 1 (2004): 71–72.

89. *Shrink*, 401.

90. *Shrink*, 401.

91. *Buckley*, 48–49.

92. *Shrink*, 402.

93. *Shrink*, 402 (emphasis added).

94. *Shrink*, 402 (citations omitted; emphasis added).

95. On this note, consider the oral argument in *Sorrell*: (Justice Kennedy): "Let's assume that some members of the Court simply accepted the proposition that money buys access. And—I don't think maybe we can take judicial of that, but I—I think that's a *common sense* conclusion that we can reach. And you tend to fight this in your brief to say that this doesn't happen. I tend to doubt that. I tend to think money does buy access."

Transcript of oral argument at 9–10, *Vermont Republican State Committee v. Sorrell* (no. 04–1530) (emphasis added; parties named were those involved at the time of oral argument).

96. Interviewee #27.

97. Brief for petitioners at 27, *Shrink* (citations omitted; emphasis added).

98. Brief for petitioners at 27–28, *Shrink* (emphasis added).

99. Brief for petitioners at 27, *Shrink* (emphasis added).

100. Reply Brief for petitioners at 14, *Shrink.*

101. Brief of the Secretaries of State of Arkansas, et al. as amici curiae in support of respondents at 21–22, *Shrink* ("If, as respondents claim, large contributions effectively determine the viability of candidacies and the outcome of elections, it follows that an electoral regime without limits significantly impairs nonwealthy citizens' opportunity for meaningful electoral participation. . . . Citizens without disposable income cannot purchase access or representation. Accordingly, large contributions from small numbers of people actually diminish the number of voices in the political arena. To the extent that contribution limits help mitigate the exclusionary effects of money in politics, they are justified by this Court's longstanding dedication to the 'free and unfettered' functioning of the electoral marketplace of ideas").

102. *Shrink* (1998, Dist.), 738.

103. *Shrink* (1998, Dist.), 738.

104. *Shrink* (1998, Dist.), 738 (citations omitted; emphasis added). Interestingly, she also proposed that "in some sense, the vote on Proposition A might be viewed as such a poll." That is, while Proposition A imposed lower (and unconstitutional) limits, it was at least a strong indication that the voters of Missouri were *troubled* by the prevalence of money in politics. By interpreting and responding to public opinion then, the legislature seemed to be doing its job. *Shrink* (1998, Dist.), 739, n. 7.

Along the same lines, Judge Gibson, dissenting at the Eighth Circuit Court of Appeals, reasoned that it was "hardly *counterintuitive* that large campaign contributions might corrupt politics and invite public cynicism," and thus because the restrictions were relatively modest, the state "need not justify them with scientific precision." *Shrink* (1998, 8th Circ.), 527. See, too, *St. Louis Post-Dispatch*, December 3, 1998 ("It doesn't take a Ph.D. in political science to figure out big contributions buy favored treatment").

105. *Shrink* (1998, 8th Circ.), 522 (emphasis added).

106. Interviewee #34.

107. Brief for petitioners at 30, *Shrink* (emphasis added).

108. *Shrink*, 391.

109. And so, the Court found that Shrink had failed to show that the statute would "have any dramatically adverse effect on the funding of campaigns and political associations." *Shrink*, 390.

110. *Shrink*, 397.

111. See *Shrink*, 389 ("In speaking of 'improper influence' and 'opportunities for abuse' in addition to '*quid pro quo* arrangements,' we recognized a concern not confined to bribery of public officials, but extending to the broader threat from politicians too compliant with the wishes of large contributors").

112. "Rethinking the Unconstitutionality of Contribution and Expenditure Limits in Ballot Measure Campaigns," *Southern California Law Review* 78, no. 4 (May 2005): 918.

113. Transcript of oral argument at 28–29, *Shrink*. Indeed, such *assumptions* about corruption do appear to be well entrenched—at least according to one recent study which found, in response to the question: "In general, do you *think* most elected officials in Washington make policy decisions or take actions as a direct result of money they receive

from major campaign contributors?" to which 65 percent of respondents answered "Yes," while 21 percent answered "No," and 14 percent were "Unsure." See Thomas H. Silver, ed., "Corruption in Washington," *Polling Report* 22, no. 1 (January 16, 2006): 1 (emphasis added).

More dramatic still were the findings of a survey conducted by the Pew Research Center for the People and the Press which, in response to the question "Do you think recent reports of lobbyists bribing members of Congress are isolated incidents of corruption, or do you think this kind of behavior is common in Congress?" reported that 81 percent of respondents said such incidents were "Common," while 13 percent said they were "Isolated," and 6 percent were "Unsure." Reported in Thomas H. Silver, ed., "Corruption in Congress," *Polling Report* 22, no. 3 (February 13, 2006): 8.

114. Transcript of oral argument at 28–29, *Shrink* (emphasis added).

115. Transcript of oral argument at 30, *Shrink* (emphasis added).

116. *Shrink* (2000), 388.

117. *Shrink* (2000), 390.

118. *Shrink* (2000), 390 (quoting *United States v. Mississippi Valley Generating Co.*, 364 U.S. 520, 562 [1961]).

119. *Auto Workers*, 577–78. See, too, Senator Robinson, stressing along the same lines, "We all know . . . that one of the great political evils of the time is the apparent hold on political parties which business interests and certain organizations seek and sometimes obtain by reason of liberal campaign contributions." *Auto Workers*, 576.

120. Seth Waxman, "Free Speech and Campaign Reform Don't Conflict," *New York Times*, July 10, 2002. And yet, in an ironic turn which offers grist to both reform advocates and critics, Nathaniel Persily and Kelli Lammie have recently concluded from their extensive review of polling data over time that "trends in public perception of corruption may have little to do with the campaign finance system" in part because "the share of the population describing government as corrupt went down even as soft money contributions skyrocketed," and because, when accounting for the demographics of the respondents, perceptions of corruption are also determined in important ways by one's "(1) position in society (race, income, education level); (2) opinion of the incumbent President and performance of the economy over the previous year; (3) attitudes concerning taxation and 'big government'; and (4) propensity to trust other people, in general." "Symposium: The Law of Democracy: Campaign Finance After McCain-Feingold; Perceptions of Corruption and Campaign Finance; When Public Opinion Determines Constitutional Law," *University of Pennsylvania Law Review* 153 (November 2004): 119.

121. Persily and Lammie, "Perceptions of Corruption and Campaign Finance," 121–22.

122. Brief of National Right to Life PAC State Fund et al. as amici curiae in support of respondents at 16, *Shrink*.

123. Ibid.

124. Ibid.

125. 548 U.S. ___ (2006).

CONCLUSION: A CONSTITUTION WE ARE EXPOUNDING

1. 17 U.S. (4 Wheat.) 316, 407 (1819).

2. See, e.g., Jeffrey Segal and Harold Spaeth, *The Supreme Court and the Attitudinal Model Revisited* (New York: Cambridge University Press, 2002).

3. See Mark Tushnet, *A Court Divided: The Rehnquist Court and the Future of Constitutional Law* (New York: W. W. Norton, 2005), 9 (surmising of the Rehnquist Court in general that "It's not enough to do a scorecard of 'conservative' or 'liberal' victories, although that's part of the story").

4. See Ken Kersch, *Constructing Civil Liberties* (New York: Cambridge University Press, 2004), 8 ("It is becoming increasingly difficult to label particular arguments and holdings as self-evidently 'liberal,' or 'conservative'").

5. Such calculations comport with those findings of Eugene Volokh, who concluded that, considering the entire realm of free speech cases between 1994 and 2000, the two Democratic appointees on the Court (Ginsburg and Breyer) are ranked fourth and ninth, respectively, in terms of their voting support for the asserted free speech claims—for an average rate of support of 49 percent, while the average for Republican appointees was 57.1 percent. See "How the Justices Voted in Free Speech Cases, 1994–2000," *UCLA Law Review* 48 (2001): 1193.

6. See Stevens (concurring), *Nixon v. Shrink Missouri Government PAC*, 528 U.S. 377, 398 (2000) ("Money is property; it is not speech").

7. See George Orwell, *Animal Farm* (New York: Harcourt, Brace, and Jovanovich, 1946).

8. See Nat Hentoff, "First Friend," *Legal Times* (Washington, D.C.), July 3, 2000, 62 (comparing Justice Clarence Thomas to Justices William O. Douglas and William Brennan in this regard). See, too, Tushnet, *A Court Divided*, 302 (noting that the Rehnquist Court was distinguished by the fact that it was the conservatives who "insisted that the First Amendment protected speech absolutely, brooking no exceptions").

9. The eight cases are: *Republican Party of Minnesota v. White* 536 U.S. 765 (2002); *Buckley v. American Constitutional Law Foundation* (*ACLF*) 525 U.S. 182 (1999); *Arkansas Educational Television Commission v. Forbes* (*AETC*) 523 U.S. 666 (1998); *McIntyre v. Ohio Elections Commission* 514 U.S. 334 (1995); *Burson v. Freeman* 504 U.S. 191 (1992); *Renne v. Geary*, 501 U.S. 312 (1991); *Eu v. San Francisco Democratic Committee* 489 U.S. 214 (1989); and *Meyer v. Grant* 486 U.S. 414 (1988).

10. *FEC v. Wisconsin Right to Life* (06–969); consolidated with *McCain v. Wisconsin Right to Life* (06–970). See www.supremecourtus.gov/qp/06–00969qp.pdf (accessed February 12, 2007).

11. 546 U.S. ____ (2006) (per curiam).

12. *WRTL* (slip opinion), 2 (noting that in upholding § 203 "against a facial challenge" in *McConnell v. Federal Election Commission*, 540 U.S. 93 (2003), "we did not purport to resolve future as-applied challenges"). WRTL is a "nonprofit, nonstock, Wisconsin, ideological advocacy corporation," recognized by the Internal Revenue Service as a tax-exempt entity. See *Wisconsin Right to Life, Inc. v. Federal Election Commission and Senator John McCain*, intervening (civ. no. 04–1260).

13. The three ads in question were broadcast (the first two by radio, the last by television) in July 2004 and encouraged listeners to contact Senators Russell Feingold and Herbert Kohl and to urge them to oppose the filibustering of federal judicial nominees, though none of the ads references either senator's previous votes on such filibusters; nor did they contain or direct the critical "PASO" elements (promotion, attack, support, or opposition) toward either official.

14. *WRTL v. FEC*, 15.

15. *WRTL v. FEC*, 20.

16. *WRTL v. FEC*, 17.
17. *WRTL v. FEC*, 18.
18. *WRTL v. FEC*, 18.
19. *WRTL v. FEC*, 20.
20. *WRTL v. FEC*, 22 (emphasis in original).
21. *WRTL v. FEC*, 25.
22. *WRTL v. FEC*, 25 (emphasis in original).
23. *WRTL v. FEC*, 33.
24. *WRTL v. FEC*, 34.
25. While I prefer the Python reference, Richard Hasen was quick to assess this ruling as a "see no evil" approach. His account is available at: http://electionlawblog.org/archives/007502.html (accessed December 22, 2006).
26. *WRTL v. FEC*, 17.
27. *Shrink Missouri Government PAC v. Adams*, 5 F.Supp. 2d 734, 738 (1998).
28. *WRTL v. FEC*, 38.
29. The text of the act, to "prohibit deceptive practices in Federal elections" (110th Cong., 1st Sess.) is available at the National Campaign for Fair Elections Web site, www.nationalcampaignforfairelections.org/page/-/obama%20deceptive%20practices%20bill%20013007.pdf (accessed January 30, 2007).
30. Ibid., 1–2.
31. Ibid., 4.
32. Ibid., 5 (quoting *Garrison v. Louisiana*, 379 U.S. 64, 75 [1964]).
33. Ibid., 2–4.
34. Ibid., 6 (emphasis in original).
35. 376 U.S. 254 (1964). On the issue of regulating "false speech" for a variety of reasons and with respect to a multitude of state interests, see Donald Lively, "The Supreme Court's Emerging Vision of False Speech: A First Amendment Blind Spot," *Rutgers Law Review* 38 (1986): 479; Jack Winsbro, "Misrepresentation in Political Advertising: The Role of Legal Sanctions," *Emory Law Journal* 36 (1987): 853; Robert M. O'Neil, "Regulating Speech to Cleanse Political Campaigns," *Capital University Law Review* 22 (1992): 575; Carlton Larson, "Bearing False Witness," *Yale Law Journal* 108 (March 1999): 1155; and Becky Kruse, "The Truth in Masquerade: Regulating False Ballot Proposition Ads Through State Anti-False Speech Statutes," *California Law Review* 89 (January 2001): 129.
36. *Jacobellis v. Ohio*, 378 U.S. 184 (1964) (concurring, and explaining, "I shall not today attempt further to define the kinds of material I understand to be embraced within that shorthand description, and perhaps I never could succeed in intelligibly doing so. But I know it when I see it").
37. *Randall v. Sorrell*, 548 U.S. ___ (2006) (slip opinion), 14.
38. *Sorrell* (slip op.), 18.
39. *Sorrell* (slip op.), 18.
40. 528 U.S. 377 (2000).
41. The Court could find only seven states that imposed limits on contributions to candidates for statewide office at or below $500, including Arizona, Colorado, Florida, Maine, Massachusetts, Montana, and South Dakota. *Sorrell* (slip op.), 16.
42. *Sorrell* (slip op.) (Thomas, concurring in judgment), 5.
43. *Sorrell* (slip op.), 21 (emphasis in original).
44. *Sorrell* (slip op.), 22.

45. *Sorrell* (slip op.), 26.

46. One wonders whether this linkage—between *Shrink* and *Buckley*—was sufficient to bring Chief Justice Rehnquist into the majority, concerned as he may have been for the legacy of "his" Court and the implications for overturning a precedent as established as *Buckley*. Such a concern appears to have figured prominently in the rationale for his majority opinion upholding the core of *Miranda v. Arizona*, 384 U.S. 436 (1966) in *Dickerson v. United States*, 530 U.S. 428 (2000).

47. *Sorrell* (slip op.), 10.

48. *Sorrell* (slip op.), 2.

49. See *Sorrell* (slip op.), 1–2 ("I am convinced that *Buckley*'s holding on expenditure limits is wrong, and that the time has come to overrule it").

Index

www.ingramcontent.com/pod-product-compliance
Lightning Source LLC
LaVergne TN
LVHW091515200926
848483LV00005B/424/J
* 9 7 8 0 8 0 4 7 5 7 2 4 9 *